Canadian Microeconomics

Problems and Policies

Third Edition

Canadian Microeconomics

Problems and Policies

Third Edition

BRIAN LYONS
Sheridan College

PRENTICE-HALL CANADA INC.,
SCARBOROUGH, ONTARIO

for Barbie, Marnie and Amber

Canadian Cataloguing in Publication Data
Lyons, Brian.
  Canadian microeconomics: problems and policies
3rd ed.

Includes index.
ISBN 0-13-116658-1

1. Macroeconomics.   2. Canada — Economic conditions.
I. Title.

HB172.L8   1990   338.5'0971   C90-095614-3

Prentice-Hall, Inc., Englewood Cliffs, New Jersey
Prentice-Hall International, Inc., London
Prentice-Hall of Australia, Pty., Ltd., Sydney
Prentice-Hall of India Pvt., Ltd., New Delhi
Prentice-Hall of Japan, Inc. Tokyo
Prentice-Hall of Southeast Asia (Pte.) Ltd., Singapore
Editora Prentice-Hall do Brasil Ltda., Rio de Janeiro
Prentice-Hall Hispanoamericana, S.A., Mexico

ISBN 0-13-116658-1

Production Editor: Amy Lui-Ma
Copy Editor: Chelsea Donaldson
Cover Design: Deborah-Anne Bailey
Manufacturing: Anna Orodi

2 3 4   AP   91 92

Typesetting by Compeer Typographic Services Limited
Printed and Bound in Canada by Alger Press

All quotations from the Royal Commission on Economic
Union and Development Prospects are reprinted by
permission of the Privy Council, Minister of Supply and
Services Canada.

TABLE OF CONTENTS

6. The nature of demand 83

7. The nature of supply 102

8. The dynamics of competition 119

PREFACE

This book is an introductory microeconomics text that addresses itself to many of the economic problems facing Canada and Canadians today, and the policy choices confronting governments in dealing with these issues. It is not oriented toward rigorous, abstract or elegant economic theory, nor to a mathematical approach to economics—students of introductory economics neither want nor need these. Rather, its approach tends to be practical and pragmatic, introducing theory only insofar as it contributes to an understanding of the problems being discussed.

Following an examination of the structure of the Canadian economy, the text examines the basic tools of microeconomics—supply and demand—and how these interact to determine prices under a variety of conditions, ranging from highly competitive to monopolistic industries. Consideration is given to many economic problems and policy issues, including corporate concentration, labor unions, the growth of government, rent controls, oil and energy policy, the environment, and agricultural policy, with the emphasis in each case placed upon the *basic economic principles* involved.

Many economists believe that, until recently, economic progress occurred so readily that some of these "basics" of economics were forgotten or ignored by Canadians and their governments. Now, however, that the economic situation has become much more challenging, it is more important than ever that "the basics" be remembered and emphasized: only by doing this can Canada achieve its tremendous economic potential. The relationship between government economic policy and the public's understanding of economic issues is fundamentally important here. If political necessity dictates that government policy must be framed to appeal to the public, the present economic situation makes it vital that the public understand economic realities, issues and policies.

Only such knowledge can ensure that economic policy will be directed toward the long-term economic advantage of Canadians rather than framed for short-term political expediency. If governments must be more responsive to the public than to their economic advisers, perhaps the time has come when economics is too important to be left to the economists.

Some people believe that this task is impossible—that economics is too difficult a subject to be comprehended by most people, and must therefore be left to the experts. This view is not correct. Economics is not a particularly difficult subject at all—the real task in teaching introductory economics is to organize many things that people either already know or can grasp quite readily into a systematic framework that promotes greater understanding of important economic problems. Hopefully, this book can help people to do this in a readable, not unduly painful, and maybe even occasionally enjoyable way.

A person undertaking a project such as this is indebted to a great number of people. In particular, I would like to express my gratitude to Bill Trimble, who said I should do it, Len Rosen, who didn't let me say I wouldn't, and all those instructors and students who used the first two editions and offered helpful comments and suggestions. I would also like to thank the people whose reviews of all three editions of the manuscript were so helpful: for the first edition, Ray Canon, Gord Cleveland, Ward Levine, Jim Thompson and Ian Wilson, for the second, Alan Idiens and Chuck Casson, and for the third, Linda Nitsou, Bo Renneckendorf, Gord Enemark, L.W. Van Niekerk, Stephen Wise and Ann Dunkley. In addition, I would like to express my appreciation to the many excellent Prentice-Hall editing and marketing people whose help and support have been indispensable, especially Chelsea Donaldson for her conscientious, patient and instructive editing. Finally, I want to acknowledge my indebtedness to my family—Barbie, Marnie and Amber—who have provided support and understanding over unduly long periods of time.

I have no doubts that there are many improvements that can be made to this book, and welcome any suggestions from teachers or students. Please write to me at Sheridan College, Box 7500, McLaughlin Road, Brampton, Ontario L6V 1G6.

Brian Lyons, Sheridan College, 1990

CHAPTER 1

What is economics?

What is "economics"? To the householder, economics is the difficult task of balancing the family budget in the face of rising prices, so that there is not too much month left over at the end of the money. To the business leader, economics is the problem of producing a product at sufficiently low cost that it can be marketed profitably in competition with the products of other producers. To a government leader, economics means difficult policy choices between goals that often conflict with each other, making it impossible to please everyone and thus ensure re-election. To the general public, economics is usually associated with vague, incomprehensible and often contradictory pronouncements by people called "economists," concerning matters of great national and international importance that seem impossible to understand, much less resolve.

While each of these views may be accurate, each is only a part of the real meaning of economics, because each represents only the viewpoint of a particular group (householders, business leaders, government leaders, voters). From the viewpoint of the economist, however, economics covers a broader field, dealing in the widest sense with how well a society's economic system satisfies the economic needs and wants of its people. Since the basic task of an economic system is to produce goods and services and to distribute them among the people of a society, the most commonly used definition of **economics** is

> the study of the decisions a society makes concerning the production of goods and services and how the society distributes these goods and services among its members.

1

This somewhat dull and simple definition leads us into a variety of areas of much broader concern and greater interest, such as:

- How likely is it that severe inflation such as we experienced in the 1970's will return?
- Will we have another major economic downturn such as the recession of the early 1980's?
- Why are economists concerned about the federal government's large budget deficits?
- Will free trade with the United States bring economic prosperity or economic hardship to Canadians?
- Will the relaxation of Canada's restrictions on US investment under the Free Trade Agreement mean more jobs for Canadians, or US domination of Canada?
- Why did the international value of the Canadian dollar fall by nearly one-third from 1974 to 1985, then rise by 20 percent by 1989, and what does this mean for Canadians?
- Must a million Canadians be unemployed?
- Are strikes severely damaging to the Canadian economy?
- Why are some people paid hundreds of thousands of dollars per year, while others receive less than one percent of that?
- Should the government place legal limits on the rent charged by landlords?

Some aspects of economic matters such as those above raise *philosophical* questions; for instance, is it proper for the government to control apartment rents, or people's wages, or workers' strikes? Other aspects of economics, however, involve more *technical economic analysis*. For example, if apartment rents are kept low by law, how will this affect the construction of new apartments? In many cases, also, economics becomes involved with *value judgments*. For example, if the government acts to reduce unemployment, inflation may well become more severe: is this a worthwhile price to pay for reducing unemployment? This question involves a value judgment, in the sense that even people who agree concerning the economic analysis of the issue may disagree on what policy the government should follow: one may be concerned about the effect of unemployment on young people, while the other may place greater emphasis on how inflation affects pensioners.

Folklore versus economic analysis

Probably the greatest obstacle to the effective learning of economics is the fact that most people already think that they know a great deal about the subject. In fact, much of this knowledge consists of widely believed but not necessarily accurate ideas, such as:

- The way to eliminate poverty is to increase the minimum wage dramatically.
- Increases in the National Debt are always bad.
- Proper use of government policies can eliminate both unemployment and inflation.
- Reductions in interest rates will help to combat inflation.
- A decline in the international value of the Canadian dollar is economically harmful to all Canadians.
- The government should always balance its budget.

None of the above statements is true, but they are widely believed by the public. The objective of this book is to replace this type of folklore about economics with the tools for accurate analysis of economic issues of importance to Canadians.

The limitations of economic analysis

Because it deals with the behavior of people (consumers, business people, government policy-makers), economics cannot be a precise science such as physics or mathematics. Similarly, economic analysis does not provide clear and simple answers to important questions, such as whether the government should reduce taxes. However, economic analysis can do a great deal to illuminate the consequences of reducing (or not reducing) taxes, thus clarifying the choices to be made. Therefore, while economic analysis does not provide us with decisions, it provides us with a much better basis for making decisions.

Can economists agree on anything?

"Ask five economists what should be done about a problem and you'll get six different recommendations" is a jibe frequently directed at economists, whose credibility is often considered in the same category as that of weather forecasters. Given the disagreements among economists (and others who describe themselves as such) on matters of importance, it is easy to get the impression that the field of economics is one of confusion and chaos. While economics, like all other fields of study, is continually evolving toward a fuller understanding of its subject matter, the present state of the subject is not as chaotic as it may seem. First, many of the disagreements among economists arise not from economic analysis but rather from differences concerning policy recommendations (value judgments) which arise from that analysis. Second, there are many generally accepted facts, concepts and theories that constitute a sort of mainstream of economic thought that is less publicized but more important than disputes between various economists. This book attempts to build

SOME SCIENCES ARE MORE EXACT THAN OTHERS

An alumnus, returning to his college for a reunion, found his old economics professor preparing the examination for her course. "But professor," said the former student, "don't you realize that these are exactly the same questions that were on my exam 20 years ago?" "Yes," answered the professor, "We always use the same ones." "But don't you know," asked the graduate, "that students pass these around, and therefore will surely know by now what questions will be on their exam?" "It doesn't matter," said the professor. "In economics, we don't change the questions, we change the answers."

around this mainstream of thought, while considering the major alternatives to it where these are important.

What is economics about, then?

Economics used to be known as the "dismal science," because of the economic theories of Thomas Malthus (1766–1834). Malthus, an English clergyman, theorized that because population could grow faster than the world's food supply, humanity was destined to live with a constant struggle with starvation. While no one can say what the future will bring, a combination of lower birthrates and modern production technology has raised living standards in many societies far beyond anything dreamed of in Malthusian theories, and has brought the study of economics to matters which, while serious, are much less depressing.

Economics, then, is about many matters both large and small. On a large scale, *macroeconomics* (based on *macro*, for big) deals with broader matters pertaining to the performance of the economy as a whole, such as recession, inflation and unemployment.

On a small scale, *microeconomics* (after the Greek word *micro*, for small) focuses on particular aspects of economics, such as consumer demand, supply, demand and prices under various conditions, the role of big business, labor unions and government in the economy, and the economics of particular industries such as agriculture and oil. The purpose of this book is to develop an understanding of these microeconomic matters which are of importance to all Canadians. Before examining these issues, however, we will consider the basic problems of economics and the various types of economic systems that exist, in Chapters 2 and 3 respectively.

Isn't this all terribly difficult?

Not really. Probably the most insightful observation ever made about economics as a field of study is that it is a *complex* subject but not a *difficult* one. Unlike nuclear physics or differential calculus, there is little in economics that many people find conceptually difficult. Rather, economics deals with people and their behavior and decisions as consumers, business people and government policy-makers. Much of this behavior is already known to the student of introductory economics; what needs to be done is to organize these fragments of knowledge into a framework for analyzing and understanding economic events. This book attempts to do this in a way that eliminates the use of abstract theories and higher-level mathematics, instead focusing on developing an understanding of real and relevant Canadian economic problems in a readable and, hopefully, enjoyable way.

QUESTIONS

1. What has economics meant to you? From what viewpoints have you viewed the economic system?

2. How well does Canada's economic system fill the needs and wants of Canadians? What shortcomings do you perceive, and what do you think could be done about them?

3. "The inability of economists to make accurate economic forecasts shows that they know so little about the workings of the economy that their advice on economic matters should be disregarded." Do you agree with this statement? Why?

4. What are some of the specific developments that have enabled us to escape the dismal predictions of Malthus? Do you believe that Malthus's theories will eventually come true? Why?

CHAPTER 2

The economic problem

As we have said, **economics** is basically the study of the decisions a society makes regarding the production of goods and services and the division of these among its people. As we shall see, different societies make these decisions in very different ways, but all societies are faced with essentially the same problems—how to use their economic resources to the best possible advantage.

Using economic resources to satisfy human wants

A modern industrial economy is a very complex mechanism, involving a baffling number of factors, such as the level of output, employment, unemployment, prices, interest rates, money supply, exports, imports, the international value of the nation's currency, government tax revenues, government spending, consumer spending, banks, stock markets, big corporations, small businesses, labor unions and many others. Furthermore, each of these factors is related to the others in ways that are often subtle and complex. It is no wonder that many people find economics confusing and have difficulty ''seeing the forest for the trees.'' Worst of all, such complexities often make it difficult to see the *basic economic principles* involved in an issue.

In examining basic economic principles, it can be very helpful to eliminate the many complexities associated with a modern economy that tend to obscure the principles involved. Suppose, then, that we are part of a group of people stranded on a desert island. With none of the complexities of a modern economy to distract us, our group must come to grips with the most basic economic problem: how best to satisfy our

6

economic wants and needs using the three types of economic resources, or **inputs**, available to us—labor, capital equipment and the natural resources of the island.

(a) Labor

The largest single economic resource, or input, available to any society is the **labor** of its people, including all types of work, mental as well as physical, from manual labor to professional employment. In our desert-island mini-society, people will have various skills (hunting, fishing, building and so on) appropriate to the situation.

(b) Capital equipment

A vitally important economic resource is society's stock of **capital equipment**, which contributes greatly to the production of goods and services. While a modern industrial economy possesses a vast array of factories, machinery, equipment and tools, your desert-island mini-society has built only a few basic tools, such as spears, fish nets and hoes.

Capital equipment is of crucial importance because it increases *production per person (productivity)*, making possible a higher material standard of living (more goods per person) for the people of the society. Thus, while the mini-society's stock of capital equipment is presently low, its people may wish to increase it, and thus increase their standard of living. Figure 2-1 illustrates this point.

FIGURE 2-1 *The Importance of Capital Equipment*

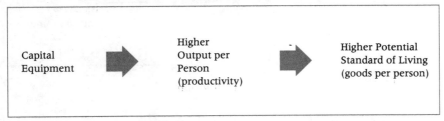

(c) Land (natural resources)

The third economic resource available to the mini-society is the *natural resources* of the island, including land and plants, streams and fish, forests and animals, minerals, and so on. Economists lump these together under the name **land**. A difference between land and capital is that capital equipment is man-made and reproducible while not all natural resources are reproducible. On the other hand, there is a relationship between a society's technology and stock of capital equipment, and what it can use as natural resources. For example, until the development of nuclear reactors, uranium could not reasonably be considered an economic resource. Many people hope that technology can, in similar ways, develop other new energy resources. Thus, while some natural resources become depleted, new technologies may be developed using more plentiful resources.

The task of an economic system

The task of any economic system is to organize and use these economic resources, or productive inputs, to produce goods and services (**output**) of the types and quantities that will best satisfy the needs and wants of the people of the society, as shown in Figure 2-2. This process can sometimes be quite complex. For instance, the production of an automobile involves people (labor) with a wide variety of skills and talents, very sophisticated capital equipment, and resources of various types. On the other hand, food production in some countries consists of peasant farmers tilling the soil with only the most primitive equipment. In organizing and using their economic resources, however, all societies face the same basic problem.

FIGURE 2-2 ***The Basic Operation of Any Economic System***

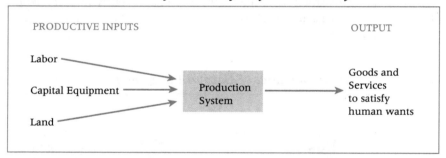

The "economic problem": Scarcity

The basic problem of economics is simply that society's economic resources, or productive inputs, are in limited supply, while people's wants seem to be unlimited. This is known as the problem of **scarcity**. Like all societies, our desert-island mini-society would like to have more goods and services than it is able to produce with its available inputs.

The production-possibilities curve

One way of illustrating the problem of scarcity is with a **production-possibilities curve**. Suppose our desert islanders can only produce two items—vegetables and fish. If all their economic inputs were devoted to producing vegetables, they could produce 15 kilograms of vegetables daily, but no fish. This option is shown as combination **A** in Figure 2-3 which indicates vegetable production of 15 kg and fish production of 0. If the desert islanders went to the opposite extreme and used all their productive inputs to produce fish, the result would be fish production of 5 kg and vegetable production of 0, as shown by combination **F** in Figure 2-3.

Of course, it is more likely that the islanders would choose to produce some combination of fish and vegetables, such as combinations **B** (14 kg vegetables and 1 kg fish), **C** (12 kg and 2 kg), **D** (9 kg and 3 kg) or **E** (5 kg and 4 kg). In making their choice, however, they will be restricted by the limitations of the production-possibilities curve: since their economic resources are limited, *producing more of one product necessarily means being able to produce less of the other.* The islanders may want to have 4 kg of fish and 12 kg of vegetables (combination **X**), but they will not be able to. Resource scarcity dictates that if they want 4 kg of fish, they can only have 5 kg of vegetables, and if they are to have 12 kg of vegetables, fish production can only be 2 kg. Thus, while it is possible to produce 4 kg of fish or 12 kg of vegetables per day, it is not possible to produce this much of both on the same day. The islanders must make choices among various combinations of products, and the production-possibilities curve reflects the limitations that resource scarcity imposes upon their choices.

FIGURE 2-3 *Production-Possibilities Curve*

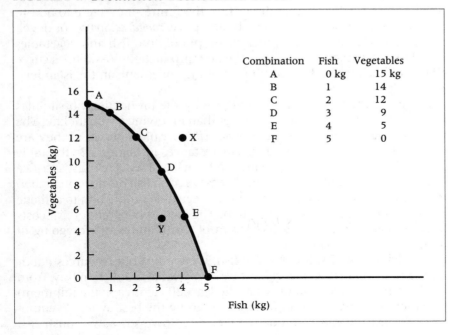

Combination	Fish	Vegetables
A	0 kg	15 kg
B	1	14
C	2	12
D	3	9
E	4	5
F	5	0

However, the combinations shown by the production-possibilities curve are based on two important assumptions—that the islanders use *all of their available productive inputs,* and that they utilize them as *efficiently as possible.* If some of their productive inputs were not used (if, for instance, some of the workers were sick, or one of their fish spears was broken) output would be below the potential level shown by the production-possibilities curve. Point **Y**, at which fish production is 3 kg and vegetable production is 5 kg, reflects such a situation. With fish production at 3 kg, vegetable production could be as high as 9 kg rather than 5 kg, and with vegetable production at 5 kg, fish production could be as high as 4 kg rather than 3 kg. However, if the islanders do not employ all of their productive inputs, their production will be below its potential. In fact, even if all inputs are employed, production may fall short of its potential. If the islanders' inputs (labor and capital equipment) were not producing fish and vegetables as efficiently as possible, production could be below its potential level and the islanders could still wind up at point **Y**.

It is important to recognize that the production-possibilities curve indicates the economy's *potential* output, assuming that economic inputs are fully employed and efficiently utilized. Production can be at any point on the production-possibilities curve (if inputs are fully and efficiently utilized) or within the shaded area (if they are not), but cannot be outside the curve.

However, the islanders need not live forever within the limitations imposed by the curve shown in Figure 2-3. This curve represents the situation at a *particular point in time,* given the economic resources available to the islanders at that time. If, in the future, they were to add to their economic resources, say, by building *new capital equipment* or developing *new technologies,* their potential output of both fish and vegetables could increase. Figure 2-4 shows the new production-possibilities curve that could be created by additions to or improvements in the islanders' economic resources.

The inquisitive reader may wonder why the production-possibilities curve is bowed outward as it is, rather than following a straight line. The shape of the curve reflects the *changing efficiency* of resources as they are shifted from one use to another. For instance, in Figure 2-3, the table shows that to increase fish production from 0 to 1 kg, we must sacrifice only 1 kg of vegetable production. But as we push fish production higher, we must forego ever-higher amounts of vegetable production to achieve the same increases in fish production. The second kilogram of fish costs 2 kg of vegetables, the third kilogram of fish requires the foregoing of 3 kg of vegetables, and so on.

To produce the first kilogram of fish, we would shift resources (labor and capital) out of their *least efficient use* in vegetable production (say, from the least productive land or using the least efficient capital equipment) into their *most efficient use* in fishing (say, using the best available equipment to fish the most productive waters). However, as we push fish

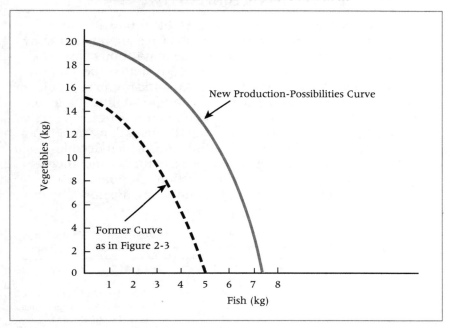

production higher and higher, the trade-off between fish and vegetable production becomes less attractive. Increasingly, we have to shift labor and capital out of more efficient uses in vegetable production and into less efficient uses in fishing. The fifth kilogram of fish production is particularly costly in terms of vegetable production lost (5 kg of vegetables), as it requires that we shift labor and capital out of our last (and most efficient) use in vegetable production and into our least efficient use in fish production. As a result of these factors, the production-possibilities curve is not a straight line, which would reflect a constant trade-off between fish and vegetable production, but rather a curve which reflects *changing efficiencies* and trade-offs.

We have used a very simplified situation, involving a production-possibilities curve for only two products, in order to illustrate the basic nature of the problem of scarcity. While the real world is much more complex, involving many more inputs and outputs, the basic reality shown by our simple production-possibilities curve still exists. Because our economic resources are limited, our output of goods and services is also limited, and society must somehow make choices between various goods and services: we cannot have as much of everything as we would like.

The task of any economic system, then, is to use its scarce economic inputs in the way that best satisfies the needs and wants of the people

THE CONCEPT OF OPPORTUNITY COST

The trade-offs between fish and vegetable production as shown by the production-possibilities curve are referred to by economists as **opportunity costs**. The opportunity cost of using economic resources to produce any item is the amount of any other item that those same economic resources could have produced instead. The production-possibilities table in Figure 2-3 provides a good illustration of this concept.

The opportunity cost of producing the first kilogram of fish is the loss of 1 kg of vegetable production, which declines from 15 to 14 kg. The opportunity cost of the second kilogram of fish is the 2 kg of vegetable production lost when their production falls from 14 to 12 kg, and so on, as shown by the following table.

Combination	Fish Production	Vegetable Production	Opportunity Cost of:
A	0 kg	15 kg	
B	1	14	The 1st kg of fish = 1 kg vegetables
C	2	12	The 2nd kg of fish = 2 kg vegetables
D	3	9	The 3rd kg of fish = 3 kg vegetables
E	4	5	The 4th kg of fish = 4 kg vegetables
F	5	0	The 5th kg of fish = 5 kg vegetables

We can express opportunity cost in terms of vegetable production foregone for *each additional kilogram* of fish, as shown in the table. Alternatively, we can calculate the opportunity cost of *any given amount* of fish production. For instance, the table shows that the opportunity cost of the third kilogram of fish production is 3 kg of vegetables, while the opportunity cost of 3 kg of fish production is 6 kg of vegetables, because if the entire 3 kg of fish had not been produced, vegetable production could have been 15 kg rather than 9 kg.

To calculate the opportunity cost of anything, ask yourself, "What could have been produced instead of it?" For instance, the opportunity cost of building a $15 billion oil and gas pipeline is not the $15 billion, but rather the other products (housing, roads, machinery and so on) that could have been produced by the inputs used to produce the pipeline. And, to a student, the opportunity cost of riotous living on the weekend could be viewed as the 16 extra marks that he or she could have obtained on the economics test if the time had been spent studying.

of the society. This task, however, is not nearly as simple as it may seem. First we will have to develop answers to three specific questions:

- How do we determine what people's needs and wants really are, so that we can produce appropriate goods and services?
- How do we organize ourselves so as to produce those goods and services as well as possible?
- How do we decide who will get how much of the goods and services that we manage to produce? Should some groups or individuals get more than others, and, if so, how much more? Conversely, is there a minimum amount that anyone should have, and how little should that be?

These are the three most basic economic questions that every society must answer, regardless of the particular type of economic system it has chosen.

The three basic questions of economics

(a) What to produce?

Because economic resources, or productive inputs, are scarce, no society can have all the goods and services it would like to have. Instead, it must make choices. For example, the people in our desert-island mini-society would have to decide whether they should use their inputs to produce fish, vegetables, shelter, nets, spears, traps, plows or other things. These choices will not be easy to make, because the more they produce of one thing they want (such as fish), the less they will be able to produce of other things they want (such as vegetables).

Even wealthy societies such as Canada cannot avoid the necessity of having to choose what to produce (and therefore what not to produce). Should Canada produce more housing? More schools? More hospitals? More gas and oil pipelines? More highways? More cars? More boats? More color televisions?

One of the most basic "what to produce" decisions that must be made is whether *consumer goods* or *capital goods* will be produced. Consumer goods (such as food, clothing and automobiles) can be enjoyed now, but do not contribute to longer-term economic prosperity. Capital goods (such as tools and equipment), on the other hand, provide less immediate enjoyment but will contribute to society's production and prosperity for many years. Obviously, the degree to which a society decides to produce capital goods (as opposed to consumer goods) will have a strong bearing on the direction and growth of its economy. Figure 2-5 illustrates this dilemma.

As noted, the decision to use scarce economic resources to produce more of one good involves a decision not to produce other goods. Who should make these choices: consumers? business people? the government? Different societies make these decisions in different ways, as we will see.

FIGURE 2-5 *Consumer Goods Versus Capital Goods*

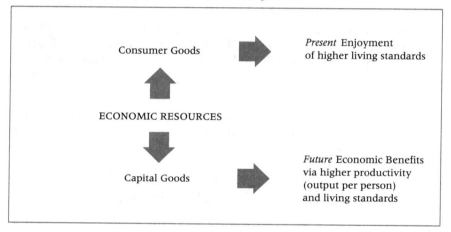

(b) How to produce it?

Once we have decided *what* we want to produce, we must decide *how* each product or service is to be produced. This is a question of production methods: how should we combine our scarce inputs of labor, capital equipment and land for use in production?

As a simple example, suppose our desert-island mini-society has decided to produce (catch) fish. The next question is, how should it do this? Should it catch them by hand? Or use spears? Or nets? Before the people can actually produce the fish they want, it is essential that they make a decision about how to produce them.

Production methods vary greatly from product to product; some are almost completely manual while others are almost totally automated. In general, we try to use inputs in the most efficient way possible, so as to get the *maximum output per unit of input*. This avoids wasting our scarce inputs and thus increases our economic prosperity.

Different societies often produce the same products in quite different ways. For example, farming in North America uses a great deal of capital equipment and very little labor, while farming in Southeast Asia uses a great deal of manual labor and very little capital equipment. Yet both production methods make economic sense, because labor is relatively scarce and thus costly in North America while capital equipment is scarce and labor is plentiful in Southeast Asia. So both production methods are efficient, in the sense that they economize on the use of those inputs which are most scarce relative to the others: capital equipment in Asia and labor in North America.

(c) Who gets what?

The final basic question is: *how will the society divide its output of goods and services among its members?* Who will receive what share of the output?

Suppose our desert-island mini-society consists of 10 people whose daily total output of food is 20 fish. How should these be divided among the 10 people? Should everyone receive the same share? Or should some have more than others? If so, who? And why? Should each person get only as many fish as he or she catches? What if someone can't catch any?

Somehow, our mini-society must answer this basic question, as must every society. This is certainly the most controversial of the three questions; indeed, revolutions have been fought over it.

Obviously, in an economy such as Canada's, which uses money, a person's share of the society's output depends on how much he or she can buy—it depends on his or her *income*. If an accountant's income is twice as large as a laborer's, the accountant's share of the economic pie will be twice that of the laborer.

But how should society decide who gets what share? Should doctors have a larger share (income) than dentists? Should engineers have a larger share than accountants? Should teachers have a larger share than nurses? Should professional athletes have a larger share than doctors? Somehow, every society has to work out how to divide up the economic pie.

Answering the three questions

In this chapter we have considered the three basic questions of economics, which every society must answer—what to produce, how to produce it and how to divide it up. As noted earlier, different societies answer these questions in very different ways. In the next chapter, we will examine the different types of economic systems that exist in the world today, and how they approach the basic questions of economics.

DEFINITIONS OF NEW TERMS

Economics   The study of the decisions a society makes regarding the production of goods and services and the division of these among its people.

Inputs   Economic resources such as labor, capital equipment and natural resources that are used to produce goods and services.

Labor   The largest single productive input available to any economy, labor includes all of the productive talents of the people of a society, mental as well as physical.

Capital (Equipment)   The tools, equipment, machinery and factories used by labor to increase production per person and thus living standards.

Land   Short form for all the natural resources available to a society's economy as economic inputs.

Output   The goods and services produced by a society using its productive inputs.

Scarcity   The problem that, while economic inputs (and thus potential output) are limited in availability, people's wants and needs are apparently unlimited.

Production-Possibilities Curve   A graph showing the maximum possible output of one product that can be combined with any given output of another product, assuming full and efficient utilization of all available productive inputs.

Opportunity Cost   The concept that the real economic cost of producing something is the foregone opportunity to produce something else that could have been produced with the same inputs.

CHAPTER SUMMARY

1. The basic task of an economic system is to use its productive *inputs* (labor, capital equipment and land) to produce goods and services so as to satisfy the wants and needs of the people of the society.

2. This task encounters the problem of *scarcity*: whereas society's economic resources are limited in quantity, people's wants and needs are apparently unlimited; thus, not all wants and needs can be satisfied.

3. The task of an economic system, then, is to make the best possible use of its scarce economic resources by providing answers to the following three questions:

(a) *what* to produce

(b) *how* to produce it, and

(c) *how to divide it* among the people so as best to satisfy the needs and wants of the society.

QUESTIONS

1. In the affluent society of Canada today, have we overcome the problem of scarcity or do we still face it?

2. Of the three productive inputs (labor, capital and land), which is the most important today? Which is gaining in importance the most rapidly?

3. In some societies, old people who are unable to work any longer are left to die. What might explain such a custom?

4. How does the custom referred to above compare to Canada's attitudes toward those who are unable to support themselves? What might explain this difference?

5. Ed Schreyer, while Premier of Manitoba, suggested that the highest paid people in industry and government should receive no more than two-and-a-half times as much take-home pay as the lowest-paid workers. Do you agree with him? Why? What do you believe would happen if such a policy were implemented?

6. Following is a table showing the production possibilities for widgets and reemistrams.

Combination	Number of Widgets	Number of Reemistrams
A	0	20
B	1	18
C	2	14
D	3	8
E	4	0

What is the opportunity cost of producing:

(a) the first widget? **(e)** three widgets?

(b) the second widget? **(f)** the fourth widget?

(c) two widgets? **(g)** four widgets?

(d) the third widget?

7. While all economic resources are scarce in the sense of being in limited supply, the problem of scarcity is particularly dramatic when the physical amount of a resource is actually diminishing, as with some agricultural land.

According to a government inventory of Canada's land resources carried out in the 1960's and 1970's, only 11 percent of Canada's land is capable of sustaining agriculture of any kind, less than 5 percent is capable of sustaining crops and less than 0.5 percent is valuable, class-one land capable of sustaining the whole range of Canadian crops. Thirty-seven percent of Canada's class-one agricultural land and 25 percent of the nation's class-two land can be seen from the top of Toronto's CN Tower. Under pressure of "urban sprawl," this prime agricultural land continues to be converted to residential, commercial and industrial uses.

(a) Why does this high-quality agricultural land continue to be converted to other uses?

(b) Should the goverment permit this to happen?

(c) What could be done to arrest this trend and protect our agricultural land?

8. The following table shows production possibilities for two commodities—fradistats and kadiddles.

Combination	Fradistats	Kadiddles
A	0	6
B	8	5
C	15	4
D	21	3
E	26	2
F	30	1
G	33	0

(a) What is the opportunity cost of producing:
the first kadiddle: _____
the second kadiddle: _____
the third kadiddle: _____
the fourth kadiddle: _____
the fifth kadiddle: _____
the sixth kadiddle: _____

(b) Draw the production-possibilities curve for fradistats and kadiddles on a graph, placing kadiddles on the vertical axis and fradistats on the horizontal axis.

(c) If the economy achieved greater efficiency in the production of kadiddles, how would the production-possibilities curve change?

(d) If a more efficient method of producing fradistats were developed, how would the curve change?

(e) Suppose more economic resources (labor, materials and capital) became available. How would the curve change?

9. Fred's Fradistats Ltd. can produce fradistats using either of two production methods: manual or mechanized. Using the manual

production method, 10 employees are required, working 8 hours per day at $10 per hour. Overhead costs (rent, office, etc.) are $200 per day and material costs are $5 per fradistat. The manual method produces 50 fradistats per day.

Using the mechanized production method, 5 employees are required, working 8 hours per day at $10 per hour. Overhead costs (rent, office, etc.) are $200 per day and material costs are $5 per fradistat. Depreciation expenses on the fradistat-forming machine are $300 per day and the machine uses $150 of energy per day. The mechanized production method also produces 50 fradistats per day.

(a) Use the table below to calculate the cost of producing each fradistat using each of these two production methods.

	Manual Method	*Mechanized Method*
Labor cost per fradistat	$	$
Material cost per fradistat		
Overhead cost per fradistat		
Depreciation cost per fradistat		
Energy cost per fradistat		
Total cost per fradistat	$	$

According to the above figures, which production method would be chosen as the most efficient method?

(b) Suppose wage rates increased to $12 per hour. What effect would this have on:
   (i)   production cost per unit under the manual method.
   (ii) production cost per unit under the mechanized method.
   (iii) the choice of production methods.
   (iv) the number of workers employed.
(c) Suppose wage rates were still $10 per hour and energy prices declined by 40 percent. What effect would this have on:
   (i)   production cost per unit under the manual method.
   (ii) production cost per unit under the mechanized method.
   (iii) the choice of production methods.
   (iv) the number of workers employed.
(d) Suppose a new fradistat-forming machine is developed which still requires 5 workers, costs twice as much as the old machine (making depreciation expenses $600 per day), uses $320 of energy per day (compared with $150 for the old machine), and produces 80 fradistats per day. Would it be economical for the company to introduce the new machine?
(e) Sections (b), (c) and (d) show that the most efficient production method depends on _____, _____, and _____.

CHAPTER 3

Types of economic systems

In Chapter 2, we identified the three basic economic questions faced by any society: what to produce, how to produce it, and how to divide it up. In order to focus on these basic problems, and possible solutions to them, we placed ourselves in a desert island setting. Now that we have identified our basic economic problems, our island mini-society will have to devise an *economic system* to decide the answers to these questions. While there are in reality a great variety of economic systems, the two most basic types from which we may choose are the **command system** and the **market system**.

The command system

If the economy is organized along command lines, all basic economic decisions will be made *by the government*. In the case of a large-scale modern economy, these decisions would probably be made through a central government economic planning committee or agency. On our desert island, however, the "government" might consist of one individual, or a small group, who would take over the task of directing, planning and overseeing production. This government would consider the economic resources (labor, capital equipment and natural resources) available to the islanders, and establish priorities for their use (for instance, whether to spend time producing capital goods or consumer goods, and what types of each). In establishing these priorities and translating them into specific requirements for particular products, an economic plan would be established. The person or group in charge would then make decisions regarding the three basic economic questions.

How the command system answers the three questions

The virtue of the command system, at least in the context of our theoretical mini-society, is its *simplicity*. As Figure 3-1 shows, all three questions are decided by the same person, or group. The government decides what to produce, and directs individuals as to their *production quotas*, so that the types and volumes of goods produced conform to the overall plan that has been set. The government would also decide how to produce each good, by designating the *production methods* to be used by each worker and allocating them the equipment necessary to reach their quotas. Finally, the government would settle who receives what share of the economic pie, by determining what *economic reward* (how much fish, or vegetables, or meat) each individual deserves for his or her contribution to the society's welfare. The command system, then, can help to ensure an equal or fair distribution of goods among the islanders by allocating more to people who are in need.

FIGURE 3-1 *The Command System*

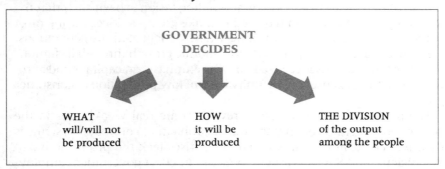

Practical experience with the command system

The command system has certain attractions in a situation such as our desert island mini-society. It offers a relatively simple way to organize people's economic activities according to a *plan*. The very concept of a plan is attractive, as it implies the provision of order to the complex tasks of deciding how best to utilize society's scarce economic resources and determining what to produce, how to produce it and how to share it among the people. In short, the government makes the basic economic decisions, and requires the people to follow these decisions, for their own economic benefit.

Actual experience with command systems has been considerably more complex—and less favorable—than this simple introduction suggests. In the Soviet Union, after the Bolshevik Revolution of 1917, the Communists established what has become the world's most famous command economic system. The state owned all production facilities (factories, farms, mines and so on), and each produced according to production quotas determined by the government's central economic planners, in conjunction with a grand economic plan covering the entire economic system. Since virtually everyone worked for the state, the central economic planners also decided the incomes that various types of workers would receive, and thus decided the division of the economic pie among these groups.

The single greatest achievement of the Soviet Union's command system was the transformation of an economically backward nation into an industrial power in a remarkably short period of time. The command system can achieve such *rapid industrialization* because the economic planners can dictate that great emphasis be placed on producing the capital goods (basic industrial facilities, factories, machinery, and so on) that are required for industrial development. Because economic resources are scarce, such a strong emphasis on the production of capital goods necessarily means that the population must accept low levels of consumer-goods production, and therefore a *low material standard of living*. The magnitude of the Soviet Union's capital-building task has been such that the Russian people have been required to make great sacrifices during most of the twentieth century, for the longer-term benefit of future generations. The Soviet government planned its economic growth through its famous *Five-Year Plans*, the essence of which was emphasis on capital-goods production at the expense (opportunity cost) of low production of consumer goods.

The Soviet Union's experience reveals some real weaknesses in the command system. Probably the major problem of command systems is their *lack of incentives*: state-owned enterprises lack the profit motive to be efficient, and Soviet workers, who are in effect government employees, lack motivation to work efficiently. As a result, productive efficiency tends to be weak, which in turn impairs economic progress; at present, the Soviet authorities' major economic concern is to improve productivity, or output per worker. Productivity has been a particularly severe problem in the agricultural sector of the economy, in which the most capitalistic group in the society—the farmers—have been transformed from self-employed entrepreneurs into less-than-enthusiastic government employees on state-owned farms.

> We've got the perfect economy. We pretend to work, and they pretend to pay us.
>
> Popular Soviet joke

Another increasingly severe problem has been the inability of the *central economic planning system* to cope with the task of planning, directing and coordinating the production and distribution of the vast number of products of a modern industrial economy. While central planning was able to direct the development of the basic industrial facilities of the Soviet Union in the 1920's and 1930's, the planning and coordination of the millions of products associated with today's modern economy is an infinitely more complex task. The task is made more difficult by the fact that today's output includes many more consumer goods, which by their nature are less suited to planning by a central authority than are basic industrial projects.

As a result, the Soviet Union's economic planning system has had increasing difficulty coping with the tremendously complex task of coordinating all aspects of a large modern industrial economy, and has increasingly tended to make errors. Some of these errors (such as the production of large numbers of eyeglass lenses but not the frames to hold them), seem somewhat amusing, but others are more serious. For instance, long delays in the opening of a major electrical generating plant were caused by the omission of a few vital components. Planning problems have been particularly persistent in the consumer-goods sector of the economy because the planners have been unable or unwilling to anticipate or cater to consumer preferences. As a result, despite the general shortage of all consumer goods, and severe shortages of some, the system produces many consumer goods that are so inappropriate or of such poor quality that consumers will not buy them. Such problems constitute a serious misuse of scarce economic resources.

Not only are such planning problems quite common; they can also be difficult to correct. A master economic plan for a nation is an incredibly complex document that must be drawn up for a considerable period of time (at least one year), making it very rigid. The complexity of the plan causes errors to be quite frequent, while its rigidity makes it difficult if not impossible to correct the errors promptly. This situation represents a fundamental problem of the command system with which Soviet authorities have wrestled, with little success, for many years.

A completely planned economy ensures that when no bacon is delivered, no eggs are delivered at the same time.

Another popular Soviet joke

The latest index of products has twenty million articles. The plan can't detail that amount.

Official of Gosplan, the Soviet State Planning Committee

KARL MARX (1818–1883)

Karl Marx was a German philosopher who began studying economics seriously after moving to London in 1849, when he became a prominent member of the British classical school of economics. His theories have always been highly controversial.

Marx's views were undoubtedly influenced by the era in which he lived and wrote—the period of the Industrial Revolution, with its extreme exploitation of labor. In his *labor theory of value*, Marx turned the predominant economic theory of the day—that the value of goods is mainly determined by the amount of labor required to produce them—against capitalism itself, attacking it at its very base.

Marx argued that because labor was the source of economic value, workers should receive the entire value of the products they produced. So, where capitalists view profits as a necessary and justifiable incentive, a reward to producers for supplying desired commodities, Marx viewed them as a *surplus value* gleaned from the unfair exploitation of other people's labor.

Marx developed an extensive definition of *social class*, and claimed that, since the capitalist system relied on the exploitation of a particular group (workers), class differences and inequalities could never be abolished under capitalism. In the increasing alienation of workers from owners, Marx foresaw the seeds of a possible socialist revolution, in which the working class would take over the means of production and the economic planning for the whole state, to the equal benefit of all members of the society.

Unfortunately, Marx never set down his ideas on exactly how a post-revolutionary socialist economy would operate. Nevertheless, his ideas have inspired many to attempt to work out a systematic approach to a state-run economy, with varying degrees of success. While he did not foresee that the Industrial Revolution would create such a broadly-based middle class in the West, it is important to remember that today, more people world-wide live under some form of socialism than live under capitalism. Where communist revolutions have occurred, the societies have usually been agrarian, rather than industrial, in nature, and have used communism and economic planning to build an industrial state.

The command system in perspective

The greatest strength of a centrally-directed command system is its ability to *direct economic resources* toward the achievement of the state's goals. In the case of the Soviet Union, high-priority goals have included *industrial development* (which means stressing capital-goods production), *national security* (which involves focusing labor and capital on the military and space areas), and *national image* (which has meant emphasizing athletic and cultural achievement). These are the "showcase" sectors of the Soviet economy.

However, the reality of scarcity means that this concentration on some sectors of the economy must occur at the expense of other areas. In the USSR, the consumer-goods sector has been particularly neglected. In addition, centrally-planned economies like the Soviet Union's tend to be both *ineffective* and *inefficient* in their use of economic resources. Such systems are *not responsive* to consumer demand, and *lack incentives* for enterprises, managers and workers to produce what consumers want and to produce it efficiently. As the Soviet economy has grown, it has become increasingly difficult for the planning system to cope with the volume and complexity of the decisions to be made. Errors inevitably occur and proliferate, and, due to the *rigidity* of the plan, the system is slow to correct its errors.

Recently, in an attempt to deal with these economic problems, the Soviet Union has introduced a sweeping reform program called **Perestroika**, which means "restructuring." The goal of Perestroika is to invigorate the Soviet economy by reducing the amount of central economic planning. In its place, there is to be a more decentralized system of economic decision-making, in which consumers and plant managers play a larger role. The reforms also include the introduction of limited elements of private enterprise, in the form of small businesses (including some private farming) and increased financial incentives for employees and managers, to promote efficiency. Most of the Perestroika reforms are characteristic of the market system type of economy that is discussed in the next section.

The market system

Under the command system, all economic decisions are made centrally by the government. The market system provides a completely different way of organizing society's economic resources, with no central planning or control. The process of economic decision-making is completely *decentralized*, with individuals, rather than the government, making the decisions.

What is a market?

Simply stated, markets are where buyers and sellers come together to exchange goods and services for money, or to buy and sell things. Figure 3-2 illustrates this concept a little more formally, using the market for fradistats as an example.

Figure 3-2 shows that the market for fradistats consists of:

(a) a number of sellers offering to sell fradistats, in competition with each other (economists call this the "supply side" of the market), and

(b) many buyers offering to buy fradistats, in competition with each other (economists call this the "demand side" of the market).

From the interaction between buyers and sellers in the marketplace emerges the price of fradistats ($5.00 each) and the sales of fradistats (100 per day). If the willingness of buyers to buy fradistats or the willingness of sellers to sell them were to change, the price and sales of fradistats would also change.

FIGURE 3-2 *The Market for Fradistats*

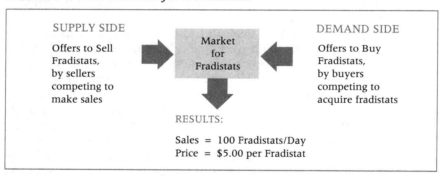

How do markets work?

Markets respond to changes in buyers' demand. For instance, if the demand for fradistats increased (because there were more buyers, or buyers had more money, or they just liked fradistats better than before), the increased demand would cause the price of fradistats to increase. This would make it more profitable to produce fradistats, so that more fradistats would be produced in response to the increased demand for them.

Conversely, if the demand for fradistats were to fall, this would cause their price to fall, making it less profitable to produce them. As a result, producers would produce fewer fradistats, in response to the lower demand of consumers.

```
┌─────────────────────────────────────────────────────────────────────┐
│                                                                       │
│   DEMAND ↑ → PRICE ↑ → AMOUNT PRODUCED ↑                              │
│                                                                       │
└─────────────────────────────────────────────────────────────────────┘

┌─────────────────────────────────────────────────────────────────────┐
│                                                                       │
│   DEMAND ↓ → PRICE ↓ → AMOUNT PRODUCED ↓                              │
│                                                                       │
└─────────────────────────────────────────────────────────────────────┘
```

A market system for our island mini-society

To introduce a market system into our island mini-society, suppose that
some form of money is introduced and each person is encouraged to
produce, sell and buy whatever he or she wishes. Obviously, this would
lead to the production, buying and selling of a great variety of goods and
services. To simplify our examination of this system, we will consider
the production of two items—vegetables and meat. From this simplified
analysis we can gain insight into the overall workings of a market system.

Suppose that vegetables are quite plentiful and are relatively easy to
pick, while meat is much more difficult to obtain. Let's say that the
animals are not plentiful, must be hunted in comparatively inaccessible
and inhospitable parts of the island and have been known to fight back,
a fact that introduces some risk into hunting. As a result of these considerations, on the first day of economic activity, eight people decide to pick
vegetables because it is the easier activity, while only two people are
prepared to undertake the harder work and greater risk of hunting animals. At the end of the first day, when the people come to sell their
products, there will be many more vegetables than people want, and
much less meat than people want. Clearly, our mini-society did not use
its economic resources very wisely on the first day—it produced too
much of one product and too little of the other. Equally clearly, the mini-
society would be better off if it were to shift some economic resources
(mostly labor) out of vegetable production and into meat production, or
hunting.

In a market type of economy, this will tend to happen *automatically*.
Because there is an oversupply of vegetables on the market, the price of
vegetables—and therefore the incomes of vegetable pickers—will be *low*.
Conversely, the shortage of meat on the market will cause the price of
meat—and the incomes of hunters—to be *high*. Thus, there will be an
economic incentive for people to shift out of vegetable production and
into hunting, or meat production. That is, there is an economic incentive
for producers to produce what consumers will buy. There is also, of
course, an economic incentive for producers to produce their products
as efficiently as possible, because higher efficiency means lower costs
and greater profits.

Market equilibrium

When the adjustments referred to above have worked themselves out, the market is said to have reached a state of *equilibrium*, or a more or less stable condition. Perhaps six people will be picking vegetables, compared to eight before. Vegetable pickers' incomes, while higher than they were originally, will still be low compared to the hunters' incomes. However, the difference between their incomes is less than it was originally, so that the remaining vegetable pickers do not view the incomes of hunters as being sufficiently high to attract them into that more difficult task. As for hunters, there will now be four of them, compared to the original two. As a result, the supply of meat will be greater than it was originally and the price of meat (and the incomes of hunters) lower. While hunters' incomes are not as high, compared to those of vegetable pickers, as they were originally, they are still sufficiently high that the four hunters are content to remain as hunters rather than switch to the easier (but less well-paying) task of picking vegetables.

Changes in equilibrium

But, having reached equilibrium, will the island economy remain the same forever and ever? Probably not, since changes can occur that can alter the equilibrium. Here are a few examples of changes that would require adjustments within the economy.

(a) A change in the demand for a product

If the demand for vegetables increased relative to the demand for meat, the *price* of vegetables would *rise*.

Thus, vegetable pickers' incomes would rise, attracting more people into that field and increasing the supply of vegetables, *automatically*, in response to consumer demand.

(b) A change in the supply of a product

Suppose that the existing vegetable plots became less productive, causing a decline in the supply of vegetables. The *price* of vegetables would once again *rise*, making it feasible for producers to buy and use better fertilizers and equipment, or to extend cultivation to new areas, thus increasing the supply of vegetables. If more labor were required for vegetable production, the higher incomes of vegetable pickers would attract people into that field. Thus, a shortage of a product *automatically* causes, through *price changes*, developments that tend to offset the shortage.

(c) Changes affecting production methods

Suppose that a particular productive input, such as the fertilizer used in farming, were to become less plentiful. Obviously, it would be economically desirable to use less of this scarce resource. In a market system, the price of this fertilizer would rise, increasing farmers' costs and reducing their profits, creating an economic incentive for them to use less of this fertilizer or to turn to an alternative. Furthermore, the higher price of this fertilizer would provide an incentive for fertilizer producers to increase their production of it or of alternatives to it. As before, the necessary economic adjustments take place *automatically*, in response to *price changes*.

The foregoing examples show how a market type of economic system adapts to changing circumstances: the system adjusts its production or production methods automatically as people respond to the *economic incentives* created by price changes. Because of the key role played by prices and price changes in such a system, the market system is sometimes referred to as the ''price system.''

How the market system answers the three questions

The operation of the market system stands in strong contrast to the command type of economic system. In a very decentralized way, without any direction or control from the government, the people of the island community have themselves provided answers to the three basic questions.

What to produce is decided by the demand of consumers, as the profit motive and price changes give producers an economic incentive to produce what consumers want.

How to produce each product is decided by the producers. The profit motive provides an incentive for each producer to use the most efficient production methods available, thus contributing to the economic efficiency and prosperity of the society.

The question of *for whom to produce it*, or how to divide the economy's output among various individuals and groups, is a more complex matter. The answer is determined by the incomes of individuals and groups, which are in turn determined in the marketplace by the supply of and demand for each type of productive skill. The *demand* for a particular productive skill depends ultimately on the demand for the product produced by it. The *supply* of that type of labor depends on the number of people who are willing and able to do that type of work. Thus, in a very real sense, no one decides incomes and the division of the economic pie—this is determined quite impersonally in the marketplace, by supply and demand.

The market system in a modern economy

In the simple desert island economy, individual people were both producers and consumers of products. In a modern economic system, the *production* of goods and services is done by privately owned businesses— mostly by **corporations** (owned by many shareholders and managed by hired professional managers) and also by smaller enterprises owned by one or more individuals (sole proprietorships and partnerships, respectively). *Consumption*, on the other hand, is done by households, which buy and use consumer goods and services. Members of households contribute to the production of goods and services by providing businesses with productive inputs, the most important of which is labor. Also, by purchasing **stocks** and **bonds**[1] issued by businesses, households provide businesses with funds (capital) for the purchase of capital equipment. In exchange for productive inputs such as these, businesses pay households incomes in the form of wages, salaries, **interest** and **dividends**.[2]

As Figure 3-3 shows, this process involves two pairs of flows within the economy. The black lines represent the flows of money between the business and household sectors, while the blue lines depict the ''real flows''of real goods and services and real productive inputs. The real flows depict the most basic and essential economic activities—the production and distribution of goods and services.

A modern market-system economy (also known as a ''free enterprise'' or ''capitalist'' system) answers the three basic questions of economics

FIGURE 3-3 *The Operation of a Market Economy*

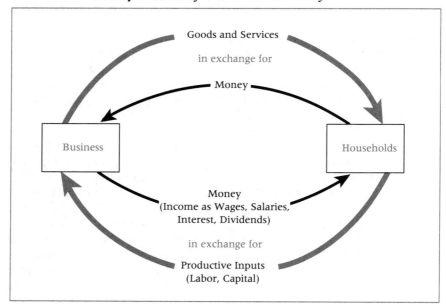

[1] *Stocks*, or corporate *shares*, represent part ownership of a corporation. *Bonds* are the equivalent of IOU's issued by businesses to people who lend money, or ''capital,'' to the business. Both stocks and bonds are sold by businesses to the public to raise capital to finance the expansion of the businesses' productive facilities.

[2] *Interest* is money paid by a borrower (here, a business) to lenders (here, bondholders) for the use of the lenders' money; it can be likened to rent paid for the use of bondholders' funds. *Dividends* are the share of the corporation's profits received by shareholders as owners of the corporation. While interest payments to bondholders must be made regularly by a business, dividends may or may not be paid to the shareholders, depending on the level of profits.

in essentially the same way as our simplified desert island market system did. Since the fundamental goal of business is to earn a profit, businesses will produce those goods and services that are in demand. Therefore, ultimately, the question of *what to produce* can be said to be decided by the consumer. This process is described by the phrases "consumer sovereignty" (meaning that the consumer is viewed as "king of the marketplace") and "dollar votes" (meaning that the consumer's purchase of a product is, in effect, casting a vote for the production of that product).

The question of *how to produce it* is decided by producers, or businesses, who will strive for the most efficient possible method of producing the product. Lower costs means higher profits, and, in a highly competitive industry, may mean survival. The most efficient method may change as the relative cost and productivity of various inputs changes. For example, rising wages may cause businesses to substitute capital equipment for labor (to automate). On the other hand, if labor is inexpensive relative to capital equipment, a business would use less capital equipment and more labor in its production processes. Whatever the decision, in a market type of economy it is privately owned producers—businesses—that make the decision.

The *division of the economic pie* among various individuals and groups is influenced by many factors, the most important one being the interplay between the supply of and the demand for various productive skills. For example, highly skilled people are in short supply as compared with the demand for them, so their incomes (and share of the economic pie) tend to be quite high. There may be an even larger demand for semi-skilled labor (as measured by the numbers employed), but their incomes are quite low because of the large supply of them as compared with the demand for them. As the contrasts between the incomes of professional

---

PRODUCTION METHODS IN THE CANADIAN ECONOMY

The production methods used in the Canadian economy vary widely, with the greatest degree of mechanization in "capital-intensive" primary industries such as prairie grain, forest products and mining. In the manufacturing sector of the economy, production methods range from technologically sophisticated automobile plants and steel mills to "labor-intensive" industries such as clothing and footwear, which use considerable amounts of labor. Generally, Canadian industries that are capital-intensive are best able to compete internationally, while labor-intensive industries suffer from heavy foreign competition. We will consider the problems and choices facing Canadians with respect to such matters in more depth later in this book.

athletes, nurses and farm laborers show, market forces (supply and demand) can generate some incomes that are extremely high and others that are extremely low, in a way that is quite unrelated to how hard people work or to most people's view of the social value of the work done. On the other hand, such a system provides strong incentives for people to move into occupations that are in demand and to work harder. Both of these factors contribute to society's economic prosperity.

ADAM SMITH (1723–1790)

Adam Smith was a Scottish professor of moral philosophy who in 1776 wrote *The Wealth of Nations*, which was to become the most famous and enduring book in the (as yet not founded) field of economics. The essence of *The Wealth of Nations* was that economic liberty, in the form of sellers and buyers competing freely in the marketplace, was the best way to promote the general economic welfare of society. In perhaps the most famous quotation from the book, Smith said, "Every individual endeavours to employ his capital so that its produce may be of greatest value. He generally neither intends to promote the public interest, nor knows how much he is promoting it. He intends only his own security, only his own gain. And he is in this led by an invisible hand to promote an end which was no part of his intention. By pursuing his own interest he frequently promotes that of society more effectually than when he really intends to promote it."

Smith was very critical of monopolies, which restricted the competition that he saw as vital for economic prosperity. He also disliked government policies that protected the monopoly positions of some groups, such as apprenticeship laws restricting the entry of people into certain occupations. By showing how economic freedom could promote the interests of the general public, *The Wealth of Nations* became the rallying point for those who believed in economic liberty and free markets, unhampered by government regulation—that is, "laissez-faire" capitalism.

It is interesting that, more than 200 years after *The Wealth of* able. After a long period of growing government regulation of business and the economy in North America, the trend after the mid-1980's was toward "deregulation," on the grounds that competition would promote efficiency and prosperity more effectively than an extensive system of government regulations.

Thus, people's incomes (and the division of the economic pie) are basically determined in markets, by the forces of supply and demand. There are, of course, other factors, including labor unions and government regulations such as minimum wage and taxation policies, that influence the distribution of society's output among various groups and individuals. These matters, however, are microeconomic in nature and are considered in a separate text.

The role of profits in the market system

Of all the aspects of a free enterprise economy, the most misunderstood is **profits**. The very word "profit" evokes for many people images of exploitation of workers and consumers. As Figure 3-4 illustrates, the *level* of manufacturers' profits is greatly exaggerated by the general public. While surveys indicate that the public believes profits to amount to 30 or 40 cents per dollar of sales, they actually amount to about 7 to 10 cents per dollar. (Ironically, the public believes 20 cents per dollar of sales to be a fair profit.) After taxes, most manufacturers' profits amount to 4 or 5 cents per dollar of sales.

The public also has many misconceptions concerning the *uses* of profits, which are widely regarded as being hoarded away in corporate coffers or being paid out lavishly as dividends to wealthy shareholders. In fact, roughly 30 percent of corporate profits go to taxes and most of the remainder is reinvested by businesses in capital equipment. Dividends to shareholders generally amount to about a 5.5 percent return on their investment, and these "capitalists" include not only the wealthy but all

FIGURE 3-4 *The Public's Attitude to Manufacturers' Profits*

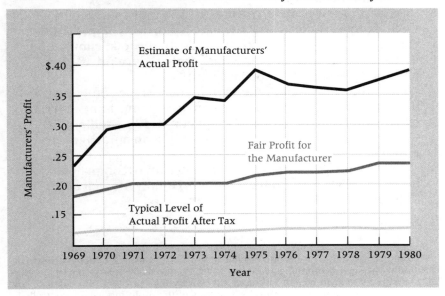

Canadians who have money in pension funds, bank or trust company deposits, life insurance policies, mutual funds and so on. Because of the public's misconceptions about profits and the negative emotional overtones to the word, many companies prefer to call their profits "earnings."

From the viewpoint of the economist, profits play two vital roles in the operation of a market system economy. First, profits provide *incentives* for businesses to produce those goods and services that consumers want, and to produce them as efficiently as possible so as to maximize economic benefits and minimize waste of scarce economic resources. It must be emphasized that using economic resources *effectively* (producing goods that are valued, or wanted) and *efficiently* (so as to maximize production and minimize waste of scarce inputs) are two fundamentally important economic objectives, and that no better way has ever been devised to attain them. Even some communist command systems have moved in recent years to introduce the profit motive into their systems, to give plant managers incentives to be both more efficient and more responsive to consumers' wants.[3]

PROFITS: IT'S ALL IN HOW YOU LOOK AT IT

Suppose a corporation has annual sales of $600 million, profits after taxes of $24 million, 4000 employees and $300 million of shareholders' capital invested in the company.

From the viewpoint of *the employees*, it might seem that they are being underpaid. If the $24 million of profits were divided among them, each would receive $6000 more ($24 million ÷ 4000).

From the viewpoint of *consumers*, $24 million in profits might seem to indicate that they are being overcharged for this company's product. Realistically though, the total elimination of the manufacturer's profits would only reduce prices by 4 percent ($24 million ÷ $600 million).

From the viewpoint of *the shareholders* of the company, their capital invested in the company is earning a rate of return (after tax) of only 8 percent ($24 million ÷ $300 million). Compared to other investments, this is not an attractive rate of return.

Thus, while employees and consumers may complain about this company's high profits, investors could very well be deciding to sell their shares in the company.

---

[3] It should be noted that profits also provide incentives for business to behave in socially harmful ways, such as dumping pollutants (cheaply) into the air and water and monopolizing markets so as to be able to charge excessively high prices. It is the task of government to ensure that these harmful side effects of the profit motive are controlled.

The second important role of profits is the provision of funds for the *financing of purchases of capital equipment*. While businesses do this to improve their own efficiency and profitability, the result, on a wider scale, is improved productivity. This is the basic source of higher living standards for society generally. Thus, reinvestment of profits by business contributes to a society's economic prosperity.

Thus, profits not only serve essential economic purposes, but are also not nearly as high as is generally believed. Many economists are concerned, in fact, that the level of profits may be too low to provide the heavy investment in capital goods needed in the near future to ensure energy supplies, keep Canadian industry internationally competitive and provide Canadians with the rising **standard of living** to which they have become accustomed.

The role of competition in a market economy

We have emphasized that a major advantage of the market system type of economy is its responsiveness to consumer demand. The market system is widely recognized as being particularly able to increase or decrease production of items in response to increases or decreases in demand, as producers seek to produce those items that are most profitable. For this reason, the market system is generally seen as being the system that best serves the interests of the consumer.

For this to be the case, however, there must be competition among producers and sellers. If one producer is able to obtain a **monopoly** of a particular market, it will no longer find it necessary to serve the consumer well. If demand increases, a monopolist may decide not to increase production in response; rather, it may increase prices sharply instead. Worse yet, a monopolist could actually reduce production in order to force prices to higher levels. When there are no other producers to whom consumers can turn for competitive products at a more reasonable price, such strategies can prove very profitable. Because of its ability to restrict supply and raise prices in this manner, a monopolist is said to possess "**market power**."

For such market power to exist does not require that an industry be reduced to a single monopoly producer. Where there are only a *few producers* in an industry, it is sometimes possible for them to act much in the way that a monopolist would, by reaching an agreement among themselves not to compete too aggressively. Firms in this position often agree not to compete regarding prices, and not to seek to expand their production and share of the market beyond certain limits. When this happens, the dominant firms are behaving much as a monopolist would—they are holding output down and prices up.

Thus, monopoly power is a threat to one of the major advantages of the market system—its service to the consumer. That is why many nations, including Canada, have *laws* that try to encourage competition and discourage the formation of monopolies. Without competition between producers, a system of free markets can turn to the advantage of the producer instead of the consumer.

An illustration of a smoothly functioning market system

Figure 3-5 expands upon the concepts in Figure 3-2 to show the operation of a smoothly-functioning market system. While Figure 3-2 showed a single market, Figure 3-5 represents the entire economy, and thus includes markets for all of the economy's goods and services.

On the supply side of the economy, there is a strong ability to produce efficiently the goods and services that are in demand. The economy possesses all of the productive inputs necessary to produce goods and services efficiently: a capable labor force, good capital equipment and ample natural resources or raw materials. In addition, the economy provides producers with strong incentives to use these inputs as efficiently as possible, in the form of the "carrot" of profits (after taxes) and the "stick" of strong competition. In short, the supply side of the economy is capable of efficient production. All that it requires is an appropriate level of demand to ensure that it produces as much as it can.

On the demand side of the economy, what is an appropriate level of demand? If demand is too low, the supply side will produce less than it can produce. Factories and equipment will be idle and workers will be unemployed: there will be a **recession**. On the other hand, if demand is too high, the output of the supply side will be unable to keep up with demand and prices will therefore rise very rapidly: there will be **inflation**.

Ideally, then, the amount of demand would be neither too low nor too high. The demand side would generate high enough demand to prompt the supply side to produce as much output as possible, but not excessive demand that will only cause inflation.

FIGURE 3-5 *A Smoothly Functioning Market System*

SUPPLY SIDE

Strong Ability to
Produce Goods and
Services Efficiently
  i.e. - labor
       - capital equipment
       - natural resources

Plus Incentives to
be Efficient
       - profits (after taxes)
       - competition

Interaction
of
Supply Side
and
Demand Side

DEMAND SIDE

Demand High Enough
to Keep Production
High and Unemployment
Low (avoid a recession)

But Demand Not So
High That Supply
Cannot Keep Up,
Causing Inflation

ECONOMIC PROSPERITY

• high output
• low unemployment
• little or no inflation

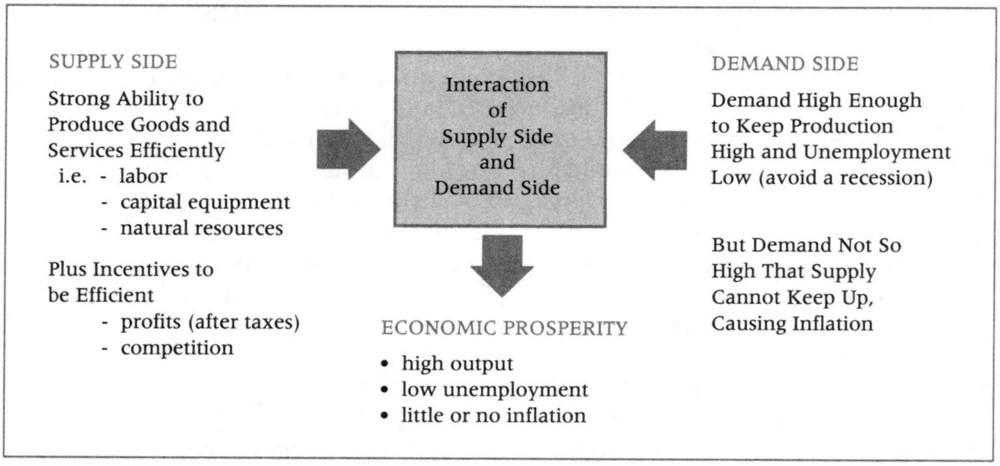

A baffling and contentious concept, profit has been the subject of debate, discussion and misunderstanding for centuries. Eminent men have variously extolled or denied its value to the community. Those who today consider profit as a "corporate rip-off" are, probably unknowingly, echoing the assertion of Michel de Montaigne, the 16th century philosopher, who said: "No man can profit except by the loss of others, and by this reasoning all manner of profit must be condemned." To this way of thinking, it follows, profit is by definition a "rip-off," and the profit motive nothing more than institutionalized greed and covetousness.

On the other side of the question, 19th century economist David Ricardo declared: "Nothing contributes so much to the prosperity and happiness of a country as high profits."

Reprinted from the Annual Report of the Royal Bank of Canada, 1974.

If the economy has a strong supply side and neither too little nor too much demand on the demand side, the results will be as shown at the bottom of Figure 3-5:

- high output of goods and services (i.e.—at or near the economy's potential output),
- high levels of employment (or low unemployment), and
- little or no inflation.

Of course, market economies do not always perform as well as the smoothly-functioning economy shown in Figure 3-5. There are three basic types of problems that a market economy can develop:

- weaknesses on the supply side that prevent it from producing goods and services efficiently, such as a poorly-trained labor force or out-dated capital equipment,

PROFITS ARE EVERYBODY'S BUSINESS

About one dollar of every four in *pension funds* in Canada is invested in corporate shares. Thus, millions of Canadians have billions of dollars invested in shares. Not only do these Canadians receive part of corporate profits; they are in part dependent upon the prosperity of those corporations for their future financial security.

- inadequate demand for goods and services on the demand side, which will cause unemployment and a recession, and
- excessive demand for goods and services on the demand side, which will cause inflation (rapid increases in prices).

Economy-wide problems such as these are the subject of *macroeconomics*, which is covered in the companion text to this one. In this *microeconomics* text, we focus on particular sectors of the economy, such as consumers, business, labour and government.

The market system in perspective

There is no economic system that is more responsive to consumer demand than the market system, which will adjust its production automatically to reflect changes in consumer preferences. Also, no system provides greater incentives for efficient use of economic inputs than the profit motive; as we have seen, it can contribute greatly to productivity and prosperity. The ability of this economic system to automatically coordinate the decisions of millions of businesses and individuals in response to changes in consumer demand has been referred to as "the miracle of the market." Adam Smith, the earliest advocate of this system, described businesspeople as being led by an "invisible hand" (the profit motive) "to promote (the interest of) the society more effectually than when they really intend to promote it."[4]

On the other hand, the market system is not without its weaknesses and problems, some of which we will examine in subsequent chapters. One problem is its tendency to slump into periodic recessions, during which economic progress slows and unemployment rises. Also, the modern large corporation is not as powerless as the producers portrayed in our desert island illustration. In some cases, industries or markets can to a degree become monopolized either by one monopolist or by a few large producers acting together to increase prices and profits by reducing competition among themselves. A similar situation can develop in labor markets when strong labor unions can sometimes secure for their members a disproportionate share of the economic pie, leaving less for less powerful groups. Another problem is the tendency in market economies for great inequalities to develop in the distribution of income, with a few people enjoying very high incomes while others live in poverty. Subsequent chapters will consider many of these problems as well as the efforts of governments to remedy them.

---

[4] Adam Smith, *the Wealth of Nations* (1776).

THE MARKET AND COMMAND SYSTEMS COMPARED

To demonstrate the different ways in which the market and command systems operate, let's consider how each would address an everyday economic problem such as a shortage of bicycles. By a shortage of bicycles, we mean that at the current price, consumers are prepared to buy more bicycles than producers are manufacturing.

In a *market system*, as the demand outran the supply, the price of bicycles would increase, making it more profitable to produce bicycles. In response to this incentive, production of bicycles would increase, as existing manufacturers (and possibly new firms) increased their output. Manufacturers would order more bicycle parts from suppliers, who would order additional parts and materials as needed from their suppliers. At each stage of this process, decisions would be made by the business(es) involved, without central direction or control. The end result would be that, as quickly as possible, more bicycles would become available to consumers at the retail level, but at a higher price than before.

In a *command system*, changes would only be made if the central economic planners directed that this be done. We will assume that the planners have been made aware of the shortage of bicycles, although this is not a certainty, due to the lack of feedback from consumers in this system. The planners must then decide whether to increase bicycle production or not. Again, this is not a certainty—increasing the resources devoted to bicycle production means reducing the resources available for the production of other goods, and the planners may or may not decide that bicycles are sufficiently important to divert resources from other products to bicycles.

Assuming that the planners decide to increase bicycle production, they would have to re-do the economic plan for next year (at the earliest). They would have to instruct bicycle plants, through increased quotas, to produce more bicycles. (At the same time, they would have to reduce the quotas for those products of which less would be produced.) The quotas of all plants that supply parts to the bicycle plants would be increased, and instructions given as to how much of each part to deliver to each bicycle plant, as well as when and how the parts would be delivered. Similar adjustments would be made to the plans of all enterprises that supply parts and materials to the parts suppliers—quotas would have to be changed, and instructions for delivery provided. Increased numbers of workers would have to be allocated to each enterprise that required them under the new plan; again, the planners would have to decide which enterprises would lose workers due to the new emphasis on bicycles, and how the plans and quotas of these enterprises should be adjusted.

Finally, if there were any errors in these detailed plans, or any enterprise could not fulfil its quota, the entire plan to increase bicycle production could be jeopardized. For instance, a shortfall of rubber production could mean too few bicycle tires, as available rubber is allocated to higher-priority products. To correct such problems would require changes to the plan for the next year, at the earliest.

The mixed economic system of Canada

The command and market systems described in the foregoing were quite pure in form, with the government making all economic decisions in the one case and playing virtually no role in the economy in the other. In actual practice, neither extreme has proven workable, and neither exists—virtually every major economic system involves some combination of command and market forces.

Canada's economic system is best described as a "mixed free-enterprise" system, in which both markets (or free enterprise) and government play important roles. Basically, the Canadian economy is a market system, in which most Canadians work for privately owned businesses operating in a market environment, producing goods and services for sale for a profit. However, there are also extensive elements of government involvement (command) in the Canadian economy.

Governments *buy* about one-quarter of all the goods and services produced in Canada. Governments are also a major *producer* of goods and services, mostly through government-owned *Crown corporations* such as Petrocan and Atomic Energy Canada Limited in the energy field, Canadian National in the transportation field, and the Post Office. By 1983, there were 60 such Crown corporations owned by the federal government alone, with assets of over $75 billion and more than 200 000 employees.

Governments also sometimes *provide capital* for certain business undertakings, one of the most notable of which has been the Syncrude Athabasca Tar Sands oil project, in which the federal and Alberta governments invested $500 million of share capital.

Furthermore, governments *regulate* in many ways the operations and practices of businesses; for example, the prohibition of monopolistic practices, the regulation of the conduct of labor relations, laws regulating advertising practices, and the regulation of the production of some farm products by government-sponsored marketing boards. Also, many prices are regulated by governments, including electrical rates, many rents and transportation rates, some energy prices and tobacco and alcohol prices. It is estimated that about 25 percent of all the prices included in the Consumer Price Index are government-regulated prices.

Another major activity of government is the _redistribution of income_ through transfer payments such as unemployment insurance, welfare, old age security allowances, family allowances and so on. Finally, as we shall see in more detail in subsequent chapters, governments undertake to use certain large-scale economic policy _tools_ to steer the entire economy away from the extremes of inflation and depression.

Taken together, these involve a great deal of government participation in and regulation of the economy, making the term _mixed free-enterprise_ an appropriate description of the Canadian economy.

The traditional system

To complete our discussion of economic systems, we should consider the _traditional_ system. Under this system, all economic decisions are made according to historic tradition. Today, this type of system is quite rare, existing mostly in tribal societies in remote regions such as the Amazon region of Brazil. In such societies, a person's economic activities and status are dictated by tradition. People perform the same economic activities (hunting, fishing, cultivating) as their parents did, using the same production methods and dividing up the economic pie into the traditional shares for various groups. This is a very static economic and social system that is of little interest to economists.

DEFINITIONS OF NEW TERMS

Command System   An economic system in which economic decisions are made mainly by the government, in a centralized manner.

Market System   An economic system in which economic decisions are made mainly by consumers and privately owned producers, in a decentralized manner.

Perestroika (Restructuring)   A program to reform the Soviet economy by making it less centralized and by introducing some elements of free enterprise.

Corporation   A business firm owned by shareholders who, in many cases, are numerous and do not take part in the management of the corporation; most large business firms are corporations.

Stocks (Shares)   Financial securities representing part ownership of a corporation.

Bonds   Financial securities issued by businesses to people who have loaned funds (capital) to the business.

Interest Money paid by a borrower to a lender for the use of the lender's money.

Dividends That proportion of a corporation's profit paid to shareholders as owners of the corporation.

Profit(s) Those funds left from a business' sales revenues after all expenses have been paid; such funds are therefore available (after taxes have been paid) for dividends to shareholders and reinvestment in the business.

Standard of Living A measure of the economic prosperity of the people of a society, usually expressed in terms of the volume of consumer goods and services consumed per household (per year). Also referred to as *material* standard of living, because it ignores other factors that influence human welfare.

Monopoly The control of an industry or a market by a single seller.

Market Power The ability to raise one's price; usually associated with a dominant or monopolistic position in a market.

Recession A situation in which the economy is producing considerably less than its potential output, and unemployment is high. (See also Chapter 7.)

Inflation A situation in which prices in general in the economy are rising rapidly.

CHAPTER SUMMARY

1. There are two basic types of economic system—the command system and the market system.

2. In a command system, the government's central economic planners decide what to produce, how it will be produced and the division of the economic pie.

3. The main strength of the command system is its ability to generate rapid economic growth, while its main weaknesses are a lack of incentives and the errors and inflexibilities associated with the complex task of planning in detail the operations of an entire economic system.

4. The market system (also called the price system and the free enterprise system) operates in a decentralized manner, through markets. In these markets, what to produce is decided by consumer demand, how to produce it is decided by producers, and the division of the economic pie is decided by people's incomes.

5. Profits play a vital role in the operation of a market system. Profits provide incentives for the efficient use of economic resources and are a major source of funds for capital investment, which contributes to economic prosperity by increasing output per worker.

6. Competition is essential to the effective operation of a market economy. Competition polices producers, keeping prices and profits down and forcing producers to be responsive to consumers.

7. The main strength of the market system is its high living standards, which are the result of the strong incentives this system provides for efficient use of resources. The main weaknesses of the market system are its tendency toward periodic recessions, the domination of some markets by monopolistic corporations and strong labor unions, and a tendency for incomes to be distributed very unevenly.

8. Canada's economic system is a mixed free-enterprise system: while it is basically a market or free-enterprise system, it includes significant elements of government involvement in the economy, or "command."

QUESTIONS

1. Three of the following are essential to the operation of a free-enterprise market economy. Which one might such an economy operate without?
   (a) the profit motive
   (b) markets
   (c) corporations
   (d) prices

2. Not all economists agree that we in North America have "consumer sovereignty." Some economists argue that big business is able to control the consumer to the point where the situation would be better called "producer sovereignty." Do you agree or disagree? Why?

3. Our economic system is not purely a free-enterprise market system because the government (command) is involved in the economic process to a significant degree.
   (a) What are some of the "rules of the game" that the government sets and enforces?
   (b) To what extent does the government (that is, command) play a role in deciding what to produce, how to produce it, and the division of the economic pie?

4. Do you agree with de Montaigne's statement that "No man can profit except by the loss of others, and by this reasoning all manner of profit must be condemned"? Does every economic transaction necessarily involve a winner and a loser?

5. If you were a Soviet economic planner,
   (a) how would you make decisions about what to produce (and not to produce)?
   (b) how would you decide which consumer goods to produce (and not produce)?
   (c) how would you decide to divide the economic pie (that is, the wages and salaries to be received by each type of occupation)?
   (d) how would you encourage your workers and managers to work efficiently?

CHAPTER 4

Introduction to microeconomics

What is microeconomics?

We have described the Canadian economy as basically a market type of economy, in which economic decisions are largely made in a decentralized manner by households (consumers) and businesses (producers). The operation of such an economic system involves billions of individual decisions by consumers, business firms and workers regarding such matters as consumer purchases, prices, production levels, wages, capital investment and so on. Taken together, these make up the overall *macroeconomic* flows shown in Figure 4-1: the total volume of goods and services and of productive inputs, and the money spent on them. Macroeconomics studies these overall flows and what determines the size of them, with particular emphasis on what causes the entire economy to alternate between periods of recession and periods of prosperity and inflation. In macroeconomic analysis, we emphasize the interaction between the level of *aggregate demand*, or total spending in the economy, and *aggregate supply*, or the economy's capacity to produce goods and services. If aggregate demand is too low, the economy will not produce all the output that it can, and there will be a recession, with high unemployment. On the other hand, if aggregate demand is excessively high, supply will not be able to keep up with demand, and the prices of goods and services will rise—there will be inflation.

Inflation and recession are important macroeconomic problems that affect the entire economy. However, it is also important and interesting to narrow the focus of our attention onto the specific goods and services that comprise these overall macro flows. For each of these individual

FIGURE 4-1 *The Organization of a Market Economy*

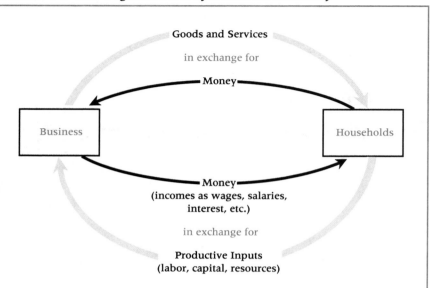

goods and services, and each productive input, a specific *amount* is
bought and sold, at a specific *price*.

Microeconomics is largely concerned with the processes whereby individual prices are determined. It analyzes the prices of goods and services
produced by various types of industries, from small farms to monopolistic corporations, and the price (wages and salaries) of labor under
varying conditions, from migrant farm labor to plumbers to professional
athletes. These prices and the processes that determine them are
extremely important, for they will determine how much Canadians will
pay for their houses, cars, mortgages, gasoline, food and so on, and how
much they will receive for their labor.

How are prices determined?

Having established the importance of prices in the operation of our economic system, we must now turn to the question of how prices are
actually determined. The question of prices has occupied people's minds
for centuries. In the Church-dominated society of medieval times, the
Church's concept of a **just price** had great influence: no one was to sell
anything for more than it was "worth." Perhaps understandably, many
people found this guideline a little vague for making actual decisions
about specific prices for specific products. For instance, when there was
a shortage of grain, the price of bread tended to rise far above the "just

price," calling into question the ability of this concept to explain prices.

Another early theory regarding prices was the **utility theory of value**, which stated that the value, or price, of something should reflect its usefulness, or utility. While both the just price and utility theories held a certain amount of superficial appeal, they both suffered from the fact that they in no way related to or explained the actual prices of things in the real world. Not only were many prices far removed from many people's idea of what was fair, but many useless items commanded much higher prices than items that were essential. A famous example of the latter is the "paradox of value": why does water, which is essential to life, have such a low price, while diamonds, which are of little practical value, are very expensive?

The answer to the paradox of value lies in the economic concepts of *supply and demand*. While water is essential and is bought and used in great quantities, the supply of it is so great relative to the demand that its price is low. On the other hand, while diamonds are not in particularly great demand (many people may want them, but few can afford them, so the demand is not really large), they are in even shorter supply, so their price is high. If the supply of clean water were to decline drastically, our analysis suggests that the price of clean water should rise significantly—as residents of more polluted urban areas already know. Similarly, if the supply of diamonds (that is, the volume of diamonds offered for sale on the market) rose significantly, they would no longer command such a high price—as those who control the supply of diamonds understand clearly.

These examples provide only a cursory glance at the concepts of supply and demand, and how they interact to determine prices. Nonetheless, they illustrate an important basic point. In our microeconomic analysis of the prices of specific products and services, we will use the same basic tools that we use in studying macroeconomics. In macroeconomics, we are concerned with *aggregate* demand for and supply of goods and services, whereas in microeconomics, we shift our focus onto the supply of and demand for *individual* goods and services.

The role of markets

The determination of prices has a great deal to do with the way in which the most fundamental economic forces—supply and demand—operate in markets for goods, services and productive inputs. Through the operation of these markets, answers will be reached to the three basic economic questions: what to produce, how to produce it and how to divide it up. In answering all of these questions, *prices* are of central importance.

Prices help to decide *what will be produced* in a market economy. For instance, if the demand for sailboats increases, the price of sailboats will rise, making the production of sailboats more profitable and creating an incentive for producers to produce more sailboats. Similarly, if there is a shortage of computer programmers, the price of computer programmers (their incomes) will rise, which will induce more people to enter that field. Conversely, if there is an oversupply of a product, its price will fall (or, in an inflationary economy, not rise as rapidly as the cost of producing it), which will discourage the production of that product. Also, an oversupply of a particular occupational skill, such as photography, will depress its value, discouraging people from entering that field. Thus, in a market system, prices, and changes in prices, play a vital role in deciding what will be produced.

Prices also help to decide *how goods and services will be produced*. To produce its output of goods and services, society will want to use the most efficient production methods possible. Obviously, this will involve economizing the most on those inputs that are most scarce. For example, if lumber is scarce, the society should cut wastage of lumber to a minimum, and use substitutes for it wherever possible. In a market economy, this will be done, for the following reasons. If lumber is scarce, its price will be high. Since it is such a costly input, producers will cut wastage of it to a minimum and use substitutes when they can. As a result, the production methods used by businesses will economize the most on the scarcest inputs, because of their high prices. This is obviously a desirable situation, and prices help to bring it about.

Finally, in a market economy, prices play a key role in deciding *how the economic pie will be divided up*. Since no society can have all the goods and services it wants, it is necessary to find a way of distributing, or rationing, the limited output. In a basically market economy, this function is largely performed by prices. As we have seen, a person's overall share of the economic pie is determined by his or her income (after taxes)—by the price of his or her productive services. Also, the prices of individual goods and services largely determine who will get them. For instance, potatoes are plentiful and therefore inexpensive, so that virtually everyone can have potatoes if they want them; but vacations in Hawaii are scarce and therefore very expensive, which restricts such vacations to those who can pay high prices. Most goods and services in our society are rationed out in this way, with the more scarce ones going to those who can and will pay the higher prices for them.[1]

---

[1] Many people will object to a rationing system that gives many goods to people who have money, and few to those who do not have money. They might accept such a system for luxuries (such as trips to Bermuda) but not for necessities (such as milk). During the Second World War, when there were shortages of essential foodstuffs such as milk and meat, the government used a different rationing system. Instead of letting the prices of milk, meat, and other essentials rise so that only the wealthy could have them, the government gave families coupons with which they could buy those things. In effect, then, these goods were rationed out according to family need rather than family income.

The importance of competition and information

For a market system to operate effectively, there must be a reasonable amount of *competition* among sellers. Competition not only gives consumers a choice of different products in the marketplace, but also spurs producers to be as efficient as possible and to keep prices as low as possible, to the advantage of the consumer. By contrast, where competition is lacking, producers have a tendency to grow complacent and inefficient. In these circumstances, the market serves the interests of the producer rather than those of the consumer.

COMPETITION AND THE POST OFFICE

Possibly the most-criticized monopoly in Canada is Canada Post. Most of this criticism pertains to first class mail delivery, on which Canada Post has a virtually complete monopoly, since competitors are required by law to charge three times the rate charged by Canada Post on first class mail. Many Canadians have come to regard Canada Post as synonymous with poor service.

That, however, is not necessarily so. Canada Post's Priority Post service is widely regarded as an effective and efficient courier service. In the view of most observers, the reason for the difference is that Priority Post has to compete with private couriers.

Information also plays a vital role in the effective functioning of markets. A free marketplace can best serve the interests of consumers if those consumers are well informed. Well informed means not only that they can judge the quality of the products available to them, but also that they are aware of what products are available and at what prices. Only if consumers are well informed in both these senses will they be able to take advantage of the opportunities offered by a free and competitive marketplace.

The "price system": Supply, demand and markets

Since, in a market economy, prices play such a central role in determining the answers to the most basic economic questions facing society, some people prefer the name *price system* for this approach to economics. Underlying the price system, however, are the basic economic forces of *supply* and *demand*.

Supply and demand interact to determine prices, wages and salaries

A COMPETITIVE MARKET FOR EDUCATION?

In most school systems, students are assigned to schools according to where they live, and have little or no choice which school they will attend. However, some critics would like to see competition introduced into the education "industry." They recommend that students (or their parents) be given vouchers for each year's education and allowed to "spend" their vouchers at any school they wish. The more students (and vouchers) a school attracted, the more revenue it would have. The theory is that this competition would put pressure on schools to improve the quality of their education.

Such a plan would work best if parents and/or students were knowledgeable concerning what was a good education. This would put pressure on schools to provide quality education, or risk "losing business" to schools that did. According to advocates of the voucher system, this approach would create more pressure for improved education than the present process of lobbying school boards politically.

On the other hand, to the extent that parents and/or students were not knowledgable, such a system would be less effective. At least some schools (just like some businesses) would be able to offer a lower-quality "product" to unsuspecting or uninformed consumers. In some cases, the quality of education could even decline in such a marketplace.

under a wide range of conditions. In markets for goods and services, these conditions range from extremely competitive industries involving a great number of small business firms (such as many service industries) to industries dominated by a few corporate giants (such as automobile manufacturing and steel) to monopolies (such as telephone service). In each of these cases, the process whereby prices and production levels are determined is different, and we will consider each separately, in Chapters 7 through 11.

Another major area of concern is *labor markets*, and the processes that determine the incomes of individuals and occupational groups, and thus the division of the economic pie. As with the prices of goods and services, wages and salaries (the prices of various types of labor) are determined under a wide variety of conditions, ranging from very open markets (such as part-time student labor) to markets where labor unions have a great deal of influence (such as many skilled trades).

In considering how supply and demand determine the prices of various goods and services and the incomes of various types of labor, we will be examining the operation of three of the four major sectors of the economy—*households* (or consumers), *business* and *labor*. However, not all prices in the economy are determined freely by the forces of supply and demand. To complete our microeconomic study of the economy, we must also consider the fourth major sector of the economy—*government*. The government intervenes in the marketplace to hold prices down in some cases (such as rent controls) so as to benefit consumers, and to hold prices up in other cases (such as farm price supports and minimum wages) in order to benefit producers and workers.

In studying microeconomics, then, we will examine the four basic sectors of the economy—consumers, business, labor and government. After considering in Chapter 5 the various forms that business organization takes in Canada, in Chapter 6 we will begin our analysis of the microeconomy with the consumer, and the nature of demand.

The Economic Organization of a Prisoner of War Camp

[As a prisoner in a German Prisoner of War camp during the Second World War, R.A. Radford watched the spontaneous development within the camp of a miniature "market system" for the purpose of allocating resources, determining incomes and distributing goods and services. In its operation, this small-scale, primitive "price system" displayed many of the characteristics and encountered many of the problems of the more sophisticated and complex price systems of modern economies.]

By R.A. Radford

One aspect of social organisation is to be found in economic activity, and this, along with other manifestations of a group existence, is to be found in any P.O.W. camp. Everyone receives a roughly equal share of essentials; it is by trade that individual preferences are given expression and comfort increased. All at some time, and most people regularly, make exchanges of one sort or another.

Our supplies consisted of rations provided by the detaining power and (principally) the contents of Red Cross food parcels—tinned milk, jam, butter, biscuits, bully, chocolate, sugar, etc., and cigarettes. So far the supplies to each person were equal and regular. Private parcels of clothing, toilet requisites and cigarettes were also received, and here equality ceased owing to the different numbers despatched and the vagaries of the post. All these articles were the subject of trade and exchange.

The development and organisation of the market

We reached a transit camp in Italy about a fortnight after capture and received ¼ of a Red Cross food parcel each a week later. At once exchanges, already established, multiplied in volume. Starting with simple direct barter, such as a non-smoker giving a smoker friend his cigarette issue in exchange for a chocolate ration, more complex exchanges soon became an accepted custom.

In this camp we did not visit other bungalows very much and prices varied from place to place. By the end of a month, when we reached our permanent camp, there was a lively trade in all commodities and their relative values were well known, and expressed not in terms of one another—one didn't quote bully in terms of sugar—but in terms of cigarettes. The cigarette became the standard of value. In the permanent camp people started by wandering through the bungalows calling their offers—"cheese for seven" (cigarettes)—and the hours after parcel issue were Bedlam. The inconveniences of this system soon led to its replacement by an Exchange and Mart notice board in every bungalow, where under the headings "name," "room number," "wanted" and "offered" sales and wants were advertised. When a deal went through, it was crossed off the board. The public and semipermanent records of transactions led to cigarette prices being well known and thus tending to equality throughout the camp, although there were always opportunities for an astute trader to make a profit from arbitrage. With this development everyone, including non-smokers, was willing to sell for cigarettes, using them to buy at another time and place. Cigarettes became the normal currency, though, of course, barter was never extinguished.

The permanent camps in Germany saw the highest level of commercial organisation. In addition to the Exchange and Mart notice boards, a shop was organised as a public utility, controlled by representatives of the Senior British Officer, on a no profit basis. People left their surplus clothing, toilet requisites and food there until they were sold at a fixed price in cigarettes. Only sales in cigarettes were accepted—there was no barter. Of food, the shop carried small stocks for convenience; the capital was provided by a loan from the bulk store of Red Cross cigarettes and repaid by a small commission taken on the first transactions. Thus the cigarette attained its fullest currency status, and the market was almost completely unified.

Actually there was an embryo labour market. Even when cigarettes were not scarce, there was usually some unlucky person willing to perform services for them. Laundrymen advertised at two cigarettes a garment. Battledress was scrubbed and pressed and a pair of trousers lent for the interim period for twelve. A good pastel portrait cost thirty or a tin of "Kam." Odd tailoring and other jobs similarly had their prices.

There were also entrepreneurial services. There was a coffee stall owner who sold tea, coffee or cocoa at two cigarettes a cup, buying his raw materials at market prices and hiring labour to gather fuel and to stoke; he actually enjoyed the services of a chartered accountant at one stage. After a period of great prosperity he overreached himself and failed disastrously for several hundred cigarettes. Such large-scale private enterprise

was rare but several middlemen or professional traders existed. The more subdivided the market, the less perfect the advertisement of prices, and the less stable the prices, the greater was the scope for these operators.

The cigarette currency

Although cigarettes as currency exhibited certain peculiarities, they performed all the functions of a metallic currency as a unit of account, as a measure of value and as a store of value, and shared most of its characteristics. They were homogeneous, reasonably durable, and of convenient size for the smallest or, in packets, for the largest transactions.

Machine-made cigarettes were always universally acceptable, both for what they would buy and for themselves. It was this intrinsic value which gave rise to their principal disadvantage as currency, a disadvantage which exists, but to a far smaller extent, in the case of metallic currency;—that is, a strong demand for non-monetary purposes. Consequently our economy was repeatedly subject to deflation and to periods of monetary stringency. While the Red Cross issue of 50 or 25 cigarettes per man per week came in regularly, and while there were fair stocks held, the cigarette currency suited its purpose admirably. But when the issue was interrupted, stocks soon ran out, prices fell, trading declined in volume and became increasingly a matter of barter. This deflationary tendency was periodically offset by the sudden injection of new currency. Private cigarette parcels arrived in a trickle throughout the year, but the big numbers came in quarterly when the Red Cross received its allocation of transport. Several hundred thousand cigarettes might arrive in the space of a fortnight. Prices soared, and then began to fall, slowly at first but with increasing rapidity as stocks ran out, until the next big delivery. Most of our economic troubles could be attributed to this fundamental instability.

More interesting than changes in the general price level were changes in the price structure. Changes in the supply of a commodity, in the German ration scale or in the make-up of Red Cross parcels, would raise the price of one commodity relative to others. Tins of oatmeal, once a rare and much sought after luxury in the parcels, became a commonplace in 1943, and the price fell. In hot weather the demand for cocoa fell, and that for soap rose. A new recipe would be reflected in the price level: the discovery that raisins and sugar could be turned into an alcoholic liquor of remarkable potency reacted permanently on the dried fruit market.

As soon as prices began to fall with a cigarette shortage, a clamour arose, particularly against those who held reserves and who bought at reduced prices. Sellers at cut prices were criticised and their activities referred to as the black market. In every period of dearth the explosive question of "should non-smokers receive a cigarette ration?" was discussed to profitless length. Unfortunately, it was the non-smoker, or the light smoker, with his reserves, along with the hated middleman, who weathered the storm most easily.

SOURCE *Economica*, November 1945, pp. 189-201, abridged. Reprinted by permission.

QUESTIONS

1. Why was it inevitable that a market system would develop in the POW camps?
2. Using examples from the POW camps, explain the importance to the effective operation of a market system of:
   (a) information (as through the bulletin boards);
   (b) the ability of buyers and sellers to move freely from place to place.
3. Why was it inevitable that a form of currency would be developed, and why were cigarettes suitable as a currency?
4. What caused the prices of goods in general to rise or fall substantially?
5. What caused the prices of particular goods to fluctuate relative to the prices of other goods?

DEFINITION OF NEW TERMS

Just Price   The medieval concept that there was a fair ("just") price for various goods.

Utility Theory of Value   The theory that the price (value) of something should reflect its usefulness (utility).

CHAPTER SUMMARY

1. In a basically market type of economic system, economic decisions are made in a largely decentralized manner by households (consumers) and businesses (producers), through markets.

2. Through markets, *prices* (which are determined basically by supply and demand) play an important role in answering the three basic economic questions: what to produce, how to produce it, and for whom to produce it (or how to divide up the economic pie).

3. The next few chapters will undertake to develop a fuller understanding of the key concepts of supply and demand, and how they interact to determine prices under various conditions.

QUESTIONS

1. Suppose there is a shortage of a product (such as apartments) but that the law forbids any increase in its price (rent). What would be the results of such a situation?

2. The text refers to the practice of rationing certain scarce essential items through coupons rather than allowing high prices. Suppose that, due to an interruption of international crude oil supplies, it became necessary to ration gasoline.
   (a) If you were administering such a rationing system, how would you decide who gets how many gas coupons and at what price?
   (b) Suppose that some people get more gasoline coupons than they need, while others get less than they need. How could you resolve this problem?

3. Why are professional hockey players able to earn much higher incomes than in the past, despite the fact that it is generally agreed that the quality of hockey played by them is lower than in the past?

4. Since 1973, the price of oil has increased dramatically. What effect would you expect this to have on the production methods used by industry? What effect could this be expected to have on economic progress and living standards?

5. The just price is discussed in this chapter as a medieval concept. Is the concept of the just price completely dead in today's society?

Appendix 1 Graphs as tools

In economics, graphs are frequently used, not only to illustrate statistical data, but also as tools of analysis. This appendix is intended to introduce students who are not familiar with graphs to the types of graphs we will use in the remainder of this text.

The most common type of graph, and the one with which most people are quite familiar, is the *historical series graph*, which shows the behavior of a statistic over a period of time. Figure 4-2 is an example of such a graph. It shows the fluctuations in the number of Canadians unemployed each year from 1970 to 1980. The actual statistics from which the graph was constructed are shown in the table in Figure 4-3. Since we have only the statistics shown in the table—one for each year—only the dots can be drawn on the graph with certainty. However, to allow the graph to give us a better visual presentation of the trends it shows, we usually

FIGURE 4-2   *Historical Series Graph*

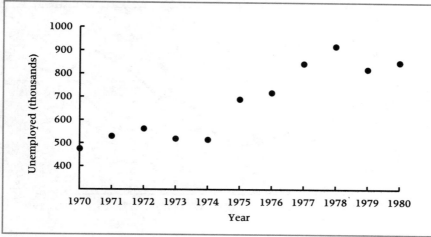

FIGURE 4-3   *Unemployment Statistics 1970-1980*

Year	Unemployed (thousands)
1970	470
1971	530
1972	560
1973	515
1974	510
1975	680
1976	720
1977	850
1978	920
1979	830
1980	860

join the dots together with a line, as in Figure 4-4. Because such a graph describes a trend visually, it is often called a *descriptive graph*.

There is, however, another type of graph that we use in economics, particularly in microeconomics, partly to *describe* a situation, but also to *analyze* it. Suppose that we wish to show how many coats Kathy's Coat Shop could sell at various prices: this information could be shown in a *table,* as in the first part of Figure 4-5. The table tells us that, at low prices, Kathy can sell more coats per week than she can at high prices. This information can also be shown on a graph, as in the second part of Figure

FIGURE 4-4 *Descriptive Graph*

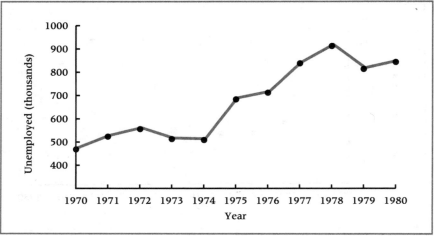

FIGURE 4-5 *Analytical Table and Graph*

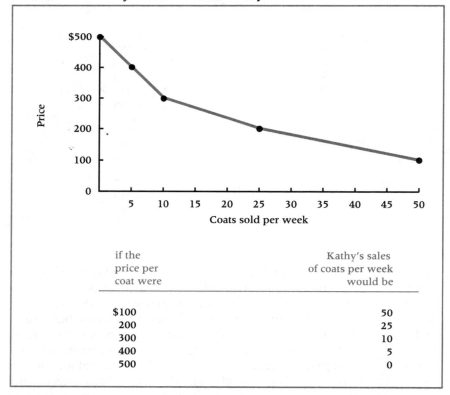

if the price per coat were	Kathy's sales of coats per week would be
$100	50
200	25
300	10
400	5
500	0

4-5. This graph shows the same information as the table, but it shows it visually (again, we only have the five specific pieces of information represented by the dots, but join them together with a line, to provide a better visual presentation of the information).

It is important to understand the nature of graphs such as the one in Figure 4-5, because it is different from graphs such as Figure 4-4. In Figure 4-4, it is easy to see the time dimension: the graph shows unemployment in each of a series of years shown on the horizontal axis. However, what is the time element in Figure 4-5, in which time is not shown on the axis of the graph? The answer to this question is that Figure 4-5 shows the relationship between the price of coats and coat sales at a *particular point in time* (January 1990 in our example). It is possible (indeed, inevitable) that this relationship would be quite different at other times, such as July, when coat sales would be less at each price shown on the graph.

The most important function of graphs like the one in Figure 4-5, then, is not to show changes over time, but to show the *relationship between two variables*: the price of coats (on the vertical axis) and the sales of coats (on the horizontal axis). The two types of relationships which such a graph can describe are called *inverse* and *direct*. The graph in Figure 4-6 tells us that, at high prices, sales will be low (at $300 per coat, sales will be 10 coats per week, as shown by point A), while at lower prices, sales will be higher (at $200 per coat, sales will be 25 coats per week, as shown by point B). When higher amounts of one variable are associated with

FIGURE 4-6 *An Inverse Relationship*

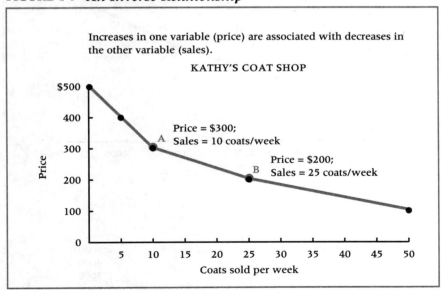

lower amounts of the other in this way, the line on the graph slopes down to the right, and we say that the two variables are *inversely related*.

Conversely, if higher quantities of one variable are associated with higher quantities of the other, the two variables are said to be *directly related*. An example of a direct relationship could be the relationship between the wage rate offered for part-time student help by a college's athletic department and the number of hours of work offered by students: the higher the wage rate, the greater the number of hours the students will be prepared to work. Such a relationship is shown in Figure 4-7.

Finally, while graphs such as Figure 4-6 and 4-7 can describe a relationship, they can also analyze or explain the connection between two variables. That is, the graph can portray a *cause-and-effect* relationship between the price and the sales of coats. If Kathy raises her price from $200 to $300, this will cause her sales to decline from 25 to 10 coats per week. Graphs such as Figure 4-6 are sometimes called *analytical graphs*, in contrast to descriptive graphs such as Figure 4-4, because of this explanatory function.

FIGURE 4-7 *A Direct Relationship Between Two Variables*

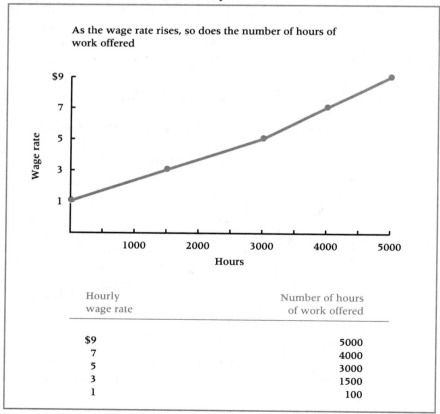

As the wage rate rises, so does the number of hours of work offered

Hourly wage rate	Number of hours of work offered
$9	5000
7	4000
5	3000
3	1500
1	100

CHAPTER 5

Business organization in Canada

We have seen that in a market economy prices are determined by supply and demand. Before examining supply and demand in detail, in this chapter we will examine the various forms that business enterprise most commonly takes in Canada, so as to gain more insight into the business sector of the economy, which produces the supply of goods and services. The most common forms of business enterprise are the sole proprietorship, the partnership, and the corporation, each of which has certain characteristics, advantages and disadvantages. Rather than list and describe these, which tends to be quite dull, we will illustrate the pros and cons of the different forms of business organization through the story of Dan's Doughnut Den.

Dan's Doughnut Den

Dan, an enterprising young man employed by a large multinational corporation, decided that he was tired of working for someone else and would go into business for himself. He found it quite simple to start up his own business—after obtaining a licence from the municipal government, he rented an appropriate building and purchased equipment and supplies with $15 000 of capital obtained from his own savings, a small inheritance and some loans from his relatives. Before long, ''Dan's Doughnut Den'' opened. The business was a **sole proprietorship**; that is, it was totally owned by Dan.

At first, things went exceptionally well: enjoying his new-found freedom and independence, Dan worked harder than he ever had, and the results showed, as sales were good and the business seemed headed for success. As the business grew more complex, Dan was working very long hours, many of which were spent recruiting, training and supervising staff, and dealing with his bank manager. Dan found financial matters a continual hassle—his bank manager was reluctant to provide the kind of credit Dan felt he needed, and was always pestering Dan for financial information which Dan was too busy to prepare carefully. Keeping the books for the business was a constant and time-consuming chore, and one at which Dan was not too skilled. Partly as a result of this, his income tax was a nightmare which tied up much of his time for a month. Finally, he hired an accountant to sort it out, and was horrified to learn that he owed nearly $4000 in taxes, most of which he didn't have: he had plowed practically all of the earnings back into the business, including the opening of another Doughnut Den across town. The sales at the new location were good, too, but having two outlets put an even greater strain on Dan's limited time and talents. For Dan, the crunch came when some of his suppliers and Revenue Canada threatened to sue him for unpaid debts and taxes. Upon consulting his lawyer, Dan learned, to his dismay, that as the sole proprietor of a business he was subject to *unlimited liability*. That is, if the business went bankrupt, he could lose not only the assets of the business, but also his personal assets, such as house and car and dog.

Still, Dan thought, the business had a lot of promise, with strong sales at both locations. What was required, he concluded, was more than just hard work; he needed more *management experience* and more *capital*. To get these, Dan decided to change the business from a sole proprietorship to a **partnership**. One of his new partners was Sally, an old high-school friend of Dan's who had graduated from Sheridan College's Business Administration program. Due to the untimely accidental death of her uncle, Sally had $15 000 to contribute to the capital of the business. Perhaps more important, Sally brought a more systematic approach to the management of the business, which soon began to show up in the profit figures. These figures were calculated (much more proficiently) by the other new partner, Ed, who contributed $20 000 to the capital of the business and kept the books, working in the evening after his regular job in an accountant's office. Unlike Dan and Sally, Ed took no active part in the management of the business and was therefore a **limited partner**: if the business went bankrupt, his liability was limited—all he could lose was the $20 000 he had invested. Dan and Sally, on the other hand, were **general partners**, who had unlimited liability and could therefore lose their personal assets if the business went bankrupt. As is customary in partnerships, the partners all took out life insurance policies on each other's lives, so that if one died, the others would have sufficient cash to buy the deceased partner's share from his or her heirs; thus, the death of a partner would not force the business to dissolve. The three partners signed an agreement outlining their respective rights and responsibilities, and agreeing to share the profits equally.

The infusion of new capital and managerial expertise improved the business's operations considerably, and things went quite well for a while. However, after a period of time, disagreements began to develop among the partners. Dan continued to work almost as hard as before, and began to resent sharing the profits equally with the others who, he felt, weren't working as hard as he was. He found this particularly hard to accept because he was the one who had undertaken the effort and risk necessary to found the business originally. Sally felt that, if anything, she was contributing more to the business than Dan, due to her superior business knowledge. Sally's increasingly frequent reminders to Dan that her capital and know-how had saved the business only aggravated the situation (Sally's grade in Human Relations at Sheridan College had been a low D). Ed was annoyed by these attitudes on the part of his partners: while he didn't work full-time at the business, his after-hours accounting tasks made for a long day. Furthermore, he knew that without the accounting data he prepared, Sally couldn't manage the business nearly as effectively as she did. Also, he had contributed more money to the business than either of the other two (the $20 000). The disagreements came to a head when, after a heated exchange with Ed, Dan learned that Sally had signed certain long-term contracts on behalf of the business which Dan believed to be extremely unwise. Since Sally was a partner, there was no way Dan could cancel these contracts—he was bound by Sally's decisions. Dan was furious that unilateral decisions by someone else could possibly cause the bankruptcy of the business and the loss of Dan's personal assets (house, car, dog, etc.). The other two partners made threats that they would pull out of the partnership, which would almost certainly mean the end of the business. Dan went home that night wishing that there were some way that he could collect on the insurance on the lives of his partners.

Finally, Dan decided that too much was enough; the partnership just couldn't work over the long haul. On the advice of his lawyer, Dan decided to change the form of the business into a **corporation**. As the lawyer explained to him, the corporation would be owned and controlled by **shareholders**, and would be a separate legal entity from the shareholders, whose liability in the event of bankruptcy would be limited to their investment in the corporation's stock. Control of the corporation would lie with its **Board of Directors**, which would be selected by the shareholders, based on one vote per share held. As the lawyer pointed out, Dan could control the Board of Directors, and thus the corporation, by owning (or controlling the votes of) 51 percent of the shares of the company.

The corporation was set up so that Dan and his wife held 85 percent of the shares, with Dan owning 45 percent and the other 40 percent being registered in his wife's name, in order to split their dividend income and reduce their total personal income taxes. The other 15 percent of the shares were bought by a few family friends, who had been impressed by the prospects for the business. Some of them had been reluctant to invest, but were attracted by the limited liability of shareholders and the tax treatment of the gains from their investments, since both dividend income from their shares and any capital gains realized from sale of their shares for a profit would be subject to favorable tax rates. Indeed, as the lawyer pointed out, if the business were ever to expand, the corporate form of organization would prove very advantageous for raising the necessary capital.

The incorporation process was complex and quite costly, but seemed like an excellent idea. The two partners were bought out, improved equipment was purchased and the facilities were renovated. A qualified manager was hired and a sophisticated sales promotion campaign undertaken. Sales in both outlets rose, as did profits; there were bonuses for the managers and substantial dividends for the shareholders. Dan found that incorporation brought tax advantages to the business, too. When the business was a sole proprietorship and partnership, its income (profit) was taxed as personal income, at personal income tax rates, which became quite high as the income of the owners rose. However, the profits of the corporation were taxed at *corporate income tax rates*, which were lower unless profits were quite low. (On the other hand, the shareholders were somewhat disappointed to find that they were subject to "double taxation": not only were the profits of the corporation taxed, but the dividends they received out of after-tax profits were also taxed, although at reduced rates, as their personal income.) Bank credit became more available as the business prospered, with three more outlets opened and consideration being given to selling an issue of shares to the public to raise capital to finance expansion into other provinces.

While Dan found being president of a successful and rapidly growing corporation exciting (not to mention financially rewarding), he also found that, as president, he seemed to spend all of his time in his office, working on paperwork, meeting with managers and committees and lawyers on matters such as financing arrangements, short-range, medium-range and long-range plans, reorganization plans, controls systems and seemingly endless government regulations which had to be followed. At times, Dan longed for the days when he worked in the shop, spent time talking with his customers, and life was simple.

Dan's wishes were soon to be answered. Fed up with Dan's heavy responsibilities and long working hours (and impressed by the assets he had accumulated), his wife established a relationship with the manager of Dan's largest outlet (an ambitious young man anxious to get ahead in the organization) and divorced Dan. She then teamed up with the other shareholders (her friends) against Dan at a shareholders' meeting. While Dan's 45 percent of the shares made him the largest single shareholder, the other shareholders (including his wife) were able to outvote him and remove him from the presidency. The new Board of Directors offered Dan a job as manager of the company's largest outlet (an opening created by the promotion of its former manager to the presidency of the company), but Dan had lost interest in the business. He declined the offer and went to work for the Post Office, where he wouldn't ever have to worry about anything. As a shareholder in Dan's Doughnut Dens, Ltd., Dan is entitled to any dividends per share which are paid to the other shareholders, and he lives quite comfortably on this income plus his Post Office salary. He does not attend shareholders' meetings of the company.

Update: Recently, Dan has been spending an increasing amount of time with Ermyntrude, an old friend of his wife's whom Dan never did like very much at all. Ermyntrude is the owner of 5.1 percent of the shares of Dan's Doughnut Dens, Ltd.

QUESTIONS

From the story about Dan's Doughnut Dens, compile a list of the advantages and disadvantages of each of the three forms of business organization: the sole proprietorship, the partnership and the corporation. Why do you think that virtually all medium- and large-sized businesses are corporations?

Small business in Canada[1]

Small business in Canada includes such a wide range of enterprises that no simple definition can cover them. According to one definition used by the Department of Industry, Science and Technology (DIST), small business includes manufacturing firms employing fewer than 100 workers and non-manufacturing firms employing fewer than 50 workers. For tax purposes, the size of the firm is less important than its profits: all Canadian-controlled private corporations qualify for a small business deduction and pay a lower tax rate of approximately 25 percent on the first $200 000 of active business income per year. The Canadian Federation of Independent Business (CFIB) takes the number of employees as the yardstick, and counts independently-owned firms with less than 50 employees as "small," and firms with between 50 and 499 employees as "medium-sized."

The extent of small business

Small business encompasses all the forms of business organization: while over half are sole proprietorships or partnerships, many are corporations—especially private corporations, meaning that they have fewer than 50 shareholders. By becoming a private corporation, a small business can gain the income tax advantages of incorporation without having

[1] This section has benefited greatly from the assistance of Pat Thompson of the CFIB.

to comply with the regulations governing public corporations.[2] The latter can sell shares and bonds to the general public to raise capital, but are required to publish considerable financial information in order to protect the investing public.

Whether incorporated or unincorporated, and however defined, small business includes a tremendous variety of individuals, firms and economic activities: professionals such as doctors and lawyers; farmers; small-scale manufacturers producing toys, boats, clothing, furniture and a host of other products; retailers such as drug stores, gift shops, grocery stores, clothing stores, bookstores, music stores and variety stores; service industry operations such as dry cleaning, hairdressing, restaurants, motels, real estate, insurance, services to business, employment agencies, repairs and landscaping; and construction, which is characterized by large numbers of small contractors and sub-contractors.

Women are increasingly entering the ranks of business owners in Canada. Census data for 1986 show that between 1981 and 1986, women were starting businesses at five times the rate of men. In addition, by 1986 women represented nearly a quarter of all business owners in the country. There is every indication that these trends will continue in the future.

Small businesses play a highly significant role in the Canadian economy, with the various different definitions of what constitutes a small business shedding different light on the contribution made by this sector. One sales-based definition shows that businesses with annual revenues of less than $5 million account for about one-quarter of both total business sales and profits. If we accept the definition based on numbers of employees, then the vast majority of all businesses in Canada can be categorized as small. In 1987, there was a total number of 880 000 firms with paid employees operating in Canada and, of these, about 98 percent had less than 50 full-year equivalent employees. These smaller companies maintained a labor force of some 3.5 million, equivalent to over a third of total private-sector employment. In addition, small firms accounted for about a third of the value of total payrolls in the private sector.

Small and new businesses have dominated the job creation scene in recent years. According to the Canadian Federation of Independent Business, between 1978 and 1987 (the most recent period for which data are available), businesses with less than 50 employees were responsible for as much as 90 percent of the nearly 2 million net jobs created by the private sector across Canada; very small firms employing less than five employees accounted for 56 percent of the total. Performance during the recession was particularly impressive. Very small firms continued to

---

[2] As noted in the case of Dan's Doughnut Dens, sole proprietors and partners pay taxes according to personal income tax rates, which are considerably higher than corporate tax rates on profits above a certain level.

provide much needed jobs across Canada, at a time when other size categories of firms, particularly large businesses, were shedding workers.

This valuable job creation record results from the fact that small businesses are highly varied in nature and in their contribution to the economy. The sector provides both the solid base of economic stability and the flywheel of economic growth and change—vital ingredients for a sound economy with the ability to adapt quickly in response to new domestic and global market conditions.

SMALL BUSINESS FACTS

According to Statistics Canada:

- Between 1975 and 1986, the number of self-employed people rose by 54 percent—more than double the rate of increase for paid workers.
- By 1986, 1.6 million Canadians (one in seven working Canadians) were working for themselves.
- From 1975 to 1986, 85 percent of new jobs created in Canada were in the small business sector.
- Self-employment is more common among men than women: 17 percent of all male workers were self-employed in 1986 as compared to 8 percent of women.
- However, self-employment is growing more rapidly among women: between 1975 and 1986, the number of self-employed women grew by 118 percent as compared to 39 percent for men.

Problems of small business

Despite their advantages and their importance, small businesses face serious problems. The most difficult time is the first year or so of operation. CFIB estimates that about 140 000 new businesses became operational during the fiscal year ending March 31, 1989. This estimate of actual business births was substantially lower than the 364 000 new incorporations, proprietorships and partnerships registered during the course of the year, the shortfall largely comprising business ideas which did not come to fruition. Once operational, many small firms lead a precarious existence and some fail every year—although it should be noted that firms may go out of operation for reasons other than failure, some being sold, some merged with other firms, while others are wound down when the owners retire.

There are many reasons for the serious problems facing small business, a key one being that management is often stretched too thinly. In many small businesses, a single owner-manager is required to perform more functions than time or expertise permit; as a result, the business often suffers from inadequate management.

According to a survey by the Canadian Federation of Independent Business, taxation, government regulation and labor supply issues are the major impediments to the operations and growth of small and medium-sized businesses in Canada. CFIB members view their total tax burden as their most pressing business problem. Concern over the substantial tax hikes contained in the 1989 federal and provincial budgets has been heightened by the prospect of the proposed federal Goods and Services Tax (GST). In addition, tax concessions made by governments to large firms tilt the competitive balance against small businesses, and are considered a poor substitute for a fair and balanced tax policy.

Government red tape and paper burden was the second most frequently identified problem in the survey. Small business owners cannot afford the considerable amount of time they are required to divert from managing their operation to filling out government forms relating to statistical information and tax collection.

Shortage of qualified labor ranks as the third most important problem for smaller firms. Small firms have traditionally given young entrants into the work force their first job, but many are now facing increasing difficulties due to the declining numbers of young people entering the work force. In addition, legislated barriers, such as limits restricting the number of apprentices in relation to trained staff, create labor shortages for many firms. In recent years, the shortage of qualified labor has developed into a problem of major proportions for smaller firms, with the result that many have decided that the best solution is to train their own staff. An October 1988 CFIB survey on education and training showed that seven of ten smaller firms provide some type of training for their workers, and that the bulk of these provided on-the-job training, sometimes in conjunction with other types of training or assistance. However, small firms often do such a good job of training and upgrading workers' skills that they frequently lose these employees to larger companies once they are trained.

Other labor issues are also high on the small business list of problems. Provincial *workers' compensation boards* (WCBs) were identified as a source of concern by CFIB members. These are entirely funded by business, yet business has little say in how the funds are used. In addition, provincial *labor laws* were a significant problem for many members.

Financing problems often create serious handicaps. Small firms face considerable problems in attempting to raise sufficient equity and risk capital, and also tend to lack the access that larger businesses have to bank and other credit sources. Not only are small businesses considered a greater risk than larger ones, but small firm owner-managers often have difficulty identifying sources of funds and preparing the necessary financial plans and forecasts required to obtain loans.

Finally, *inflation* is particularly hard on small businesses, whose heavy reliance on credit (rather than profits) for financing makes them vulnerable to high interest rates. And small businesses are less able than large corporations to recover rising costs by increasing their prices, due to the strongly competitive situation faced by most of them.

Assistance to small business

Because small businesses are in many ways at a disadvantage in an economy characterized by large corporations, a wide variety of government programs is available to assist them. Both the federal and provincial governments offer loan guarantees or lower cost, longer-term *financing* for small businesses. At the federal level, the Federal Business Development Bank makes term loans to new or existing businesses that are unable to obtain the required funds from other lenders on reasonable terms and conditions, and offers an extensive management training program. Most provincial governments offer financial help through similar agencies, with loan guarantees arranged through regular financial institutions and screening processes to minimize failure rates.

Bank lending to small business received a boost from the 1977 revisions to the Small Business Loans Act (SBLA), which redefined eligibility requirements and increased the interest rate that banks could charge on

---

In general, small businesses have relied heavily on debt financing. Individual entrepreneurs have tended not to seek external equity, apparently because they desire to keep full control of their operations. There is, however, concern on the part of small business about access to funds, particularly for start-up purposes.

Finally, when small businesses apply for government assistance or bid on government contracts, they face a sea of forms and paperwork. They find themselves at a competitive disadvantage with larger companies which have tax, legal, financial and technical expertise readily at hand.

If small business is to play its role in economic renewal, it is essential that federal and provincial governments and private financial institutions respond to their special needs.

Hon. Michael H. Wilson,
A New Direction for Canada: An Agenda for Economic Renewal,
Department of Finance, November 1984

such loans. However, a 1987 CFIB survey showed that the present SBLA system now needs to be thoroughly overhauled in order to more effectively support bank lending to small business. A significant finding of the study was a general lack of financing for small firms. About one in five respondents indicated that they were either turned down or cut back in their most recent financing application, with smallest and newest firms most frequently affected by this problem.

Counseling programs are also available from the federal government and most provinces, to assist small business owners with their management problems. Such programs help small businesses that are unable to afford expert counseling, utilizing various people, including MBA students, retired executives and professional counselors. Also, marketing programs are offered by all provincial governments, intended to assist small businesses in the opening up of new markets, both in Canada and abroad. Usually, these are designed to complement programs offered through the Federal Export Development Corporation. Some provinces also offer personnel assistance programs to help small businesses find skilled employees, and in some cases the wages of employees are subsidized by the government. Finally, government programs provide subsidies for research and development and help small business to make use of new technology in various ways.

In total, there is a bewildering array of well over 500 programs for small business offered by the federal, provincial and municipal governments. According to some observers, a major problem facing many small business owners is finding the time to evaluate the wide variety of programs that could be of value, and to work through the extensive paperwork that many of them require. To aid in these matters, many governments have set up *information centers* to help small businesses determine where to look for aid, and have undertaken to reduce the amount of paperwork involved.

Finally, there is the question of how much assistance should actually be given to small businesses. Sometimes, businesses should be allowed to fail because they are not viable, or the people involved do not have the abilities required to operate a successful business. No one would argue that the government should use taxpayers' funds to keep businesses operating in such circumstances. But neither the government, nor anyone else, quite knows how to recognize the potential of a new, small business or how much assistance is appropriate. Nonetheless, the importance of small business to the Canadian economy has led to a variety of government programs intended to help small businesses, particularly in their early years.

Canadian Federation of Independent Business

Until the early 1970's, small business owners in Canada felt that they lacked a voice in the federal and provincial governments. As a result, they believed, government policies were often formulated without consideration of their effects on small business, which was being threatened by the expansion of taxation and regulations, and the proliferation of red tape associated with these. In response to these problems, several organizations of small businesses have developed, the most important of which is the *Canadian Federation of Independent Business* (CFIB).

The CFIB was formed in 1971, and by 1990 it included 85 000 small and medium-sized Canadian-owned businesses in its membership. With offices located across the country, the federation employed a full-time staff of 80, including legislative specialists and economists, and a 120-person field staff to sell memberships nationwide. A major function of the CFIB's staff is the conduct of surveys and other research. The analysis of this information provides the basis for its presentations to governments.

The CFIB acts as the small business lobby with government, raising issues such as taxation, financing, government regulations and red tape. It claims to have saved small business several billions of dollars through its influence on government decisions. CFIB's stated objective is to promote and protect a system of free competitive enterprise in Canada and to give the independent business owner a greater voice in the laws governing business and the nation. With its sizeable cross-country membership base and its lines of communication with each provincial government as well as the federal government, CFIB is by far the most important and influential of the groups representing small business in Canada.

Big business in Canada

As Figures 5-1 and 5-2 show, big business in Canada is a totally different world from the small business sector, a world dominated by corporate giants that are household names. All such large businesses are incorporated, mostly in the form of *public corporations* that have the ability to raise capital through the sale of stocks and bonds to the public.[3] Their shares are traded on the various stock exchanges in Canada, such as Toronto, Montreal and Vancouver. Through these stock exchanges, corporations can issue new shares to raise capital, and the investing public can buy and sell shares from and to each other. The ability to buy and sell corporate shares freely, together with the limited liability of shareholders, makes it possible for public corporations to raise the vast amounts of capital they need, not only from the general public but also from large institutional investors such as pension funds.

[3] Many large businesses take the form of *private corporations*, which have less than 50 shareholders and are not required to publish nearly as much financial information as public corporations. In particular, subsidiaries of foreign companies and family-owned firms tend to take this form, because it ensures greater privacy.

FIGURE 5–1 *Canada's 35 Largest Industrial Corporations by Sales, 1988*

Rank by Sales 1988	1987	Sales or operating revenue ($ thousands)	Company (head office)	Foreign ownership (percent)	Major shareholders
1	1	19 310 538	General Motors of Canada Ltd. (Oshawa, Ont.)	%100	General Motors, Detroit
2	3	15 943 300	Ford Motor Co. of Canada (Oakville, Ont.)	97	Ford Motor, Detroit 94%
3	2	15 253 000	BCE Inc. (Montreal)	8	Wide distribution
4	4	12 016 300	Canadian Pacific Ltd. (Montreal)	27	Wide distribution
5	5	10 831 200	George Weston Ltd. (Toronto)		Wittington Investments 57%
6	6	10 497 000ᵃ	Alcan Aluminium Ltd. (Montreal)	46	Wide distribution
7	21	10 394 650ᵇ	Campeau Corp. (Toronto) Jan./89		R. Campeau family 50%, Olympia & York 28%
8	8	8 858 000	Noranda Inc. (Toronto)	–	Brascan 45%
9	9	8 667 900	Chrysler Canada Ltd. (Windsor)	100	Chrysler, Detroit
10	10	7 378 500	Provigo Inc. (Montreal) Jan./89	–	Unigesco 26%, Empire 25%, Caisse de dépôt 12%
11	7	7 105 000	Imperial Oil Ltd. (Toronto)	70	Exxon, New York
12	13	7 051 000ᶜ	Brascan Ltd. (Toronto)	16	Brascan 49%
13	11	5 813 000	Ontario Hydro (Toronto)	–	Ontario government 100%
14	14	5 222 996	Hydro-Québec (Montreal)	–	Quebec government 100%
15	16	4 968 000	Shell Canada Ltd. (Calgary)	71	Shell, Netherlands/Britain
16	12	4 847 000	Petro-Canada (Calgary)	–	Federal government 100%
17	17	4 845 000	Imasco Ltd. (Montreal)	42	B.A.T. Industries, Britain 40%
18	26	4 811 526ᵃ	Seagram Co. (Montreal) Jan./89	47	Bronfman family 38%
19	18	4 676 194	Canadian National Railway Co. (Montreal)	–	Federal government 100%
20	15	4 671 740	Hudson's Bay Co. (Toronto) Jan./89	–	Thomson family 74%
21	25	4 610 984	John Labatt Ltd. (London, Ont.) Apr./88	–	Brascan 39%
22	19	4 608 972ᵃ	International Thomson Organisation Ltd. (Toronto)	8	Thomson family 74%ᵈ
23	20	4 584 685	Steinberg Inc. (Montreal) July/88	–	Steinberg family 87%
24	22	4 327 200	Sears Canada Inc. (Toronto)	61	Sears, Roebuck, Chicago
25	24	4 274 535	Oshawa Group Ltd. (Toronto) Jan./89	–	Wolfe family 100% voting
26	23	4 041 385ᵃ	Canada Safeway Ltd. (Calgary) Jan./89	100	Kohlberg, Kravis, Roberts, New York
27	43	4 015 841ᵃ	Inco Ltd. (Toronto)	54	Wide distribution
28	44	3 941 000ᵉ	Nova Corp. (Calgary)	–	Wide distribution
29	32	3 693 000	IBM Canada Ltd. (Markham, Ont.)	100	IBM, Armonk, N.Y.
30	31	3 426 400	Air Canada (Montreal)	–	Federal government 57%, employee share plan 16%
31	29	3 342 664	Canada Packers Inc. (Toronto) Mar./88	–	Cedcasac Holdings, company pension plan 11% each
32	34	3 304 500	Abitibi-Price Inc. (Toronto)	–	Olympia & York 79%
33	27	3 268 700	TransCanada PipeLines Ltd. (Calgary)	–	BCE Inc. 49%
34	35	3 138 552	Canada Post Corp. (Ottawa) Mar./88	–	Federal government 100%
35	33	3 130 924ᵃ	Moore Corp. (Toronto)	17	Royal Trustco 10%

ᵃConverted from US$. ᵇEstimate. Converted from US$. ᶜIncludes beneficial interest in gross revenues of consumer products, natural resources and other operations, but excludes financial services. ᵈSubsequent to yearend proposed amalgamation with Thomson Newspapers. ᵉReflects acquisition of Polysar Energy in July, 1988.

SOURCE *The Financial Post 500*, Summer 1989, pp. 84–85.

FIGURE 5-2 *Canada's 10 Largest Banks and Financial Institutions, 1988*

Rank by Assets		Assets		Revenue	Foreign ownership	
1988	1987	($ thousands)	Company (head office)	($ thousands)	(percent)	Major shareholders
1	1	110 054 340	Royal Bank of Canada (Montreal) Oct./88	10 594 976	–	Wide distribution
2	2	94 687 528	Canadian Imperial Bank of Commerce (Toronto) Oct./88	9 157 580	–	Wide distribution
3	3	78 908 911	Bank of Montreal (Montreal) Oct./88	9 180 181	–	Wide distribution
4	4	74 674 837	Bank of Nova Scotia (Halifax) Oct./88	7 032 561	3	Wide distribution
5	5	59 285 378	Toronto Dominion Bank (Toronto) Oct./88	5 862 035	–	Wide distribution
6	7	34 246 830[a]	La confédération des caisses populaires Desjardins du Québec (Quebec City)	3 531 851	–	Member federations
7	9	31 825 000[b]	Trilon Financial Corp. (Toronto)	3 883 000	1	Brascan 46%, Olympia & York 14%
8	8	31 798 000	Caisse de dépôt et placement du Québec (Quebec City)	2 633 000	–	Quebec government 100%
9	6	30 922 587	National Bank of Canada (Montreal) Oct./88	3 097 613	–	Wide distribution
10	10	29 219 217[c]	CT Financial Services Inc. (London, Ont.)	3 264 964	–	Imasco 99%

[a]Includes assets of caisses populaires, member federations and Caisse centrale Desjardins, but excludes those of Trustco Desjardins Inc.
[b]Consolidates results of Royal Trustco. Assets at yearend were $28.5 billion.
[c]Consolidates results of Canada Trustco. Assets figure not available.
SOURCE *The Financial Post 500*, Summer 1989 (pp. 162–163)

Figure 5-1 shows that ownership of big business in Canada is quite diverse. Foreign-owned and family-owned companies each accounted for about one-quarter of Canada's 35 largest companies in 1988, while widely-held[4] and government-owned enterprises each comprised nearly one-fifth. Figure 5-2 indicates that most of Canada's largest banks and financial institutions are widely-held, and none are foreign-owned.

Corporate concentration

In Canada, much business activity is concentrated in the hands of relatively few very large corporations. In 1985, the largest 25 enterprises (ranked by sales) controlled over one-third of all corporate non-financial assets in Canada. The 500 largest enterprises, which represented less than one percent of Canada's non-financial corporations, had over 67 percent of corporate assets, over 50 percent of total sales and 67 percent

---

[4] A widely-held company is one in which ownership is spread among a large number of relatively small shareholders.

of total profits. This corporate concentration is the result of various factors, including the growth of the sales and assets of the most successful corporations and the tendency of corporations to purchase control of, or merge with, other corporations. As a result, as we will see in Chapter 10, some industries and markets in Canada have come to be dominated by a few large corporations, to an even greater degree than in the USA. When a few firms dominate an industry, concerns are raised about whether there is sufficiently strong competition in the industry; the handful of "competitors" may tend to agree among themselves, especially with respect to prices, so that all of them can live together more comfortably and profitably. In these cases, it is viewed as necessary for the government to set down rules for corporate behavior that, in effect, outlaw the monopolization of markets and fixing of prices, a matter that will be considered further in Chapter 12.

Conglomerates and holding companies

Not all corporate mergers and takeovers have the effect of increasing the control of a few firms over a particular industry. A different form of corporate concentration is the **conglomerate**, a group of seemingly unrelated types of corporations controlled in varying degrees by a central management group. This control is exercised through *holding companies*, whose purpose is simply to hold (own) shares of other companies. The various corporations that are owned and controlled by a holding company are not absorbed into it, but rather are allowed to continue operating as separate businesses, with the resulting group of companies referred to as a conglomerate. Conglomerates are a relatively recent development in business; most have been formed since the 1950's. In the view of some observers, the depressed stock prices of many corporations since then have made them easy targets for takeovers by acquisition-minded holding companies.

One major Canadian conglomerate is *Power Corporation*, which has controlled roughly 200 corporations, including Canada Steamship Lines, Investors Group, Montreal Trust, Great-West Life Assurance, Consolidated Bathurst, Dominion Glass, Imperial Life Assurance, Laurentide Financial Corp., and Shawinigan Industries. Another major Canadian conglomerate is *George Weston Ltd.*, whose holdings include (or have included, since these change quickly) Loblaws, Tamblyns, Eddy Paper, Weston Bakeries, McCormick's (biscuits), William Neilson (chocolates), Willard's Chocolates, Donland's Dairy and many other companies in Canada and around the world. Another conglomerate, whose financial details are, for the most part, confidential, is the *Irving Group* based in the Maritimes. Irving interests are reported to involve 140 corporations, including Irving Oil, Irving Steamships, Key Anacon Mines, Moncton Publishing, St. John Shipbuilding and Dry Dock Co., and St. George Pulp and Paper. The oldest and most venerable Canadian conglomerate is *Argus Corporation*, whose holdings have included Standard Broadcasting (CFRB), Dominion Stores, Hollinger Mines, Domtar, Noranda Mines, Labrador Mining and Exploration, and B.C. Forest Products. Unlike Power Corporation, Argus has not traditionally held over 50 percent of the voting shares of its companies, although this has not prevented Argus from exercising considerable influence over them through positions on their Boards of Directors. In the past, Argus' image was conservative and sedate compared to Power's. However, since the late 1970's, under the leadership of Conrad Black, Argus has been more aggressive, selling off

CANADIAN SHAREHOLDERS

Periodically, the Toronto Stock Exchange conducts a survey to determine the characteristics of Canadian share owners. According to its mid-1986 survey (The Toronto Stock Exchange, *Canadian Shareowners: Their Profile and Attitudes*, 1986):

- 3.2 million Canadians (18 percent of the adult population) owned shares, either directly or through mutual funds. This represented an increase of about 1 million from 1983, when 13 percent of the adult population owned shares.

- Only 36 percent of all share owners were women, but 44 percent of new share owners were women.

- 29 percent of all share owners had bought shares for the first time since 1982.

- Most share owners had small portfolios. About 60 percent of them owned stocks worth less than $10 000.

- Most share owners were quite cautious investors. Nearly all cited long-term potential for capital appreciation and a good dividend yield as key factors in their decision to invest in stocks. Less than half responded that they were aiming at short-term profits in buying shares.

In a similar survey conducted in 1984, Canadian share owners were described as a small but vitally important group in the nation, particularly because their contribution to raising new share capital helps businesses to grow and create jobs. As TSE Chairman Robin Younger said, wider participation by Canadians in the stock market "will allow corporations to reduce their debt loads and invest in new plants, new products, new technologies and new markets."

unprofitable companies and increasing its interests in (and control of) the more profitable ones.[5]

Observers' attitudes toward conglomerates vary widely. Some people believe that being part of a large corporate group brings advantages to a company, including diversification, better management and perhaps improved access to credit. Others disagree, and are uneasy about the concentration of so much corporate control in the hands of a few people (or even one person). They view conglomerates as the rather unattractive toys of power-hungry rich people, at best, and as a vague threat to society at worst, due to their political and economic influence.

One major Canadian conglomerate is the Thomson Group, which includes (or has included) 80 business publications in the USA, business magazines in Britain, Singapore, Germany, Denmark, Australia and South Africa, 83 newspapers and 12 consumer publications in Britain, 143 newspapers in Canada and the USA, educational and reference publishers in the USA and Britain, various specialized professional publishing enterprises in Canada, the USA and Britain and various information services in several countries. In addition to its publishing interests, the Thomson organization includes several travel and tourism companies in the USA and Britain and retail interests in Canada such as the Bay, Zeller's and Simpsons. Until late 1988, the Thomson Group also included British North Sea oil and gas interests valued at approximately $450 million US. However, these were sold off, with the intention of using the proceeds to expand further into the publishing and travel fields with which Thomson is most familiar.

Who controls the corporation?

In theory, this is a simple question, since the *shareholders* of a corporation vote to elect the Board of Directors, which in turn selects top management and directs them as to the corporation's objectives and the policies to be followed. In reality, however, the matter is often not so simple. In many large corporations, the shares are so widely held that the shareholders are too numerous and too dispersed to exercise any effective control. A typical shareholders' meeting of a large corporation attracts only a handful of shareholders, few of whom seriously question or challenge the executive officers of the corporation.

If the small shareholders are often not in a position to exercise control over the large corporation collectively, then who does control it? Given

---

[5] In late February of 1986, Black clinched an enormously complex deal with Peter and Edward Bronfman, in which the corporate empire of the Bronfmans and that of Conrad and Montegu Black became intertwined. Essentially, Black traded control of Norcen for a minority interest in most of the Bronfmans' corporate holdings. Both families also have extensive connections to the Reichmann brothers, another powerful Toronto family.

the importance of large corporations in the economy, this is an important question. Unfortunately, the answer is not always clear, since it depends on the circumstances.

If the corporation's stock is so widely held that there is no major shareholder or organized group of shareholders, it will be impossible for the shareholders to exercise control through their meetings. Rather, control will often fall to the *top management* of the corporation, which can control the shareholders' meetings through **proxies**.[6] Under these circumstances, the top management of a corporation can exercise complete control of the firm, even to the point of nominating and selecting the members of the Board of Directors to which top management reports. In such cases, the management of the corporation can usually retain secure control as long as the corporation performs well enough to keep the shareholders content. Those shareholders who disagree strongly with management's decisions will generally sell their stocks rather than engage in a struggle for control that will probably prove futile.

While the circumstances described above can give top management *control* of a large corporation, this does not mean that the top managers make all the *decisions* in such corporations. Unlike a small business, in which decision-making is dominated by one or a few people, large corporations employ large numbers of specialists in areas such as marketing, product design, finance, personnel, law, data processing and so on. The role of top management is not so much to make decisions in these people's areas as it is to set down plans and objectives for the corporation, and to select and organize people and to coordinate their efforts, establishing an environment in which they can work effectively, making the maximum contribution to the corporation with their skills and knowledge. Such people—called the *technostructure* by economist John Kenneth Galbraith and *knowledge workers* by Peter Drucker, the management theorist—are vital to the success of the large corporation, and the art (or task) of the top manager is to utilize them effectively. The fact that their main contribution lies not in their product knowledge, but rather in their ability to organize and coordinate the activities of other managers, helps to explain the high mobility of chief executive officers, many of whom move quite freely between corporations in different industries, and between corporations and top positions in government agencies. It also explains the fact that, whereas the loss of its president would likely be a catastrophe for a small business, the loss of the chief executive officer of a large corporation often goes almost unnoticed on the stock market and

[6] A proxy is a legal instrument whereby a shareholder in effect delegates to another person authority to vote on his or her behalf, either according to specific directions or as the person holding the proxy sees fit. Usually, proxies are solicited by and given to people representing the management of the corporation, as noted above. Occasionally, however, a dissident group of shareholders will attempt to use proxies to gain control of the corporation, setting off a ''proxy war'' in which it and the management compete for the proxies of the shareholders (and control of the corporation).

in the operations of the company. If the chief executive officer's job has been done well, the company will continue to function effectively until a replacement is selected. In a sense, then, it can be argued that the key to effective corporate decision-making lies in the middle-level specialists of its technostructure and, while it cannot be said that these people *control* the corporation, it also cannot be denied that their knowledge and expertise gives them great *influence* over its decisions.

In summary, when the shareholders are numerous and dispersed, control of large corporations often resides with the top management; however, it is also true that in these situations the corporation's decision-making process is strongly influenced by its personnel who are specialists in various areas. This situation is generally accepted as being quite common in large corporations in the USA, as well as in many corporations in Canada.

In Canada, it is widely accepted that in many large corporations, the *Board of Directors* takes a more active part in company policies and decisions than is suggested in the preceding paragraphs. Sometimes such control is exercised through Boards of Directors by majority shareholders, such as family interests or other corporations that own a majority of the shares. However, the situation is not always so clear-cut: under certain conditions, a group of shareholders (individuals or other corporations) can maintain control of a corporation's Board of Directors even though it holds only a small percentage of the total shares outstanding; such control can be achieved through proxy votes or simply through personal relationships between the people involved. For instance, Argus Corporation traditionally exercised considerable influence over corporations in which it held interests, even though these were not majority interests.

While these corporate directors are seldom major stockholders themselves, they are in a position to decide the policies of some of the country's most important corporations.[7] Who exactly are these people? The Financial Post's "Directory of Directors" has in the past listed approximately 14 000 names, but it was generally considered that less than 1 000 of them possessed any significant influence. Traditionally, corporate boards of directors have been regarded as closed clubs dominated by older men of very conservative values. Many of them were senior executives of the company itself and many others were associated with large, politically-affiliated law firms of possible value to a company. Often, the board would include some "establishment names" to add prestige to the board and the company. This structure has led to the creation of a Canadian *corporate business elite*: a relatively small group of people who can exercise a great deal of influence on business decisions through their strategic

[7] The entire board of Canadian Pacific Railways, comprising 24 of the most influential businessmen in Canada and setting the company's policies, owned in the late 1970's a combined total of only about 0.17 percent of CPR's stock.

positions in the large corporations of the nation. The importance of this 'elite' is increased further by the fact that many directors serve on the boards of several companies, in what are called *interlocking directorships*. About one-quarter of Canadian corporate directors have significant interlocking connections, many of which are effected through Canada's large and powerful chartered banks, as senior personnel from large corporations often serve on the boards of the banks and vice versa. There are different views concerning the significance of this so-called corporate business elite, with some observers feeling reassured by the stability that it provides, others seeing in it something threatening, and still others doubting whether its significance with respect to the actual operational decisions of Canada's major corporations is as great as is often supposed.

While corporate directorships have often been thought of as sinecure positions involving some status but relatively little responsibility, there are signs that the situation is changing. Directors now face increased responsibilities due to changes in the law that place more liability upon them for their companies' actions. Partly as a result of this, and partly in response to increasing concerns that board members be impartial and independent in providing shareholders with information about their companies, corporations are seeking directors with more expertise and dedication than ever before, and are increasingly going outside their own companies for them. Also, while boards are still dominated by men, participation by women is growing.

While the question of who controls the large corporation is not a simple one, it can be said, in conclusion, that large corporations play a very important role in the Canadian economy, even greater relative to the size of the economy than in the USA, and that in these large corporations, *control is often separated from ownership*. Widespread small shareholders are not in a position to exercise active control. As a result, control tends to shift, depending on the circumstances, to the top management of the corporation or to groups of influential members of the Board of Directors. Generally, neither top managers nor directors are major shareholders in their corporation; their claim to control over the corporation is based on their *expertise* rather than on ownership.

Government enterprises

No discussion of big business in Canada would be complete without reference to government-owned enterprises. Comprising roughly 10 percent of Canada's very large corporations, government enterprises often take the form of **Crown corporations**. Crown corporations, like other corporations, are legally independent, separate entities. However, most or all of their shares are owned by the government, and they are ultimately responsible to the government, through a cabinet minister. In addition to Crown corporations, government enterprises often take the form of *boards* or *commissions*, such as hydroelectric commissions.

Whatever legal forms they take, government enterprises constitute an important part of big business in Canada. Their largest single activity is the *provision of electricity*: the combined sales of the provinces' electricity utilities would place them second among Canada's industrial corporations, with sales ahead of Ford and only slightly behind those of General Motors. Traditionally, government enterprises have also been important in the fields of *transportation and communications* in Canada, including, at various times, Canadian National Railways, Air Canada, Pacific Western Airlines, British Columbia Railway and Nordair. More recently, government enterprises such as PetroCan, Atomic Energy of Canada, Eldorado Nuclear, the Canada Development Corporation and the Potash Corporation of Saskatchewan have established a significant presence in the *energy and resources* sector of the Canadian economy. While government enterprises play a smaller role in the *manufacturing sector*, they include some well-known names (such as Canadair at the federal level). Some provincial governments have acted as partners in manufacturing firms in attempts to stimulate growth and employment in their regions. Finally, in 1981, the *Post Office* was converted from a government department into a Crown corporation, in the hope that doing so would reduce the political element and would allow it to concentrate on improving efficiency and employee relations. Figure 5-3 lists the ten largest government enterprises in Canada, ranked by sales in 1988.

The question of government enterprises has been a controversial one in Canada. Supporters argue that government enterprises have contrib-

FIGURE 5-3 *Canada's Top 10 Government Enterprises, 1988*

Rank	1988 Sales ($ thousands)	Name	Rank in FP 500	Number of employees	Ownership
1	$5 813 000	Ontario Hydro	13	32 473	Ontario government 100%
2	5 222 996	Hydro-Québec	14	19 252	Quebec government 100%
3	4 847 000	Petro-Canada	16	7 373	Federal government 100%
4	4 676 194	Canadian National Railway Co.	19	43 933	Federal government 100%
5	3 426 400	Air Canada	30	22 640	Federal government 57%, employee share plan 16%
6	3 138 552	Canada Post Corporation	34	61 558	Federal government 100%
7	2 862 936	Canadian Wheat Board	38	485	Federal government 100%
8	2 110 000	B.C. Hydro and Power Authority	55	6 419	B.C. government 100%
9	1 071 418	AGT	107	11 592	Alberta government 100%
10	910 000	Saskatchewan Power Corp.	119	2 856	Saskatchewan government 100%

SOURCE *The Financial Post 500*, Summer 1989.

uted enormously to the economic development and unity of the nation. They point out that in a far-flung country such as Canada, the costs of operating such enterprises are so great that it is necessary for the government to subsidize their operation in order to provide a reasonable level of service to all Canadians. Critics of government enterprises tend to stress the fact that their numbers have increased greatly over the years (by 1985, the federal government owned 60 Crown corporations) and have come to include money-losing businesses that the government acquired mainly for political reasons, to "save jobs." They point out that many government enterprises pay above-market wages to their employees and/or operate inefficiently, losing money regularly and falling back on taxpayers for subsidies. As the federal government's budget deficits mounted in the 1980's, pressures to reassess the government's commitment to many of its money-losing enterprises grew.

In 1985, the federal government undertook a critical review of the performance of its Crown corporations. It decided to sell some of them to private interests, or **privatize** them. Ambitious plans were made to sell off as many as five federal companies per year, possibly including such notables as Air Canada, Canadair and Petro-Canada, which had started in the 1970's with the objective of frontier oil exploration and development, but had by the mid-1980's acquired a nation-wide system of retail gasoline outlets. The privatization program started with the high-profile sale of De Havilland Aircraft of Canada Ltd. to Boeing Corp. of the United States. And in 1989, the sale of Air Canada to private interests was completed. However, the privatization program did not proceed as rapidly as planned, possibly due to political opposition and the public's coolness towards it.

To summarize, government enterprises are big business in Canada, many of them being household names and major forces in the economy. The objectives of these enterprises are not only profits—some of them, such as Canadian National Railways and the Canadian Broadcasting Corporation, are intended to provide particular services throughout the country whether doing so is profitable or not, or to aid in the development of particular industries, products or regions. The matter of government enterprises has always been a controversial one; critics argue that such operations tend to be very inefficient because of political interference and the absence of the profit motive, and supporters argue that they are an essential component of the Canadian economy, performing functions that private enterprise would not or could not.

Market structure

In this chapter we have considered the nature of the "business sector" of the economy, which produces the supply of goods and services. In Chapters 6 through 10, we will see how supply and demand interact to determine prices. This task is complicated somewhat by the fact that supply—the production of goods and services by business—occurs under various conditions, ranging from industries comprised of large numbers of small firms to industries dominated by a few large firms to industries in which there is only one producer (a monopoly). These different conditions—referred to as *market structures* by economists—are of great significance to the supply of goods and services. If there is only one firm in an industry (a monopoly), it is in a position to control the supply of the product, thereby raising the price of the product and increasing its profits. In industries dominated by a few large firms, it is sometimes possible for these firms to get together to avoid competing on prices and thus increase their profits. On the other hand, in industries in which there are a large number of small firms, such collective action is very difficult or impossible to achieve; as a result, competition in such industries tends to be more intense, and profits lower, than in either of the first two cases. In Chapter 6, we will examine the concept of demand, then in Chapter 7, we will begin our examination of supply (and its interactions with demand) in those industries in which there are a large number of small firms—industries that economists call *competitive*.

DEFINITIONS OF NEW TERMS

Sole Proprietorship   A business firm owned (and usually managed) by a single person who bears full legal liability for the firm's debts.

Partnership   A business firm owned by two or more persons, with each person bearing full legal liability for the firm's debts.

Limited Partner   A partner who invests in a business but takes no active part in the management of it, and whose liability is limited to the amount invested.

General Partner   A partner who takes active part in the management of the business and who has unlimited personal liability for its debts.

Corporation   A business firm which is a separate legal entity from its owners, or shareholders, each of whose liability is limited to the amount of his or her investment in the firm.

Shareholder   The owner of shares (stocks) in a corporation; shareholders may or may not have voting rights and their liability is limited to the amount invested.

Board of Directors   A group of people elected by the shareholders of a corporation to provide direction to the management of the corporation.

Conglomerate   A group of seemingly unrelated types of corporations controlled in varying degrees by a central management group, through holding companies which own shares in those corporations.

Proxy A legal instrument whereby a shareholder's right to vote at shareholders' meetings is delegated to another person, either with or without specific instructions as to how that vote will be exercised.

Crown Corporation A corporation owned by a government, being ultimately responsible, through a cabinet minister, to that government.

Privatization The process of selling government enterprises (usually Crown corporations) to private interests.

CHAPTER SUMMARY

1. The sole proprietorship and the partnership have the advantages of being easy to form, and of providing strong motivation and a high degree of independence. Disadvantages include lack of access to financing, lack of managerial expertise, the unlimited personal liability of the owner(s) and higher tax rates once the income of the business exceeds a certain amount. An added disadvantage of the partnership is the possibility of disagreements among the partners.

2. The corporation, the typical form taken by larger businesses, has the advantages of being able to raise larger amounts of capital due to the limited liability of its shareholders, and of lower tax rates on income above a certain level. Disadvantages include the initial costs of incorporation and a greater degree of government regulation, especially with respect to public corporations.

3. Small business is an important and dynamic sector of the Canadian economy, consisting of many hundreds of thousands of firms and employing up to 40 percent of the nation's labor force.

4. Major problems faced by small business include lack of management expertise, financing problems, government regulations and paperwork, difficulties attracting and retaining skilled employees, and coping with inflation.

5. A wide variety of government programs exists to assist small business in areas such as financing, management counseling, marketing, personnel recruitment, and research and development.

6. The Canadian Federation of Independent Business is an organization of over 85 000 small- and medium-sized Canadian businesses which acts as the small business lobby with government, promoting free competitive enterprise.

7. Big business is another major component of the Canadian economy, accounting for as much as half the economy's output, according to some measures. While these large corporations are important to the Canadian economy, the domination of some industries by a

few large corporations raises questions as to whether such corporate concentration is in the public interest.

8. A different form of business concentration is the conglomerate, in which companies in a variety of industries are controlled by a central management group, through holding companies.

9. Control of the modern large corporation is not usually in the hands of the shareholders as a group; rather, it tends to rest with top management and/or the Board of Directors, neither of which are usually major shareholders.

10. A significant number of Canada's large corporations are government-owned, particularly in the areas of electrical utilities, transportation and communications, and energy and resources.

QUESTIONS

1. Do you believe that small business will become more or less important in the Canadian economy in the future? Why?

2. As a career, which would you prefer to do:
   (a) Own and operate your own small business?
   (b) Work for a small or medium-sized business?
   (c) Work for a large corporation?
   (d) Work for a government enterprise such as a Crown corporation?

   What are the main reasons for your preference?

3. "Interlocking directorships" as referred to in the text are illegal in the USA. Why do you think this is so?

4. Do you believe that the fact that shareholders seldom really control large corporations tends to improve or worsen the management of those corporations? Why?

5. Do you believe that conglomerates pose a threat to society? If not, why not? If so, what would you suggest be done about this?

6. In the late 1980's, Canada Post recorded a profit for the first time. However, this improved financial performance resulted, at least in part, from cutbacks in services to rural areas. Some observers saw the changes as responsible and appropriate, while others argued that maintaining postal service to *all* areas was more important than turning a profit. What do you think, and why?

7. Petro-Can represents the most ambitious government enterprise ever undertaken in Canada. Is Petro-Can generally regarded as having been successful in increasing oil exploration and development in Canada, and in increasing Canadian ownership of the oil industry?

CHAPTER 6

The nature of demand

In Chapter 4, we saw that, in the operation of a market type of economic system, prices play a vitally important role in determining the answers to the three basic economic questions of what to produce, how to produce it and how to divide up society's output of goods and services. Furthermore, we saw that the basic forces determining prices are supply and demand. Before we examine how supply and demand interact to determine prices (in Chapter 7), we need to consider the concept of demand in more detail.

PART A: What is demand?

Suppose we took a survey of all the households in Cantown to determine how much steak people would buy each week in March 1990 if the price were $10 per kilogram, $8 per kilogram, $6 per kilogram, $4 per kilogram and $2 per kilogram respectively. While surveys such as this are an imprecise way of gathering information, especially when they ask people to estimate what they might do under different circumstances, we would expect that people would buy more steak at lower prices than at higher prices. Let us assume, then, that the results of the survey are as shown in Figure 6-1.

Figure 6-1 shows the relationship between the price of steak and the quantity of steaks sold (bought): *as the price rises, the quantity demanded falls*. This drop occurs for two reasons: higher prices cause some people to become *unwilling* to buy steak and others to become *unable* to buy steak. Those who do not buy steak at the higher prices can either substitute another product (such as chicken) for steak, or they can do without steak (that is, buy smaller cuts or none at all).

FIGURE 6-1 *Demand Schedule for Steak in Cantown, March 1990*

If the price per kilogram were	The quantity sold (bought) per week would be
$10	20 000 kg
8	30 000
6	50 000
4	80 000
2	120 000

This relationship between price and quantity demanded, known as **demand**, can be shown in a *demand schedule* as in Figure 6-1, or a *demand curve* on a graph as in Figure 6-2. The demand curve is simply another way of showing the same information that is contained in the demand schedule—that as the price rises, the quantity falls.

FIGURE 6-2 *Demand Curve for Steak in Cantown, March 1990*

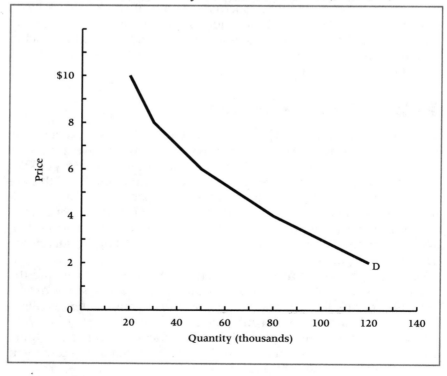

What demand is not

Suppose that, in the example discussed above, the actual price of steak was $6 per kilogram, and that the actual quantity sold was 50 000 kilograms. Under these circumstances, it is tempting to conclude that the demand for steak is 50 000 kilograms, but this is incorrect and misleading. Demand refers to much more than the actual price and quantity bought; it also includes the idea that if the price of steak had been higher, less would have been sold, and that lower prices would have been associated with higher sales. When we say demand we mean *the entire relationship between the various possible prices and the quantity demanded at each price*. Think of demand as the entire results of our hypothetical survey, or as the entire demand schedule or curve, as shown in Figures 6-1 and 6-2.

Shifts in the demand curve

In Figure 6-3, the demand curve labelled D is the same curve used to illustrate the demand for steak earlier in the chapter. Suppose that, since we did the consumer survey that provided the data from which curve D was drawn, a more recent survey has been done. This survey reveals that certain changes have occurred in the demand for steak. The data from the new survey are reflected in demand curve D_1, located *further to the right* on the graph than curve D, indicating that at every possible price, consumers are buying more steak than in the situation shown by curve D. This new relationship can be seen clearly from the demand schedules below the graph: at a price of $10 per kilogram, people used to buy 20 000 kilograms but are now buying 40 000 kilograms; at a price of $8 per kilogram, they have increased their purchases from 30 000 kilograms to 50 000 kilograms; at a price of $6 per kilogram, sales used to be 50 000 kilograms but are now 70 000 kilograms, and so on. Where consumers are buying more of a product at every possible price, so that the demand curve shifts to the right, we say that there has been an *increase in demand*.

Causes of increased demand

Clearly, some of the basic conditions underlying the demand for steak must have changed in the time between the survey that produced demand curve D and the more recent survey reflected in curve D_1. What could explain this shift of the demand curve to the right?

One possible cause is a *change in consumers' tastes:* if people's preferences had changed such that they preferred steak to other meats more strongly than in the past, they would be willing to buy more steak at every possible price and the demand curve would shift to the right. This change

FIGURE 6-3 *Demand Curve and Schedule Showing an Increase
in Demand*

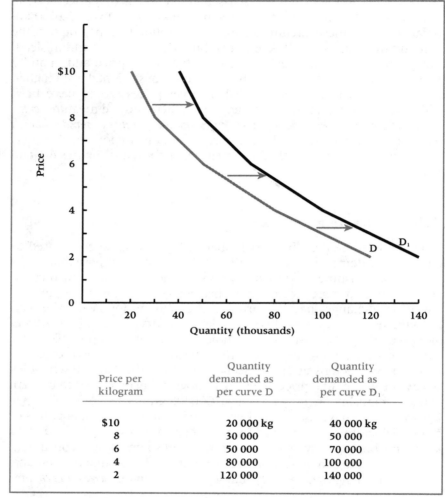

Price per kilogram	Quantity demanded as per curve D	Quantity demanded as per curve D_1
$10	20 000 kg	40 000 kg
8	30 000	50 000
6	50 000	70 000
4	80 000	100 000
2	120 000	140 000

in preferences could be long-term or seasonal in nature: for instance,
demand curve D may reflect preferences in March, whereas curve D_1
may reflect tastes in July, during the barbecue season.

Another possible explanation of the demand curve's shift to the right
could lie in a *change in people's incomes*. Suppose that, between the surveys
that produced the two curves, people's disposable incomes increased
significantly, enabling them to buy more of the products they preferred.
Quite likely, steak would be one such product, so that the demand for

steak would increase and the demand curve would shift to the right. A further explanation of such a change in demand could be a *change in the prices of other products.* For example, an increase in the prices of chicken, pork or other meats would make steak a better buy by comparison, causing an increase in the demand for steak that would shift the demand curve for steak to the right. Still another explanation for an increase in demand such as this is a *change in consumer expectations concerning the price or availability of a product.* If consumers expected that, in the near future, steak would be in shorter supply and considerably more expensive, many of them would buy more steak now and freeze it, again causing an increase in demand and a shift to the right in the demand curve.

Causes of decreased demand

Everything discussed in the preceding sections on increases in demand can be reversed for the purpose of discussing decreases in demand. As Figure 6-4 shows, when the demand for steak decreases, less steak is bought at every possible price (as shown by the demand schedule), and the demand curve shifts to the left (as shown by the new demand curve D_2).

A shift to the left indicates that the factors underlying the demand for steak have changed in such a way that the demand for steak has decreased. Such a change can be explained by reference to the factors discussed earlier. Perhaps people's *incomes* have fallen (or at least not kept up with inflation), leaving them less able to buy as much steak as before, or perhaps their *tastes* have changed, such that they prefer steak less strongly than before (curve D_2 could reflect preferences in the period around Thanksgiving, when the barbecue season is over and people are buying turkey). An alternative explanation could be that the *prices of other products* have fallen: if other meats had become significantly cheaper than they were, consumers would buy more of them, causing a decline in the demand for steak. Finally, a change in people's *expectations* could cause a decline in the demand for a product. If people expect lower prices in the future, they may very well reduce their purchases at present and wait for the lower prices that are anticipated. Our example of steaks does not illustrate the importance of expectations as well as mortgage interest rates, which periodically rise to very high levels, then decline again. In fact, many house buyers postpone purchase decisions when mortgage rates are high, with the expectation that the future will bring lower rates again.

Factors underlying demand

In summary, demand is the relationship between the *price* of a product and the *quantity demanded* by buyers. This relationship can be expressed numerically, in a demand schedule, or graphically, in a demand curve.

FIGURE 6-4 *Demand Curve and Schedule showing a Decrease
in Demand*

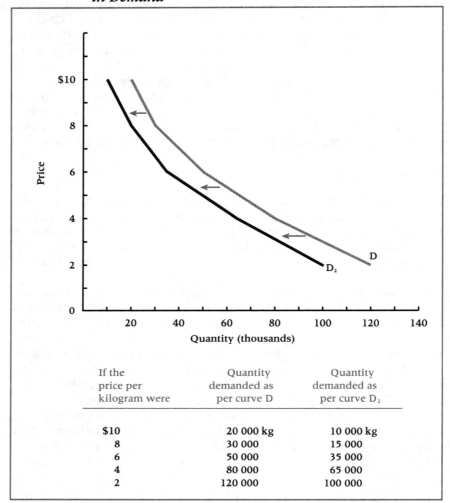

If the price per kilogram were	Quantity demanded as per curve D	Quantity demanded as per curve D₂
$10	20 000 kg	10 000 kg
8	30 000	15 000
6	50 000	35 000
4	80 000	65 000
2	120 000	100 000

The location of the demand curve for a product depends on such factors as buyers' tastes and incomes, the prices of other products and buyers' expectations of future price changes. Should these change so as to increase the demand for the product, the demand curve will shift to the right, whereas changes that reduce the demand for the product will cause the demand curve to shift to the left.

PART B: Elasticity

In Part A we saw that, as the price of a product rises, the amount that buyers will purchase (the quantity demanded) will generally fall. A very

"CHANGES IN DEMAND" VERSUS "CHANGES IN QUANTITY DEMANDED"

We have seen that, if the tastes, incomes or expectations of consumers change, or the prices of other products change, the demand for a product will change—the demand curve will *shift*, either to the left or to the right.

But what if the price of that product fluctuates—will the demand for the product also fluctuate? Certainly, the quantity demanded (or sales) will change, as Figure 6-5 shows: an increase in the price from $1 to $3 causes a reduction in quantity demanded (sales) from 400 to 200.

FIGURE 6-5   *Demand Curve Showing Price Fluctuation*

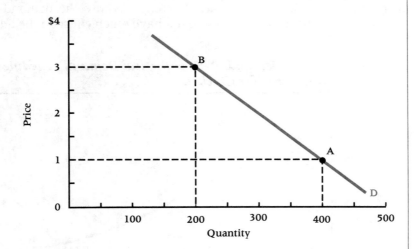

But demand as we have explained it in this chapter has not changed—there has been no shift of the demand curve as occurs when demand changes, only a movement along the demand curve, from point A to point B. Thus, while a change in price does cause a change in *quantity demanded* (sales), it does not alter *demand*. The entire relationship between price and quantity demanded does not change; there is merely a movement, to a different price and quantity demanded, within the same relationship (that is, to a different point on the same demand curve).

important question, which will be examined in the remainder of this chapter, is *how much* will sales fall when prices rise? How sensitive are buyers to changes in price? Obviously, the answer to this question depends on the specific product or service being discussed. For example, an increase in the price of chicken will have a much greater impact on chicken sales than a similar increase in the price of gasoline will have on sales of gasoline. Economists use the terms elastic and inelastic to describe how buyers respond to price changes: when buyers change their purchases a great deal in response to price changes (as with chicken), demand is said to be *elastic*, while demand is called *inelastic* if buyers do not adjust their purchases much in response to price changes.

The difference between elastic and inelastic demand is shown in Figures 6-6 and 6-7. In Figure 6-6, as the price of chicken rises, the quantity demanded declines quite quickly. (Conversely, as the price falls, the quantity demanded rises quite rapidly.)

In Figure 6-7, which shows a hypothetical demand schedule and curve for gasoline, the situation is quite different. Because the demand for gasoline is inelastic, price changes do not have much effect on the quan-

FIGURE 6-6 *Elastic Demand: A Hypothetical Demand Schedule and Curve for Chicken*

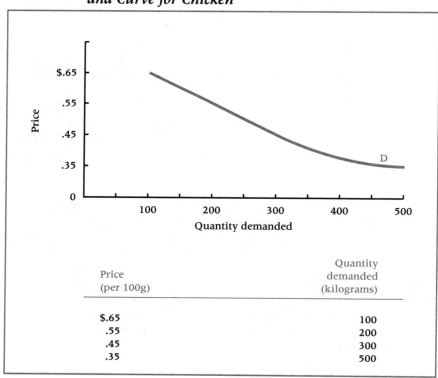

Price (per 100g)	Quantity demanded (kilograms)
$.65	100
.55	200
.45	300
.35	500

tity demanded: as the price rises, buyers do not reduce their purchases by much, and price reductions do not cause buyers to buy much more gasoline. The result, as a comparison of Figures 6-6 and 6-7 shows, is a quite different demand curve—one that is considerably steeper than the elastic demand curve for chicken.[1]

FIGURE 6-7 *Inelastic Demand: A Hypothetical Demand Schedule and Curve for Gasoline*

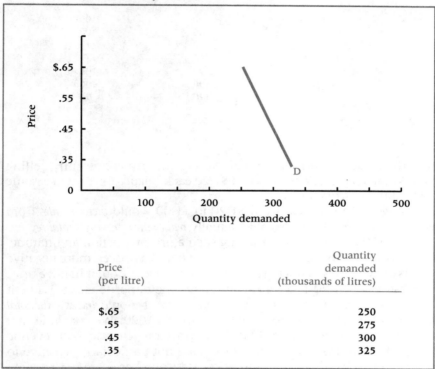

Price (per litre)	Quantity demanded (thousands of litres)
$.65	250
.55	275
.45	300
.35	325

Defining the terms

The preceding examples provide an illustration of the concepts of elastic and inelastic demand, but no proper definitions of these terms. To define elastic and inelastic more precisely, we will use as an example the demand for Supersmooth Shaving Cream as illustrated in Figure 6-8.

In Figure 6-8, we have added a third column—*total revenue*, which is the total sales revenue, or price times quantity demanded. If we assume

[1] Of course, the actual steepness of the demand curve depends on the scales used on the price and quantity axes of the graph. However, the graphs in Figures 6-6 and 6-7 have been drawn with the same scales, so as to make them comparable.

FIGURE 6-8 *Demand Schedule and Total Revenue for Supersmooth Shaving Cream*

Price (per can)	Quantity demanded (thousands of cans per week)	Total revenue ($ thousands) (price x quantity demanded)
$2.00	50	$100
1.80	60	108
1.60	70	112
1.40	80	112
1.20	90	108
1.00	100	100
.80	120	96

that the Supersmooth Shaving Cream Company is presently selling 90 000 cans per week at a price of $1.20 each, Figure 6-8 provides some interesting information.

First, while a price cut from $1.20 to $1.00 would *increase sales* from 90 000 to 100 000 cans, it would actually *reduce the company's total revenue* from $108 000 to $100 000, making such a price reduction an unattractive decision.[2] A price reduction to $.80 would have even more negative effects on revenues, reducing them to $96 000. On the other hand, a price increase from $1.20 to $1.40 would have the opposite effect: while it would *reduce sales* from 90 000 to 80 000 cans, it would *increase the total revenue* of the company from $108 000 to $112 000. We conclude that price increases within the $.80 to $1.40 price range cause total revenue to rise. Within this price range, buyers are not particularly sensitive to price changes, so that when the price rises, purchases are not reduced by so much that total revenue falls. We have said that when buyers are relatively unresponsive to price changes, demand is said to be inelastic. Our formal definition, then, is that *if a price increase causes total revenue to rise, demand is inelastic.*

As the Supersmooth Shaving Cream example shows, though, price increases beyond a certain point tend to backfire. This point is almost reached when the price rises from $1.40 to $1.60, leaving total revenue unchanged at $112 000. (In this borderline case, when the effects of the higher price are exactly offset by effects of the reduced sales, so that total revenue remains unchanged, we say that demand is of *unitary elasticity*.)

---

[2] Note that we say *total revenue* not *profits*. The effect on profits is more complex—it depends on the combined effect of the increased sales and output on total sales revenue *and* total production costs, respectively. For our purposes, however, we can simply assume that higher total revenue means higher profits, and vice versa.

Beyond $1.60, however, price increases cause *declines* in total revenue: price increases to $1.80 and $2.00 cause total revenue to fall to $108 000 and $100 000 respectively, as these higher prices cut more deeply into sales. In this price range, where buyers are quite sensitive to price changes, demand is elastic. Our definition, then, is that *if a price increase causes total revenue to fall, demand is* elastic.

In summary, elasticity of demand refers to the responsiveness of buyers to changes in price. Demand is said to be elastic if a price increase causes total revenue to fall, and inelastic if a price increase causes total revenue to rise. Similar rules can be worked out for the effects of price reductions, but these tend to be confusing. A simple rule of thumb is that if the *price* and the *total revenue* move in the same direction (up or down) demand is inelastic. These definitions are illustrated in the Supersmooth Shaving Cream demand schedule in Figure 6-9.

FIGURE 6–9 *Elasticity of Demand for Supersmooth Shaving Cream over Various Price Ranges*

Price (per can)	Quantity demanded (thousands of cans per week)	Total revenue (price X quantity demanded)	Elasticity of demand (over price range shown)
$2.00	50	$100	elastic from $1.80 to $2.00
1.80	60	108	elastic from $1.60 to $1.80
1.60	70	112	unitary[a] elasticity from $1.40 to $1.60
1.40	80	112	inelastic from $1.20 to $1.40
1.20	90	108	inelastic from $1.00 to $1.20
1.00	100	100	inelastic from $ .80 to $1.00
.80	120	96	

[a]**Unitary elasticity** means there is no change in total revenue as a result of price increases.

The Supersmooth Shaving Cream example illustrates another point concerning elasticity: the elasticity of the demand for a product *depends upon the price range under discussion.* Over the lower price ranges, the demand for Supersmooth Shaving Cream is inelastic, presumably because its relatively low price makes buyers less responsive to price increases. Over the higher price ranges, however, the demand becomes elastic, as further price increases drive away more and more buyers. Therefore, we cannot properly say that the demand for a certain product is elastic or inelastic—the elasticity depends on the price range we have in mind. However, we often say that the demand for a product (say, gasoline) is inelastic. When we do so, we are implicitly referring to the price range around its *present actual price.* Obviously, at $5 per litre, the elasticity of the demand for gasoline would be quite different.

Characteristics of products with inelastic and elastic demand

When the price of a product or service increases, buyers of it have basically three alternatives:

(a) they can continue buying it as before,

(b) they can substitute; that is, buy another product instead, or

(c) they can do without it.

Of course, buyers do not need to choose (a) *or* (b) *or* (c); they can combine them. For instance, in response to an increase in steak prices, a family may buy smaller steaks than previously and buy more chicken—a combination of all three alternatives. Nonetheless, these are the basic choices open to buyers facing higher prices.

If the demand for a product is *inelastic,* higher prices will not reduce sales by much. That is, buyers must mostly choose alternative (a), despite the higher price, under the following two conditions. First, buyers must be *unable or unwilling to do without* the product; it must be a necessity (such as food) or it must be treated as such (for instance, a television set). We are not really interested here in whether a product is a real physical necessity or is more of a psychological necessity. We are only concerned with the fact that buyers will continue to buy it despite the higher price. Second, there must be *no close substitutes* available; otherwise, buyers could simply switch to another product. For demand to be inelastic, *both* these conditions must apply: for buyers to be forced to continue buying the product at the higher price, they must be not only unable or unwilling to do without it, but also unable to switch to a close substitute.

For demand to be *elastic,* buyers must reduce their purchases substantially in response to higher prices. Such a reduction could happen for

THIS ELASTICITY'S FOR YOU!

The market for beer in Ontario in the summer of 1989 provides a good example of elasticity of demand in action. The events unfolded in three stages.

First, in the spring and early summer, imported US beer was selling through the government-controlled Liquor Control Board of Ontario (LCBO) for as little as $4.30 per six-pack, as compared to $6.60 for a six-pack of Canadian beer. Sales of US beer soared to the point where it claimed 7 percent of the Ontario market, up from only 1 percent in the previous year. This prompted complaints to the LCBO that Canadian beer sales—and jobs—were being jeopardized.

On July 9, the LCBO moved to protect the Canadian beer industry by increasing the price of US beer to $5.50. At the same time, Canadian breweries dropped their price to $6.25. Sales of US beer promptly dried up over the peak month of July.

However, this left the unfortunate LCBO with 48 million cans of unsold (and perishable) US beer, and the prospective loss of millions of dollars. So the LCBO reversed gears again, cutting the price of its US beer on August 9 to $4.70. Sales of US beer picked up again briskly.

This example of elasticity of demand in action is particularly interesting because breweries spend millions of dollars in advertising to promote what is known as "brand loyalty" to their product. Apparently, in the face of a price difference of 25 to 35 percent, brand loyalty is quickly forgotten by consumers.

two different reasons: perhaps they were able to switch to another product because a reasonably close substitute was available, or perhaps they were able to do without the product because it was not (or was not regarded as) a necessity. To make the demand elastic, all that is necessary is that one of these conditions apply, so that buyers do not have to continue buying the product at the higher price.

Real world elasticity

Elasticity of demand is a very important factor in many business and economic decisions. One obvious area is that of *business pricing policies*, since it is the elasticity of demand that will determine whether a price change will increase or reduce the firm's total revenue. Suppose, for instance, that the Glace Bay Bombers hockey team is presently pricing tickets to its games at an average price of $4 each, and that average ticket sales per game are 2400, well below the arena's capacity of 3000. Should the Bombers' management seek to increase ticket sales to 3000 and fill the arena for their games? The answer is not as simple as it seems, if increasing attendance requires the kind of price reductions shown in the demand schedule in Figure 6-10. If the demand for tickets is as shown, ticket prices will have to be cut to $3 to lure 3000 people to support the Bombers—a price that would *reduce* the club's total revenue by $600 per game.

FIGURE 6-10 *Hypothetical Demand Schedule for Tickets to Glace Bay Bombers' Home Games*

Average price per ticket	Quantity of tickets demanded per game	Total revenue per game
$3	3 000	$9 000
4	2 400	9 600
5	2 000	10 000
6	1 650	9 900

In fact, the schedule indicates that, financially, the Bombers would be better off if they *raised* ticket prices to $5, as the loss of sales would be more than offset by the higher price per ticket. Even at a price of $6 per ticket, there are still enough diehard Bomber fans to make a nearly half-empty arena more profitable for the club than one with 2400 fans paying $4 each.

On the other hand, suppose the demand schedule is as shown in Figure 6-11. In this case, it would pay the club to reduce ticket prices. A reduction would increase attendance as well as total revenue, whereas price increases would have the opposite effect. Obviously, it is of great importance that the Bombers' management know the elasticity of the demand for their tickets. However, in the real world, sellers do not have neat and precise demand schedules, such as those shown in Figures 6-10 and 6-7, to guide them in their pricing decisions. While the market research departments of larger corporations may expend considerable effort in attempts to estimate the elasticity of demand for their products,[3] many smaller businesses operate on a trial-and-error basis, gaining a rough

[3] Usually the elasticity is expressed numerically, as a **coefficient of elasticity**. For instance, a coefficient of 1.2 means that a 1-percent increase in price causes a 1.2-percent reduction in quantity demanded, while a coefficient of 0.4 means that if price rises 1 percent, quantity demanded declines only 0.4 percent. Demand is *elastic* if the coefficient is greater than 1.0 and *inelastic* if the coefficient is less than 1.0. For example, the coefficient of elasticity for food has been estimated at 0.4, while for durable goods the coefficient has been estimated at 1.1.

idea of the elasticity of demand by testing the market with small price increases or reductions. But this lack of a reliable method for determining elasticity of demand does not mean that sellers operate in the dark in their pricing decisions. Obviously, the Organization of Petroleum Exporting Countries had a reasonable understanding that the industrialized nations' demand for oil was quite inelastic in the 1970's. Small retailers sense clearly that if their prices rise above those of their competitors, the demand for their products will be quite elastic, and discount retailers operate on the basis that at least a certain segment of consumers is quite sensitive to prices.

FIGURE 6-11 *Another Hypothetical Demand Schedule for Tickets to Glace Bay Bombers' Home Games*

Average price per ticket	Quantity of tickets demanded per game	Total revenue per game
$3.25	3 000	$9 750
4.00	2 400	9 600
5.00	1 900	9 500
6.00	1 500	9 000

In a similar way, elasticity of demand influences the ability of workers to increase their *wages*. For instance, the demand for certain highly skilled workers, such as computer programmers, is very inelastic. Such work has to be done, and there is no substitute way of doing it. Consequently, such workers are in an excellent position to bargain for higher wages— which they do. By contrast, people in the lawn mowing industry probably face a more elastic demand, since their service is not essential and buyers have the alternative of mowing their own lawns. As a result, the demand for lawn mowing would be more elastic, making it more difficult for lawn mowers to raise their prices and incomes.

Elasticity of demand is also an important consideration underlying the *taxation policies* of governments. Three of the most heavily taxed products are liquor, tobacco and gasoline. Moral and ecological considerations aside, the main reason for these products being singled out for exceptionally high taxes is the fact that the demand for all three is inelastic: sales (and tax revenues) hold up quite well even after tax increases have raised their prices considerably. There is little point in imposing heavy taxes on products whose demand is elastic, as sales would fall drastically, devastating those industries (not to mention reducing government tax revenues).

Elasticity of demand is also a factor underlying certain *social problems*, a good example of which is the low incomes of many farmers over the years. Farmers have advanced technologically, raising productivity and the total output of farm products, but most still find themselves in a difficult position economically. While the increased output has depressed farm prices, the lower prices have not led to increased sales of farm products, because the demand for food is inelastic: people do not buy much more food just because it is a bargain. Farmers received lower prices for their crops, but were unable to sell more crops to offset the lower prices, leaving them with low incomes. This is not a new problem for farmers; it has been with them for centuries. For instance, Gregory King, an English writer, remarked in the seventeenth century that when there was a good harvest, farmers actually received less than when the harvest was poor. This latter observation is the key to the farmers' ability to overcome their problem: while they cannot control the size of the harvest, some of them are able to control how much of it reaches the market. Coffee producers in Brazil band together to burn part of any large crops they have, so as to secure higher prices and, due to the inelastic demand for coffee, higher total revenues. However, many other groups of farmers have had great difficulty uniting and have suffered low incomes as a result. In Canada recently, government-sponsored marketing boards have played an increasing role in organizing reductions in farm production and increases in farm incomes.

A final important (and interesting) example of elasticity of demand is provided by the *oil crisis*. As Canada entered the 1980's with crude oil prices less than one-half world price levels, a major debate began over whether higher prices would significantly promote oil conservation by reducing oil usage by Canadians.[4] Most Canadians seemed to feel at that time that higher prices would not significantly reduce their use of oil. But while oil use may be reduced very little *in the short run* by higher prices, *over the longer run* the demand for oil seems to be less inelastic. Given time, people will switch to smaller cars and insulate their homes in response to higher prices, and industries will convert to more energy efficient production methods. Some evidence for this prediction is provided by comparisons of the USA and Canada: from 1972 to 1978, the economy in the US (where oil prices rose more rapidly) increased its energy efficiency by about 10 percent, while Canada (with slower increases in oil prices) increased its energy efficiency by only 4 percent. It appears not only that the demand for oil may be less inelastic than had been feared, but also that the demand for oil (and energy generally) may become more elastic as higher prices prevail over a period of time. This elasticity was one of the factors that made it impossible for OPEC to maintain oil prices at the extremely high levels that they reached by 1980—buyers simply cut back on their purchases.

[4] An even more important aspect to the debate was whether higher prices would generate a higher *supply* of oil, by providing incentives and funds for exploration and development. As it turned out, high prices did generate an increased supply of oil on world markets, and were one factor that caused oil prices to drop after 1980. However, this process involves a different concept—elasticity of supply—which we will examine in Chapter 7.

Conclusion

This chapter has considered the nature of demand—one-half of the price-determining process of supply and demand. In Chapter 7, we will consider supply, and how supply and demand interact to determine prices.

DEFINITIONS OF NEW TERMS

Demand The entire relationship between the various possible prices of a product or service and the quantity demanded at each price, expressed through either a schedule or a graph.

Inelastic Demand The term used to describe demand if a price increase causes an increase in total sales revenue.

Elastic Demand The term used to describe demand if a price increase causes a reduction in total sales revenue.

Coefficient of Elasticity The percentage change in quantity demanded that results from a 1-percent change in price.

CHAPTER SUMMARY

1. A demand schedule or curve reflects the fact that, as the price of a good or service rises, the quantity demanded generally falls.

2. If consumer tastes, incomes, expectations or the prices of other products change, the demand for a product will increase (in which case more is demanded at each possible price and the curve shifts to the right) or decrease (in which case less is demanded at each possible price and the demand curve shifts to the left).

3. If buyers can do without a product or find a close substitute, a price increase will cause the seller's total sales revenue to fall, and demand will be elastic.

4. If buyers cannot do without a product and cannot find a close substitute, a price increase will cause the seller's total sales revenue to rise, and demand will be inelastic.

5. Elasticity of demand is an important factor in decisions and trends regarding prices, incomes and taxes.

QUESTIONS

1. Many economists (and merchandisers) believe that the demand curve for some products is the type of curve shown in the following graph rather than the simple downward-sloping demand curve discussed in Part A of this chapter.

(a) What is the relationship between price and quantity demanded, as shown by this curve?
(b) What could explain this peculiar type of consumer behavior?
(c) How could merchandisers use this type of consumer behavior to their advantage?

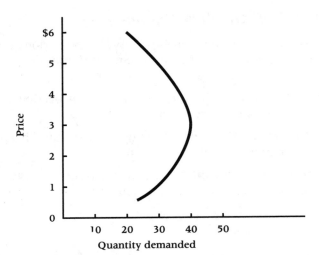

2. If the price of North American cars rose rapidly, what would happen to the demand curve for Toyotas?

3. If you were selling a product with an *inelastic* demand, what would you emphasize and not emphasize in your advertising?

4. If you were selling a product with an *elastic* demand, what would you emphasize in your advertising?

5. How does the elasticity of the demand for automobiles appear through the eyes of
   (a) top management of General Motors?
   (b) the owner of a General Motors dealership?

6. What effect would the burning of coffee by Brazilian coffee producers have if the demand for coffee were elastic?

7. "The dilemma posed by the demand curve is that, to increase *sales*, you must lower your *price*. This means that you will have to charge *less* to some buyers than they would have been prepared to pay, thus foregoing some sales revenue." Is there any way for a seller to get around this dilemma?

8. One way in which workers attempt to raise their incomes is by joining a labor union. How do a union's prospects for increasing the wages of plumbers compare with its prospects for increasing the incomes of hairdressers, and why?

9. For each of the following pairs of goods, state which one of the pair has the more *elastic* demand, and state the reason for your choice.
  (a) air conditioners/furnaces
  (b) new automobiles/licenses for automobiles
  (c) telephone service/electricity
  (d) beef/meat

10. Explain whether each of the following will make the demand for the product or service involved more elastic or more inelastic, and *why* it would do so.
  (a) Rising consumer incomes should make the demand for restaurant dinners more _____.
  (b) At Christmas, the demand for turkey should become more _____.
  (c) The development of inexpensive wigs would make the demand for hairdressing more _____.
  (d) The use of freezers in more homes should make the demand for foods that can be frozen more _____.

11. Place the following in order of elasticity of demand, the most elastic coming first.
  —chocolate ice cream
  —dairy products
  —Neilson's chocolate ice cream
  —ice cream

CHAPTER 7

The nature of supply

Competitive conditions

Before we examine how demand and supply interact to determine prices, we must begin to consider systematically the supply side of the market, or the organization and operation of the firms and industries that produce, or supply, goods and services.[1] As we saw in Chapter 5, the process of supply takes place under various conditions. In some industries, there are many small firms, while other industries are dominated by a few very large firms, and in a few markets there is only one producer (a monopoly). These different conditions—referred to as **market structures** by economists—are of great significance to the process of supply. Obviously, there is a great deal of difference between the way a small vegetable farmer and General Motors make their decisions as to how much output to produce and what price to charge for it.

Competitive industries

One basic type of market structure consists of what economists call **competitive industries**. Competitive industries have two basic characteristics: first, they are comprised of a *large number of small firms*; and second,

---

[1] The term *firm* refers to a business; the term *industry* refers to the group of business firms producing a particular product or service. For example, General Motors, Ford, and Chrysler are the three largest *firms* in the North American automobile *industry*.

it is *easy for new firms to enter (and leave) the industry.* As a result, there tends to be intense competition among producers, which holds prices and profits down to quite low levels. If, for any reason, prices and profits increase to higher levels, new producers will be attracted into the industry, increasing the amount supplied, intensifying competition and pushing prices and profits back downward. While this situation is not to the advantage of the producers in the industry, they are unable to do anything about it—because they are so numerous, it is impossible for them to get together and make agreements to restrict competition among themselves.

Competitive industries, then, are those in which a combination of numerous small firms and easy entry into the industry make it impossible for producers to band together and exercise any significant control over the supply or price of their product. Rather, such industries are characterized by vigorous competition among producers, which drives prices and profits down to minimal levels.[2] Examples of such competitive industries include much of the small business sector described in Chapter 5—small-scale retail stores, hamburger stands, many small agricultural producers, small-scale manufacturing, and many service industries such as appliance repairs and window-washing.

Non-competitive industries

Not all industries are competitive in this sense—a large proportion of the economy's output comes from industries that are of a different nature. Called **non-competitive** by economists, these industries are dominated by a few firms, making it difficult for others to enter the market.[3] These characteristics put the firms in such industries in a much more advantageous position than those in competitive industries. First, because they are *few in number,* the dominant firms will be in a better position to get together and agree among themselves not to compete vigorously on prices; as a result, profits in non-competitive industries are often higher than in competitive industries. Second, because it is so *difficult for new firms to enter* the industry, there is much less risk that the high profits of the dominant firms in the industry will attract newcomers who would increase competition and erode high profits.

In short, in non-competitive industries, the dominant producers are often in a better position to act together so as to hold the supply of their

[2] Strong competition does not mean that *all* firms will earn very low profits—in even the most competitive industries, there are usually efficient companies that earn excellent profits. However, *on the average,* profits will be low in these industries.

[3] By *non-competitive,* we do not mean that they avoid all forms of competition; often, such firms will compete quite strongly in their advertising efforts, but will try to avoid competing regarding prices.

product down and its price up, and thus receive higher profits for prolonged periods.[4] Examples of non-competitive industries include steel making, automobile manufacturing and petroleum refining.

Figure 7-1 summarizes and compares the characteristics of competitive and non-competitive industries that we have discussed. Because the production and pricing decisions associated with supply in non-competitive industries are different from those in competitive industries, we will consider the former separately, in Chapter 10. Our first look at supply will be limited to the case of competitive industries.

FIGURE 7-1 *Characteristics of Competitive and Non-Competitive Industries*

Competitive industries (Chapters 7–9)	*Non-competitive industries (Chapter 10)*
Producers have very little control over prices and profits	Producers are in a better position to influence prices and profits
because: 1. there are many small firms in the industry; and 2. it is easy for new firms to enter;	*because:* 1. there are only a few firms in the industry; and 2. it is difficult for new firms to enter;
so that: the producers are unable to control the supply—if profits become high, new firms start up, causing supply to rise and prices and profits to fall;	*so that:* the producers are in a position to make price agreements among themselves and to keep supply down and prices and profits up (above competitive levels);
with the result that: prices and profits tend to be held down to low levels.	*with the result that:* prices and profits tend to be maintained at above-competitive levels.

Supply under competitive conditions

As we have seen, competitive industries have two basic characteristics: they are comprised of many small firms and it is easy for new firms to enter the industry. As an example, suppose that, in the cattle industry, an increase in the demand for beef drives prices upward. What effect will this have on the amount of beef offered for sale? We should expect the higher prices to induce producers to offer *more* beef for sale, by making

---

[4] However, such firms and their industries are not guaranteed a comfortable position, as the problems of the North American automobile industry in the 1980's show.

it more profitable to sell beef. This does not merely mean that producers will temporarily sell more cattle out of existing herds; the higher price will make it economical (profitable) to support larger herds that will sustain higher production levels. Furthermore, the increased production will not come just from existing producers—because it is easy to enter the industry, new producers of beef will start up, adding to production levels. In competitive industries, therefore, *higher prices tend to generate an increase in the amount offered for sale*, as shown in Figure 7-2, in which a price increase from $2 to $5 causes the quantity supplied (offered for sale) to increase from 40 units per week to 80 units per week.

While this connection may seem quite obvious, it is worth noting that not all markets operate in this way. If there were only one firm in the industry (a monopoly), or a few firms acting in cooperation with each

FIGURE 7-2 *Supply in a Competitive Situation*

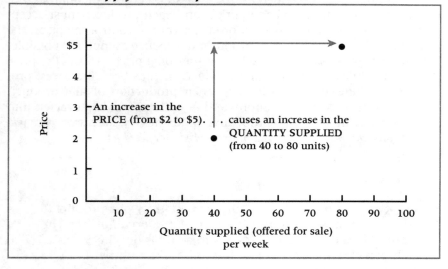

PRICE AND SUPPLY

The oil industry provides an excellent illustration of the effect of price upon supply. Following the major oil-price increases of the 1970's, there was an upsurge of oil exploration and development activity in Canada, including plans for massive investments in Tar Sands oil projects. However, when the price of oil fell after 1981, exploration and development activity declined and projects were postponed.

other, the quantity supplied would not necessarily increase in response to a price increase: the producer or producers would be in a position to restrict the supply, keeping the price and profits high. An example of this method of controlling prices is provided by the Arab oil-producing states, which acted together to increase the price of oil by restricting the quantity offered for sale on world markets. Similar action on the part of organized groups maintains high price levels for a wide variety of products, ranging from diamonds to eggs. It is important to remember, therefore, that not all markets or industries are competitive in the sense described in this chapter. Sellers who possess monopoly power are called **price-makers**, because they have the ability to determine (or at least influence) the price of the product.

However, in a competitive industry, due to the large number of disorganized sellers and the fact that new producers can enter the industry easily, it is not possible for producers to control the supply or the price. Such producers are described as **price-takers**, because the market, not the producer(s), determines the price, and each producer must accept that price. Since each individual producer cannot control the price, the economic incentive is for each producer to produce as much as possible, as efficiently as possible, and sell it for the going price. And, if the price (and profitability) of a particular product, such as beef, increases, producers can be expected to increase their production of that product. Existing firms will produce more, and new firms will be attracted into that industry. In short, in competitive industries, *an increase in price will tend to cause an increase in the quantity supplied, or offered for sale.*

THE CONCEPT OF SUPPLY

Supply does not refer to the physical quantity of a product in existence, but rather to the quantity of it *offered for sale.* The supply of used ten-speed bicycles in a city is not the 300 000 such bicycles that exist there, but rather the number that would be offered for sale at various possible prices, and the 14 000 used ten-speed bicycles presently on the market is the "quantity supplied" at the current market price of $85.

An example

In Chapter 6, we used purchases of steak as an illustration of demand. In this chapter, we will use steak to illustrate the concept of supply as well, since the beef cattle industry is a reasonable example of a competitive industry. As noted previously, the quantity of steak offered for sale will depend in large part on the price of steak: the higher the price that consumers are prepared to offer, the greater the quantity of steak that will be supplied by producers. Suppose that, using a survey or some other means, we have been able to determine the actual relationship between the various possible prices of steak and the quantity that sellers will supply at each possible price. This information is presented numerically in a **supply schedule** in Figure 7-3, and graphically in a **supply curve** in Figure 7-4. Both the supply schedule and the supply curve

FIGURE 7-3 *Supply Schedule for Steak in Cantown, March 1990*

If the price per kilogram were	The quantity supplied (offered for sale) would be
$10	100 000 kg
8	80 000
6	50 000
4	20 000
3	0

FIGURE 7-4 *Supply Curve for Steak in Cantown, March 1990*

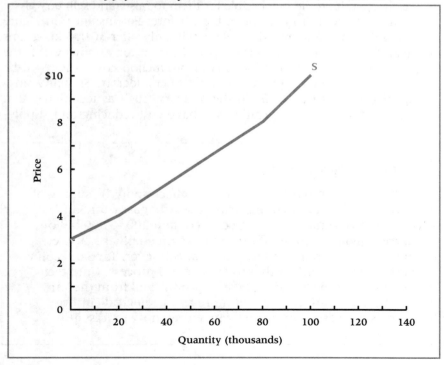

reflect the fundamental fact that we have stressed: in a competitive market, increases in price will tend to cause increases in the quantity supplied. At a price of $3 per kilogram, no one is prepared to sell steak, while higher prices cause increasing amounts to be offered for sale . . . at $10 per kilogram, cattle production and the quantity of steaks supplied have increased greatly.

As with demand, the concept of supply includes the entire supply schedule or curve—that is, supply refers to the amounts that would be offered for sale at every possible price. If the actual price were $6 per kilogram and the actual quantity supplied were 50 000 kilograms, supply is not 50 000 kilograms—supply also includes the amounts that would have been offered for sale if the price had been higher or lower.

Changes in supply

In Chapter 6, we saw that if demand increased, the demand curve shifted to the right, and that a decrease in demand caused the curve to shift to the left. Similarly, increases in supply cause the supply curve to shift to the right, as shown in Figure 7-5. Here, the curve S_1 represents an increase in supply: *at every possible price*, sellers are offering 30 000 more kilograms of steak for sale than previously. What could cause such a change in sellers' behavior? Perhaps their *costs of production* have decreased—if feed were cheaper, it would be possible for them to raise (and sell) any given amount of cattle at a lower price than before. For instance, in Figure 7-5, supply curve S shows that sellers will only offer 50 000 kilograms of steak for sale if they can get $6 per kilogram for it; however, if the supply rises to S_1 due to reductions in production costs, they will be willing to sell 50 000 kilograms for only $4 per kilogram. Similarly, anything that *increases productivity* in the industry, such as techniques that speed the maturity of the cattle, will have cost-reducing and supply-

TECHNOLOGY AND SUPPLY

Technology can have a tremendous effect upon the supply of particular products. For instance, the Athabasca Tar Sands of northern Alberta are estimated to contain 200 to 300 billion barrels of oil, or about fifteen times as much oil as has ever been discovered in western Canada. However, Tar Sands oil is very difficult—and costly—to extract and process. Until technology was developed that could produce oil from the Tar Sands, they were considered more as a geological curiosity than as the vast economic resource they now represent.

FIGURE 7-5 *An Increase in Supply*

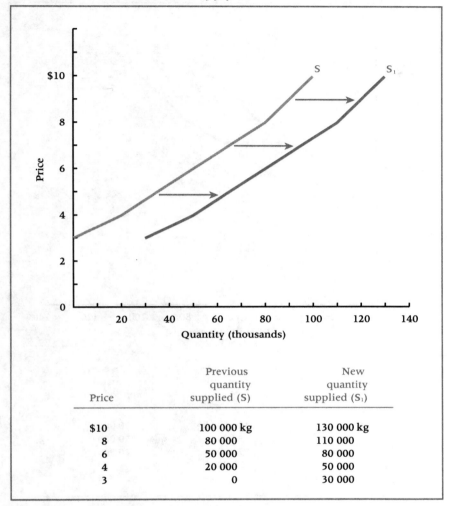

Price	Previous quantity supplied (S)	New quantity supplied (S₁)
$10	100 000 kg	130 000 kg
8	80 000	110 000
6	50 000	80 000
4	20 000	50 000
3	0	30 000

increasing effects. *Government subsidies* will have the same effect, by making it economical for producers to raise and sell more cattle. Another possibility is that *more people* will decide to enter the cattle-raising industry, either because they like the lifestyle or because they expect higher cattle prices in the future. Any of these developments would increase the supply of steak, shifting the supply curve to the right.

Conversely, anything that made cattle more difficult or costly to raise, such as higher *production costs* or higher *taxes* on producers, would reduce the supply, shifting the curve to the left, as shown in Figure 7-6. In

FIGURE 7-6 *A Decrease in Supply*

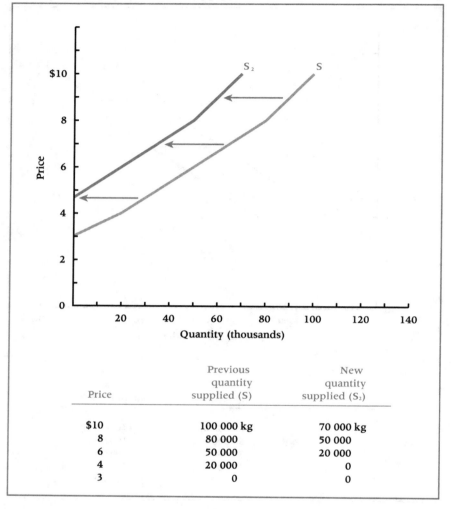

Price	Previous quantity supplied (S)	New quantity supplied (S₂)
$10	100 000 kg	70 000 kg
8	80 000	50 000
6	50 000	20 000
4	20 000	0
3	0	0

summary then, supply curves follow the same pattern as demand curves, shifting to the right when supply increases and to the left when supply decreases.

Elasticity of supply

We have seen that, as the price of a product produced in a competitive industry rises, the quantity supplied will rise. What is most important, however, is *the degree* to which the quantity supplied will rise in response to a higher price. In some cases, the higher price will cause prompt and large increases in the quantity supplied, while in other cases even very large increases in price will not cause the quantity supplied to change significantly.

If rising prices do not cause significant increases in quantity supplied, supply is said to be <u>inelastic</u>. Figure 7-7 shows an inelastic supply: here,

FIGURE 7-7   *An Inelastic Supply Curve*

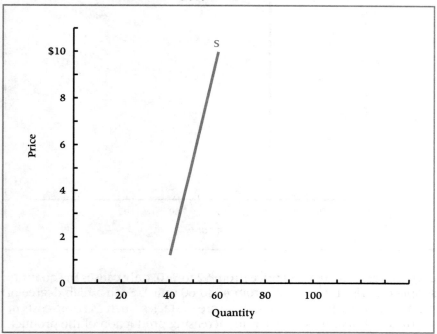

INTEREST RATES AND SUPPLY

In addition to direct production costs such as labor and materials, supply is also affected by interest rates, or the cost of borrowing capital. Obviously, higher interest rates mean higher costs of doing business and high prices for consumers. In addition, however, if interest rates become too high, businesses may postpone capital investment projects that would add to the supply of goods and services. High interest rates were a factor in the decision to abandon the Tar Sands oil projects planned for the 1980's. At a cost estimated at $13 billion per plant, these projects involved such heavy borrowing that interest rates were a major cost factor influencing the decision to proceed or not.

On a more general scale, some economists have been concerned since the early 1980's that Canada's high interest rates could slow the country's economic progress by depressing capital investment and the supply side of the economy.

FIGURE 7-8 *A Perfectly Inelastic Supply Curve*

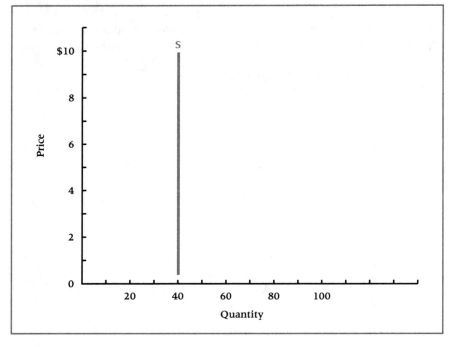

*Canadian
Microeconomics:
Problems and
policies*

even a fivefold increase in price (from $2 to $10) only causes the quantity supplied to rise by one-half (from 40 to 60 units). Such a high degree of inelasticity usually means that there are obstacles, such as rising costs or shortages of materials or labor, to increasing production of the product. The most extreme case of inelasticity of supply—perfectly inelastic supply—is illustrated in Figure 7-8: here, despite very large price increases, *no* increase in the amount offered for sale takes place. The most extreme example of such a situation would be a unique item such as an original work of art; no matter how high the price goes, there can only ever be one of it. Figure 7-9 shows an **elastic** supply curve, reflecting a situation in which a tripling of the price (from $2 to $6) causes a fivefold increase in the quantity supplied. An example of such a situation could be plastic toys—with the molds already in existence, it is a simple and low-cost matter to increase production of the toys if price increases warrant it.

Finally, as with elasticity of demand, elasticity of supply tends to *increase over a period of time*. When the price of the product first increases, it may be impossible to increase the quantity supplied for a while. However, given more time, producers are often able to increase the quantity supplied in response to price increases. The difference between elasticity of supply in the short run and in the long run is illustrated in Figure 7-10, with the supply becoming much more elastic as time passes. What is the actual difference between the short run and the long run? For plastic toys, it may be a matter of days before production can be increased significantly; for annual agricultural products, up to a year. For higher

FIGURE 7-9 *An Elastic Supply Curve*

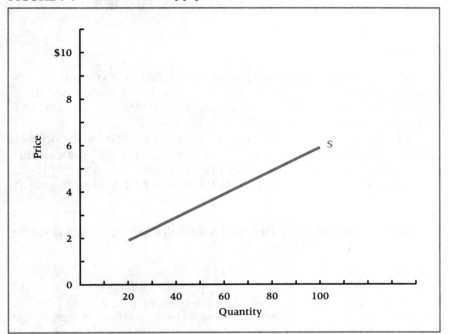

FIGURE 7-10 *Elasticity of Supply in the Short Run and the
Long Run*

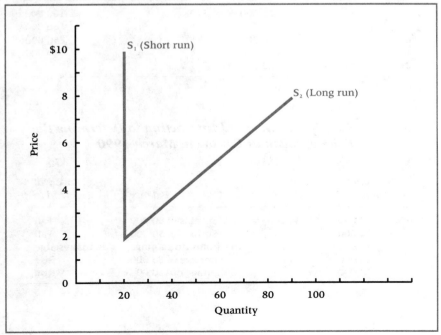

oil prices to stimulate increased exploration, development and production of oil on a large scale, ten to fifteen years are required.

Summary

We have now examined both demand (in Chapter 6) and supply under competitive conditions (in this chapter); these two concepts are summarized in Figure 7-11. We are now ready to consider how demand and supply interact, by combining them, as in Figure 7-12.

As the supply and demand schedules in Figure 7-12 show, the price of steak will tend to stabilize at $6 per kilogram. This is called the **equilibrium price**. It is not possible for the price to stabilize at any other level, because all other prices lead to either a shortage or a surplus, which

FIGURE 7-11 **Supply and Demand Schedules for Steak in Cantown, March 1990**

DEMAND		SUPPLY	
The relationship between the price of the product and the number of units buyers will offer to buy		The relationship between the price of the product and the number of units producers will offer to sell	
Price of steak per kilogram	*Quantity demanded (kilograms)*	*Price of steak per kilogram*	*Quantity supplied (kilograms)*
$10	20 000	$10	100 000
8	30 000	8	80 000
6	50 000	6	50 000
4	80 000	4	20 000
2	120 000	2	0

FIGURE 7-12 **Supply and Demand Interacting to Determine the Price of Steak in Cantown, March 1990**

Price	*Quantity demanded*	*Quantity supplied*	*Balance*	*Price will tend to*
$10	20 000	100 000	Surplus of 80 000	Fall
8	30 000	80 000	Surplus of 50 000	Fall
6	50 000	50 000	No surplus/no shortage	Remain stable
4	80 000	20 000	Shortage of 60 000	Rise
2	120 000	0	Shortage of 120 000	Rise

would cause the price to change. For instance, at a price of $10 per kilogram, the quantity supplied exceeds the quantity demanded, generating a surplus of 80 000 kilograms on the market. Under these circumstances, competition among sellers will drive the price down toward the equilibrium level of $6. Similarly, prices below $6 discourage production but encourage demand, causing shortages on the market. As buyers compete for the limited supply, the price will be bid up toward the equilibrium level of $6. Only at a price of $6 per kilogram are the actions of both buyers and sellers in harmony, so that there is neither a surplus nor a shortage. As a result, the price will stabilize at the equilibrium level of $6 per kilogram.

The interaction of supply and demand can also be shown on a graph, as in Figure 7-13. On the graph, the equilibrium price of $6 is determined by the intersection of the supply curve and the demand curve at the *equilibrium point* (E). The intersection of the curves also determines the quantity that will be bought (and sold), or the **equilibrium quantity** of 50 000 kilograms.

In summary, the way in which supply and demand interact to determine the price of a product or service can be represented on a schedule such as Figure 7-12, or on a graph such as Figure 7-13. Both the schedule

FIGURE 7-13   *Supply, Demand and the Price of Steak in Cantown, March 1990*

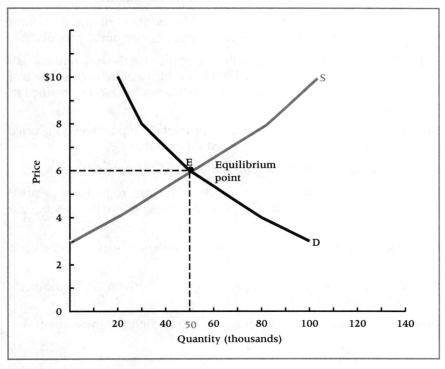

and the graph depict the behavior of buyers (demand) and sellers (supply) in the market for a particular good or service, and the equilibrium price and quantity that will emerge in that market.

Figure 7-13 is a very static representation of a market, showing the demand for and supply of steak *at a particular time* (March 1990). In reality, however, markets are very dynamic, with constant changes in supply and demand occurring, causing continual changes in equilibrium prices and quantities. In effect, then, Figure 7-13 is a snapshot of a dynamic, changing situation at a particular point in time. In the next chapter, we will consider how markets change and adjust in response to changes in both supply and demand.

DEFINITIONS OF NEW TERMS

Market Structure   Term used to describe the organization and nature of a market or an industry, particularly whether it is competitive or non-competitive in nature.

Competitive Industry   An industry that consists of many small firms and is easily entered by new competitors.

Non-Competitive Industry   An industry that is dominated by a few large firms and is not easily entered by new competitors.

Price-Maker   Term used to describe the position of the dominant firm(s) in an industry, which can influence the price of the product.

Price-Taker   Term used to describe the position of the individual small firm in a competitive industry, which is unable to influence the price of its product and is forced to accept (take) whatever price is determined in the market.

Supply Schedule   A table depicting the relationship between the price of a product and the quantity supplied (offered for sale).

Supply Curve   A graphical representation of a supply schedule.

Elastic Supply   A situation in which sellers are responsive to price changes; that is, the quantity supplied increases readily when the price rises.

Inelastic Supply   A situation in which quantity supplied does not increase readily when the price rises.

Equilibrium Price   A price determined in the marketplace by the interaction of supply and demand.

Equilibrium Quantity   The quantity sold (bought) at the equilibrium price.

CHAPTER SUMMARY

1. In competitive industries, the nature of supply is such that increases in the price of a product will cause increases in the quantity supplied.

2. Increases in supply will shift the supply curve to the right, while decreases in supply will shift the curve to the left.

3. If the quantity supplied does not increase significantly in response to a price increase, supply is *inelastic*, while supply is *elastic* if price increases cause large increases in the quantity supplied.

4. In competitive markets, supply and demand interact freely to determine the equilibrium price and quantity, which will change as supply or demand change.

QUESTIONS

1. Many schools employ labor for various purposes, such as part-time help in the athletic department. Try to draw the supply curve and the demand curve for student labor in your school, so as to estimate the equilibrium wage rate for student help. (Hints: for the supply curve, survey your friends to try to determine how many hours per week they would be willing to work at various wage rates. For the demand side, determine or estimate the school budget for student help so as to calculate how many hours of student help could be bought at various wage rates. The equilibrium price will be a wage rate, while the equilibrium quantity will be the total number of hours of work purchased by the school.)

2. "The supply of good professional hockey players is very inelastic." Debate this statement.

3. Ever since the Middle Ages, when the Church decreed that it was improper to charge interest on borrowed money, there has been support for legal restrictions on interest rates. Suppose that the government set a legal maximum on the interest rate on consumer credit that was below the current rate of interest: what would you expect to be the results of such legislation?

4. Each winter, the price of fresh fruit in Canada rises, sometimes to very high levels.
   (a) Draw a graph explaining such seasonal increases in fresh fruit prices.
   (b) Why does the government not attempt to protect consumers against such price increases by placing legal limits on fruit prices?

5. Following are the supply and demand schedules for hoojikumflips.

Price	Quantity Demanded		Price	Quantity Supplied
$6	20		$6	50
5	40		5	40
4	60		4	30
3	80		3	20
2	100		2	10

(a) On a graph, draw the supply and demand curves for hoojikum-flips, and indicate the equilibrium price.

(b) Suppose that improvements in efficiency cause the supply of hoojikumflips to increase by 30 at each price shown. Draw the new supply curve and indicate the new equilibrium price.

6.

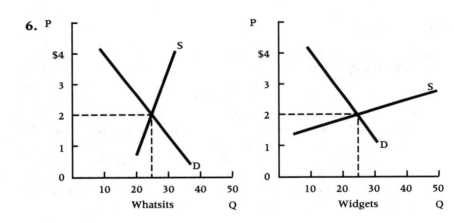

In the preceding graphs, the demand curves are identical and the equilibrium price is $2 in each case. However, the supply curves are of different shapes.

(a) What might explain the different shapes of the two supply curves?

(b) How would this affect the price of the products if the demand were to increase? (Hint: draw a new demand curve on each graph showing an identical increase in demand.)

CHAPTER 8

The dynamics of competition

In Chapter 7, we considered how supply and demand interact in competitive markets to determine equilibrium prices and quantities, using as our example the market for steak, reproduced in Figure 8-1. The equilibrium price and quantity of $6 per kilogram and 50 000 kilograms in

FIGURE 8-1   *Supply, Demand and the Price of Steak in Cantown, March 1990*

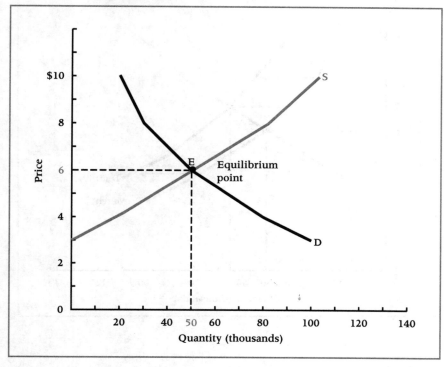

Figure 8-1 must be interpreted carefully. They do not mean that the "proper" price is $6, or that the price will necessarily *stay* at $6. All they mean is that, given the behavior of sellers (supply) and buyers (demand) *at that time* (March 1990), the equilibrium price will be $6. However, the behavior of buyers and sellers is not static, but continually changing. As a result, the supply and demand curves in Figure 8-1 are best viewed as a *snapshot* of a dynamic, changing situation. As supply or demand change, the supply and demand curves will shift, causing changes in the equilibrium price and quantity. In the following sections, we will consider a few such changes, and in doing so, see how competitive markets actually operate.

Changes in supply and demand

An increase in demand

The demand curve in Figure 8-1 depicts buyer behavior in March 1990. By July, with the barbecue season in progress, the demand for steak will likely have increased, causing the demand curve to *shift to the right*, as

FIGURE 8-2   *An Increase in Demand*

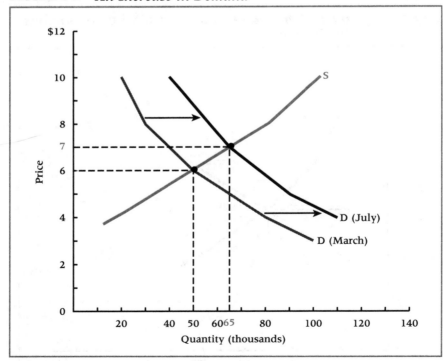

shown in Figure 8-2. The new demand curve, shown by the solid black line, intersects the supply curve at a higher point, resulting in a *higher equilibrium price* of $7 per kilogram. This higher price creates an incentive for producers to offer more steak for sale. As a result, there is an *increase in quantity supplied* to a level of 65 000 kilograms. Thus, an increase in demand (without a change in supply) causes increases in both the equilibrium price and quantity, as the market responds to the higher demand.

A decrease in demand

Figure 8-3 shows the results of a decrease in demand for steak, such as might occur between August and September, when barbecuing activity declines. As the graph shows, such a decrease in demand will cause the *equilibrium price to decline* (from $7 to $6), which will lead producers to *reduce the quantity supplied* (from 65 000 to 50 000 kilograms). Thus, the market responds to a decrease in demand by reducing both the equilibrium price and quantity.

FIGURE 8-3 *A Decrease in Demand*

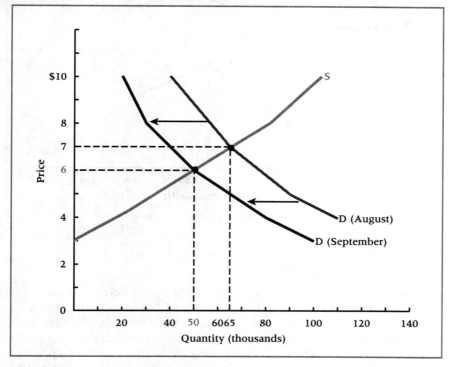

An increase in supply

Suppose that for some reason, such as reduced production costs or increased productivity, the supply of beef (and therefore steak) increased. Such an increase in supply would cause the supply curve to *shift to the right*, as shown by curve S₁ in Figure 8-4. This increase in supply would *decrease the equilibrium price* from $6.00 to $4.50, and this price reduction would induce an *increase in the quantity demanded*, from 50 000 to 70 000 kilograms. The market's response to an increase in supply, then, is to reduce the equilibrium price and increase the equilibrium quantity.

FIGURE 8-4   *An Increase in Supply*

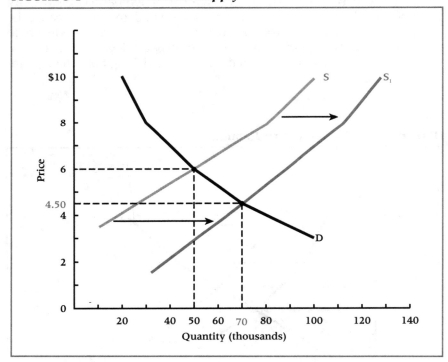

A decrease in supply

If factors such as increases in production costs led to a *decrease in the supply* of steak, the supply curve would *shift to the left*, as shown by curve S₂ in Figure 8-5. With the supply lower, *the equilibrium price would increase* from $6 to $7 and this price increase would induce a *reduction in the quantity demanded* from 50 000 to 40 000 kilograms. When the supply of a product decreases, the market's response is to increase the equilibrium price and reduce the equilibrium quantity.

FIGURE 8-5 *A Decrease in Supply*

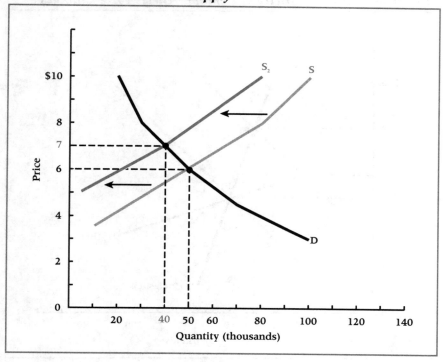

Elasticity

Elasticity—the responsiveness of buyers and sellers to changes in prices—has a great bearing on how markets respond to changes in supply and demand.

Elasticity of demand

The importance of elasticity of demand is shown in Figure 8-6, when the market is faced with a reduction in supply, causing the supply curve to shift from S to S_1. If the demand for the product is *inelastic*, as shown by curve D, the equilibrium point shifts from E_1 to E_2, and the equilibrium price rises a great deal, from $5 to $8. The price increase is so large because demand is *inelastic*—buyers are unable or unwilling to substitute or do without this product, so they bid actively for the reduced supply, forcing the price up rapidly. If, on the other hand, the demand were *elastic*, as shown by curve D_1, the situation would be quite different, with the equilibrium point shifting to E_3 instead of E_2. The same reduction in supply would cause a much smaller price increase, to only $6. This is because the demand is elastic—since buyers are able to substitute for this product or do without it, they do not bid up its price nearly as much

FIGURE 8-6   *How Elasticity of Demand Affects Price Changes*

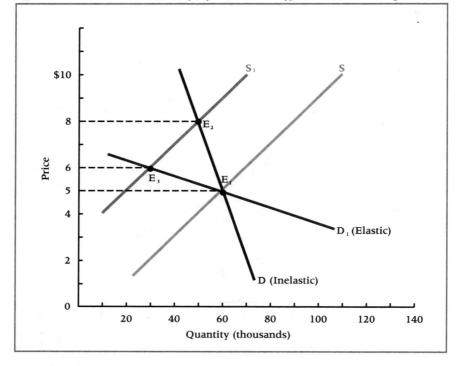

when it is in short supply. Thus, the effect of changes in supply on prices depends to a great extent on the elasticity of demand, with the price changes being greater the more inelastic the demand is.

Elasticity of supply

Elasticity of supply also has a large bearing on prices when changes result from changes in demand. Figure 8-7 shows the effect of an increase in demand (from curve D to D_1) on the price of the product when supply is inelastic and when supply is elastic. If supply is perfectly inelastic, as shown by curve S, the increase in demand causes the equilibrium point to shift from E_1 to E_2 and the price to increase greatly from $5 to $8. An example of such an inelastic supply would be an agricultural product: the harvest (60 000 units) is in, and the quantity supplied cannot be increased beyond 60 000 units regardless of how high demand and prices go.[1] However, if the supply had been elastic, as shown by curve S_1, the

---

[1] This inelasticity of supply (together with fluctuations in supply due to the weather) explains much of the volatility of the prices of many agricultural products.

FIGURE 8-7 *How Elasticity of Supply Affects Price Changes*

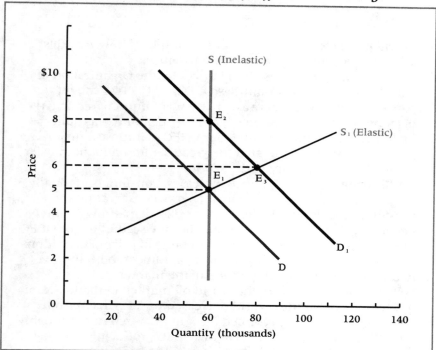

equilibrium point would have shifted to E_3 instead of E_2, so that the price increase would have been much smaller, to only $6. The reason for the smaller price increase is that supply is elastic—as the price rises, producers increase the quantity supplied, holding the price increase down. To continue the example of the agricultural product, curve S_1 could represent the supply curve after a period of one year, when farmers have had time to respond to the $8 price by planting and harvesting more of the product. Generally, price fluctuations are likely to be most extreme in the short run, when supply is inelastic, and more moderate over the longer run, when supply has had sufficient time to become more elastic.

Other types of markets

So far, all of our examples involving supply, demand and markets have involved products, such as steak; however, there are other markets that illustrate these same principles. An example is *labor markets*, in which the supply of and demand for various types of labor interact to determine wages and salaries (the price of labor services). Take the market for

HOW MARKETS ADJUST

World oil markets provide a good example of how markets adjust, over time, to changed circumstances.

The first major increase in oil prices by the Organization of Petroleum Exporting Countries (OPEC) in 1973-74 caught consumers unaware. Because many were unprepared to cut back on their consumption of gasoline, demand was quite inelastic. This made it possible for OPEC to impose a major price increase that generated the greatest international transfer of wealth in the history of the world.

Following the 1973-74 price increases, consumers gradually adjusted to higher prices through energy conservation measures that held down the demand for oil—demand was slowly becoming more elastic. However, after the second major OPEC price increase in 1979 (a further doubling of prices), conditions in world oil markets changed more rapidly, on both the demand side and the supply side of the market.

On the *demand side* of the world oil market, demand for oil in the non-communist world decreased by 11 percent from 1979 to 1985. This represented a cut in oil purchases of roughly six million barrels per day, leaving OPEC producing more oil than consumers were willing to buy at the current price. Developments on the *supply side* of the world oil market compounded this situation. High oil prices had attracted into world oil markets a number of new producers, including the United Kingdom, Mexico and Norway. As a result of these developments, there were considerable surpluses of oil on world markets, and prices fell sharply, from about $34 US per barrel to $12-20 US after 1985.

These price adjustments reflect the elasticity of both demand and supply. They also show why it is naive to project that because a price *has risen* sharply, it will *continue to rise* rapidly. In 1980, Canada's federal government based its entire energy policy on the assumption that oil prices would continue to rise in the 1980's, to $70 US per barrel by 1990. But by the late 1980's, the price was fluctuating between $10 US and $21 US.

professional hockey players, as illustrated in Figure 8-8. Demand curve D represents the demand for players before the expansion of professional hockey, and E_1 represents the original equilibrium point, with an average

FIGURE 8-8 *The Market for Professional Hockey Players*

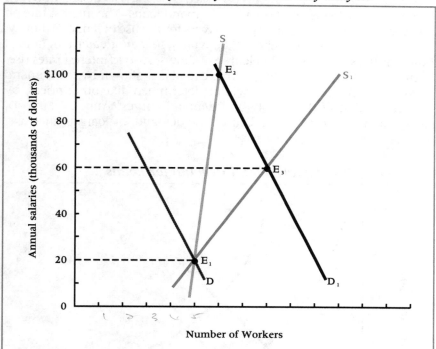

salary of $20 000.'When the number of professional teams expanded in the late 1960's, the demand for players increased dramatically, as shown by the curve D_1. However, the supply of good hockey players was highly inelastic, at least in the short run, as shown by curve S. Consequently, players' salaries increased phenomenally, as the equilibrium point shifted from E_1 to E_2, despite the fact that the quality of the average player deteriorated noticeably. Since then, the market has quietly operated. The higher salaries attracted more young players into professional hockey, with the result that, after a few years, the supply curve became more elastic, as shown by curve S_1. As a result, average salaries actually declined, despite the fact that the quality of players was improving.[2] In response to the demand for hockey players (as expressed through higher prices in the marketplace), the supply of players was increasing. Similar adjustments are constantly occurring in markets for various types of labor, as rising incomes attract people into some fields and declining incomes discourage people from entering others.

[2] The salary figures used on the graph are approximate, and make some allowance for inflation, which generally increased salaries quite rapidly during the 1970's.

Another example of market is provided by *markets for capital*, in which lenders supply loans and borrowers demand loans. The interest rate on those loans is the price paid by borrowers for the use of lenders' money. As interest rates rise, lenders will be willing to loan greater amounts of funds, as the supply curve in Figure 8-9 shows. Also as interest rates rise, borrowers will be less willing to make loans, as shown by the demand curve. The actual interest rate will be determined, like other prices, by the intersection of the supply and demand curves. And, as curve D_1 shows, if an economic boom caused the demand for loans to increase, interest rates would also increase.

FIGURE 8-9   *The Supply of and Demand for Loans*

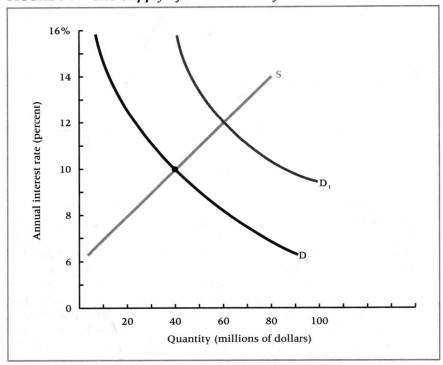

A final example is provided by the *market for gold*, which is illustrated by Figure 8-10. While the supply of gold is quite inelastic (curve S), the demand for gold fluctuates greatly, as people's expectations change. When people expect gold prices to rise, the demand for it increases rapidly, as in curve D_1, while the reverse can happen equally quickly if people expect gold prices to fall, shifting the curve to D_2. With such an inelastic supply, sudden changes in demand cause gold prices to be quite volatile (varying from P to P_1 to P_2), as followers of gold markets well know.

FIGURE 8-10 *The Market for Gold*

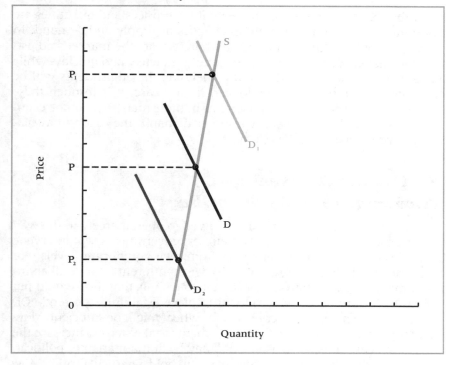

THE MARKET FOR BASEBALL TICKETS

For the 1989 American League Championship Series, prices to Toronto Blue Jays' home games approximately doubled, to an average of nearly $30 each. Had the Blue Jays played in the World Series, the average ticket price would have been nearly $50. These price increases were decided by Major League Baseball (the Commissioner's Office), in consultation with the Players' Association.

QUESTIONS

1. Why do ticket prices rise by so much for post-season games? Use a graph to illustrate this point.

2. Do you agree with those who say that it is "highway robbery" to increase prices for these games? If prices were *not* increased by the Blue Jays, what would happen?

3. What could prevent prices from being raised in this manner?

Summary

It can be said that in any market, equilibrium prices and quantities are constantly changing in response to changes in supply and demand. In those cases where supply and demand are elastic, the market's adjustment to changing conditions occurs quite completely and quickly, while in cases where supply or demand is inelastic, the adjustments will be less complete and/or will take longer. In any case, it is through these markets, and through price adjustments in these markets, that the economy adjusts to fluctuations in consumer demand, the cost and availability of products, and other changes.

Government intervention:
Price supports and price ceilings

Markets, however, are not always allowed to operate freely in the way that we have been describing. Sometimes, governments will intervene in markets in order to change prices from their equilibrium levels. For instance, an equilibrium price of $550 per month rent for a small apartment might be sufficiently unacceptable to tenants that they would put political pressure on the government to place legal limits on rents. Or, an equilibrium price of $2 per bushel for wheat might be sufficiently low that farmers might pressure the government to take steps to increase the price of wheat. Thus, for reasons that may be humanitarian or political, governments will take steps in some cases to hold a particular price *below* its equilibrium level, and in other cases to hold prices *above* the equilibrium level. On the surface, this seems like a fairly simple solution to problems, but as we consider each of these policies in turn, we will see that they are not as simple as they appear.

Price supports

A good example of a government price support program designed to hold prices above their equilibrium level is the method used to subsidize farmers. For many years, North American farmers have suffered from a tendency to oversupply the market. Improved technology and farming methods greatly increased the potential output of farm products, and, due to the competitive nature of farming (farmers were not organized so as to restrict the supply of food), farmers tended to produce as much as possible, oversupplying the market and driving prices down. The problem was aggravated by the inelastic demand for food generally; as prices fell, people would not buy significantly more food, and the increased supply of food drove prices down sharply. In some cases, there were concerns that this problem was depressing farm prices and incomes to the point of threatening the long-term survival of much of the nation's agricultural capacity.

Unable to solve the problem on their own, some groups of farmers turned to the government, which provided assistance in a number of ways. The program we will consider here is *farm price supports*, under which the government prevents the price of, say, wheat, from falling below a certain level, such as $2 per bushel. The government can achieve this by simply *offering to buy wheat* from the farmers at $2 per bushel, so that no farmer need sell for less, and all farmers are guaranteed that price for their entire crop.

While such a program will support farm prices and incomes, it will have complicating side effects, which are illustrated in Figure 8-11. As the graph shows, the equilibrium point would have been E, making the equilibrium price $1.25 per bushel and the equilibrium quantity 50 million bushels. However, if the government supports the price at $2, two adjustments will take place. First, at the higher price, somewhat *less wheat will be demanded*; on the graph, point A shows that at a price of $2, 45 million bushels will be bought, a decline in sales of 5 million bushels.

This is a fairly small change, because the demand for wheat is quite

FIGURE 8-11 *The Effects of Farm Price Supports*

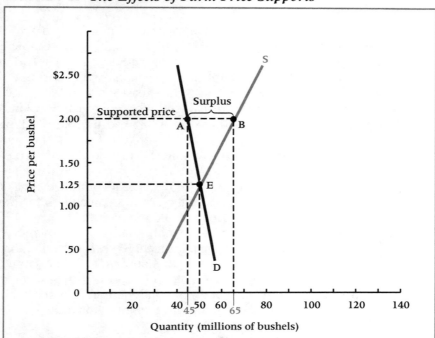

inelastic. The second change, however, could be considerably greater: because they are now assured a price of $2, farmers will *increase their production.* On the graph, point B shows that the quantity supplied increases from 50 to 65 million bushels as farmers respond to the incentive of a guaranteed higher price. The combined effect of these two adjustments to the new, higher price (a 5 million-bushel increase in quantity supplied) will be a *surplus* of 20 million bushels . . . 20 million more bushels of wheat will be produced than people are willing to buy at the $2 price.

Where will this surplus go? It will wind up in the possession of the government, which acts as a *reserve buyer* in the wheat market, supporting the price by buying whatever the farmers produce at a price of $2. In some cases, such surpluses have grown to sizes that have caused some political embarrassment, so governments have turned to other ways of supporting farm prices and incomes. These include paying farmers *not* to grow certain crops and setting up marketing boards empowered to set maximum production limits for individual producers so as to reduce the supply of products and support their prices. Regardless of the specific method used, the government is in effect doing for the farmers what they, as a disorganized group, have been unable to do for themselves in order to support their prices and incomes.

Price ceilings

Rent controls (legal limits on the level of rents and/or on the rent increases charged by landlords) are probably the best illustration of government programs intended to hold prices below their equilibrium level (**price ceilings**). In response to the complaints of tenants (who constitute a significant political pressure group in some areas), governments have imposed various sorts of rent controls to limit the rents charged by landlords to lower levels than could have been charged under prevailing market conditions. While rent controls are favored by tenants, they can have the unfortunate side effect of creating shortages of rental accommodation, as illustrated in Figure 8-12. While the graph shows an equilibrium rent of $450 per month and a government-controlled rent of $350 per month, this should not be interpreted as meaning that the government reduced rents arbitrarily by $100 per month.

Rather, it should be interpreted as meaning that rent controls were imposed some time ago and have held rents to $350 per month, but that demand has increased to the point that, without the controls, rents *would now be* $450 per month in a free market. Point E represents what would have happened if rents were not controlled—the equilibrium price (rent) would have been $450 and the equilibrium quantity would have been 55 000 rental units on the market.

At the controlled rent of $350 per month, the situation is quite different. As point B shows, the lower rent has caused a small (5000-unit) increase in the quantity demanded, from 55 000 to 60 000 units. There is a much

FIGURE 8-12   *The Effects of Rent Controls*

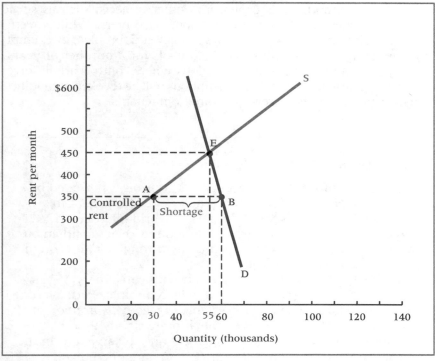

more important adjustment on the supply side. Here, as point A shows, the quantity supplied at the controlled rent of $350 is only 30 000 units, whereas at the uncontrolled rent of $450 the quantity supplied would have been 55 000 units. In other words, there are 25 000 fewer rental units on the market at the $350 controlled rent than there would have been without the rent controls. When this 25 000-unit reduction in quantity supplied is added to the 5000-unit increase in quantity demanded due to the lower rents, the effect of the rent controls is to create a *shortage* of apartments to the extent of 30 000 units. The reason for the shortage is not that the landlords of existing buildings refuse to rent their apartments at the controlled rents; they have little choice but to accept the situation.[3] The shortage will occur because new apartment construction

---

[3] Some, however, may convert their apartments to condominiums, which can be sold as private residences at prices not subject to government controls. If they are prevented by law from converting to condominiums, owners of apartment buildings may cut back on maintenance and repairs, allowing buildings to deteriorate; in extreme cases, land-lords have abandoned buildings, simply writing off their investment. Another side-effect of rent controls, once apartment shortages become severe, is the appearance of black markets—desperate tenants willingly pay cash "under the table" to building super-intendents, or pay rental rates for "furnished" apartments, the furnishing of which consists of little more than junk, in order to obtain an apartment.

will be depressed by the controls, which make apartments a less attractive investment and divert capital into other projects, such as single family dwellings, condominiums or shopping centers. While governments have attempted at various times to relieve this problem by exempting new apartment buildings from controls for a number of years, developers still tend to avoid jurisdictions where controls are in force, apparently due to fears that such exemptions will be revoked or modified by governments in response to pressure from tenants.

CANADA'S "CHEAP-OIL" POLICY

Another example of the effect of price controls is provided by the federal government's "cheap oil" policy from 1974 to 1985. Following the sharp increases in world oil prices in 1973-74, the Canadian government undertook to keep Canadian oil prices well below world prices, mainly through controls on the price of Alberta's crude oil.

While this policy was very popular with consumers (especially those in central Canada), its economic effects were not so beneficial. The low prices *encouraged consumption* of oil by Canadians, who moved much more slowly than consumers in other nations toward energy conservation. In the meantime, the low controlled price of Canadian crude oil *discouraged exploration and development* in Canada, as oil companies found Canadian projects less attractive.

Over time, price controls were leading toward oil shortages in Canada. Partly because of this, the federal government abandoned controls on oil prices in 1985.

A perspective

Prices are much more than tags telling buyers how much they must pay to get items; prices are *signals to buyers and to sellers* as to how much of an item to buy or to offer for sale. Once a competitive market has established an equilibrium price, governments cannot change that price without affecting the amounts that buyers are willing to buy and sellers are willing to offer for sale. Programs to support prices above the equilibrium level will have the side effects of generating surpluses of that product, while controls that hold prices below their equilibrium level will create shortages of those products.

DEFINITIONS OF NEW TERMS

Price Support   An artificially high price, held above the equilibrium level by the government.

Price Ceiling   A legal limit on a price or on increases in a price, which holds the price below its equilibrium level.

CHAPTER SUMMARY

1. In competitive markets, supply and demand interact freely to determine the equilibrium price and quantity, which will change as supply or demand change.

2. Generally, the more elastic the supply and the demand, the more rapid and complete will be the adjustments to changes in supply or demand.

3. Markets that operate in these ways include not only markets for goods and services, but also markets for labor and capital.

4. If the government intervenes in a market to hold the price above its equilibrium level, the result will be a surplus of that product.

5. If the government intervenes in a market to hold the price below its equilibrium level, the result will be a shortage of that product.

QUESTIONS

1. An interesting peculiarity concerning the cattle industry is that if ranchers decide to cut their herds (reduce supply) in response to rising feed costs, the price of beef *drops* temporarily, before increasing. Conversely, when ranchers decide to build up their herds so as to increase supply, beef prices *rise* temporarily. Can you explain these phenomena?

2. According to some estimates, the total revenues from the sale of pornographic materials in Denmark actually *declined* by about 25 percent in the year immediately following the legalization of such pornography. From this evidence, some researchers have concluded that the legalization of pornography actually reduces the demand for it, by making it less forbidden and exciting. What is another (and probably more likely) explanation of the decline in total revenues from the sale of pornography?

3. In late 1969, the US government greatly increased the policing of the US-Mexican border, in order to stop the flow of marijuana into the USA. In early 1970, the associate medical examiner for New York City observed a sudden sharp increase in heroin use by the young in New York. Trace in detail the probable relationships between these events.

4. Many governments have passed minimum wage laws in order to protect the less skilled members of the labor force against exploitation by unscrupulous employers. The following figure shows the market for such labor, with an equilibrium wage rate of $3 per hour. What effects would a minimum wage rate of $5 per hour have on this market and on the labor force in this market?

surplus of 40 = (60-20)

5. Some people have suggested that, to make it possible for more Canadians to buy their own homes, a legal ceiling, or maximum, should be placed on mortgage interest rates. Do you agree that such a policy would be beneficial?

6. At a September 1989 Rolling Stones concern in Toronto, scalpers sold $32.50 floor tickets for prices between $125 and $500.
   (a) Explain why scalpers could charge such high prices.
   (b) Should the law permit scalping of tickets in this manner? (At that time, the penalty for scalping was a small fine.)
   (c) If the government wanted to prevent scalping, how could it do so?

CHAPTER 9

Competitive industries

In Chapters 7 and 8 we saw how, in competitive markets, supply and demand interact to determine the prices of goods, services and labor. In such markets, the large numbers of both buyers and sellers, plus the fact that neither buyers nor sellers are organized so as to be able to influence the price, mean that the price will be determined impersonally and automatically by the total supply of all sellers and the total demand of all buyers in the marketplace, as illustrated in Figure 9-1. Once the market

FIGURE 9-1 *Determination of the Equilibrium Price in a Competitive Market*

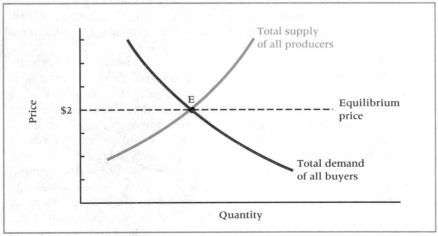

price for the product has been determined in the marketplace, all producers and sellers will have to keep their prices at or very near the market price, in order to be competitive.

This, then, is the essence of what we have called competitive industries—industries in which there are so many small firms and it is so easy for new firms to enter the industry that producers have little or no influence over the price. The market determines the price, and each individual producer is a *price-taker*. In studying these competitive industries, economists divide them into two types: perfect competition and monopolistic competition.

Perfect competition

Perfect competition is the *most competitive situation* possible. It is considered to exist only if the following three conditions are met:

(a) there are *many small firms* in the industry
(b) it is *easy for new firms to enter* the industry, and
(c) all firms in the industry sell *identical products*.

It is the last condition that makes perfect competition so unique and so extremely competitive. If each producer's product is *identical* to those sold by the other producers, each producer will be forced to charge *exactly* the same price as the others; in Figure 9-1, all will have to charge the market price of $2 per kilogram. If any producer charges more than $2, that producer's *sales will fall to zero*, as buyers will buy instead from the numerous competitors, who would be charging less for an identical product.

For example, suppose the product is tuna fish, the buyers are fish canneries, and the sellers consist of a large number of very small fishing boat operators, each selling the same (identical) product—tuna. If the going price for tuna is $2 per kilogram, each boat will be able to sell its entire catch of tuna. But if one boat (say, Sonja's) charges more than $2 per kilogram, its sales will be zero. The buyers will be able to get plenty of fish from the other boats, and will not even miss Sonja's tiny contribution to the total supply.

Thus, the demand curve for Sonja's tuna will consist of a perfectly horizontal line, as in Figure 9-2. This is an unusual demand curve, and it illustrates an unusual situation. The curve shows that, at a price of $2 per kilogram, Sonja can sell 10 kilograms, 100 kilograms, or all the tuna her boat can catch (500 kilograms). She is, after all, only a small producer, so variations in her production level cannot affect either the total market supply or the price of tuna. However, if Sonja raises the price of her tuna over $2, her sales will fall to zero. This is a **perfectly elastic** demand curve, reflecting the fact that *any* increase in price will cause *all* sales to be lost. Obviously, the case of perfect competition is the most competitive situation imaginable, one in which the seller has no control over the price of the product, because there are so many sellers competing to sell identical products.

FIGURE 9-2 *Market Demand, Market Supply and the Demand Curve for the Individual Producer's Product in a Perfectly Competitive Market*

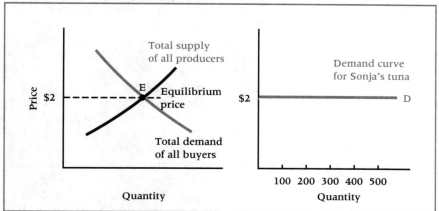

Because it is restricted to industries with many small firms, easy entry into the industry and identical products, perfect competition is a rare case. It is for the most part restricted to certain agricultural products and natural-resource products, where buyers can be sure that the products are identical, and to markets in which the buyers are processors or wholesalers.[1]

Incentives for producers

Since the producer has no control over the price of the product and cannot develop a product that is different from those of competitors, the only strategy available to such a producer for maximizing profits is

(a) to reduce production costs per unit of output to the lowest possible level; that is, *maximize productive efficiency*;

(b) to produce as much *output* as is economical at these low unit cost levels; and

(c) to sell the product for *whatever price the market determines*.[2]

---

[1] Retail markets and consumer products can very seldom be considered perfectly competitive, not only because the consumer often perceives products to be different, but also because retail outlets—even those selling identical product lines—cannot be considered identical, due to their different locations. A litre of milk for sale for $.80 in a store two minutes from my home is not identical to a litre of milk for sale for $.80 twenty minutes away, because retail stores provide not only *products*, but also the *service* of making products conveniently available to consumers.

[2] At first, it may seem that *any* firm would make exactly the same decisions described here; however, that is not the case. If the industry were controlled by one firm, it could very well be more profitable for that monopoly to change decisions (b) and (c) by producing a smaller output and forcing the price (and profits) to higher levels. In a competitive industry, however, the numerous disorganized small producers are unable to achieve this.

This is essentially what producers in such industries actually do—small vegetable farmers cultivate as large a crop as they can afford, as efficiently as possible (at the lowest possible cost per unit), harvest it and, together with all the other farmers, throw it on the market for whatever price they can get for it. In seeking to maximize their own profits in this way, these competitive producers contribute to the welfare of consumers, not only by producing what consumers want to buy, but also by maximizing their output of it, and minimizing production costs and prices.

While such behavior is beneficial to the consumer, it makes matters quite difficult for the producers. Generally, the intensity of competition in such industries will force the profits of the average firm to very low levels, and there will be many marginal producers who are barely able to stay in business. Unable to develop a product that is different from a competitors' and unable to charge a higher price, the only way a producer in such industries can earn an above-average profit is to increase productive efficiency so as to reduce production costs per unit and thereby increase profits per unit of output. Those producers who are able to achieve this will be able to earn profits above the average for the industry, representing a reasonable rate of return on their capital.

As noted above, perfect competition is a very rare situation. Much more common (but still very competitive) is the case of monopolistic competition.

Economists' descriptions of competitive industries sometimes place such emphasis on *prices* that students get the impression that an industry cannot be classified as competitive unless producers practice *aggressive price-cutting* tactics against each other on a day-to-day basis, to the point of nearly driving each other out of business. Since few industries fit this description, the concept of "competitive" industries can seem more theoretical than realistic.

However, the economics of competitive industries are more subtle than this. Because producers as a group are *unable to control supply* (partly because there are so many of them and partly because it is easy to enter the industry), the incentive for *each* is to produce as much as possible. When *all* producers do so, the result is a high supply and downward pressure on prices.

The *result*—low prices and profits—is the same. However, the *origin* of this situation lies in the inability of producers to control supply rather than in any extraordinary tendency on their part to slash prices.

Monopolistic competition

Typically, even in competitive industries, each producer is not selling an identical product or service. While there may be large numbers of sellers selling products that are very similar, each seller's product is usually a little different from the rest, particularly in industries that cater to the consumer. We will use the term monopolistic competition to describe such industries.[3] Monopolistic competition has three characteristics:

(a) there are *many small firms* in the industry,
(b) it is *easy for new firms to enter* the industry, and
(c) all firms' products are *not identical*—each firm's product or service is in some way different from those of its competitors.

The facts that there are many small firms and that it is easy to enter the industry ensure that there will be strong competition and that prices and profits will be held down to low levels. However, the fact that each firm sells a product that is in some way different from the other firms' products adds a new dimension to the situation: because the products of different firms are not identical, their *prices do not need to be identical*. Thus, a firm in a monopolistically competitive industry has some (small) opportunity to increase the price of its product—although not by much, because the large number of competitors selling similar products would cause many sales to be lost if one firm's price increased by much. This limited leeway reflects the fact (illustrated in Figure 9-3) that, while the demand for the individual firm's product is not *perfectly* elastic, as in perfect competition, it is still *highly* elastic, due to the competitiveness of the industry.

Product differentiation

The demand curve in Figure 9-3 indicates that, while the firm *could* raise its price, the demand for its product is so elastic that it would be unprofitable to do so—too many sales would be lost. However, the firm in monopolistic competition is not always in such a helpless condition. To the extent that a firm can make its product or service *different* from those of its competitors—that is, practice product differentiation—it can increase its ability to raise prices (within limits) without losing too many sales.

For instance, Harry's Hamburg Stand is a firm in a monopolistically competitive industry (fast foods) comprised of a large number of small outlets, each with its own characteristics such as product, service and

[3] The term monopolistic competition is meant to convey the impression that, while the industry is highly *competitive* (due to the large number of firms), each producer's position can be regarded (to a slight degree only) as similar to that of a monopoly, because its product is different from those of other firms. In some small way, it could be said to be unique. It is essential, however, to avoid confusing this with the position of a real monopoly, such as Bell Canada, which is the only producer in a particular market. We will examine the case of such real monopolies in the next chapter.

FIGURE 9-3 *Demand Curve for the Individual Firm in Perfect and Monopolistic Competition*

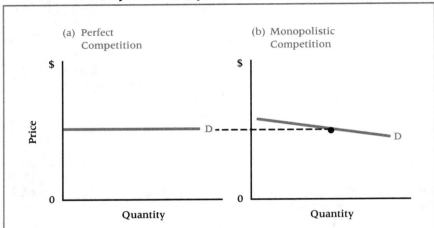

location. Harry's Hamburg Stand is differentiated by its location (between the beer store and the drive-in theater), its product (Harry's hamburgers are not prepackaged, but charbroiled and dressed to the customer's taste), its service (Harry's employees are known to be very polite and efficient), and the fact that Harry was the highly popular penalty leader for the local hockey team for several years. At a price of $1 per hamburger (the same price charged by most others in the area), Harry sells 2000 hamburgers per week, as indicated by the dot on the diagram in Figure 9-4.

FIGURE 9-4 *Demand Curve for Harry's Hamburg Stand*

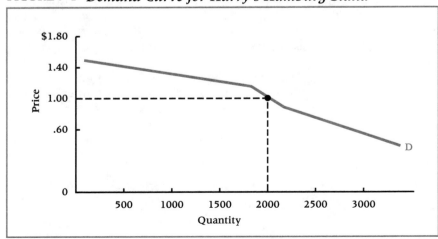

The demand curve in Figure 9-4 is quite elastic, due to the competitiveness of the industry, but around the market price of $1, it is less elastic, due to the fact that Harry's product is differentiated from his competitors'. For instance, Harry could raise his price *a little* (say, to $1.10) without losing many sales. While some of his customers would abandon him, the vast majority would stay with him. Although not happy about paying the premium price, they would feel that the combination of location, product and service made Harry's hamburgers worth a little more. Thus, for a small price increase, the demand for Harry's hamburgers could be *inelastic*, making it profitable for Harry to raise his price a little. However, if Harry were to raise his price *a lot* (say, to $1.20), he would likely find that the demand for his burgers becomes *elastic*, as numerous customers decide that Harry's burgers are not worth the extra $.20 each and switch to other hamburger stands, causing Harry's sales (and profits) to fall seriously. At prices above $1.40, not even his mother will eat at Harry's. Thus, under monopolistic competition, the fact that each firm's product is somewhat different from its competitors' can give it an opportunity to raise its price a little.[4]

A similar effect occurs with price reductions: while large price reductions will attract many sales, for small price reductions demand will not be so elastic. A *small* price cut by Harry will not likely attract many more customers from his competitors . . . these customers are patronizing Harry's competitors because they prefer their product, location or other features, and will not likely be lured away by the prospect of saving 5 or 10 cents per burger at Harry's. A *large* price cut is out of the question— while it would increase Harry's sales greatly, he would lose money on every sale and go bankrupt.

In summary, then, the demand curve for the differentiated product of a firm in monopolistic competition is basically very *elastic*, but for small changes around the market price, it is less elastic, and possibly even inelastic. As a result, the firm has the opportunity to increase its price, within quite narrow limits, although it may or may not decide to actually do so.

Incentives for producers

As in perfect competition, there is a strong incentive for producers in monopolistic competition to *increase productive efficiency*: faced with very little scope for increasing prices, firms in this situation find it very important to produce at the lowest possible cost per unit. Under monopolistic competition, however, there is the additional incentive to practise *product differentiation*, so as to widen the difference between your product and

---

[4] This is not to say that Harry *will* raise his price to $1.10, only that he *could*. Harry's problem is that he doesn't know how far he can raise his price without losing too many sales; as a result, he is likely to be cautious about increases. Many firms in this situation would decide to charge the same price as their competitors ($1.00), rather than risk a price increase that could have negative effects on their sales and profits.

your competitors', and thus gain an advantage in the marketplace. Such an advantage could be achieved by actually making your product or service different from those of your competitors and by trying to persuade consumers that whatever differences exist are of importance to them.

Accordingly, sellers in monopolistically competitive industries will try to use considerable ingenuity in their advertising and promotion to establish the ways in which they are different from their competitors. Restaurants stress their special menus, drinks, atmosphere, type of entertainment and so on. Retailers strive to establish their own identity through the character of their shops, special product lines, special services (delivery, exchanges, refunds, credit and so on). Some businesses providing services (such as dry cleaning) emphasize the speed of service, others stress quality, others offer extended hours. To the extent that a firm is successful in these efforts at product differentiation, it can alter its demand curve by making it more inelastic. For instance, Harry's competitive position would be enhanced strongly if his were the only hamburger stand in a prime location, or if he developed a unique and highly popular product line. On the other hand, a monopolistically competitive market is a very dynamic situation, and Harry must face the risk that his competitors—or a brand new firm starting up—may successfully imitate his advantages, reducing the degree to which Harry's firm is differentiated, and making the demand for his hamburgers more elastic again. Worse yet (from Harry's viewpoint), some of them may come up with even better ideas to differentiate their products, placing Harry at a disadvantage. People who have operated small businesses successfully in this kind of environment for years tend to discount flashy promotional stunts as short-term strategies, and stress instead the importance of establishing (or earning) a reputation as an honest, reliable firm, if long-term success is to be achieved. They claim that this is the most valuable type of product differentiation that a firm can claim.

In conclusion, product differentiation, however achieved, can benefit the firm in two ways. First, it can build *consumer loyalty* to the firm and its products, and thus protect the firm against competition; and second, it can provide an opportunity for the firm to *charge higher prices* for its products, to the extent that consumers believe the product differentiation to be worth a higher price. All firms welcome the advantages of consumer loyalty; some will also charge a higher price. Product differentiation introduces into a situation that is *basically very competitive* a slight degree of *monopoly power*, due to the fact that each firm's product or service can be different from those of its competitors. Obviously, the degree to which this occurs varies: it is one thing to be the only one of eight hamburger stands in town with a particular location, and quite another to be the only Chinese restaurant in town *and* the only restaurant with a liquor licence in town. Nonetheless, new restaurants can easily open, emphasizing the fact that, while monopolistic competition is less extremely competitive than perfect competition, it still represents a highly competitive situation. As a result, profits in monopolistically competitive industries generally tend to be low, with many firms earning only marginal profits. However, firms that enjoy cost advantages, or that have succeeded in practising product differentiation to their advantage, will earn above-average profits.

Extent of competitive industries

Determining the actual number of competitive industries is not a simple matter, because of the difficulties in defining "small business" and deciding whether a particular firm is in a competitive industry or not.[5] As we have said, perfect competition is a rare situation because of the requirement that products be identical; however, monopolistic competition is a very common form of market structure that includes most of the small business sector of the economy discussed in Chapter 5. Taken together,

---

Now That's A Price War

Monday, August 27, 1983. That's the day of the Great Winnipeg Gasoline Price War. The hostilities began on Saturday the 25th when a new Domo gas station reduced prices as an opening promotion. Two neighbouring stations owned by Mohawk Oil and Petro-Canada matched the Domo price. But Domo had a big sign announcing that it would keep its price four-tenths of a cent per litre below the competition.

On Monday the war began in earnest, reduction-matching-reduction, all day long. At the peak of the battle a Domo worker used binoculars to spy on the prices on the Petro-Canada pumps, shouting numbers to a fellow worker sitting on the top of a stepladder while he changed prices on the Domo sign.

Regular leaded gas went from 47 cents per litre on Saturday to 1.6 cents per litre on Monday. In a last charge for victory Domo offered to *pay* customers .3 cents per litre to take gas away. (No one ever said that the demand curve cannot cross the axis.)

Customers were delighted to help out. But the lines for the stations were so long they produced a traffic jam 1.5 kilometers long and a police officer asked the stations to close in order to relieve the congestion. The stations may have provided permanent relief: the next day prices were stable at the pre-war level of about 47 cents per litre.

SOURCE *Common Sense Economics*, Issue 13, Vol. 7, No. 1, University of Waterloo.

QUESTION

What factors might contribute to exceptional outbreaks of competition such as this?

---

[5] For instance, drugstores are generally considered to be a competitive industry, but what about the only drugstore in a small and quiet remote town?

FIGURE 9-5 *Characteristics and Incentives of Competitive and
Non-Competitive Industries*

Perfect competition	Monopolistic competition	Non-competitive industries
1. many firms 2. easy to enter 3. identical products	1. many firms 2. easy to enter 3. differentiated products	1. few firms 2. difficult to enter
Prices and profits are held down, and producers have *no control* over the price of their product.	Prices and profits are held down, but producers have *a small degree of control* over the price of their product.	Prices and profits tend to be higher than in the competitive situation.
Economic incentive for each producer is to (a) maximize efficiency (minimize production costs per unit), (b) produce as much output as is economical, and (c) sell it for whatever price the market establishes.	Economic incentive for each producer is to (a) maximize efficiency (minimize production costs per unit), (b) practise product differentiation, and (c) (possibly) increase price by a small amount only.	Economic incentive for all producers is to act together so as to restrict competition and raise prices significantly.

competitive industries probably account for roughly half of the economy's output, concentrated for the most part in some sectors of agriculture and fishing, retail trade, small-scale manufacturing and especially the large number of service industries (restaurants, fast-food outlets, travel agencies, and so on) that have expanded rapidly in recent years. Figure 9-5 summarizes the characteristics of the two types of competitive industries we have been considering, together with the incentives that each situation provides to producers. For comparative purposes, a brief summary of non-competitive industries, which will be examined in Chapter 10, is also included.

Laissez-faire

Generally, economists have tended to prefer competitive industries to non-competitive ones, on the grounds that the consumer is best served by vigorous competition among producers. In competitive industries, consumer demand (through price changes) in effect directs producers to supply whatever consumers desire. Producers are encouraged, by competition and the profit motive, to be efficient—not to waste scarce (and costly) productive inputs. The high degree of competition among producers ensures that profits will not be excessive, and that consumers will pay reasonable prices for products. Business firms are small, so there is no danger that they will establish monopolies and charge excessive prices. If the entire economy were competitive in this way, it would in large part be an effective, self-regulating system for deciding the basic economic questions of what to produce, how to produce it, and how to divide up the output. Such an economic system would require relatively little government intervention in order to make it work better—at least, much less government intervention than an economy dominated by monopolistic producers.

This theory of a competitive economy, which serves the consumer so well that there is little (or no) need for government to regulate businesses or intervene in the economy, is the theoretical basis for the doctrine of **laissez-faire** the belief that it is best for the government to minimize its intervention in the economy and regulation business. The concept of laissez-faire originated in France at the time of Louis XIV, as a reaction to a web of government regulations of business that was so complex and so restrictive that it stifled incentives and caused economic activity to stagnate. By comparison, a free competitive economy would be much more effective in promoting economic activity and serving the consumer.

Thus the doctrine of laissez-faire is based on the assumption that the economy is in fact very competitive, so that monopolies will not take advantage of the freedom provided by the lack of government regulations. As we will see in Chapter 10, however, this assumption does not fit a modern economy like Canada's, in which many industries are dominated by a few large firms. This sector of the economy operates quite differently from the competitive industries discussed in this chapter, and, as we will see in Chapter 12, can be regarded not only as posing a threat to the public interest, but also as providing advantages to consumers and society generally.

DEFINITIONS OF NEW TERMS

Perfect Competition   A term describing industries that consist of a large number of small firms, where entry to the industry by new firms is easy, and where all firms in the industry sell identical products.

Perfectly Elastic Demand   A situation in which any price increase above the market price will cause a firm's sales to fall to zero; represented by a horizontal demand curve.

Monopolistic Competition   A term describing industries that consist of many small firms, where entry to the industry by new firms is easy, and where the products or services of individual firms, while basically similar, are differentiated from each other to a degree.

Product Differentiation Attempts by individual firms to distinguish their products or services from those of their competitors.

Laissez-Faire The doctrine or philosophy that it is neither necessary nor beneficial from the viewpoint of the public interest for governments to intervene in the operation of the economy.

CHAPTER SUMMARY

1. *Perfect competition* is the most competitive situation possible, in which the individual firm has no control over the price of its product since it faces a perfectly elastic demand curve.

2. The options for a firm in perfect competition are to minimize production costs per unit (maximize efficiency), produce as much output as it can afford to, and sell its output for whatever price the market determines.

3. Generally, profits in perfectly competitive industries will be very low, with only those firms that have below-average production costs able to earn above-average profits.

4. Monopolistically competitive industries are also very competitive, but differ from perfect competition in that firms have an opportunity to practise product differentiation, thereby making demand somewhat less elastic, and (possibly) to increase prices a little.

5. Competitive industries, consisting mainly of the small business sector of the economy, constitute an important part of the economy, probably producing about half of its output.

QUESTIONS

1. Can you think of additional examples of perfectly competitive industries or monopolistically competitive industries? If you went into business for yourself in any of these industries, what strategy would you follow in order to be successful?

2. The example in the text of the restaurant with a liquor licence illustrates the point that some important aspects of product differentiation could be the result of actions by governments, or government agencies. Can you think of other examples of such actions by governments affecting the competitive positions of small businesses vis-à-vis each other?

3. The example in footnote 5 of the drugstore in a remote town illustrates that the line between a competitive and non-competitive situation may sometimes be vague. Can you think of situations in

your experience in which there are quite a few competitors in a field, but where only one or two are considered sufficiently convenient or reliable that they have a substantial advantage over the others? Do they take advantage of their situation by charging a premium price?

4. Economists like to assume (because it makes people's behavior easier to predict) that business firms always seek to maximize their profits. From your experience, do you believe that small businesses always seek to maximize their profits in every way possible? If so, how do they do this? If not, in what ways do they not, and why not?

5. The text notes that service industries are generally very competitive. Why would this be the case?

6. Would you classify professionals such as doctors and lawyers as being in monopolistic competition? Why?

7. The text refers to vegetable farming as a possible example of perfect competition, in which the only way to earn above-minimal profits would be to have below-average production costs per unit. In vegetable farming, what factors could contribute to lower-than-average costs and thus make some firms quite profitable even in a competitive industry such as this?

CHAPTER 10

Non-competitive industries

In Chapter 9 we examined competitive industries, in which there are many firms and which it is easy for new firms to enter. As a result, competition in such industries is particularly strong, and is constantly pushing downwards on profits. Such a situation benefits the consumer, but certainly not the producers, who probably wish that they were fewer in number and could somehow prevent (or at least regulate) the entry of new firms into the industry. Then they would be in a position to restrict the supply of the product and (if demand were inelastic) increase their revenues.[1] However, the difficulties in organizing such numerous producers to act collectively, plus the impossibility of preventing new firms from entering the industry, make it impossible for producers in competitive industries to achieve this. In short, then, the major problem facing producers in competitive industries is that they are unable to control the *supply* and therefore the *price* of their product. In this chapter, we will consider noncompetitive industries, in which producers are in a better position to control the supply and price of their products. Such industries are divided into two categories—**monopolies**, in which there is only one producer, and **oligopolies**,[2] which are dominated by a few large producers. We will begin by considering the simplest case of a noncompetitive industry—monopoly.

[1] Note that we say "revenues," not profits. At this point, we are not including in our discussion how the production costs of business firms interact with their sales revenues to determine their profits—this will be done in Chapter 11.

[2] From Greek words meaning "one seller" for monopoly and "few sellers" for oligopoly. Quite possibly the single most misspelled word in the entire field of economics is "oligopolistic."

Monopoly

Suppose that the fradistat industry is a monopoly, in which Consolidated Fradistats is the only producer. Since Consolidated Fradistats *is* the entire industry, the entire market demand for fradistats is the demand for Consolidated Fradistats' product. This demand is illustrated in Figure 10-1, in both schedule and graph form.

FIGURE 10-1 **Demand for Consolidated Fradistats' Product**

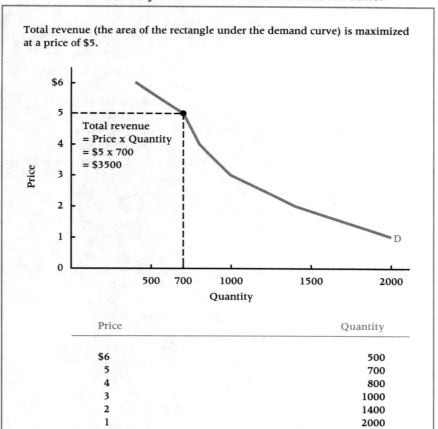

Total revenue (the area of the rectangle under the demand curve) is maximized at a price of $5.

Total revenue
= Price x Quantity
= $5 x 700
= $3500

Price	Quantity
$6	500
5	700
4	800
3	1000
2	1400
1	2000

What price will the monopoly charge for fradistats? While our initial reaction may be that the monopoly will select the highest price, Figure 10-1 shows that *the highest price may not be the most profitable*: by charging a price of $5 and producing 700 units, the monopoly can make a higher total revenue than if, for instance, the price were raised to $6, and sales dropped to 500 units. Note that we are only looking at the *revenue* side of the picture, and are ignoring the *cost*. In effect, we are assuming that

THE INTERNATIONAL DIAMOND MONOPOLY

One of the most profitable monopolies of all time is the international diamond monopoly organized by De Beers Consolidated Mines, Ltd. of South Africa. For most of the twentieth century, De Beers has owned or controlled all the diamond mines in South Africa and owned diamoned-trading companies in England, Portugal, Israel, Belgium, Holland and Switzerland.

De Beers' success has stemmed not only from its control of the *supply* of diamonds, but also from its ability to influence the *demand* for them. Starting in 1938 (at which time diamond prices had declined badly due to the Depression), the demand for diamonds in the USA was promoted by a sophisticated advertising campaign that virtually *created* a tradition: the diamond engagement ring, and the association of diamonds with romance and permanence ("A Diamond is Forever"). By the late 1950's a diamond was generally considered essential to an engagement in North America. In 1967, an advertising campaign was started in Japan, a potentially large market in which only 5 percent of brides wore a diamond engagement ring. By 1980, 60 percent of engaged Japanese women received diamonds, and diamond sales in Japan had reached $1 billion per year.

Even a monopoly as powerful as De Beers is not without problems. As with most monopolies, its main concern involves losing control of the supply. In the 1960's the diamond market was threatened by a large inflow of Russian diamonds, almost all of which were considerably smaller than De Beers' "traditional" South African gems. To avoid a depressed market due to this new source of supply, De Beers undertook to market these diamonds for the Soviets, in effect making Russia a partner in the highly capitalistic diamond cartel. An advertising campaign was mounted to shift demand toward smaller diamonds, many of which were sold in new "eternity rings", which contained as many as 25 small Soviet diamonds and were targeted at older married women. This campaign was remarkably successful; however, it had the side-effect of undercutting the market for De Beers' traditional larger diamonds. By the late 1970's these were being discounted by as much as 20 percent.

Meanwhile, other developments threatened De Beers'

control of the diamond market. In the late 1970's the discovery of vast diamond deposits in Western Australia made it even more difficult for De Beers to control the supply. In addition, political instability in South Africa made it uncertain whether De Beers would be able to hold together the key suppliers in that region.

When De Beers had tight control of the world supply of diamonds, it could control the price simply by cutting back on the volume of diamonds that it allotted each year to about 300 hand-picked dealers. However, as other suppliers came into play, De Beers found it increasingly necessary to keep their diamonds off the market, by buying diamonds at the wholesale level. By the early 1980's, De Beers had accumulated an inventory of diamonds worth over a billion dollars, and was finding itself short of cash to buy up additional diamonds in order to support the price.

And support of the price of diamonds is crucial to De Beers' strategy. According to conservative estimates, the public holds more than 500 million carats of gem diamonds—over 500 times the volume produced by the cartel in any one year. Since new demand each year is satisfied by new production from the world's diamond mines, it is essential that this half-billion carat stock of diamonds be retained by its owners, and not placed on the market. If only a small proportion were sold in any one year, the price could collapse. While it is unlikely that people would sell their engagement rings (a diamond is, after all, forever), there was an increasingly large stock of "investment diamonds" in the hands of both wealthy individuals and financial institutions. In the event of price declines, these "investment diamonds" might well be dumped onto the market, depressing prices further.

Ironically, only by maintaining the price of diamonds (described by some observers as the "diamond illusion") can De Beers prevent such a selloff of diamonds, and the risk of a price collapse that this could bring. Yet, as additional suppliers come onto the diamond market, it becomes more difficult to preserve that price by controlling the supply.

QUESTION

According to some economists, monopoly can never be more than a temporary market condition. Explain the reasoning behind this theory, and why you agree or disagree with it.

if the monopoly maximizes total revenue, it is maximizing profits also. Under these assumptions, the monopoly will raise its price as long as the demand is inelastic—it is because the demand becomes elastic above a price of $5 that higher prices will not be charged.

Monopoly compared to competition

By making *prices higher* and *output lower* than they would otherwise be, monopoly imposes a twofold burden on society economically. As an example, suppose that the minimum price for which widgets could be sold profitably were $3. If there were strong competition in the widget industry, the price would fall to $3 (instead of $5) and production would be 1000 units (instead of 700). But with a monopoly in the industry, the public is burdened with both higher prices and lower output than would exist under competition, as Figure 10-2 shows.

In a competitive industry, it is the consumer who is most powerful in the marketplace. If consumer demand for a product increases, higher prices and profits will attract more firms into production. Furthermore, they will offer it for sale to the consumer at the lowest possible price, due to the intense competition they face. In a monopolistic situation, on the other hand, the shoe is on the other foot. The monopolist is in the dominant position: since the consumer must deal with the monopolist, the monopolist can restrict the supply of the product, forcing its price to higher levels. The higher price and profits will not call forth increased supply, because new firms cannot enter the field. Obviously, the key to the monopolist's position lies in the *control of the supply* of the product.

FIGURE 10-2 *The Two-Fold Economic Burdens of a Monopoly*

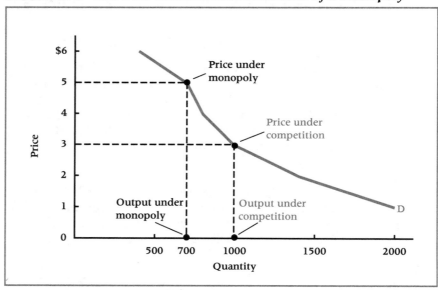

Two approaches

There are two related but different approaches to the exercise of monopoly power. One approach is to state the price of the product, then produce only as much as can be sold at that price. This approach is most suited to a manufacturing operation, in which a list price is often established for an entire year, and production levels are adjusted during the year to ensure that there is no overproduction of the product. This approach can be summarized as *raising the price, then restricting the output*.

However, not all producers can schedule their output quite so precisely. In the case of agricultural products, crop sizes vary with the weather and other circumstances, and cannot be tailored to suit a predetermined price—in such cases, there is a risk of overproduction driving prices downwards. To deal with this danger, producers sometimes hold part of their output off the market so as to prevent prices from falling. In some cases, such as Brazilian coffee, part of a large crop is actually destroyed, while in other cases, such as Canadian wheat and industrial skim milk powder, it is put into storage, usually with the assistance of government agencies. This approach can be summarized as one of *restricting the supply so that the price moves to a higher level on its own, in the marketplace*.

Natural monopolies

Despite the criticisms of monopolies, there are certain industries in which monopoly is the only logical form of organization. The best examples of such industries are public utilities and services: the public interest would not be served by having a dozen different companies providing gas, water, electricity, telephone service and local public transportation. Such a situation would not only be chaotic, but also probably inefficient.[3] Such industries are sometimes referred to as **natural monopolies**, since they lend themselves by nature to control by a single supplier.

While monopoly is the only logical situation in such industries, there would be dangers in leaving such economic power in the hands of private businesses. As a result, natural monopolies are typically either *nationalized* (placed under government ownership and operation) or subjected to *regulation* of their prices. Sometimes their rates (prices) are regulated in such a way as to permit the company to earn a certain rate of return on its shareholders' investment, so as to be fair to both consumers and shareholders.

Many people believe that when natural monopolies are regulated by the government or by a board, these monopolies are therefore subject to

---

[3] The proper definition of natural monopoly is an industry in which average production costs per unit would be lowered by having a single producer. Usually (as in the case of many public utilities) this is because of the heavy capital investment involved in rendering the service to the public. By spreading these heavy capital costs over more clients and output, a monopoly producer can be more efficient.

156

Canadian Microeconomics: Problems and policies

CAN MONOPOLY BE BENEFICIAL?

While economists generally believe that the public interest is better served by competition than by monopoly, there are economic circumstances in which the opposite can be argued.

Suppose that there is a natural resource, such as timber or fish, that is capable of regenerating itself but could become seriously depleted if current production is excessively high. If the industry that is exploiting this resource consists of a large number of competitive firms, the economic incentive for each firm is to produce as much as possible in the short run, without regard for the long-run consequences of its depletion. Such free competition will serve the short-run interests of consumers by making current output high and prices low; however, in the longer run, timber and fish stocks will become depleted. Knowing that if it doesn't catch more fish, others will, the incentive for each firm is to maximize its short-run production. And investing in regeneration of the resource, such as by restocking fish, would be uneconomical for each individual firm because others would catch most of the fish.

Suppose that, on the other hand, exploitation of such resources were carried out by a monopoly. The monopolist would have a strong economic incentive to preserve the long-run position of the industry (and thus its own long-run profits) by avoiding depletion of the resource. It could achieve this in part by limiting current production, which a monopolist would do anyway, to keep prices up. Also, it would pay the monopolist to invest in replenishing the resource, in order to maintain its long-run production.

Thus, it can be argued, the long-run interests of society would be better served by establishing monopolies in those industries where resource depletion is a concern.

QUESTIONS
Do you agree with this argument? Why or why not?
If not, what alternatives would you propose for dealing with this problem? What problems might these encounter?

control by the public. However, the matter of regulating monopolies is not quite as simple as that. In order to regulate the prices to be charged by a natural monopoly, the people responsible for determining the regulations must possess considerable *knowledge* about that industry, its operations and its costs. Where can people with such knowledge and experience be found? One likely source is the industry itself: retired senior officials, such as executives and board members, of the company being regulated. Even if the regulators come from outside the natural monopoly being regulated, they must depend heavily for their information on the management of the company. Thus, the process of regulation is far from the clear cut, objective procedure it is often believed to be, since the people who impose the regulations may be influenced by the corporation they are intended to regulate. This raises the question of whether regulatory boards can always be counted upon to act in the best interests of the consumer, or whether the interests of the producer might not take precedence, as has been suggested in the case of the regulation of the airlines. It is neither possible nor fair to generalize concerning the effectiveness of regulatory boards, since some seem to be much more effective protectors of the consumer's interests than others.

Postscript

We have said that monopoly is defined as a situation in which there is only one seller of a particular good or service. This definition, however, is not as simple as it may seem. For example, each individual barbershop could be said to offer a unique particular service, because it has its own barbers with their own personalities and styles, its own magazines, location, and so on. Yet it would be silly to call each local barbershop a monopoly, because there are many competing barbershops within a reasonable distance—in short, one individual barbershop may possess certain elements of uniqueness and monopoly, but it does not have that degree of economic power over the consumer that we associate with monopoly.

At the other end of the scale, consider the example of telephone services, a case that is generally considered to be a monopoly.[4] Even in this case things are not so simple, because Bell (or your local phone company) does not have a complete monopoly on communications; there are other forms of communication available, even if these are not very close substitutes for telephone communications. So even Bell's monopoly is not as pure as one might think.

So there is some element of monopoly even in highly competitive situations, and some element of competition even in highly monopolistic situations. There is probably no such thing as absolute monopoly, so in defining monopoly we have to fall back mostly on common sense. Thus, we could call Bell Telephone a monopoly, and we would not call a barbershop a monopoly.

---

[4] The fact that there continue to exist a few local companies other than Bell in certain localities does alter this situation. These companies do not compete with Bell; they merely *service other areas*. In each one of those areas, the monopoly is the local company, instead of Bell. If you want to use a phone, you must deal with the local monopoly.

Oligopoly

Like perfect competition, monopoly is quite a rare situation, restricted to a relatively small proportion of the output of the economy. Of much greater importance and interest is the last of our four types of market structures—oligopoly, which accounts for an estimated 40 to 50 percent of the economy's output. Figure 10-3 shows the four types of market structure ranked according to competitiveness, and indicates roughly the relative size and importance of each.

FIGURE 10-3 *The Four Basic Types of Market Structure*

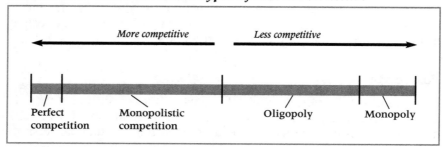

Oligopoly refers to a situation in which a few sellers (or producers) dominate a market (or industry). More specifically, an industry is called oligopolistic if *four (or fewer) producers account for 50 percent or more of the industry's sales.*

Behind this somewhat technical definition lie certain economic realities that are important to understand. When only a few firms dominate an industry, there exists the possibility that they will band together to increase their prices and profits. For such oligopolistic power to exist, it is not necessary that the industry consist of *only* four or fewer firms. As long as the dominant four firms account for half the industry's sales, the rest of the sales could be split up among, say, twenty or thirty small firms. In these circumstances, the smaller firms would very likely follow the price set by the dominant firms, making the industry oligopolistic despite the presence of considerably more than four firms. Similarly, there could be hundreds of firms in an industry across Canada, but if they are fragmented into relatively small local markets with a few firms in each market, these markets will be oligopolistic. There are probably hundreds of road paving firms in Canada, but all do not serve a national market: if a municipality offers a contract for road paving, bids may be received from only four or five local firms, a situation that certainly looks oligopolistic. In deciding whether an industry is oligopolistic, then, *the total number of producers is less important than the number that the buyer actually has to choose from.*

This is the key about oligopoly: unlike the competitive situations we looked at earlier, the buyer's choice among sellers or producers is limited to a relatively small number. This limitation on the buyer increases the potential market power of the producers—it increases their ability to raise prices.

The extent of oligopoly

Industries that are oligopolistic in nature are a very important part of the Canadian economy, accounting by some estimates for as much as half the economy's output. Oligopoly is particularly common in the manufacturing sector of the economy. We can get an indication of its importance by listing some of the industries that can be classed as oligopolistic: steel, automobile manufacturing, heavy machinery, farm implements, pulp and paper, tobacco, beer, liquor, soft drinks, electrical apparatus, aircraft, transportation equipment, explosives and ammunition, sugar, petroleum refining, cement, meat packing and soap. As these examples show, a substantial proportion of the goods produced and consumed in the Canadian economy comes from oligopolistic industries.

Why so few producers?

With greater control over prices, oligopolistic industries will generally enjoy higher rates of profit than competitive industries. In competitive industries, above-average rates of profit usually attract new producers into the industry, causing output (supply) to rise and prices and profits to fall. This does not happen so readily in oligopolistic industries because of the *barriers to entry* to an industry.

A major barrier to entry into many oligopolistic industries, such as steel mills and automobile manufacturing, is the vast amount of *capital* required to start business on a large enough scale to be efficient and competitive. A related problem for newcomers is that of securing a *sufficient volume of sales* to support an efficient level of production. A tremendous volume and *extensive advertising* are often required to compete on a level with the industry leaders. Some oligopolists spend from $.15 to $.40 of every sales dollar on advertising—something a struggling newcomer could scarcely afford. Another problem that a newcomer would face would be *consumer acceptance*. Regardless of how good the products of the existing producers are (or aren't), the consumer has become familiar with them over the years, and the familiarity is strongly reinforced by the heavy advertising that oligopolists usually do. It is quite difficult for a newcomer to break down these attitudes. Another problem that prevents newcomers from imitating an established producer's product is the *patent*, which is a legal device that has been used to great advantage by the drug companies.

In the past, it was quite common for the established firms to engage in *predatory pricing*, or price wars, to drive newcomers out of business. However, such tactics are regarded today as somewhat crude, and it is much more common now for the established firms to use the *merger* tactic of buying out new competitors.

Another obstacle facing new entrants to some industries is *government licencing*; for example, obtaining a taxi, commercial airline licence or a farm product quota can pose major barriers to entry. Ironically, government licencing, which is usually intended to protect the consumer against unqualified businesses, sometimes has the effect of reducing competition and supporting higher prices.

The problem of foreign competition is more difficult, because it is beyond the direct control of oligopolists. To deal with foreign competition requires that oligopolists secure the assistance of government, usually in the form of high *tariffs* or other barriers to imports. In some cases, industries have been quite successful in convincing government that they are sufficiently important to the economy that protection against foreign competition is warranted, even at considerable cost to the consumer.

These barriers to entry provide formidable obstacles to the entry of new firms into some industries, and are less formidable in other cases. Generally, their effect is to *limit competition* and *increase profits*. Studies have shown that, while there are exceptions, the greater the barriers to entry into an industry, the higher the profit rates (expressed in terms of rate of return on investment) of the firms in that industry tend to be.

Price-fixing

When an industry is dominated by a few producers, there exists a possibility that they will reach an agreement among themselves to avoid price competition, so that all of them can earn higher profits than otherwise would have been possible. While business firms in all types of industries prefer to avoid price competition that harms *all* producers, it is generally only feasible to make and keep agreements on prices when there are relatively few producers involved, as in oligopolistic industries. As a result, the pricing policies of many oligopolists reflect a ''live and let live'' approach to competition, rather than the ruthless approach that often characterizes competitive industries. Also, oligopolists tend to channel their competitive activities into less mutually destructive, non-price areas, which we will consider shortly.

The control of prices by producers is sometimes referred to as **price fixing**, or administered prices. In order to successfully fix prices, oligopolists, like monopolists, must *control the supply* of their product; price-fixing agreements must include an understanding concerning how much of the product should, therefore, be produced at the price selected by the oligopolists.

Typically, then, once the oligopolists have set the price of the product for a given period (say, one year, as with automobiles), they make every effort to maintain that price for the entire period. Such **administered prices** tend to be particularly resistant to downward movements. Should the demand for their product prove weaker than expected, the oligopolists will usually cut back their production schedules rather than reduce their prices and risk an outbreak of price-cutting.

While cutting production to protect profits may seem an obvious response to weak demand, it is worth noting that not all industries do this. Different types of industries respond differently to recessions, with the bulk of the downward adjustment falling on *prices* in competitive industries and on *output* in oligopolistic ones. Generally, the prices of the products in highly competitive industries tend to fluctuate considerably more than oligopolistic prices. In competitive markets, prices vary as supply and demand fluctuate, with seasonal vegetable prices providing a good example. By contrast, the administered prices of oligopolists tend to remain at the level set by the producers until the oligopolists *decide* to change them.

Price stickiness

The reason why oligopolistic prices, once set by the industry, tend to remain unchanged for considerable periods of time, is shown in Figure 10-4. The demand curve in Figure 10-4 represents the demand for the

FIGURE 10-4 *Kinked Demand Curve of an Oligopolist*

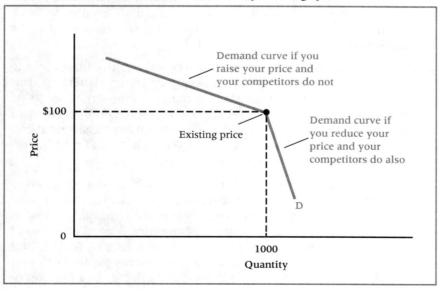

product of one of a few oligopolistic firms in an industry in which all companies are pricing their product at $100. The unusual kink in the oligopolist's demand curve is the result of the following two situations.

First, if an oligopolistic firm increases prices (independently, in violation of the agreement among the producers), it will lose a considerable volume of sales—that is, the demand will be *elastic for price increases*. On the other hand, we must assume that any *price cut* by our oligopolist (in violation of the agreement, of course) would be met by the others doing the same, so that our oligopolist's strategy would not gain many sales—that is, the demand will be *inelastic for price reductions*. With the demand for a product elastic for price increases and inelastic for price reductions, the oligopolist finds that neither price increases nor price reductions are profitable—the best strategy is to let the price remain at the present level. Thus, once set by the producers, oligopolistic prices tend to be quite *sticky*, or resistant to change. Even if demand turns out to be weaker than expected, oligopolists will often reduce production so as to maintain prices, rather than cut prices so as to maintain sales.

Price-fixing techniques

There are several ways in which businesses can actually go about fixing prices among themselves; three of the most important ways are described here.

(a) Price leadership is probably the most common technique employed for fixing prices. Under **price leadership**, the price leader in the industry (usually the largest firm) announces an increase in prices, and all the other firms follow suit in short order. This technique is particularily appropriate when all firms are selling undifferentiated products, such as steel, aluminum or gasoline, whose prices need to be identical because the products are identical.

(b) Formal agreements are sometimes worked out by oligopolists to avoid competition. Such agreements generally cover matters such as prices, product quality, the division of markets into territories to be reserved for each firm, and techniques for fixing bids on government contracts. Such conspiracies to restrict competition are illegal and therefore somewhat risky for those people involved; as a result, formal agreements tend to be used less frequently than price leadership.

(c) Informal understanding is a situation in which there is no apparent communication among the oligopolists and no clear evidence of price leadership, yet the different firms' prices come out remarkably close to each other. The automobile industry has provided a good example of such a situation: knowing each other's ways of changing models and calculating prices, knowing each other's costs reasonably well and knowing the general economic conditions, each firm is in a position to

work out its prices, being reasonably confident that they will come very close to the prices of the other firms. This process will not yield identical prices (as price leadership does), but automobiles themselves are sufficiently differentiated that identical prices are not necessary.

THE OPEC OIL CARTEL

The most famous oligopolistic price-fixing agreement of all time is that of the **Organization of Petroleum Exporting Countries**, or **OPEC**. OPEC consists mainly of Arab states that export oil to the industrialized world. Their control of much of the world's known oil reserves and the inelastic nature of the demand for oil created the potential for a price-fixing agreement—but for years the OPEC nations were unable to reach such an agreement.

Finally, in 1973-74, the OPEC states succeeded in presenting a united front on oil prices, which soared from about $3 US to $12 US per barrel in a few months. Again in 1979, OPEC prices skyrocketed, from about $13 US to $32 US per barrel.

However, even as OPEC's power reached its peak in 1980, with oil revenues of $287 billion US, underlying market forces were working against the cartel, on both the demand side and the supply side of the world oil markets.

On the *demand side*, after a time lag, demand growth slowed as oil users adjusted to higher prices in various ways—adding insulation to their homes and switching to smaller cars and natural gas, etc. This trend toward oil conservation became more pronounced after the huge 1979 price increase: from 1979 to 1985, demand for oil in the non-communist world fell by 11 percent. This decline in demand made it particularly important for OPEC to control the supply in order to maintain its price.

However, on the *supply side* of the market, OPEC was not very successful in controlling the supply of oil, from either its own member nations or from non-OPEC countries. While the OPEC nations had agreed on *price increases*, they had never really reached agreement on *production quotas* for each OPEC member. As a result, the OPEC cartel found itself producing more oil than could readily be sold at the price it had set, so that from 1974 to 1979, there were surpluses of oil on world markets and real oil prices (adjusted for inflation) actually *fell*.

After the 1979 price increase, the surpluses became larger, as several OPEC member states persistently violated production quotas. To make matters worse for OPEC, the high prices had attracted into world markets a number of new non-OPEC oil producers, including the United Kingdom, Mexico and Norway. Non-OPEC oil production in the non-communist world, which had increased by 20 percent from 1973 to 1979, rose by another 27 percent from 1979 to 1985. The result was a growing glut of oil on world markets.

By 1985, OPEC's price was totally unsustainable. The price of oil fell from a peak of nearly $35 US per barrel to below $12 US.

By this time, OPEC was no longer in a position to control world oil prices. OPEC's share of the world non-socialist oil market had fallen from nearly 60 percent in 1979 to less than 38 percent in 1985. In its attempts to maintain oil prices, OPEC's production had been reduced from 31 million barrels per day to only 14 million. These reductions were mainly due to the efforts of OPEC's largest member, Saudi Arabia, which repeatedly cut its own production to offset increases by other producers. Finally, however, the Saudis abandoned this effort as futile and too costly to themselves, and increased their own production, leading to the price collapse.

As of 1989, OPEC was still trying to regroup so as to be in a position to control world oil prices. A new "official" price of $18 US per barrel was set and new production quotas totalling 19.5 million barrels per day for OPEC members were established. However, OPEC members had been producing nearly 21 million barrels per day prior to this agreement, and some (especially the United Arab Emirates and Kuwait) showed every intention of exceeding their quotas.

Perhaps most tellingly, OPEC's official price of $18 US per barrel was, after adjustment for inflation, considerably *lower* than it had been after OPEC's first price increases more than 15 years earlier.

QUESTIONS
1. How does the OPEC experience illustrate the conditions that must exist in order for a cartel to function effectively?
2. What changes could occur that would restore OPEC's power over world oil prices?

Non-price competition

While oligopolists often do try to work together to avoid price competition, it would be a mistake to assume they are sufficently friendly to forego other forms of competition. In fact, there is strong rivalry between firms in many oligopolistic industries, such as soft drinks, automobiles, and soaps and detergents. This rivalry, which uses a variety of methods other than price cuts, is directed toward *increasing sales*. To a considerable extent, the success of an oligopoly is measured by its *market share* (its percentage of the total sales of the industry). Oligopolistic firms tend to be quite concerned with the size of their market share and whether (and at what pace) it is growing.

This competition for market share, however tends to be concentrated on *non-price factors*, particularly *product differentiation* and *advertising*—the arts of making your product distinctive from those of your competitors, and of persuading consumers that these differences are important. Non-price competition offers oligopolists significant advantages over price competition, which forces all involved to cut prices, with the result that all lose. If you can develop a new product, a new design, or a uniquely effective advertising approach, you may gain an advantage which your competitors cannot quickly or completely offset. To the extent that these tactics are effective, you will be able to increase your share of the market without the risk of provoking a ruinous price war with your competitors. This last point illustrates the *controlled* nature of non-price competition: the costs of it can be kept within bounds (for instance, many corporations set their advertising budgets as a certain percentage of their sales), whereas price competition can escalate ruinously.

Some of these efforts at product differentiation (such as more fuel-efficient cars) will serve consumer needs; others (such as minor styling changes) will be trivial; and some (such as the Ford Edsel) will be unsuccessful. Many of them will be costly, as will the heavy advertising and promotion campaigns used to promote them. In some industries, advertising alone amounts to $.15 to $.40 of every sales dollar. Generally, oligopolists are heavy spenders in the areas of market research, advertising and product design and differentiation. Non-price competition is not cheap competition, but it does offer oligopolists two major advantages: its extent can be controlled so that price wars can be avoided, and the costs of it can be passed on to the consumer through higher prices. As a result oligopolists prefer, when possible, to practise non-price competition rather than price competition.

Predicting behavior

Earlier, we noted that once oligopolists have set the price of their product, that price tends to be sticky, or resistant to change. However, we have not yet considered how oligopolists make their price and output decisions in the first place. Considering the importance of oligopolistic industries in the economy, this is a very important question. Unfortunately, it is quite difficult to generalize about or predict the pricing behavior of oligopolists. While we can predict that in competitive industries prices will be driven downwards toward production costs (plus a minimal profit), oligopolists have considerably more discretion over the prices of their products, making the analysis of their pricing decisions much more difficult.

While the domination of an industry by a few firms creates the *potential* for price-fixing, many factors will influence the *actual* pricing decisions of oligopolists. The possible range of their power over prices is quite wide: at one extreme, a tightly-organized group of oligopolists facing a highly inelastic demand for its product is in an excellent position to raise prices to very high levels. At the other extreme, oligopolists facing strong foreign competition may find themselves without any real power over prices at all. In the following section, we will consider some of the limits on the market power of oligopolists.

Limits on prices

Obviously, one crucial factor determining the market power of oligopolists will be the *degree of cooperation* among them, or the extent to which they are able to act together and stick together regarding price-raising. If any of them have tendencies toward price-cutting, this will tend to affect the pricing policies of all of them, and reduce the profits of all. If any of the major firms in the industry are not party to the price agreement, or cut prices secretly (as sometimes happens when business is slow), the others will be unable to fix prices as they would like to. If each firm is uncertain as to how the other will react to a price increase, it may be reluctant to risk leading the way. On the other hand, if the group is well organized and all involved are willing to refrain from price-cutting, the group of oligopolists will be in a position to behave in the same way as a monopolist.

Another important factor in oligopolists' pricing decisions is the *elasticity of demand* for their product. Even a monopolist would not raise the price if the demand for the product were elastic, since the loss of sales would be too costly. Typically, since oligopolists control their entire industry (such as steel, tobacco or petroleum), there are few if any substitutes for their product—demand is inelastic and the oligopolists have the power to increase prices. Sometimes, however, oligopolists do suffer from competition from other industries. For instance, steel can be in competition with aluminum, plastics with glass, and the airline industry is to some extent in competition with other vacation packages. While this kind of inter-industry competition is less direct, it can nonetheless impose some limitations on oligopolists' pricing decisions by making the demand for their products more elastic.

Probably the greatest single factor that can increase the elasticity of demand for oligopolists' products, though, is *foreign competition*, as many major North American industries such as automobiles, steel, electronics and textiles have discovered in recent years. The increased competitiveness of Japanese and European industry has significantly reduced the price-fixing power of some North American oligopolies.

The *stage of development of the industry* can also have a bearing on the nature of competition. Generally, a rapidly expanding market lends itself more to a competitive free-for-all involving all sorts of competition (including price competition) even among the dominant firms (such was the case with the personal computer market a while back); whereas a mature, relatively stable industry (such as automobiles) lends itself more to oligopolistic agreements than to unrestrained battling for market dominance.

Fear of government action could also be a factor restraining some oligopolists' decisions. Abuse of market power (such as price-fixing) by oligopolists is illegal, and while prosecutions have been rare, oligopolists would prefer to avoid such open clashes with the government. Other possible courses of action available to the government include withdrawal of government contracts from offending firms, withdrawal of government subsidies or tariff protection, or public inquiries or reports that could arouse hostile public opinion against the oligopolists. Such tactics are only rarely used, so it is really the fear of what might be done that is the key factor. It is impossible to measure the effectiveness of this deterrent, but it is probably a consideration for at least some large corporations when making price decisions.

Another limitation on oligopolists' pricing practices arises from the fact that many corporations have goals other than short-term profit maximization. For example, two other corporate goals are a favorable public image and the long-term growth of the corporation in terms of sales, assets and personnel. According to some observers, the modern large corporation, under the direction of hired managers rather than shareholders, values *growth* more highly than profits. Whether or not this is true, growth remains an important objective for many corporations, and one which poses a problem for corporation decision makers: should they charge the maximum possible prices to maximize profits today, or should they charge lower prices to promote the growth of sales and the corporation generally? There is a *conflict of goals* here, or a trade-off, in which some corporations may charge lower prices than they could have in order to achieve corporate growth. Some analysts of the behavior of large corporations believe that this conflict also tends to restrain oligopolists' prices.

How much market power?

There is no simple answer to the question of how much market power oligopolists possess—it varies widely from industry to industry and from time to time, making it impossible to generalize about how much power oligopolists have over prices. In some cases, the factors referred to in the previous section can impose quite strict limits on oligopolists' prices, while in other cases, these limits are not effective and prices and profits can rise to high levels. Furthermore, the effectiveness of these limits can vary from time to time, as conditions change. For many years, the automobile industry enjoyed a very strong position in the marketplace, as a few dominant firms kept competition within bounds and enjoyed high

FIGURE 10-5 *Summary of the Four Types of Market Structure*

PERFECT COMPETITION	MONOPOLISTIC COMPETITION	OLIGOPOLY	MONOPOLY
Characteristics			
(a) many firms (b) easy to enter (c) identical products	(a) many firms (b) easy to enter (c) differentiated products	(a) few firms (b) difficult to enter	(a) one firm (b) difficult to enter
Economic Incentives			
Each producer gains by (a) maximizing efficiency, (b) producing as much output as is economical, and (c) selling output for the market price.	Each producer gains by (a) maximizing efficiency, and (b) using product differentiation (and possibly relatively small price increases).	All producers can gain by acting together to restrict competition, restrict supply and raise prices; competition is restricted to non-price areas.	The monopolist controls the entire supply and gains by restricting it so as to maximize profits.
Results			
Downward pressure on prices and profits: each firm has *no* control over the price of its product.	Downward pressure on prices and profits: each firm has a *potential, slight degree of control* over the price of its product.	Depending on the circumstances in each situation, producers may (or may not) be able to exercise *considerable control* over the prices of their products and to earn profits well above competitive levels.	Monopolists can maximize their profits by exercising the *maximum degree of control* over the prices of their products (in cases of public utilities, subject to rate regulation or government ownership).
Extent			
Very rare—it exists with some agricultural products and resource products.	It exists to a wide extent, producing up to two-fifths of the economy's output—mostly in service industries, retail trade and small-scale manufacturing.	It exists to a wide extent, producing up to half of the economy's output—concentrated in the manufacturing and resource sectors.	It is relatively rare—mostly restricted to public utilities such as electricity, water, and telephone service.

profits. Since then, however, the auto industry has experienced very strong competition from foreign producers.

Regardless of the factors that may (or may not) restrain the pricing decisions of oligopolists, the fact remains that many large corporations possess considerable control over prices. These large corporations, and the market power they possess, are a long way from the competitive industries of Chapter 9 and the ideal of a highly competitive economy. (Figure 10-5 summarizes and compares all four types of market structures.) This wide variation, together with the sheer size and importance of the oligopolistic sector of the economy, raises important questions about whether such concentration of economic power in a few large corporations is in the best interests of society at large. These questions will be considered more fully in Chapter 12.

DEFINITIONS OF NEW TERMS

Monopoly   A situation in which there is only one seller of a particular good or service.

Oligopoly   A situation in which four or fewer firms account for at least half of the sales of an industry.

Natural Monopoly   An industry, such as public utilities, that by its nature lends itself to a monopolistic form of organization.

Price-Fixing   Collusive action by oligopolists to raise their prices above levels that would prevail in a competitive situation.

Administered Prices   A term used to describe prices that have been fixed by producers.

Price Leadership   A technique of price-fixing in which one firm (the price leader) sets its prices and the rest of the firms in the industry follow suit.

Organization of Petroleum Exporting Countries (OPEC)   An international cartel of oil-producing countries, mostly Arabian states. (A cartel is a formal agreement among producers to coordinate their price and output decisions so as to earn monopoly profits.)

CHAPTER SUMMARY

1. A monopoly is able to restrict the supply and thus raise the price of its product so as to maximize its profits.

2. Monopoly is quite rare, being restricted mainly to public utilities, which tend to be "natural monopolies" that are regulated or owned by the government.

3. Oligopolies consist of sufficiently few firms that they often act together so as to fix prices, using various techniques of price-fixing.

4. The high profits of many oligopolistic industries are protected by various barriers to entry that keep new entrants out of these industries.

. Oligopolistic industries constitute a major portion of the Canadian economy, being concentrated in the manufacturing sector and accounting for up to half the economy's output.

. Once oligopolistic prices have been set by the producers, each firm tends to leave its prices unchanged (until the industry changes the price), but oligopolistic firms often do compete quite strongly in non-price areas such as advertising and product differentiation.

. Depending on the circumstances, oligopolists can possess considerable power over their prices or they can be subject to a variety of limitations which restrict their pricing freedom severely; as a result, oligopolistic pricing decisions are difficult to predict.

Canadian Microeconomics: Problems and policies

QUESTIONS

1. Would you consider the barriers to entry to each of the following industries to be very high, substantial, or moderate-to- low?

Shoes	Automobiles
Petroleum refining	Steel
Drugs	Cigarettes
Soap	Meat packing

2. What are some good recent examples of successful *advertising* and *product differentiation* by oligopolists? In each case, to whom is the seller trying to appeal, and how? If you were a competitor, how would you attempt to appeal to the same group of consumers?

3. The automobile industry is said to produce the most differentiated of all products. What are some of the most recent trends in this area? What do you believe would be a successful future trend in the differentiation of the automobile?

4. Many marketing experts regard product *packaging* as an important form of advertising and sales promotion. Name some products whose packaging reflects this approach to marketing.

5. According to one view, OPEC's price increases in the 1970's were of long-run benefit to the industrialized nations of the world. Explain the reasoning that might underlie such a view.

CHAPTER 11

The costs and revenues of the firm

In Chapters 9 and 10, we examined the behavior of the individual business firm under the four basic types of market structures—perfect competition, monopolistic competition, oligopoly and monopoly. While we discussed various strategies whereby firms could increase their profits under various conditions, we focused our attention on the total (sales) *revenue* of the firm more than its *profits*; indeed, in some cases, we treated total revenue as if it were the same as profits, speaking in terms of the firm maximizing its total revenue rather than its profits. While this approach allowed us to discuss the limitations facing the business firm and its behavior under various conditions, it is not really accurate to consider total revenue to be the same as profits. Total revenue is the result of the firm's sales, while profits are the net result of the firm's sales revenues *and* its production costs. In this chapter we will examine the nature and behavior of production costs and how they interact with sales revenues to determine not only the business firm's profits, but also its decisions regarding prices and output.

Production costs

To illustrate the nature and behavior of the production costs of the firm, we will use the example of Phil's Fradistats, one of many small manufacturing firms selling an undifferentiated product (fradistats) to large industrial buyers in a highly competitive market. Since competition lim-

171

its Phil's price to $3 per fradistat, his success is mainly dependent upon his ability to keep his production cost per fradistat as low as possible, by producing fradistats as efficiently as possible. From Phil's business, we can learn some of the basic facts related to the production costs of a business.

Fixed costs

We will suppose that Phil has leased a building and equipment (three fradistat formers) for his business, and that the cost of these, plus other overhead items such as light and heat, amounts to $120 per day. These are called Phil's **fixed costs**, meaning that they will remain at $120 per

FIGURE 11-1 *Fixed Costs per Unit*

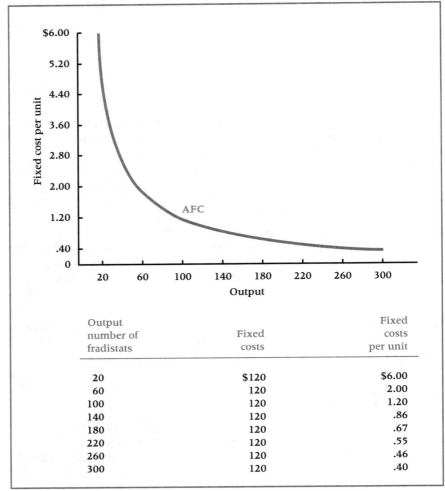

Output number of fradistats	Fixed costs	Fixed costs per unit
20	$120	$6.00
60	120	2.00
100	120	1.20
140	120	.86
180	120	.67
220	120	.55
260	120	.46
300	120	.40

day regardless of how much he produces. If he produces 10 fradistats per day or 300 fradistats per day, his fixed costs will be $120. This makes it essential that Phil produce and sell a certain number of fradistats per day, because if his production is too low, the fixed costs per item produced will be so high that he will be unable to make a profit. Phil's research into this matter is shown in Figure 11-1, which shows that fixed costs per fradistat are extremely high at low volumes of output. Considering that the market price of fradistats is $3, it is apparent that Phil can succeed only if he attains a sufficiently high volume of sales and production to spread his fixed costs over a large number of units, so as to keep fixed costs per unit low. Generally, then, fixed costs per unit of output are very high at low volumes of output, and decline as output is increased.

Variable costs

In addition to his fixed costs, Phil will have **variable costs**: these are costs, such as direct labor and materials, that will increase as Phil's output of fradistats increases.[1] To simplify our illustration, we will assume that there are no materials costs, so that the only variable cost with which we will be concerned is direct labor.

The labor cost per fradistat will depend on two factors: how much the average worker is *paid* per day, and how many fradistats he or she *produces* per day. At first glance, we might expect both of these factors to be constant regardless of how many fradistats Phil produces. That is, hiring additional workers should not affect either the daily wages or the average daily output of the workers. However, the average daily output of each worker will, in fact, change as additional workers are added to Phil's plant.

The reason for this change is that the plant is of a certain size, and is best suited to a certain level of production. If production is too far below or too far above this level, efficiency will suffer, and the average daily product of each worker will be below its peak. This is illustrated in Figure 11-2, which shows the total production and the average production per worker which will be obtained if various numbers of workers are employed. If Phil's production is so low that only one or two people are working in the plant, he will find that his operation is inefficient and that average production per worker is quite low. This is because with only one or two people working in the plant, they will not be able to *specialize* enough to produce fradistats efficiently—they will each have to spend so much time performing many different tasks that they will not be able to do any of them particularly efficiently. As a result, at low levels of production, with few workers employed, average output per worker

---

[1] "Direct" merely specifies that such labor and materials are directly used for producing the product, as distinct from office labor and materials, which are more like fixed costs or overhead items.

FIGURE 11-2 *Average Product per Worker*

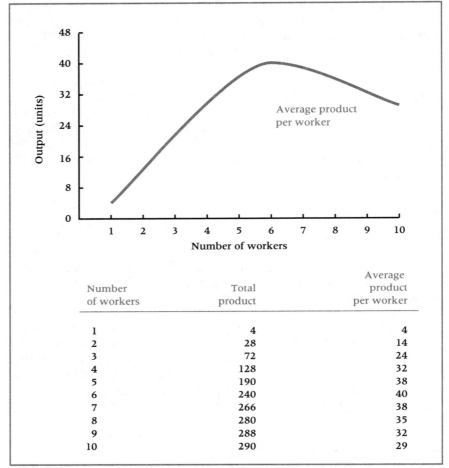

Number of workers	Total product	Average product per worker
1	4	4
2	28	14
3	72	24
4	128	32
5	190	38
6	240	40
7	266	38
8	280	35
9	288	32
10	290	29

will be very low (4 units per day if one person is employed and 14 units per day with two workers on the job).

Phil will find, however, that as he increases production and hires additional workers, average output per worker improves significantly. With more workers in the plant, each can become more specialized. Some can prepare materials for production, some can operate the fradistat-forming machinery, some can finish and paint the fradistats, while others package them for shipping. With each worker being more specialized, efficiency is greater and average output per worker rises considerably, reaching 40 units per day when six workers are employed.

However, Phil will find that hiring additional workers improves output per worker only up to a certain point. If he hires additional workers beyond the sixth, average output per worker declines, as Figure 11-2 shows. This is because Phil's plant is only so large, and we have moved beyond the point at which it operates at *peak efficiency*. The addition of more workers does not increase the opportunities for specialization, as it did earlier; in effect, the additional workers are crowding the fixed amount of equipment and therefore are actually reducing the efficiency of the work force. By *efficiency* we mean average output per worker: as Figure 11-2 shows, the addition of the seventh through tenth workers causes the plant's total output to rise, but average output per worker declines once production is past the level of peak efficiency for that plant.

This phenomenon is known as the Law of Diminishing Returns which can be stated in general terms as follows:

> If additional units of one productive input (here, labor) are combined with a fixed quantity of another productive input (here, capital equipment), the average output per unit of the variable input (labor) will increase at first, then decline.

The Law of Diminishing Returns places an important limitation on Phil's production decisions, because it means that, while Phil can increase his output to certain levels, to do so may involve such reductions in efficiency (or increases in cost per unit) that he will not find it *economical* to do so.

Marginal productivity

There is another useful way of analyzing the data in Figure 11-2: rather than looking at total output, or average output per worker, we can examine the increase in production resulting from the hiring of one additional worker, or the marginal productivity (marginal output) per worker. This information is presented in Figure 11-3, which shows that the hiring of the fifth and sixth workers add 62 and 50 units respectively to total output, while after that, additional workers add much less. The seventh worker only increases production by 26 units, the eight and ninth only add 14 and 8 units respectively, while the tenth worker barely adds to total output at all—the tenth one's marginal output is only 2 units. It is important to remember that this does not mean that the quality of the workers is declining. The reason for the decline in marginal output per worker is the Law of Diminishing Returns: once production in Phil's plant moves past the point of peak efficiency, average output per worker will decline because additional workers will not be able to add as much to output as before. This diminishing return will have an important impact on production costs, because the cost of the extra units (marginal output) produced by additional workers will rise very rapidly beyond a certain point, making it uneconomical to hire workers and increase output beyond that point. For instance, it is very doubtful that the marginal

FIGURE 11-3 *Average and Marginal Product per Worker*

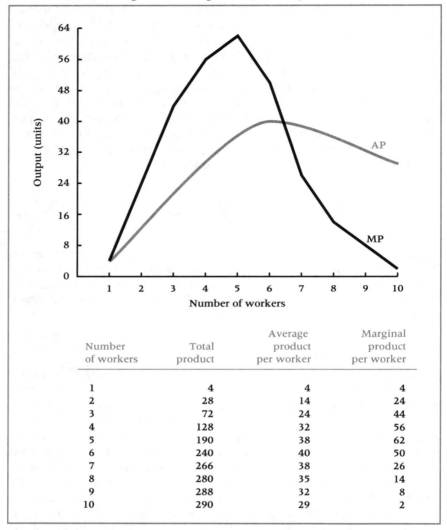

Number of workers	Total product	Average product per worker	Marginal product per worker
1	4	4	4
2	28	14	24
3	72	24	44
4	128	32	56
5	190	38	62
6	240	40	50
7	266	38	26
8	280	35	14
9	288	32	8
10	290	29	2

output of the ninth and tenth workers (8 and 2 units, respectively) warrants hiring them. Or, viewed differently, the cost per unit of increasing output from 280 to 290 units would be so high as to be uneconomical.

The cost and productivity factors that we have been discussing place limitations on Phil's production decisions. Because fixed costs per unit are very high at low levels of output, he must achieve a certain level of production (and sales) in order to operate economically. However, due to the Law of Diminishing Returns, it will not prove economical to

177

The costs and
revenues of the
firm

FIGURE 11-4 *Average Variable Costs per Unit*

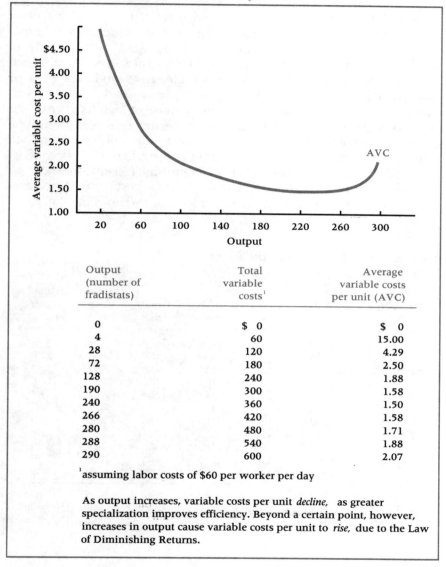

Output (number of fradistats)	Total variable costs[1]	Average variable costs per unit (AVC)
0	$ 0	$ 0
4	60	15.00
28	120	4.29
72	180	2.50
128	240	1.88
190	300	1.58
240	360	1.50
266	420	1.58
280	480	1.71
288	540	1.88
290	600	2.07

[1] assuming labor costs of $60 per worker per day

As output increases, variable costs per unit *decline*, as greater specialization improves efficiency. Beyond a certain point, however, increases in output cause variable costs per unit to *rise*, due to the Law of Diminishing Returns.

increase his output beyond a certain point, since the variable costs per unit (labor costs) will rise to higher levels, as Figure 11-4 shows.

In general terms, then, we have outlined the situation Phil faces with respect to production costs, and how this will affect his operations. On the basis of these two figures, Phil can make two more calculations which will help him decide exactly what volume of output to produce. These are the average cost per unit and the marginal cost per unit.

Average cost per unit

Figure 11-5 summarizes the production costs of Phil's fradistat plant which we have been discussing. It is based on the production information discussed earlier: *fixed costs* of $120 per day regardless of the level of output, and *variable costs* consisting only of wages of $60 per day for each worker. *Total costs* are fixed costs plus variable costs, and *average cost per unit* is total costs divided by total output. As we saw earlier, at low levels of output, average cost per unit is high, because of high fixed costs per unit. As output is expanded, the plant operates more efficiently, reaching a minimum average cost per unit of $2 at a daily output level of 240 units. Further increases in output cause the plant to operate beyond its most efficient level, so that the Law of Diminishing Returns pushes variable costs per unit up again. As a result, average cost per unit increases still further, rising to $2.48 at an output level of 290 units per day.

FIGURE 11-5 *The Costs of the Firm*

Number of workers	Total output	Fixed costs	Variable costs	Total costs	Average cost per unit[1]	Marginal cost per unit[2]
0	0	$120	$ 0	$120	—	—
1	4	120	60	180	$45.00	$15.00
2	28	120	120	240	8.57	2.50
3	72	120	180	300	4.17	1.36
4	128	120	240	360	2.81	1.07
5	190	120	300	420	2.21	.97
6	240	120	360	480	2.00	1.20
7	266	120	420	540	2.03	2.31
8	280	120	480	600	2.14	4.29
9	288	120	540	660	2.29	7.50
10	290	120	600	720	2.48	30.00

[1] $\dfrac{\text{Total costs}}{\text{Total output}}$ [2] $\dfrac{\text{Change in total costs}}{\text{Change in total output}}$

Marginal cost per unit

The last column in Figure 11-5—marginal cost per unit—requires some explanation. **Marginal cost per unit** is the addition to total costs resulting from the production of one additional unit of output. For instance, when output is increased for 4 to 28 units, total costs rise from $180 to $240. In other words, it costs $60 more to increase output by 24 units, making the cost of each additional unit (the marginal cost per unit) $2.50 ($60 ÷ 24). These calculations, together with other samples, are shown in Figure 11-6. Marginal cost per unit can be an important tool for Phil in deciding his output: obviously, if he is considering expanding his production, it would be valuable to know the cost per unit of the increased output.

Figure 11-7 presents the average cost per unit and marginal cost per unit data graphically. This graph illustrates a fact concerning the relationship between the two curves: *the marginal cost curve always intersects the*

179

The costs and
revenues of the
firm

FIGURE 11-6 *Calculation of Marginal Cost per Unit*

Total output	Total costs	Marginal cost per unit	=	Increase in total costs / Increase in total output
0	$120			
4	180	$15.00	=	$\frac{\$180 - 120}{4 - 0}$
28	240	2.50	=	$\frac{\$240 - 180}{28 - 4}$
72	300	1.36	=	$\frac{\$300 - 240}{72 - 28}$

FIGURE 11-7 *The Average Cost per Unit and Marginal Cost per Unit Curves of the Firm*

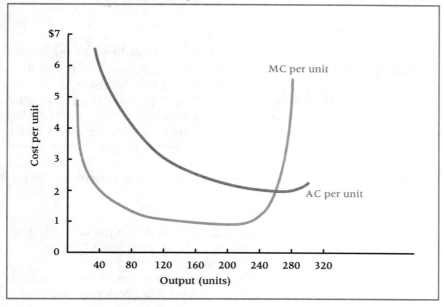

average cost curve at the lowest point on the average cost curve. If average cost per unit is falling, additional units of output are pulling the average cost down, meaning that the marginal cost of the additional units must be lower than the average cost per unit. Similarly, if average cost per unit is rising, additional units of output are pulling the average cost up, because the marginal cost of the additional units is higher than the average cost per unit. Thus, when average cost is falling, marginal cost is below the average, and when average cost is rising, marginal cost is above the average—it is only at that point where average cost is at its minimum (neither falling nor rising) that average cost per unit and marginal cost per unit are exactly the same, and the curves intersect. Beyond this output level, as Figure 11-7 shows, marginal cost per unit rises very quickly, as the Law of Diminishing Returns makes it increasingly difficult to increase output by simply adding more workers to the plant.

To summarize Phil's production costs, increasing output causes average cost per unit to decline until it reaches a minimum at an output level between 240 and 260 units per day. At output levels beyond this, average cost per unit increases again, and rapidly rising marginal cost per unit makes it uneconomical to increase output beyond a certain point. What this "certain point" is—and what level of output Phil will actually decide to produce—will depend not only on how much additional units cost to produce, but also on how much additional revenue they bring in. To complete our analysis of Phil's fradistat firm, we must now consider the revenues, or *sales* of the business.

The revenue side

Average revenue per unit

We will assume that Phil's is one of many small firms in the highly competitive fradistat industry, and that the market price of fradistats is $3 per unit. At this price, Phil can sell as many fradistats as he can produce, up to his maximum possible output of 290 per day. In other words, the demand for Phil's product is perfectly elastic, as shown by the demand schedule and demand curve in Figure 11-8. Figure 11-8 also shows that the *price* of the product can be viewed as the *average revenue per unit*; since he can sell as many as he produces for $3 a piece, the *demand curve* can be viewed as showing the *average revenue per unit sold*.

Marginal revenue per unit

From the demand for Phil's fradistats, we can develop a table of information concerning his sales revenues, as shown in Figure 11-9. Since he can only charge $3 per unit, his average revenue per unit is always $3. *Total revenue*, which is simply price (or average revenue) times quantity demanded, rises in proportion to sales. **Marginal revenue per unit** is

FIGURE 11-8 *The Demand for Phil's Fradistats*

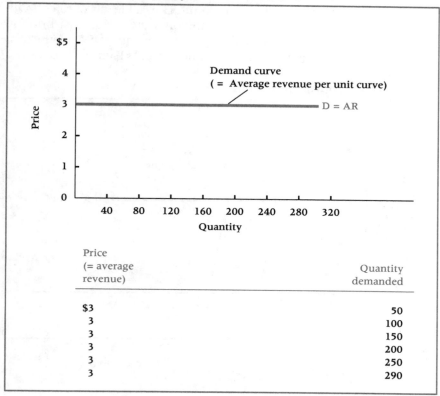

Price (= average revenue)	Quantity demanded
$3	50
3	100
3	150
3	200
3	250
3	290

FIGURE 11-9 *The Revenue Side of Phil's Fradistats*

Price (= average revenue)	×	Quantity demanded	=	Total revenue	Marginal revenue per unit[1]
$3		50		$150	
3		100		300	$3
3		150		450	3
3		200		600	3
3		250		750	3
3		290		870	3

[1] $\dfrac{\text{Increase in total revenue}}{\text{Increase in quantity demanded}}$

the addition to total revenue gained from the sale of one more unit. It can be calculated in the same way as we calculate marginal cost per unit, by dividing the increase in total revenue by the increase in units sold; in each case total revenue rises by $150 and the number of units sold by 50, making the marginal revenue per unit $3 at all levels of sales. With the price always $3 per unit, each additional unit sold must bring in marginal revenue of $3, making the marginal revenue curve identical to the demand curve and the average revenue curve, as Figure 11-10 shows.

FIGURE 11-10 *Marginal Revenue per Unit*

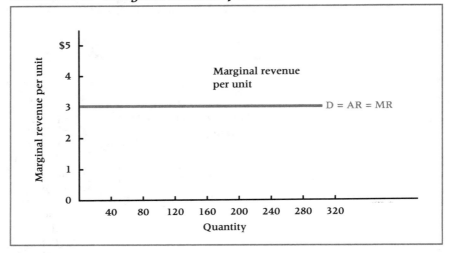

The most profitable output

We now have all of the information needed concerning Phil's costs and revenues in order to decide what level of output he should produce. Figure 11-11 summarizes all of the information we have developed about Phil's costs and revenues and adds a column for **total profits**, which are total revenue minus total costs. The table shows that low levels of output are unprofitable due to the fixed costs, and that profits are maximized at $258 per day by producing 266 units per day, using 7 workers.

Tools of analysis

While it is easy to see why Phil would choose to produce 266 fradistats per day, we can use this simple example to develop other, more sophisticated concepts. Why didn't Phil choose to produce 240 units per day? At this output level, his plant operates at peak efficiency, and production costs per unit are minimized at $2. The answer lies in the marginal cost per unit and marginal revenue per unit columns. The extra 26 units (from 240 to 266 per day) had a *marginal cost* of $2.31 each, while they brought in a *marginal revenue* of $3 each. Thus, each of these additional units added $.69 of profit to the firm. From this, we can conclude that, *whenever marginal revenue exceeds marginal cost, it is profitable to increase output.*

FIGURE 11-11 *The Costs and Revenues of Phil's Fradistats*

Number of workers	Total output	Fixed costs	Variable costs	Total costs	Total revenue	Total profit(+) or loss(−)	Average cost per unit	Marginal cost per unit	Marginal revenue per unit
0	0	$120	$ 0	$120	$ 0	−$120	—	—	—
1	4	120	60	180	12	− 168	$45.00	$15.00	$3.00
2	28	120	120	240	84	− 156	8.57	2.50	3.00
3	72	120	180	300	216	− 84	4.17	1.36	3.00
4	128	120	240	360	384	+ 24	2.81	1.07	3.00
5	190	120	300	420	570	+ 150	2.21	.97	3.00
6	240	120	360	480	720	+ 240	2.00	1.20	3.00
7	266	120	420	540	798	+ 258	2.03	2.31	3.00
8	280	120	480	600	840	+ 240	2.14	4.29	3.00
9	288	120	540	660	864	+ 204	2.29	7.50	3.00
10	290	120	600	720	870	+ 150	2.48	30.00	3.00

Why, then, did Phil *not* increase his output beyond 266 units per day? Again, the answer lies in examining marginal revenue and marginal cost per unit. While additional units beyond 266 per day will still bring in *marginal revenue* of $3 each, the production of them will involve a *marginal cost* of $4.29 each, making it unprofitable to produce these additional units. The Law of Diminishing Returns has made further output increases uneconomical by forcing marginal cost per unit to high levels.

To summarize, it will be profitable to increase output as long as marginal revenue per unit exceeds marginal cost per unit. However, as diminishing returns set in, marginal cost per unit will rise, and once marginal cost per unit becomes greater than marginal revenue per unit, it will no longer be profitable to increase production. Thus, profits will be maximized at that level of output at which marginal cost equals marginal revenue; that is, where the marginal cost curve intersects the marginal revenue curve. This principle is illustrated in Figure 11-12, in which profits are maximized by producing 100 units of output. In the remainder of this chapter, we will use this approach to analyze the price and output decisions of business firms under different market structures, starting with perfect competition as discussed in Chapter 9.

Different market structures

(a) Perfect competition

As noted in Chapter 9, perfect competition is a rare situation in which there are many small firms in an industry, it is easy for new firms to enter the industry, and all firms are selling identical products. The result is the most competitive situation imaginable, in which producers have

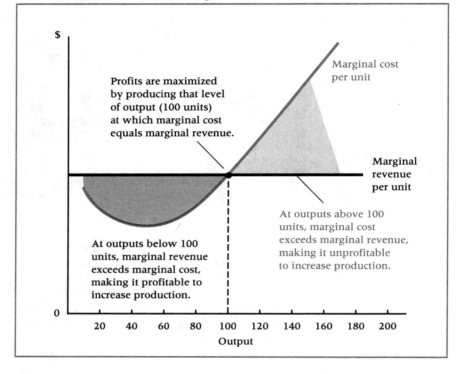

no control over the price of their product and there is constant downward pressure on profits. Using analysis based on costs and revenues as developed earlier in this chapter, we can now examine the case of perfect competition more closely.

The costs and revenues of the firm in perfect competition will be like those of Phil's fradistat firm, which we described as a small firm in a highly competitive industry. The cost curves will have the usual shapes described earlier in this chapter,[2] with average cost per unit declining as output increases up to a point, then increasing again, and the marginal cost per unit curve rising quite sharply beyond a certain output and intersecting the average cost per unit curve at that curve's minimum point, as shown in Figure 11-13. In perfect competition, the existence of many small firms selling identical products ensures that the demand for

[2] The shape of the cost curves is determined by physical factors such as the Law of Diminishing Returns; as a result, cost curves have the same general shape regardless of whether the firm is small or large, or in an industry that is highly competitive, oligopolistic or monopolistic.

FIGURE 11-13 *The Firm in Perfect Competition with Profits*

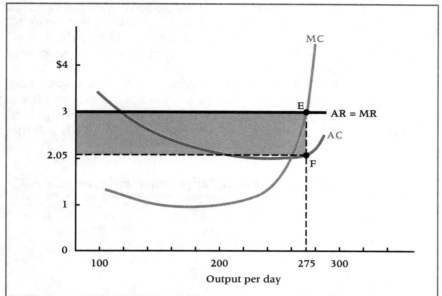

any one firm's product will be perfectly elastic. Thus, if the market price of the product is $3 per unit, the demand curve of the individual firm will consist of a horizontal line at a price of $3, as in Figure 11-13. This line will also represent the *average revenue* from each sale (AR) and the *marginal revenue* (MR) for each additional sale, as indicated on the graph.

Figure 11-13 shows an individual firm in a perfectly competitive industry which is making profits. *Profits* are maximized by producing that output at which marginal cost equals marginal revenue, or 275 units per day, as point E indicates. Total revenue will be $825 per day ($3 × 275 units). Point F indicates that, at an output level of 275 units, average cost per unit is $2.05, making total costs of $564 ($2.05 × 275 units). Thus, total daily profit will be maximized at $261 ($825 − $564) at an output level of 275 units. The shaded area on the graph represents the total profit (275 × $.95) earned by the firm in this situation.

Dynamics of perfect competition

If the firm we have been discussing is a typical firm in the industry, the situation cannot remain as it is shown in Figure 11-13. The profitability of firms in this industry will attract new competitors into the industry, increasing the supply of the product and *reducing its price*. When this happens, the demand curve (labelled AR = MR on Figure 11-13) will move downward as the price declines, reducing the profits of our firm.

How far can the price fall? Figure 11-14 shows what would happen if the price fell to $1.50: at *every* level of output, average cost per unit exceeds average revenue per unit. As a result, it would be impossible to make a profit at a price of $1.50—by producing 250 units, where marginal cost equals marginal revenue, the firm could minimize its losses, but it would still be losing money.

If the typical firm in the industry were losing money, it is obvious that some firms would have to leave the industry—a polite way of saying that they would go bankrupt. As they left, the supply of the product would decline, and the price would come back up. How high will the price rise, and at what level will it settle?

FIGURE 11-14 *The Firm in Perfect Competition with Losses*

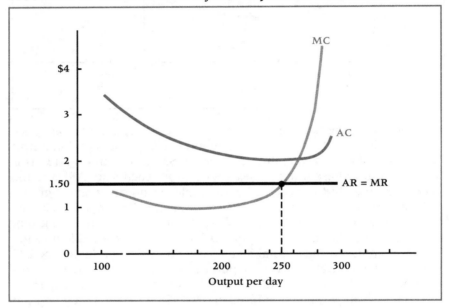

Figure 11-15 provides the answer: the price will rise to (and settle at) just under $2 per unit, at which point output will be 260 units. At this price, two conditions exist:

(a) marginal cost equals marginal revenue, so that the firm's profits are maximized, and the firm has no incentive to increase or decrease its output, and

(b) average cost equals average revenue, so that profits are zero, providing no incentive for anyone to enter or leave the industry.

Since one might wonder why anyone would even *stay* in a business with no profits, we should define profits more precisely. By **profits** we mean business income *over and above the owner-manager's salary*. Viewed differently, we assume that the owner-manager will only continue in business if a certain minimum income level is earned, and include that person's salary in the production costs of the business, as a fixed cost.

In conclusion, then, our marginal revenue/marginal cost analysis confirms what we said in Chapter 9 about the firm in perfect competition: the intense competition in such industries will exert constant downward pressure on prices and profits, tending to drive profits to minimal levels. In these circumstances, the only way an individual producer can earn profits is to operate more efficiently than average, so as to enjoy lower-than-average costs per unit.

FIGURE 11-15 *The Firm in Perfect Competition with No Profits*

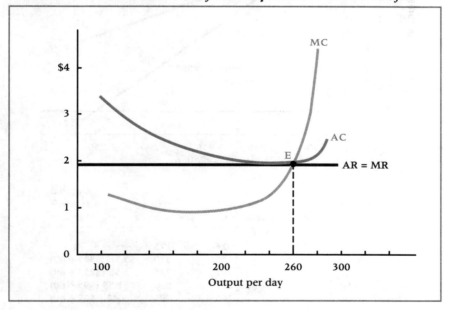

(b) Monopoly

Monopoly represents the other extreme from perfect competition: a situation in which there is only one producer in the industry, who is able to select the level of output that maximizes profits. In Chapter 10, we discussed *total revenue* as if it were profit, but now that we have both cost and revenue information, we can analyze the monopolist's price and output decisions more precisely.

For our average and marginal cost curves, we will use the same curves as we used in the example of perfect competition, so as to provide a basis for comparing the results of the two situations. Under monopoly, however, the *demand* for the product will be *less elastic*, because there is only one seller. Since monopolists have more freedom to set prices, the average revenue per unit and marginal revenue per unit curves will be significantly different from those of the firm in perfect competition, as Figure 11-16 shows.

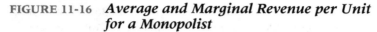

FIGURE 11-16 *Average and Marginal Revenue per Unit for a Monopolist*

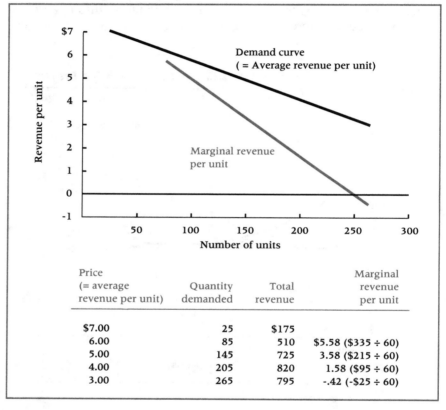

Price (= average revenue per unit)	Quantity demanded	Total revenue	Marginal revenue per unit
$7.00	25	$175	
6.00	85	510	$5.58 ($335 ÷ 60)
5.00	145	725	3.58 ($215 ÷ 60)
4.00	205	820	1.58 ($95 ÷ 60)
3.00	265	795	-.42 (-$25 ÷ 60)

As output is increased, *marginal revenue per unit falls more rapidly than average revenue per unit*, or the demand curve. The reason why this happens is that, in order to sell more units, the monopolist must reduce the price, not only on the additional units sold, but also on all units sold. For instance, when sales are increased from 85 to 145 units by reducing prices from $6 to $5, the additional 60 units sold bring in $300 ($5 × 60), but there is $85 less total revenue on the 85 units, because they are selling for $1 less per unit. Thus, the net marginal revenue on the 60 additional units is $215 ($300 − $85), or $3.85 per unit, as shown in Figure 11-16. As sales increase, the monopolist's marginal revenue curve will fall, and will fall more steeply than the demand curve—a fact that will have an important bearing on the monopolist's price and output decisions.

Price and output decisions

To maximize profits, the monopolist will follow our rule of producing that output at which marginal revenue equals marginal costs. Figure 11-17 shows that doing this will result in a decision to produce 220 units of output per day. Point P on the demand curve shows that, to sell 220 units per day, a price of $3.75 per unit must be charged. Thus, the monopolist will maximize profits by charging a price of $3.75 and producing 220 units per day.

189

The costs and
revenues of the
firm

FIGURE 11-17 *The Monopolist's Price and Output Decisions*

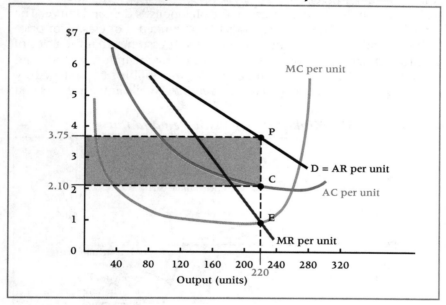

At this level of output, the monopolist's average revenue per unit will be $3.75 (the price), and average cost per unit will be $2.10 (from point C on the average cost curve). The average profit per unit will then be $1.65 ($3.75 − $2.10), and the monopolist's total profits will be $363 per days ($1.65 × 220). The shaded area on the graph in Figure 11-17 represents these profits.

Monopoly and competition compared

In a perfectly competitive industry, we saw that the price of the product would be $1.95, output would be 260 units per day (Figure 11-15), and that competition would tend to eliminate profits in excess of the salary of the owner-manager. Under monopoly, using the same cost curves, the price would be $3.75, output would be 220 units, and there would be substantial profits.[3] Furthermore, because new firms cannot enter the industry, these profits are secure from competition.

(c) Oligopoly

In Chapter 10, we saw that, while the price and output decisions of oligopolistic industries were of great importance, it was impossible to develop a theoretical basis for analyzing and predicting those decisions. In this chapter, we have developed considerably more sophisticated techniques for analyzing the costs, revenues and price and output decisions of the firm. However, these still do not enable us to analyze oligopolists' behavior precisely.

The problem lies in the nature of the oligopolist's demand curve. The curve, as Figure 11-18 shows, tends to be "kinked," or elastic for price increases and inelastic for price reductions. It assumes that the price of the product has (somehow) been established by the industry at $6, and that any price increases you make above this will *not* be matched by your competitors, causing you to *lose many sales*, while any price cuts you

FIGURE 11-18 *The Kinked Oligopolistic Demand Curve*

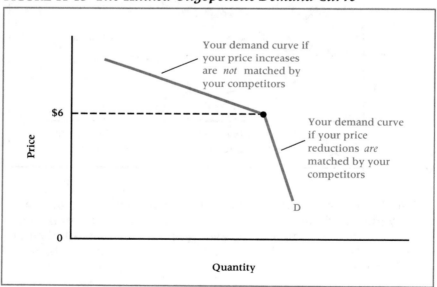

[3] For comparative purposes, we have used the same cost curves for the small firm in perfect competition and for the monopolist. This ignores the possibility that the monopolist's costs may in fact be *lower* than the small firm's, due to improved technology and mass-production techniques. We will consider this possibility further in Chapter 12.

make below $6 *will* be matched by your competitors, so that you will *gain few sales*. Therefore, once the price has been established, there is no incentive for individual oligopolists to either raise or lower their own prices. Rather, each will simply go along with the group.

Marginal cost and marginal revenue analysis do not help us to analyze oligopolists' decisions further. As Figure 11-19 shows, even the most

FIGURE 11-19 *Marginal Cost and Marginal Revenue Curves for the Oligopolist*

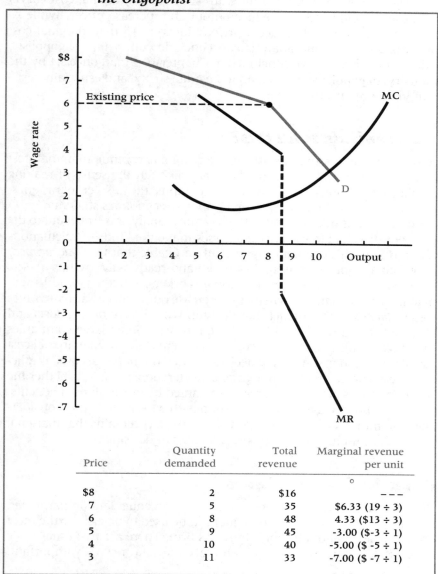

Price	Quantity demanded	Total revenue	Marginal revenue per unit
$8	2	$16	---
7	5	35	$6.33 (19 ÷ 3)
6	8	48	4.33 ($13 ÷ 3)
5	9	45	-3.00 ($-3 ÷ 1)
4	10	40	-5.00 ($ -5 ÷ 1)
3	11	33	-7.00 ($ -7 ÷ 1)

modest kink in the demand curve causes strange changes in the marginal revenue curve. At the level of output where the demand curve is kinked, the marginal revenue curve becomes *discontinuous* (see the dotted line in Figure 11-19), leaving us with no clear intersection point for the marginal cost and marginal revenue curves. As a result of this, marginal cost and marginal revenue analysis cannot help to pinpoint oligopolists' price and output decisions. All we can say is that the existence of a kinked demand curve provides a strong incentive for individual oligopolists to leave their price and output unchanged. As Figure 11-19 shows, it would take a *major increase in production costs* (upward shift of the marginal cost curve) to cause our oligopolist to reduce output and increase prices, while *no reduction in costs* would induce a price reduction. All that marginal cost and marginal revenue analysis can conclude concerning oligopolistic prices, then, is what we concluded in Chapter 10—that, once set by the industry, oligopolistic prices tend to be quite sticky, and especially resistant to downward movements.

How realistic is all this?

A student can reasonably ask about marginal revenue/marginal cost analysis: "does anybody actually *do* all this?" In the sense of making detailed calculations and drawing exact graphs, the answer to this questions is certainly "not many people—mostly economics students."

However, this does not mean that marginal analysis is irrelevant to the real world. While few if any businesses make the kinds of calculations referred to in this chapter, it is certainly arguable that the *basic approach* of marginal analysis is used, in a rough-and-ready way, by businesses. A decision whether to hire additional workers, whether to add more machinery to a plant, or whether to increase output necessarily involves some *estimates* of the impact that decision would have on the costs and revenues (and thus the profits) of the business. Some large companies that have sophisticated cost accounting systems have used marginal cost calculations and made pricing decisions based on marginal costs. Implicitly, every choice involves marginal considerations; that is, whether the additional costs of the decision are warranted by the additional benefits. While it is not always (or even often) possible to reduce these considerations to numbers as we have done here, the fact remains that marginal analysis is a useful tool for making all kinds of decisions.

Other business decisions

We have seen in this chapter how cost and revenue data (in particular, marginal cost and marginal revenue) can be used to determine the most profitable level of output for a business firm. There are two other basic business decisions for which cost and revenue data are vitally important:

whether to start a new business and whether to shut down an existing business. Using Phil's Fradistats as our example, we can use the cost and revenue data in Figure 11-5 to decide

(a) what volume of sales Phil must achieve in order to justify *starting* his business up, and

(b) how low his sales could fall before he should *close* his business.

193

The costs and
revenues of the
firm

The start-up decision

In deciding whether to start up in business, the key question facing Phil is whether he can sell enough fradistats to cover his *costs*. Because high fixed costs per unit cause the average cost per unit to be high at low levels of output, Phil must achieve a certain volume of sales in order to cover his costs, or *break even*. To make this decision, Phil will use average cost and average revenue data rather than the marginal cost and revenue data used to determine the most profitable level of output.

Figure 11-20 shows the use of average cost and average revenue in this way: if the price per fradistat (average revenue per unit) is $3, Phil must sell more than 118 fradistats per day in order to make a profit. At point A, with an output of 118 units, average cost and average revenue per unit are equal, making Phil's profit zero—he is breaking even.

At output levels below 118, average cost exceeds average revenue per unit, and Phil loses money, while at output levels above 118, average revenue exceeds average cost per unit, and Phil earns a profit. Unless Phil can realistically plan on sales in excess of 118 per day, he should not start up in business.

In business terminology, 118 units per day is said to be Phil's *break-even point*, because at this level of output he just barely covers his costs, or breaks even. Break-even analysis similar to that shown in Figure 11-20 is useful when considering whether to start a business; however, it is usually done with *total cost* and *total revenue* data, as shown in Figure 11-21, rather than with average cost and revenue data.

The total cost and total revenue data in Figure 11-21 lead Phil to the same conclusion reached earlier: he must sell more than 118 units per day in order to make a profit. At sales of 118 per day (point A), he breaks even, with total revenue equal to total costs. At lower levels of output, total costs exceed total revenue, causing him to lose money. Only by selling more than 118 units per day can Phil earn a profit.

Figure 11-21 illustrates another point seen earlier in this chapter: the firm will not maximize profits by producing as much output as is physically possible. If output is increased beyond a certain point, the Law of Diminishing Returns causes costs to increase rapidly, making it unprofitable to increase output further. Rather, profits are maximized at an output level of 266 units per day, as we saw earlier.

FIGURE 11-20 *The Start-Up Decision*

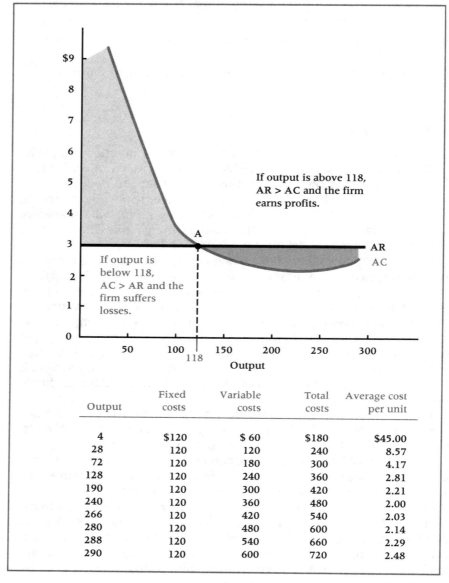

If output is above 118, AR > AC and the firm earns profits.

If output is below 118, AC > AR and the firm suffers losses.

Output	Fixed costs	Variable costs	Total costs	Average cost per unit
4	$120	$ 60	$180	$45.00
28	120	120	240	8.57
72	120	180	300	4.17
128	120	240	360	2.81
190	120	300	420	2.21
240	120	360	480	2.00
266	120	420	540	2.03
280	120	480	600	2.14
288	120	540	660	2.29
290	120	600	720	2.48

The shut-down decision

Suppose that, once he has started business, Phil's sales begin to fall. How low can they fall before Phil should decide to go out of business?

The key factor in this situation is that, even if he stops production, he must still pay his fixed costs such as rent, interest on debt and so on.[4] To

[4] These fixed costs must still be paid in the short run; for instance, rent must be paid until his lease expires. Over a longer period of time, all costs can be viewed as variable (particularly if he goes out of business).

FIGURE 11-21 *Break-Even Analysis*

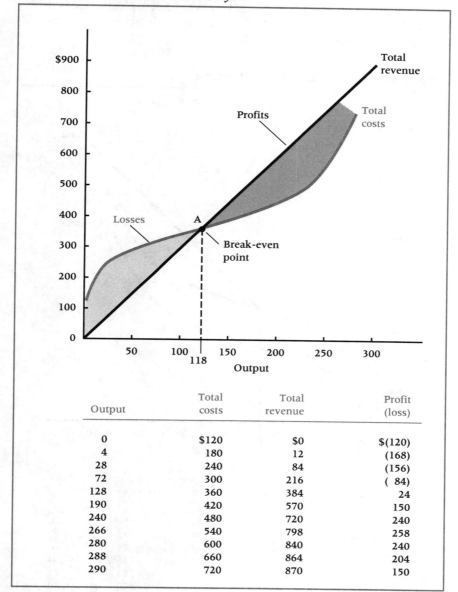

Output	Total costs	Total revenue	Profit (loss)
0	$120	$0	$(120)
4	180	12	(168)
28	240	84	(156)
72	300	216	(84)
128	360	384	24
190	420	570	150
240	480	720	240
266	540	798	258
280	600	840	240
288	660	864	204
290	720	870	150

stop production means incurring fixed costs (losses) of $120 per day. Consequently, it would be better for Phil to remain in business (at least in the short run), as long as his losses are *less* than $120 per day. For instance, the table in Figure 11-22 shows that if his sales fall to 72 units per day, Phil will lose $84 per day—$36 *less* than the $120 he would lose by stopping production altogether. Why is this so? Because, while he *is* suffering losses, his total revenue of $216 exceeds his variable costs of $180 by $36. As a result, by continuing production, he can use this

$36 to offset some of his fixed costs, so that he loses $84 rather than the $120 he would lose by stopping production completely. He is therefore $36 better off (less badly off?) to remain in business producing 72 units per day, than to stop altogether.

FIGURE 11-22 *The Shut-Down Decision*

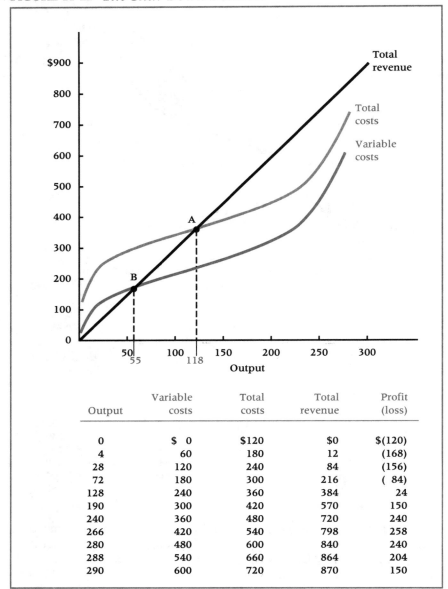

Output	Variable costs	Total costs	Total revenue	Profit (loss)
0	$ 0	$120	$0	$(120)
4	60	180	12	(168)
28	120	240	84	(156)
72	180	300	216	(84)
128	240	360	384	24
190	300	420	570	150
240	360	480	720	240
266	420	540	798	258
280	480	600	840	240
288	540	660	864	204
290	600	720	870	150

As a generality, we can conclude that *as long as total revenue exceeds variable costs, the firm should remain in business rather than close down*, because its losses will be smaller. Put differently, only when variable costs exceed total revenue should the firm close. For Phil, this occurs when his sales fall below 55 units per day, as the graph in Figure 11-22 shows. If he cannot sell 55 units per day, he should close down.

Thus, cost and revenue data can be used not only to determine the most profitable level of output for a firm, but also to determine the minimum level of sales required to start up in business, and the level of sales at which it should be decided to shut down the business.

DEFINITIONS OF NEW TERMS

Fixed Costs   Production costs that remain constant, regardless of the level of output (for example, rent).

Variable Costs   Production costs that vary with the level of output (for example, direct labor and direct materials).

Law of Diminishing Returns   A physical law stating that, if additional units of one productive input (such as labor) are combined with a fixed quantity of another productive input (such as capital), the average product per unit of the variable input (labor) will increase at first, then decline.

Marginal Productivity per Worker   The increase in production resulting from the hiring of one additional worker.

Marginal Cost per Unit   The addition to total costs resulting from the production of one additional unit of output.

Marginal Revenue per Unit   The addition to total revenue resulting from the sale of one additional unit of output.

CHAPTER SUMMARY

1. A firm's average costs per unit are high at low levels of output, due to high fixed costs, then decline as output increases. Beyond a certain output level, however, average costs per unit rise again, as variable costs per unit increase due to the Law of Diminishing Returns.

2. The marginal cost per unit curve will rise quite sharply beyond a certain output level, intersecting the average cost per unit curve at that curve's minimum point.

3. A firm's profits will be maximized by producing at the output level at which marginal cost equals marginal revenue.

4. Under perfect competition, there will be a horizontal demand (or average revenue or marginal revenue) curve, which will be forced downward by competition until the marginal revenue curve intersects the marginal cost curve at the minimum point on the average cost curve.

5. The result of this situation will be an equilibrium, in which profits are zero. There is no incentive for each firm to increase or reduce output, and no incentive for firms to enter or leave the industry.

6. Under monopoly, as output increases, marginal revenue per unit decreases, falling faster than the demand (average revenue) curve.

7. As a result, under monopoly, the marginal cost and marginal revenue curves intersect at a lower level of output than under competition, the result being lower output, higher prices and higher profits under monopoly than under competition.

8. Because an oligopolist's demand curve is "kinked," the marginal revenue curve is not continuous at the existing price and output, providing no clear intersection point for the marginal cost and marginal revenue curves and thus creating an incentive for each oligopolist to leave the price at the existing level once it has been set.

9. While marginal analysis is not usually carried out in the detailed manner employed in this chapter, it is nevertheless a useful tool for decision making, even when approximations and estimates are used.

QUESTIONS

1. Following are the prices for "cool white" fluorescent lighting tubes of various sizes:

   3' : $8.69
   8' : $7.29

   Why do you suppose the larger tube has the lower price?

2. Complete the last 5 columns of the following table:

Output	Fixed costs	Variable costs	Total costs	Average fixed costs per unit	Average variable costs per unit	Average total costs per unit	Marginal cost per unit
0	$600	$ 0	$	$ __	$ __	$ __	$ __
5	600	150					
10	600	200					
15	600	225					
20	600	340					
25	600	600					

(a) As output increases, why do:

    (i)   average fixed cost per unit,

    (ii) average variable cost per unit, and

    (iii) average total cost per unit change as they do?

(b) What does "marginal cost per unit" mean? Why does it change as it does as output increases?

3. Acme Widget Ltd. sells widgets at a price of $22 each. Acme's fixed and variable production costs are indicated in the following table:

Units of output per day	Fixed costs	Variable costs	Total costs	Average cost per unit	Average revenue per unit	Marginal cost per unit	Marginal revenue per unit
0	$200	$ 0	$	$ __	$ __	$ __	$ __
10	200	170					
20	200	320					
30	200	440					
40	200	580					
50	200	800					
60	200	1100					

(a) Complete the 5 remaining columns in the table.

(b) Draw the average cost per unit and marginal cost per unit and average revenue per unit and marginal revenue per unit curves on the following graph.

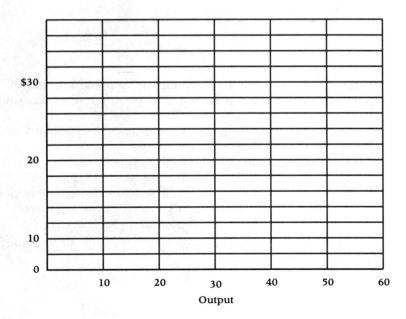

(c) Use the graph in (b) above to determine the following:

(i) The level of output at which profits will be maximized is _____ units per day.

(ii) At this level of output, the level of profits will be $_____ per day. (Show your calculation of the level of profits.)

(d) Is Acme Widget Ltd. operating in a perfectly competitive market? If this firm is in a perfectly competitive industry and is a typical firm which is making profits, what adjustment will occur in the price of the product, and how will this affect the profits of this typical firm? What will be the final equilibrium level of the price?

4.

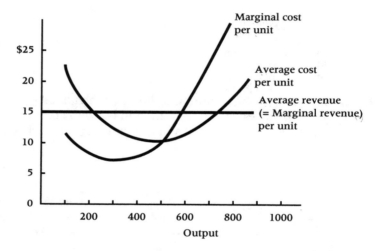

For the firm whose costs and revenues are shown in the graph,

(a) profits will be maximized at a level of output of _____ units, and

(b) at this level of output, profits will be $_____. (show your calculations)

(c) Is this firm operating in a perfectly competitive market? If this firm is in a perfectly competitive industry and is a typical firm which is making profits, what adjustment will occur in the price of the product, and how will this affect the profits of this typical firm? What will be the final equilibrium level of the price?

5. Following are the cost and revenue data for the Phaultless Fradistat Company:

If the company charges this price per fradistat:	It will sell this many fradistats per week:
$38.00	0
33.50	20
29.00	40
24.50	60
20.00	80
15.50	100
11.00	120

The company's fixed costs and variable costs are shown in the following table.

Units of output per week	Fixed costs	Variable costs	Total costs	Average cost per unit	Average revenue per unit	Marginal cost per unit	Marginal revenue per unit
0	$400	$ 0	$	$ __	$ __	$ __	$ __
20	400	180					
40	400	330					
60	400	430					
80	400	560					
100	400	780					
120	400	1080					

(a) Complete the 5 remaining columns in the table.
(b) Draw the average cost per unit and marginal cost per unit and average revenue per unit and marginal revenue per unit curves on the following graph:

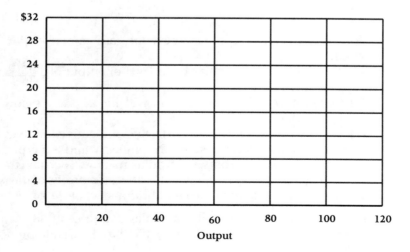

(c) Use the graph in (b) above to determine the following:
  (i) The level of output at which profits will be maximized is _____ units per week.
  (ii) At this level of output, the level of profits will be $_____ per week. (Show your calculation of the level of profits.)
(d) Is the Phaultless Fradistat Company operating in a perfectly competitive market? If this firm is operating in a perfectly competitive industry and is a typical firm which is making profits, what adjustment will occur in the price of the product and the profits of this typical firm? What would be the final equilibrium level of the price?

6.

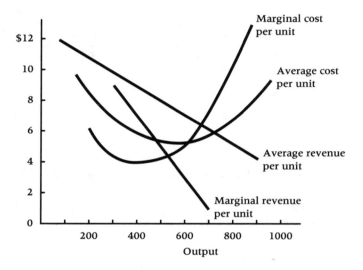

For the firm whose costs and revenues are shown in the above graph,
(a) profits will be maximized at a level of output of _____ units, and
(b) at this level of output, profits will be $_____. (Show your calculations.)
(c) Is this firm operating in a perfectly competitive market? If this firm is in a perfectly competitive industry and is a typical firm which is making profits, what adjustment will occur in the price of the product, and how will this affect the profits of the typical firm? What will the final equilibrium level of the price be?

7. Kermit's Kadiddles Ltd. sells kadiddles at a price of $8 each. Following is a table showing Kermit's fixed and variable production costs.

Units of output per day	Fixed costs	Variable costs	Total costs	Total revenue
0	$400	$ 0		
100	400	1000		
200	400	1700		
300	400	2200		
400	400	2500		
500	400	3200		
600	400	4400		

(a) Complete the remaining 2 columns in the table.

(b) On the graph below, draw the total revenue, total costs and variable costs curves.

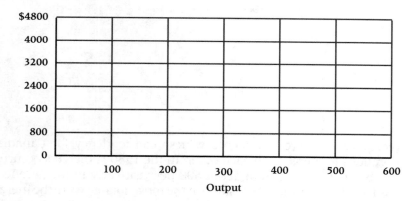

(c) The graph indicates that the minimum level of output (sales) required for this firm to start up in business (its break-even point) is _____ units per day.

(d) The graph indicates that, before this firm should go out of business, its sales should fall below a level of _____ units per day.

Explain the reasons for your answers to (c) and (d).

CHAPTER 12

Industrial concentration: Is big bad or better?

In recent years, there has been a widespread tendency for Canadian corporations to merge with each other. In the 1980's, mergers occurred at a record pace, rising from about 600 per year early in the decade to 938 in 1986 and 1082 in 1987. Some of the most notable were the merger of the Molson and Carling O'Keefe breweries, the purchase of Texaco by Imperial Oil, the takeover of Wardair by Canadian Airlines International (itself the product of an earlier purchase of Canadian Pacific Airlines by PWA Corp.) and Dofasco's acquisition of Algoma Steel. Partly as a result of this trend, a small number of corporations own an unusually large proportion of Canadian industry.[1]

Some of this ownership takes the form of *conglomerates*, which (as we saw in Chapter 5) control companies in a variety of industries rather than dominate a particular industry. However, in recent years, corporate strategists have increasingly favored a narrower focus on industries with which they are familiar. As a result, most mergers have involved an increasing *domination of particular industries or markets by a few firms* (as discussed in Chapter 10). For instance, the Molson-Carling O'Keefe merger gave the newly formed company 53 percent of the beer market, the Wardair acquisition gave PWA nearly half the airline market, the merger of Imperial Oil and Texaco resulted in a market share of over 30

---

[1] In 1985, Canada's 25 largest corporations owned 34 percent of the country's non-financial assets (that is, excluding assets of financial firms such as banks, trust companies or insurance companies). In the United States, the same share of total assets is spread more widely, among about 100 corporations.

HOSTILE TAKEOVERS AND POISON PILLS

While many corporate mergers occur with the blessing of the management and Boards of Directors of both companies involved, that is not always the case. Sometimes a company is the subject of a "hostile takeover" bid, in which its management and Board are opposed to the merger. In such cases, the company attempting the takeover may buy up the other company's shares on the stock market, or make a direct offer to its shareholders for their shares, over the objections of the management and Board of that company. If over half of the company's voting shares can be acquired in this way, the company falls under the control of the purchaser and a "hostile takeover" is completed.

To discourage hostile takeovers, some companies have introduced what is known as a "poison pill" plan. Under a typical poison pill plan, if any outside company (known as a "predator") acquires more than 20 percent of the company's stock without the approval of its Board, existing stockholders are given the opportunity to buy additional shares at half price. The result would be a large increase in the volume of shares outstanding, which would greatly increase the cost of acquiring the 50 percent of the shares needed to achieve control of the company. By making it prohibitively expensive to acquire control, the poison pill is intended to discourage anyone from attempting a hostile takeover.

percent, and Dofasco's merger with Algoma made it the largest steel-maker in Canada and the fourth largest in all of North America.

Industrial concentration

To the extent that a particular industry or market is dominated by a few firms, it is said to be **concentrated**. The Canadian economy has quite a high degree of concentration—higher than the US economy. This domination of much of Canada's economy by large corporations is viewed with concern by some, especially consumer groups and unions, who see in it a dangerous increase in monopoly power in certain sectors of the economy. On the other hand, defenders of mergers such as those just described argue that they will increase prosperity by making industry more efficient and better able to compete internationally.

In this chapter, we will consider the reasons for the high degree of industrial concentration in Canada, arguments that such concentration is both bad and good for Canadians and the important question of what government policy toward industrial concentration and mergers should be.

Reasons for concentration

There are several reasons why some industries come to be dominated by a few large firms. Probably the simplest reason is the *elimination of firms by competition*: those firms that are able to gain advantages in production costs and sales tend to expand, gaining further advantages from their ability to use mass-production techniques not available to their competitors, who fall by the wayside. Many industries that now have comfortable oligopolistic pricing arrangements were not always that way—in their early years, ruthless competition was often the rule, and the weak were eliminated. Another reason for industrial concentration is that modern production technology often establishes a *large minimum efficient size* for plants and operations: with large plants and facilities required by technology, there will only be room in the industry for relatively few firms. This is believed to be particularly true for Canada, because the small size of the Canadian market effectively limits the number of firms that can operate in many industries.

Finally, we must return to *mergers*, which often reflect the tendency of business to seek to reduce competition in their industries. Especially since the late 1960's, mergers have been a popular way for many businesses to expand. Some observers believe that mergers have increased in frequency because of the generally slower economic growth since the mid-1970's: if the market for an industry is growing slowly, the more aggressive firms in it will likely seek to buy other firms' capacity rather than build new capacity. The merger strategy is made more attractive if the stock prices of the takeover targets are depressed, as was often the case in the late 1970's and first half of the 1980's.

More recently, *changes in the international economic environment* have contributed to increased merger activity in Canada. The 1980's saw a trend toward increased international competition, or the **globalization** of some markets. This trend, together with the Canada-US Free Trade Agreement, not only created more intense foreign competition for many Canadian industries, but also expanded export opportunities for Canadian firms. To improve their ability to compete with their often-larger foreign counterparts in the USA and Europe, some Canadian firms merged with others, so as to gain economies of scale, more complete product lines, stronger marketing networks, better access to financial resources and so on. For instance, the Molson-Carling O'Keefe merger was expected to increase the efficiency and capacity of the company's Canadian brewing operations while giving it access to the worldwide distribution network of Elders IXL Ltd., Carling's Australian parent company. Elders, for its part, wanted access to Molson's extensive US distribution network for the marketing of its own beers, including Foster's. (This prompted Canada Malting Ltd. to purchase a rival US malt producer in order to be able to supply the increasingly global operations of the brewing industry.) PWA's acquisition of Wardair not only made it almost as large as Air Canada, but also added several important international routes to PWA's (Canadian Airlines International's) offerings, making it a more effective player in international airline markets. Similarly, Dofasco's merger with Algoma Steel made it the fourth largest steelmaker in North America, while giving it an expanded and balanced product line that was expected to position the company well for competing in the US market under the Free Trade Agreement.

The public interest

For whatever reasons, Canadian industry, especially manufacturing, is more concentrated than in other countries. Under these circumstances, it cannot be assumed that competition will automatically keep prices and profits in check; indeed, there is a real possibility that the oligopolists will act together so as to reduce competition among themselves. This raises the question of what government policy should be regarding industrial concentration and bigness in business. In the following sections, we will consider two opposing viewpoints on this matter: first, the view that "big is bad," and second, the view that "big can be better." Finally, we will examine how Canadian policy attempts to deal with the difficult question of bigness in business in general, and corporate mergers in particular.

The traditional view

The traditional view that big business is bad is based on some familiar facts: in cases where a few firms dominate an industry, they can band together to avoid competition, raise prices and restrict the supply of the product so as to maintain high prices and profits. If demand is inelastic, the consumer must continue to buy even at higher prices, redistributing income away from the general public in favor of the corporations and their wealthy shareholders. This view is supported by the profits earned

> People of the same trade seldom meet together, even for merriment and diversion, but the conversation ends in a conspiracy against the public, or in some contrivance to raise prices.
>
> Adam Smith, *The Wealth of Nations* (1776)

by many oligopolists: while the *average* after-tax rate of return on capital invested in business is about 10 to 12 percent, for many oligopolists it is 12 to 20 percent, or one and a half to two times the average. While not all oligopolists earn such profits, the fact that many do supports the argument that industrial concentration results in price-fixing.

How much does price-fixing increase prices?

This is a difficult question to answer, because it requires that we know (or estimate) how much lower the prices of an oligopolistic industry *would have been* if the industry were competitive rather than oligopolistic. However, it is possible to at least make an estimate of the extent to which oligopolistic practices inflate the prices of products, using some simple theory and research.

The theory is illustrated in Figure 12-1, which shows the difference between the components of a competitive price (the price that would prevail under highly competitive conditions) and an oligopolistic price. As Figure 12-1 shows, the competitive price consists of only the cost of producing (and distributing) the product plus a minimal profit for the producer, due to the strong price competition in the industry. The oligopolistic price is higher than the competitive price, for two reasons:

(a) oligopolists' *profits* are higher than those of competitive producers, because oligopolists avoid price competition, and

(b) oligopolists tend to spend much more money than competitive firms on *advertising* and other forms of non-price competition, as a substitute for price competition, which they avoid.

While this tells us *why* oligopolistic prices tend to be higher than competitive prices, it does not answer the key question of *how much* higher they are. To determine this, we would have to find a product that is sold under both competitive and oligopolistic conditions, and compare the prices.

The closest approximation to this is provided by the house brand or private label products sold by many supermarkets. In many cases, these goods are of equal quality (or are identical to) the brand name products sold by the manufacturer at considerably higher prices. The prices of the private label products are lower for two reasons: they do not include the heavy advertising costs for the brand name products, and the supermarket is able to use its buying power to eliminate most or all of the extra profit included in the price of the brand name product. In other words, the brand name product provides an example of an oligopolistic price, while the corresponding private label product—by eliminating the additional two components of the oligopolistic price in Figure 12-1— provides a reasonable estimate of a competitive price for the same product.

FIGURE 12-1 *Competitive and Oligopolistic Prices Compared*

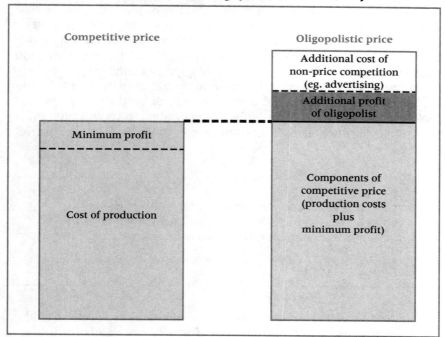

Studies of house and brand name prices showed wide variations in the amount by which the oligopolistic price exceeded the competitive price—from 17 percent on some products to 48 percent on others. On the average, however, the prices of the oligopolistic brand name products tended to be about 25 percent higher than the prices of the private label products. In situations where manufacturers practise resale price maintenance,[2] researchers have estimated that prices will be 35 to 40 percent higher than competitive levels.

It must be recognized that this research relates only to specific products and markets and cannot be used as the basis for generalizations about *all* oligopolistic industries; however, it is indicative of the effect that oligopolistic practices can have on prices.

Other criticisms

Failure to compete on prices is not the only point of criticism of oligopolistic corporations. Critics of big business also point out that a further

---

[2] A practice which allows the manufacturer to dictate the consumer price to the retailer, thereby eliminating price competition at the retail level as well as at the manufacturer's level. Resale price maintenance is illegal in Canada.

economic consequence of prices being higher is that *output* will necessarily be *lower* than under competitive conditions, placing a double burden on the consumer and reducing employment in oligopolistic industries. Furthermore, the critics add, the same forces that lead oligopolists to avoid competition on price also lead to lack of competition regarding *product quality*; consequently, oligopolistic industries often produce products of poor quality. Commonly cited examples include breakfast cereals, automobiles, and a wide variety of products with *planned obsolescence* built in, from light bulbs to major appliances. All such practices, while detrimental to the consumer, are profitable for the industries involved.

> (Mergers) reduce Canadian competition, raise prices for consumers and cause job losses. I can't see how any of those things in any way benefit Canadians or the economy.
>
> David McKendry, Consumers Association of Canada

It is also argued that industrial concentration results in an *inequitable distribution of income*. Most oligopolistic industries, especially in manufacturing, are unionized. Often, the employers grant their unionized employees above-average wage increases in response to union pressure, and pass the increased costs on to the consumer through higher prices. Over the years, this has raised the wages of workers in some such industries to quite high levels, at the expense of consumers. In effect, it can be argued that oligopolistic industries are pockets of economic power in which unionized workers *and* employers exercise monopoly power to the benefit of *both* of them and at the expense of the rest of society.[3] It is also argued that this situation contributes to *inflation*, as unions press for large wage increases and employers grant them and increase prices rather than take a costly strike.

Other critics argue that big business tends to slow down *technological progress*, because entrenched power groups such as oligopolists are conservative, having little interest in promoting significant changes of any sort. These critics believe not only that the bureaucracies of large corporations are ill-suited to promoting technological progress, but also that some oligopolists have suppressed innovations and inventions that threatened their interests.

Other lines of criticism are concerned with the more general effects of big business on the economy, on society and on the political process.

---

[3] A good example of this is the automotive industry. At the start of the 1980's, wages in the auto industry were roughly 50 percent higher than the industrial average, *and* the companies had been earning well above-average profits.

> Canadians are in danger of becoming tenants in their own nation to a few industrial landlords.
>
> Shirley Carr, President, Canadian Labour Congress

One concern is that, through sophisticated advertising, large corporations have the power to manipulate the consumer to their advantage, creating *producer sovereignty* in place of consumer sovereignty and thus calling the whole market system into question. Some critics stress the social dangers of such concentrated power, arguing that society's values are in large part shaped by its organizations, and that big business' economic power has not been matched by a sense of *social responsibility*. This argument is backed up with examples such as the pollution problem and auto safety, the basic point being that power must be accompanied by responsibility, and that such responsibility has too often been lacking.

Finally, and most broadly, there is the concern regarding the *political implications* of bigness in business, raising the danger that, in some cases, the government may act in the best interests of large, powerful and wealthy corporations rather than in the interests of the public. The importance of big business gives it a voice in the policy deliberations of governments by practical necessity, often backed up by well-financed political lobbies operated on behalf of major corporations.

A summary

The traditional view of bigness in business can be summarized as follows: there is a strong tendency for business activity in many industries to be concentrated in a few firms, which are then in a position to restrict supply and raise both prices and profits. Price competition is replaced by the less dangerous (but more costly to the consumer) practice of competition through advertising and superficial product differentiation. These practices, together with price-fixing, tend to inflate oligopolists' prices and profits considerably above competitive levels. In effect, oligopolistic industries can become bastions of economic power within the economy which extract excessive prices from consumers for the economic benefit of their shareholders, managers, and employees, all of whom tend to gain from the situation.

According to the traditional view, since competition cannot be relied upon to keep prices and profits in check in such industries, the government must set down rules for oligopolists to follow and must police their behavior. In particular, governments must prevent price-fixing and other measures that reduce competition, and must prevent mergers of companies where these would reduce competition, even breaking up excessively dominant corporations, if necessary, into smaller firms.

The traditional view challenged

Those who wish to defend big business against the charge of the traditional view that "big is bad" can begin by pointing out an important fact: while business may be bigger than ever, the consumer is prospering more than anyone would expect according to the traditional view. If this is exploitation, it is the most enjoyable form of exploitation ever devised. This raises the possibility that some of the criticisms of big business are not accurate, or that bigness in business can bring economic benefits as well as harm to the consumer. The challenge to the traditional view that "big is bad" generally takes the form of three broad arguments:

(a) Many of the criticisms of big business are not accurate.

(b) Big business is the source of significant economic benefits for society.

(c) The power of big business is exaggerated, and is subject to many limitations.

(a) Inaccurate criticisms

Many arguments against big business are vaguely phrased and tend to appeal to emotions rather than logic. For example, critics often speak of profits in dollar terms—it sounds very impressive to hear that International Reemistrams earned a profit of $63 million last year. But if shareholders' capital is $900 million, the rate of return on shareholders' investment was only 7 percent—less than they could have earned on government bonds, which also involve less risk. When critics attack profits, they never point out the fact that manufacturers' profits are generally 4 or 5 cents per sales dollar (considerably less than the sales taxes levied by governments).

Another very important point is that it is not the *level* of profits that matters so much as the *uses* made of those profits. For example, which makes the greater contribution to society: a corporation that makes a profit of 8 percent on shareholders' capital and pays it all out to shareholders as dividends, or one that makes a profit of 16 percent and uses most of it for research and development and capital investment, which boosts productivity and creates new jobs? Critics of big business demand more employment and lower prices, but ignore the role played by profits in financing the heavy capital investment (over $200 000 per job created, in many industries) required to achieve these goals.

Finally, many observers question the very relevance of the old concept of capitalists exploiting the public in today's economy, as a significant and growing proportion of the shares of major corporations are owned by the pension funds of Canadians. In other words, a wide range of Canadians have an important, albeit indirect, stake in the success of Canada's major corporations.

In conclusion, it is not accurate to generalize concerning criticisms of

> The showpieces [of American industrial achievement] are, with rare exceptions, the industries which are dominated by a handful of large firms. The foreign visitor, brought to the United States to study American production methods and associated marvels, visits the same firms as do attorneys of the Department of Justice in their search for monopoly.
>
> John Kenneth Galbraith, *American Capitalism*
> (Boston: Houghton Mifflin Company, 1952).
> Copyright J.K. Galbraith 1952, 1956.
> Reprinted by permission of Houghton Mifflin Company.

Industrial concentration: Is big bad or better?

big business and profits. While there are obviously cases of excessive corporate power and profits, it is not fair to assume that this applies to all large corporations, and that big is therefore by nature bad.

(b) Contribution to prosperity

Probably the most important argument that can be made in defence of big business is that it actually contributes to the economic prosperity of society. In particular, this argument emphasizes the productive uses of the profits of big business, such as *capital investment, improved technology* and *research and development*. According to this view, the modern large corporation can serve as an instrument of technological progress, the results of which are *higher productivity* (output per worker) and a higher standard of living due to the more efficient use of resources made possible by improving technology. This helps explain the paradox of the prosperous consumer in a world of big business: while big business may make higher profits, it can also generate *higher productivity* and increased prosperity for society. A related defence of bigness in business is that the *mass-production technology* that benefits the consumer requires large plants and thus large corporations to raise the necessary capital and administer the operations. For instance, only big businesses can function in industries such as automobiles, steel, aircraft, international banking, and many others.

It can also be pointed out that large corporations are generally *more stable* than smaller businesses. Particularly during recessions, larger corporations are more able to ride through the bad times without massive layoffs than are smaller businesses. It can, therefore, be argued that big business adds an element of increased stability to both employment and income levels.

A final argument in favor of larger-scale businesses in Canada is that much of Canada's manufacturing industry is relatively small-scale and inefficient and hence not competitive internationally. Thus, many economists believe that fewer but larger manufacturing corporations in Canada would contribute to the nation's efficiency and *international competitiveness*, a point to which we will return later in this chapter.

Canada is a small market with relatively low growth. If you want to grow your business and your earnings, you have to acquire a new business or look beyond national boundaries— and maybe put your marbles together with someone else.

Mike Jamani, mergers and acquisitions partner,
Woods Gordon/Clarkson Gordon,
in *The Financial Post*, Jan. 23, 1989, p. 1.

(c) Limits on oligopolists' power

While the domination of any industry by a few firms creates the *potential* for excessive oligopolistic power, there are a variety of limitations on this power that come into play, reducing significantly the power *actually* exercised by oligopolists. Some of these limitations have been discussed in Chapter 10; however, it is worth reviewing them briefly here.

Defenders of big business argue that its critics seem to assume that oligopolists are always able to establish comfortable price-fixing arrangements that ensure high profits. This view, they claim, underestimates the importance of *competition* as a factor limiting oligopolists' power over prices. In defense of big business, it is argued that the Canadian economy, particularly its manufacturing sector, is exposed to considerable *foreign competition*, which keeps prices and profits in check. Furthermore, it is argued, foreign competition can be expected to intensify in the future due to the Free Trade Agreement with the United States and the general trend toward the globalization of markets. Many economists believe that successful oligopolistic price-and-output agreements are essentially temporary in nature, as their high profits will attract new competitors into the field. An outstanding example of this tendency is the North American automobile industry, which was for years regarded as a classic example of oligopoly, but has in the more recent past come under heavy competition from foreign manufacturers, especially the Japanese. Competition can also arise from *new products or technologies*: for instance, the success of the international tin cartel in maintaining high prices for tin was eventually undermined by the development of other materials, such as aluminum and plastics, as substitutes for tin. Such competition has the effect of making the demand for the oligopolists' products more elastic, undermining their ability to maintain high prices.

Another factor that can limit oligopolists' power is *lack of cooperation* among them: in particular, when business is slow, there is the temptation for individual firms to chisel on their pricing agreements with competitors, in order to gain sales. Also, conspiracies to fix prices and lessen competition unduly are *illegal*, so corporations and their executives engaging in such practices risk prosecution. While we will see that this risk is relatively low, it can still be argued that it places a limitation on the practices of big business.

Another factor that restrains pricing policies is the large corporation's *desire for growth*. Traditional economic theory assumes that the only objective of business is to maximize profits, but the actual situation is not so simple. Most large corporations place a high value on growth of the corporation, but this in turn requires rising sales. They may, therefore, deliberately adopt a pricing policy that does not maximize either prices or profits, but rather strives to boost sales. In other words, they may possess the power to raise prices further, but decide not to use it.

The previous point is related to the modern large corporation's *desire to maintain a good public image*. In an era of consumerism and increased government action regarding business practices, many large corporations are reluctant to risk the bad publicity associated with prosecutions for price-fixing, false advertising, shoddy products and so on. In short, corporations may be restricted in their freedom of action by the attitudes and values of the society in which they operate. Many responsible business leaders feel that unless business behaves responsibly and earns more support from the general public, it is likely that government regulations and intervention will continue to expand, with undesirable effects not only on business, but also on the performance of the economy generally.

Still another limitation on the power of big business is provided by the fact that big corporations are not the only economic power group in society. Not only are there other such groups, but their power sometimes offsets, or limits, the economic power of big business. This is the **theory of countervailing power** developed by economist John kenneth Galbraith. He argues that bigness in business is not always bad for the public, because it may be offset by other economic power groups. For example, the power of large oligopolistic manufacturers over the consumer may be offset in part by the great buying power of the large chain store. The sale of private label products at prices held down by the purchasing power of the supermarket chains, discussed earlier in this chapter, suggests that there could be truth to this argument. Similarly, farmers' cooperatives can use their collective purchasing power to drive down the cost of farm machinery produced by large oligopolists, and can offset to a degree the buying power of the food processing corporations. Another example is labor unions, which tend to offset the effects of the economic power of large corporations in dealing with their employees. To the extent that economic power blocs offset each other rather than use their power against a disorganized and largely defenceless public, those economic power blocs are not damaging the public interest. The essence of this argument, then, is that the key question is not whether private economic power *exists*, but rather in what ways it is *used*—to offset other economic power or against the public interest.

Finally, there are natural limits on the size of businesses, due to the fact that an excessively large organization tends to become impossible to manage—the so-called "dinosaur effect." While many businesses appear on paper to be vast, centrally controlled organizations, in practice they are not. Usually their operations and decision-making are quite decentralized. The best examples of this are General Motors, with its many semi-independent divisions, and the conglomerates: corporate empires owning businesses in many industries, with each business operating quite independently rather than under the direct control of its parent company. Thus, organizational factors can make big business quite different from the vast, centralized, monolithic decision-making power center that it appears to be.

The policy dilemma

The arguments against and in favor of bigness in business present government authorities with a very real dilemma in deciding government policy toward industrial concentration: while bigness in business can certainly pose a *threat* to the welfare of consumers, it can also provide society with significant economic *benefits*. To do nothing to prevent abuses of oligopolistic power would expose consumers to exploitation by corporations possessing monopolistic powers, while to mount an all-out attack on big business would risk depressing capital investment and productivity, to the detriment of society generally. The government must try to decide, then, how far it can go in policing the antisocial behavior of oligopolists without losing the economic benefits that such large corporations bring to society.

The Canadian dilemma

This dilemma is especially troublesome in Canada, where industrial concentration is higher than in other countries, but many Canadian companies are not internationally competitive because they are smaller than their competitors in other nations. This contradictory situation was highlighted in the Macdonald Commission Report in 1978, which found that

(a) the average size of Canada's 100 largest non-financial corporations and Canada's 25 largest financial corporations is very much smaller than the average size of their counterparts in the USA and other developed countries; and

(b) industrial concentration in Canada is substantially higher than in comparable industries in the USA.

Only four Canadian corporations (George Weston Limited, Ford, General Motors of Canada Limited and Imperial Oil Limited) were on a list of the 100 largest non-financial corporations in the world. Clearly, Canadian firms in all categories are much smaller than their counterparts in the United States and other countries.

Report of the Royal Commission
on Corporate Concentration, 1978 (page 25).

*Industrial
concentration: Is
big bad or better?*

In other words, corporations that are sufficiently large to dominate markets and threaten consumers' welfare *within* Canada are small by world standards, and can only become *internationally* competitive by growing larger, and presumably more dominant here at home. These facts make the policy dilemma referred to earlier particularly severe for Canadian policy-makers: while industrial concentration is presently high enough to support the argument for strong laws restricting further growth and concentration, policies that do so could prevent Canadian corporations from growing to the size needed to be internationally competitive. And, unless the Canadian manufacturing sector becomes more competitive internationally, economic prosperity and employment in Canada will continue to be depressed by weak export performance and a strong tendency to import manufactured goods rather than produce them domestically.

Under these circumstances, the setting of government policy regarding industrial concentration is a very difficult task, leaving policy-makers open to criticism no matter what policy they choose. Either they will be criticized for exposing the public to powerful corporate interests, or they will be blamed for preventing Canadian industry from becoming more competitive internationally.

. . . the inevitable result of expansion of the large Canadian firms to the average size of the large world firms would involve a significant increase in industrial concentration in Canada, assuming that the larger firms remained primarily oriented to the Canadian market.

Report of the Royal Commission
on Corporate Concentration, 1978 (page 42).

Canadian policy toward big business

The Combines Investigation Act

Until 1986, the legislation governing restriction of competition by business firms in Canada was the Combines Investigation Act. First enacted in 1889 and largely unchanged since 1910, the Combines Investigation Act was intended to prevent actions by firms which "unduly lessen competition." More specifically, the law prohibited *agreements among producers* to fix prices, restrict output, or unduly restrict entry into an industry; *mergers* of firms that would unduly lessen competition, and a number of *restrictive trade practices* such as predatory price-cutting to eliminate competitors, misleading advertising, and resale price maintenance, whereby a producer dictates to retailers the selling price of a product.

While these laws appeared to cover most of the abuses of oligopolistic power, it was generally agreed that the Combines Investigation Act was largely ineffective, for a variety of reasons. Because violation of the Combines Investigation Act was a criminal offence, it was necessary for the prosecution to prove the charges beyond a reasonable doubt. Since most such agreements were made verbally between firms, it was extremely difficult to obtain the evidence necessary for a conviction. Furthermore, the law applied only to acts which *unduly* lessened competition, and the courts were reluctant to interpret this term broadly enough to apply to many cases. In the relatively few cases of convictions under the law, the fines levied were generally not very high. Finally, the law was particularly ineffective against *mergers*, making it possible for Canadian firms to take over other firms with virtually no legal restrictions.

In summary, the Combines Investigation Act made monopolistic practices illegal, but did relatively little to prevent them in practice. The weakness of the Act led to four different attempts at reforms during the 1971–85 period; however, little was achieved. The government would propose stronger measures against corporate mergers and anti-competitive practices, and then the business community would voice strong opposition to the proposals, causing them to be shelved pending further consideration. The business viewpoint was given weighty support by the 1978 Royal Commission on Corporate Concentration, which emphasized that, while corporate concentration posed certain threats to the interests of consumers, much of Canada's manufacturing sector consisted of firms that were small by international standards. Consequently, there was concern that laws based on the simple premise that "big is bad" could prevent Canadian firms from merging into larger enterprises that could be more competitive internationally. And in 1985, the Report of the Royal Commission on the Economic Union and Development Prospects for Canada (the Macdonald Commission) emphasized that, as a means of protecting the consumer, stronger foreign competition (such as would result from freer trade with the United States) would prove more effective and beneficial than tougher legislation placing legal limits on business.

Others disagreed strongly. They pointed out that important oligopolistic industries in Canada, such as retailing, banking and publishing, are not subject to much, if any, foreign competition. Such industries, they argued, would be free to take advantage of their economic power unless the government strengthened the law. It was also believed by many observers that stronger legislation was required to cover mergers.

As a result of these differing viewpoints, the government faced a particularly difficult task in developing new legislation to replace the Combines Investigation Act.

The changing economic environment

The Canadian government's search for new legislation was complicated by changes in the international economic environment. Historically, many government economic policies, in Canada as in other countries, had been geared to *national* markets. Two examples in Canada were its trade and competition policies.

Through its *trade policy*, government sought to foster the development of Canadian manufacturing industries by imposing tariffs to protect Canadian manufacturers against foreign competition. Thus, the government regulated *access to Canada's national market* by foreign producers. On the other hand, *competition policy* sought to protect Canadian consumers from price-fixing and other non-competitive practices by oligopolistic industries (many of which were, themselves, protected by the government against foreign competition). Thus, the government regulated the competitive behavior of businesses within Canada's national market.

However, in the 1970's and 1980's, important changes were occurring in the *international* economic environment that made the concept of gearing policies to national markets less relevant. As nations reduced tariffs and new international competitors such as Japan and Southeast Asia came onto the scene, international competition became more intense and markets became more international. The signing of the Canada-US Free Trade Agreement in 1989 left Canadian industry facing the prospect of growing US competition as tariffs were phased out, and plans for the complete economic integration of Europe into a single market of 325 million made it likely that North American producers would soon face stronger competition from larger and more efficient European firms. All of these trends toward the globalization of markets pushed policymakers away from thinking of their *national* markets, and toward *international* concerns, especially the *ability of their nation to compete* in global markets.

In short, competition legislation had always been based on the assumption that big corporations were in a strong economic position (in their national market) and that it was the role of the law to regulate their behavior and to protect consumers from them. Now, however, it was becoming necessary to also consider whether these corporations themselves were in a good position to compete with foreign producers (in international markets). This concern was particularly strong in Canada, where many industries faced tough foreign competition. The task of the government was to produce legislation that recognized both of these realities.

The 1986 Competition Act

In June 1986, the federal government passed legislation to replace the Combines Investigation Act. Under the new *Competition Act*, offences involving mergers and monopoly abuses such as price-fixing (renamed "abuses of dominant market position") became civil offences, making convictions much less difficult to obtain.

Under the Competition Act, the basic test was whether the effect of the firms' action would be (or had been) to *"Lessen competition substantially"* in a given market. That is, with respect to mergers, the key was not simply the size of the companies or their share of the market, but rather the effect of the proposed merger on competition in the marketplace.

In addition, the Act explicitly approved of mergers that would likely result in *efficiency gains* to offset any likely reduction in competition. This allowed companies to defend mergers that would increase their *ability to compete internationally*.

The Act is administered by the Bureau of Competition Policy, which is attached to the Ministry of Consumer and Corporate Affairs. The Bureau must be notified of any plan to merge or acquire businesses in which the total assets or total annual revenues of the firms exceeds $400 million. After notifying the Bureau, the parties must wait for 7 to 21 days before completing the merger.

The Bureau then reviews the proposed merger or acquisition, considering whether:

(a) it is likely to lessen competition substantially, and

(b) there are likely to be real gains in efficiency that will exceed, and offset, the lessening of competition.

Other factors to be considered include barriers to entry to the particular market (which would affect future competition), the extent of foreign competition, the effectiveness of the competition that would remain after the proposed merger and the availability of alternatives (such as an alternative buyer for all or part of a firm).

If the Bureau has concerns about the effect of the proposal on competition, it will seek to negotiate amendments. The Bureau can also grant

> The core of the policy is the likely effect of a proposed merger
> on competition, whether domestic or foreign.
>
> Professor William Stanbury,
> UBC Faculty of Commerce and Business Administration,
> in the *Financial Post*, February 18, 1988 (p. 16)

conditional approval for a merger, and then monitor the competitive conditions in the market following the merger.

Most concerns are successfully dealt with through negotiations; however, if the parties are unable to agree, the matter is taken to the Competition Tribunal for a decision. The Tribunal is chaired by a judge of the Federal Court of Canada, and consists of twelve members, including business and consumer authorities as well as judges. As noted, because the Competition Act is civil rather than criminal, convictions are easier to obtain than under the Combines Investigation Act. The Tribunal operates under the same procedural rules as a civil court and its decisions may be appealed to the Federal Court of Canada.

Experience with the Competition Act

Since the Competition Act is quite new, there has been considerable interest in its operation. From its passage in June 1986 until April 1989, the Bureau of Competition Policy completed examinations of 340 merger deals, or about 10 per month. Most of these were accepted without challenge by the Bureau. The Bureau decided to monitor 19 cases, and in 9 other cases, the Bureau convinced the parties through negotiation to restructure their proposals. In 7 other cases, the merger plans were voluntarily abandoned by the parties following objections by the Bureau; while the names of the companies involved were not revealed, it is reported that several of these plans involved large and well known firms. Only 4 cases were forwarded to the Tribunal for adjudication.

The most common type of negotiated settlement between the Bureau and the companies involved the sale of some assets to competitors in order to maintain competition in particular markets. For instance, the merger of General Foods and PepsiCo (Frito-Lay division) was approved only after they agreed to reduce their share of the potato chip market by selling certain brands and assets to another competitor. Similarly, when Weston Foods Ltd. wanted to sell off its Interbake Foods Ltd. biscuit business in 1987, it had to sell to two competing buyers rather than one as originally planned. And when Safeway bought the supermarket operations of Woodward Stores Ltd., Safeway had to agree to sell 12 Woodward Food Floor stores over a two-year period in six cities where the merger might reduce competition substantially. In the Imperial Oil-Texaco merger, the Tribunal rejected two separate proposals by Imperial for the sale of certain of Texaco's assets. Finally, Imperial agreed to sell various Texaco assets, including 638 gas stations across the country, mostly in market areas where competition would be reduced by the Imperial-Texaco merger.

Assessments of Canada's Competition Act

Generally, reaction to the new Competition Act has been favorable. Most economists prefer the new law's emphasis on economic and competitive factors to the previous law's focus on legalities involving criminal conspiracies. More specifically, the Competition Act is stronger than its predecessor in addressing the important issue of mergers and acquisitions.

The view was also emerging by the end of the 1980's that the new law was more effective than its predecessor in stopping price-fixing. The levying of a record fine ($400 000 each) against four commercial printing firms for bid-rigging enhanced the credibility of the Competition Act. This incident was followed, in the fall of 1989, by fines totalling $250 000 being incurred by five motorcycle companies and their industry association for agreeing to avoid price competition at trade shows.

Furthermore, leniency allowed under the Act towards mergers that would improve efficiency and the ability to compete with foreign firms was popular with the business community, and made the stronger provisions against mergers and price-fixing more acceptable.

This provision, however, was also a source of criticism of the new legislation. Under the Competition Act, some very large mergers have been approved that have resulted in very large domestic market shares for the companies involved: for instance, 53 percent of the beer market for Molson–Carling O'Keefe and nearly half of the domestic airline market for Canadian Airlines International/Wardair. The strongest objections have been expressed by consumer groups concerned about reduced competition in Canadian markets, and by labor unions concerned about layoffs as the merged companies move to increase efficiency and become more internationally competitive.

Considering the benefits for Canada of becoming more internationally competitive, most economists do not seem to favor the blocking of such mergers by the government. However, the fact remains that some of the merged companies will have enormous shares of the Canadian market. By the late 1980's there was a growing body of opinion that the government should move in such cases to protect consumers' interests by allowing a greater degree of foreign competition in industries where mergers had increased concentration greatly and where government regulations also prevented or limited foreign competition.

DEFINITIONS OF NEW TERMS

Industrial Concentration   The degree to which an industry is dominated by a few firms.

Globalization   A shift from national or continental markets to world markets.

Theory of Countervailing Power   The theory that there is sometimes a tendency for economic power groups to develop which offset the power of other economic power groups.

CHAPTER SUMMARY

1. The Canadian economy has a high degree of industrial concentration, higher than the USA and other nations.

2. Such industrial concentration is the result of several factors, including the elimination of firms by competition, the fact that the small size of the Canadian market leaves room for only a few plants of efficient size in some industries, and the tendency of firms to merge with or take over their competitors, sometimes for the purpose of increasing their ability to compete internationally.

3. The traditional view is that industrial concentration reduces competition and thus leads to higher prices, restriction of output, lower product quality, an excessive share of the economic pie for employees and investors in concentrated industries, a stifling of technological progress and innovation, manipulation of consumers by advertising, and excessive corporate influence on the political process.

4. The traditional view is challenged by those who argue that many criticisms of big business are emotional and do not stand up to analysis; that big business is not all-powerful, but rather is subject to a variety of limitations; and that big business generates significant economic benefits for society, mainly through capital investment and technological progress, which increase productivity and living standards.

5. The Combines Investigation Act, which was Canada's competition legislation for nearly a century, prohibited a variety of anti-competitive practices, but was not particularly effective, especially against mergers.

6. Determining an appropriate competition policy is a dilemma for Canada because, while industrial concentration is high, many Canadian industrial corporations tend to be small by international standards, and thus not competitive internationally in a world that

is becoming increasingly competitive. As a result, it can be argued not only that government policy should oppose and restrict mergers that would increase industrial concentration, but also that it is in Canada's interests for firms to merge so as to become more competitive internationally.

7. In 1986, the Combines Investigation Act was replaced by the Competition Act, which was intended to provide the public with better protection against anticompetitive behavior by firms enjoying a dominant position in the Canadian marketplace while allowing Canadian firms to merge for the purpose of increasing efficiency and thus improving their ability to compete internationally.

QUESTIONS

1. Some people argue that the theory of countervailing power, referred to in this chapter, can sometimes backfire. For instance, this can happen when large oligopolistic corporations *and* their employees' labor unions band together to overcharge the consumer for their mutual benefit. Can you think of any examples of such a situation?

2. Defenders of big business believe that large corporations *promote* technological progress, while critics argue that big businesses fail to promote technological progress effectively, and, at worst, deliberately *stifle* it. Which view do you believe is correct? Why?

3. Do you believe that the effect of advertising by large corporations is so powerful that it poses a threat to consumer sovereignty? Why or why not?

4. Has the international competitiveness of Canadian manufacturing improved or not in recent years? Why?

5. Collect a file of newspaper articles concerning recent mergers of Canadian companies. Does it seem to you that these are geared toward improving the companies' ability to compete internationally (either through increased export sales or through better ability to compete with imports), or do they seem to be aimed at increasing the companies' dominance of the Canadian market?

6. Because the Competition Act allows mergers that result in increased efficiency, there is concern that some firms will become too powerful in the Canadian market. Under these circumstances, it is important that such firms be deterred from abusing their power. Watch the newspapers for articles on prosecutions for price-fixing under the Competition Act, and for moves by the government to allow increased foreign competition in industries such as brewing and airlines, where government regulations have protected Canadian firms from foreign competition.

CHAPTER 13

Labor markets and labor unions

In the past few chapters, we have examined markets for goods and services: how prices are determined in these markets by supply and demand, and how they are affected by various conditions ranging from highly competitive situations to monopolistic ones. *Markets for labor* also exist, in which the supply of various occupational skills interacts with employers' demand for labor to determine the wages and salaries[1] (prices) of different types of labor. As in markets for products, there are some labor markets in which the sellers (workers) are highly organized, such as unionized skilled trades and some professional groups. These groups regulate entry into their trade or profession much as a monopolist would restrict the supply of a product. By contrast, other labor markets are highly competitive, consisting of numerous unorganized sellers (workers), such as most service-industry and white-collar workers, computer programmers and student labor: in these markets, there are no unions to influence workers' incomes. Between these extremes, however, lie a considerable number of Canadian workers who belong to labor unions that have only limited powers to influence their wages.

It is through these labor markets that the incomes of Canadians, and the fundamentally important question of how the economic pie will be divided up, are determined. In examining labor markets, we will consider first the non-union sector of the economy, then the unionized sector.

The non-union sector

The non-union sector of the labor force embraces a wide variety of people, including the self-employed, managers, most office workers,

---

[1] By "wages and salaries" we mean the entire compensation package of employees, including all fringe benefits as well as financial remuneration.

most service-industry employees (ranging from banking and department stores to small-scale service firms such as restaurants and retail shops) and many part-time workers in a variety of occupations.

The incomes of these groups, and of individuals within each group, are determined by a variety of complex factors; however, certain generalizations can be made. Broadly speaking, in the non-union sector, the forces determining wages and salaries are the *supply of* and *demand for* various types of labor, as shown in Figure 13-1. The supply of a particular type of labor (for instance, fradistat formers) depends on a number of factors, such as the abilities, training and preferences of potential workers; also, as the shape of the supply curve shows, higher wages will attract more of these potential workers to actually offer their services to employers.

FIGURE 13-1 *The Market for Fradistat Formers*

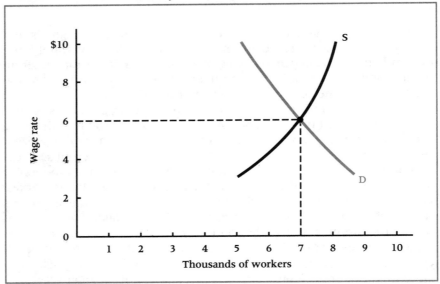

The demand for fradistat formers is a *derived demand*, because it is dependent on, or derived from, the demand for fradistats. Obviously, the higher the demand for fradistats, the higher the demand for fradistat formers. However, other factors such as technological change will affect the demand for fradistat formers, by altering the number of workers needed to produce a given volume of fradistats.

Finally, as the shape of the demand curve in Figure 13-1 shows, the number of workers actually demanded by employers will depend to a significant extent on the wages of those workers—at higher wages, it will not be economical to hire as many fradistat formers as at lower wages. Thus, a variety of factors underlie the demand and supply curves that determine the wage rate for fradistat formers and other non-union workers. As we will see, these supply and demand factors are capable of generating a tremendous range of incomes, from extremely high incomes for some to poverty-level wages for others.

Labor markets

Labor markets perform the important role of allocating labor to various occupations according to the demand of employers and, ultimately, consumers. In this role of allocating labor, *wages*—and changes in wages—play an important part. For instance, if the demand for fradistats increased, the demand for fradistat formers would increase, causing the demand curve to shift to the right, as shown in Figure 13-2. The result would be an increase in the wages of fradistat formers from $6 to $8 per hour, which would attract an additional 2000 people to accept jobs in this field. Thus, in response to increased consumer demand, employment in this industry has risen from 7000 to 9000, making possible increases in output, as desired by consumers.

FIGURE 13-2 *An Increase in the Demand for Fradistat Formers*

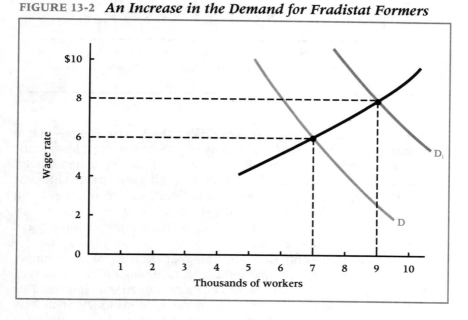

The more elastic the supply of labor, the more smoothly will the labor market operate. Figure 13-3 illustrates this by comparing the response of the market for clerical workers and the market for computer programmers to an identical increase in demand. In the case of clerical workers, homemakers provide a pool of qualified workers off the market but available for work, which makes the supply quite *elastic*—a relatively small increase in wages will attract many additional workers into the market. As a result, the increase in demand from D to D_1 causes a large increase in employment (from N_0 to N_1) and only a small increase in wages (from W_0 to W_1).

FIGURE 13-3 *Elasticity of Labor Supply and the Operation of Labor Markets*

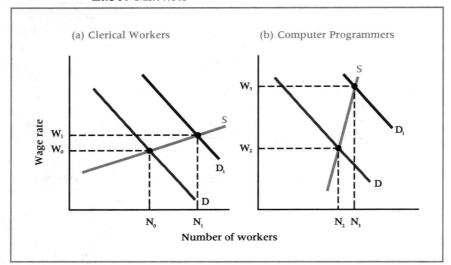

In the market for computer programmers, the reverse is true—due to the training period required, the supply of programmers (at least in the short run) is *inelastic*. As a result, the same increase in demand as for clerical workers has quite a different effect, causing only a small increase in employment (from N_2 to N_3) and a very large increase in wages (from W_2 to W_3). In the long run, the higher wages may attract additional people into computer programming; that is, the long-run supply curve may well be much more elastic.

These two examples not only illustrate that elasticity of labor supply is important to the smooth and efficient functioning of labor markets, but also point out the value of accurate labor requirement forecasts. Due to the training periods required for many occupations today, such forecasts would contribute greatly to economic prosperity. Unfortunately, it has proven extremely difficult to produce accurate forecasts of the changes in technology and demand that determine future labor requirements.

The dynamic nature of labor markets

Because of changes in underlying economic factors such as consumer demand, industrial technology and international competition, labor markets tend to be particularly dynamic. In the words of the Economic Council of Canada's *Twenty-Fifth Annual Review*,

> In the course of a working life that usually spans 40 years or more, most people change jobs several times; as the industrial structure changes, more of them will also change the type of work they do. Many will experience unemployment between jobs; many will need some retraining or some help in locating another job.

Because of this, governments provide a variety of programs designed to help workers adjust to changing job markets. Such programs range from the temporary income support provided by Unemployment Insurance to retraining and relocation assistance.

Income differentials

As mentioned earlier, the marketplace generates a tremendous range of incomes, from those of star athletes and entertainers to those of migrant farm workers and part-time student workers. In competitive markets, one might wonder why some of these income differentials exist and persist. Why, for instance, wouldn't more clerical workers be attracted by the salaries of computer programmers to become programmers, thus increasing the supply of programmers and reducing the income differential between them and clerical workers? The answer, of course, lies mainly in the fact that there are often *obstacles to entering certain occupations*.[2] Not everyone has the abilities and skills required to become a computer programmer, or the opportunity to pursue further education; so the income differentials between the two groups tend to persist. Similarly, the scarcity of people with the talents to be top athletes or entertainers, or people who will work in the far North, or people who will undertake dangerous jobs, causes their income to be very high compared to incomes for jobs that many people are able and willing to do.

Educational requirements are a major obstacle to entering certain occupations. Sometimes, educational requirements are based on specific knowledge that must be acquired in order to perform a job (such as accounting), while in other cases employers use educational requirements as a handy screening device for applicants (such as the requirement of a Bachelor of Arts degree for certain jobs). This latter example

---

[2] We will focus here on what might be called *natural* obstacles to entering certain occupations. Later, we will consider *artificial* obstacles, such as regulation of entry by labor unions and professional associations. These barriers are similar to the barriers to entry to industries described in Chapter 12, in that they reduce the numbers and increase the income in some fields.

illustrates the two aspects of education: in part, education involves the acquisition of certain skills required to do a job, and in part getting an education is a process of *making yourself more scarce* (relative to demand) in the labor market, so as to improve your prospects for earnings.

Because of the cost of higher education, *money* is sometimes an obstacle to some people entering certain occupations. For instance, medical and law schools are more accessible to the children of well-off families than poor families. Equality of educational opportunity is regarded as a fundamentally important social policy objective by many Canadians, since education is probably the main way for the children of lower-income families to break out of the "poverty trap." Still, individuals and groups who lack skills, education and experience are at a great disadvantage in labor markets, with most earning only low incomes.

Minimum wage legislation

The fact that some groups earn very low wages in an open labor market has led many governments to enact **minimum wage** legislation, setting legal minimums for wage rates so as to prevent exploitation of workers. While such legislation can raise the wages of some low-income workers. Figure 13-4 shows that it has the side effect of *increasing unemployment*. At an equilibrium wage rate of $2.50 per hour, 90 000 workers are employed, whereas at a legal minimum wage of $4 per hour, only 80 000 jobs exist (point A), because the higher wage rate reduces the number of workers employed. Furthermore, the higher wage rate attracts an additional 10 000 workers into the labor force, bringing the total to

According to Statistics Canada, in 1989 nearly 1 million Canadians, or about 8 percent of the labor force, worked for the minimum wage. The typical minimum-wage earner was under 25, and many were females working in the food service industry.

FIGURE 13-4 *The Effect of a Minimum Wage*

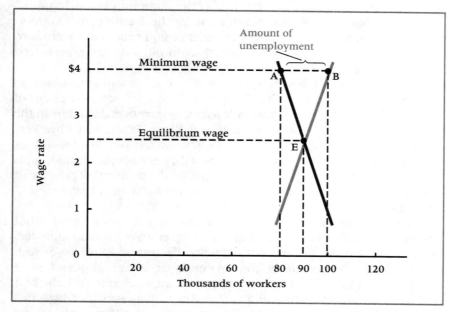

100 000 (point B), and total unemployment of this type of worker to 20 000 (the distance AB).

While there is little doubt that minimum wage laws do have a negative effect on employment, there is also considerable debate as to the extent of that effect. Generally, employers emphasize the negative aspects, while labor unions and other groups that support minimum wages argue that the drawbacks are minimal. To the extent that unemployment is increased by minimum wage legislation it probably indicates less hiring of new workers rather than layoffs of existing ones. Minimum wage laws create a sort of lottery, in which the winners are the workers who

This Commission fully accepts the important social objectives of minimum-wage legislation. Good intentions, however, do not necessarily lead to good policies. The evidence that disemployment resulted from the rapid increases in minimum wages of the 1970's suggests that Canadian governments should be careful in the future not to allow minimum wages to rise too quickly.

Royal Commission on the Economic Union and Development Prospects for Canada
(Ottawa, Minister of Supply and Services, 1985)

remain in jobs at the higher wages required by the law, while the losers are those who do not get jobs because of the minimum wage. In particular, researchers believe that minimum wages limit employment opportunities for *younger workers*, whose experience and productivity are low, and who must in many cases compete with older, more experienced workers for jobs.

While the extent of this *disemployment effect* is uncertain and subject to debate, the basic reality is that in order to lift low-wage earners out of poverty, *the legal minimum wage would have to be more than doubled* from the $4.50 to $5 per hour levels prevalent in the late 1980's. Few observers doubt that such increases in the minimum wage rate would have serious effects on the employment opportunities of the very people the minimum wage was intended to help. We will consider the problem of poverty in Canada, including other ways of assisting the poor, in subsequent chapters.

To summarize, in the non-union sector of the labor force, what amounts to "individual bargaining" between employees and employers decides employees' incomes and benefits. Each worker is free to seek the best deal he or she can get from an employer, and employers are free (subject to legislated rules such as minimum wage laws) to seek the best deal they can obtain from workers. The forces that determine how this bargaining process works out for the participants are the supply of and demand for various productive skills. If the demand for a particular type of skill is high and the supply is low, people with that skill will be able to obtain high incomes, whereas in the opposite situation, incomes will be low, because supply exceeds demand. The forces of supply and demand can, therefore, generate great differentials in incomes. Governments attempt to support the lowest incomes with minimum-wage laws; however, the ability of minimum-wage legislation to help the low-income group is limited by the fact that raising their wages has the side-effect of reducing their employment opportunities.

Unionized labor

In the unionized sector of the labor force, the situation is quite different. Individual bargaining is replaced by **collective bargaining**, in which a labor union negotiates with the employer on behalf of all the employees represented by the union. The bargaining relationship is thereby considerably altered, because while an individual bargaining on his or her own behalf can only resign as a last resort (and can perhaps be easily replaced, depending on his or her skills), a union can call a *strike* of all the employees it represents. As a result, unionized employees are often in a stronger position in negotiating with their employers.

In discussing labor unions, we move into one of the most controversial aspects of economics. Some people regard unions as saviors of the working people and others insist that they are devils, destroying the economic system and everyone with it. In fact, as we will see, neither label is justified; the actual role of labor unions is too complex to be summed up in a simple slogan.

Unions in Canada

As Figures 13-5 and 13-6 show, although total union membership in Canada has grown substantially since 1960, union membership as a percentage of the labor force has levelled off at around 30 percent since the mid-1970's.

FIGURE 13-5   *Union Membership 1960-88*

Year	Union membership (thousands)	Total non-agricultural paid workers (thousands)	Union membership as percentage of civilian labor force	Union membership as percentage of non-agricultural paid workers
1960	1459	4522	23.5%	32.3%
1961	1447	4578	22.6	31.6
1962	1423	4705	22.2	30.2
1963	1449	4867	22.3	29.8
1964	1493	5074	22.3	29.4
1965	1589	5343	23.2	29.7
1966	1736	5658	24.5	30.7
1967	1921	5953	26.1	32.3
1968	2010	6068	26.6	33.1
1969	2075	6380	26.3	32.5
1970	2173	6465	27.2	33.6
1971	2231	6637	26.8	33.6
1972	2388	6893	27.8	34.6
1973	2591	7181	29.2	36.1
1974	2732	7637	29.4	35.8
1975	2884	7817	29.8	36.9
1976	3042	8158	30.6	37.3
1977	3149	8243	31.0	38.2
1978	3278	8413	31.3	39.0
1980	3397	9027	30.5	37.6
1981	3487	9330	30.6	37.4
1982	3617	9264	31.4	39.0
1983	3563	8901	30.6	40.0
1984	3651	9220	30.6	39.6
1985	3666	9404	30.2	39.0
1986	3730	9893	29.7	37.7
1987	3782	10066	29.8	37.6
1988	3841	10483	29.6	36.6

Note: There was no survey conducted in 1979.

SOURCE Labour Canada, *Directory of Labour Organizations in Canada, 1988.*
Reproduced by permission of the Minister of Supply and Services Canada.

FIGURE 13-6 *Union Membership as a Percentage of the Civilian Labor Force, 1920-88*

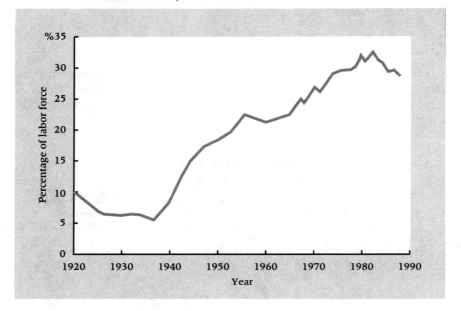

This 30-percent figure is not, however, an accurate indication of the *actual extent* of union influence in the Canadian economy, because many employees who are part of groups that are *represented* by unions have not actually *joined* a union by signing a membership card. Thus, the fact that about 30 percent of workers are union members understates the extent of union coverage, or representation, of the labor force. In fact, about 42 percent of the labor force is covered by union contracts.

The percentage of employees represented by unions is much higher in *plants* (nearly 75 percent) than in offices (less than 40 percent). Heavily

WOMEN IN UNIONS

In 1978, about 28 percent of Canada's union members were women. Ten years later, this figure had grown to more than 35 percent of union members—over 1.3 million. This growth of female union membership was attributed mostly to the more rapid growth of government unions, which include a larger proportion of women, than the "traditional" blue-collar manufacturing and skilled trades unions.

unionized sectors of the economy include public administration (with nearly 90 percent of government employees covered by union contracts), construction, transportation, manufacturing, communications, utilities, logging and mining. Generally, it is employees of *larger businesses* that tend to unionize—nearly 60 percent of employees in establishments with more than 20 employees are covered by union contracts, compared to 42 percent for the economy as a whole. Broadly speaking, unions have made relatively little progress in the small business sector, non-government offices, service industries, retail and wholesale trade and the financial sector, such as banks and insurance companies.

Union membership, like business activity in many industries, is quite *concentrated*: in 1988, the 16 largest unions in Canada accounted for 51 percent of total union membership. Some of Canada's largest unions are listed in Figure 13-7, which shows that unions of government employees are a particularly large component of organized labor in Canada.

By international standards, Canada's level of union membership is neither large nor small, falling between the USA's low level (about 18 percent of the labor force) and European levels of about 40-80 percent.

FIGURE 13-7   *Canada's Sixteen Largest Unions, 1988*

	1988 membership (thousands)
1. Canadian Union of Public Employees (CLC)	342.0
2. National Union of Provincial Government Employees (CLC)	292.3
3. Public Service Alliance of Canada (CLC)	175.7
4. United Food and Commercial Workers International Union (AFL-CIO/CLC)	170.0
5. United Steelworkers of America (AFL-CIO/CLC)	160.0
6. National Automobile, Aerospace and Agricultural Implement Workers Union of Canada (CLC)	143.0
7. Social Affairs Federation Inc. (CNTU)	96.5
8. International Brotherhood of Teamsters, Chauffeurs, Warehousemen and Helpers of America (AFL-CIO)	91.5
9. School Boards Teachers' Commission (CEQ)	75.0
10. Service Employees International Union (AFL-CIO/CLC)	70.0
11. Canadian Paperworkers Union (CLC)	69.0
12. United Brotherhood of Carpenters and Joiners of America (AFL-CIO)	66.0
13. International Brotherhood of Electrical Workers (AFL-CIO/CFL)	64.6
14. International Association of Machinists and Aerospace Workers (AFL-CIO/CLC)	58.5
15. Labourers' International Union of North America (AFL-CIO)	46.7
16. Ontario Nurses' Association (Ind.)	46.6

SOURCE Labour Canada, *Directory of Labour Organizations in Canada, 1988.*
Reproduced by permission of the Minister of Supply and Services Canada.

However, the growth of union membership in Canada since 1960 has been far more rapid than in most other countries, especially the United States. Most observers believe that this trend is largely the result of a more *favorable legislative environment* in Canada, where labor laws make it easier for unions to be certified (or voted into existence by employees) and place stronger limits on anti-union tactics by employers than American laws.

The stagnation of union growth

Figure 13-6 shows that, as a percentage of the labor force, union membership peaked at a level of about 30 percent in the mid-1970's. The main reason for the stagnation of union growth since then has been the slow growth of employment in the traditional union strongholds: the manufacturing sector and skilled trades. In these "goods-producing" sectors of the economy, the replacement of workers with machinery has slowed employment growth, as Figure 13-8 shows. Instead, employment has grown rapidly in the *services-producing sector* of the economy. Not only has the demand for services (from education to health care to entertainment and travel) grown briskly as living standards have risen, but also the service industries tend to be "labor-intensive"; that is, they lend themselves less to the use of technology than goods-producing industries such as manufacturing and mining.

In addition, many of the newly-created jobs in the services sector have been *part-time jobs* in industries such as retail trade and hospitality. From 1975 to 1988, the percentage of jobs in Canada that were part-time increased from 10.6 percent to 15.4 percent. Many of these part-time service-industry jobs went to women—in 1987, nearly 34 percent of employed Canadian women worked part-time. Both the service industries and part-time workers have proven difficult to unionize. In another area of rapid employment growth—office workers—unions have also had little success in recruiting members.

These trends have generated a *recruitment problem* that is causing the union movement considerable concern. Unless unions can succeed in recruiting members from the service industries and "white-collar" office employees, they risk becoming a declining force within the Canadian economy, representing mainly government employees and employees in government-regulated industries.

Craft and industrial unions

There are two basic types of labor unions: *craft unions*, which are unions of skilled tradesworkers practising a particular craft or trade, such as plumbing or printing; and *industrial unions*, such as the Canadian Automobile Workers, which represent all of the workers in a firm, regardless of the work they perform.

FIGURE 13-8 *Employment in Goods–Producing and Services–Producing Industries, 1970-88*

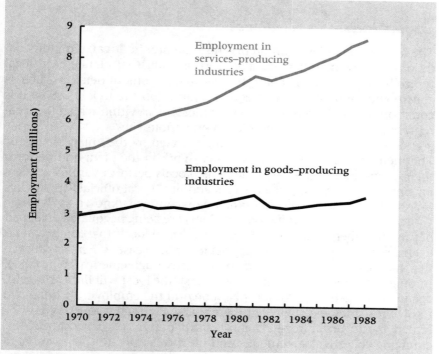

SOURCE Department of Finance, *Quarterly Economic Review* (Annual Reference Tables, June 1989).

Historically, craft unions were the first unions, mainly because the skills of such workers gave them the ability to resist employers' attempts to prevent them from unionizing. Later, as technology changed and large factories became common, industrial unions developed to represent the semi-skilled production workers employed in large numbers in such plants. The growth of the industrial unions during the 1930's posed a threat to the established craft unions, and the two types of unions remained separate—and rivals—for two decades, with each organized into its own umbrella group known as a council or congress. Finally, in 1956, they merged into one umbrella organization for Canadian unions known as the *Canadian Labour Congress (CLC)*.

The most rapid growth in union membership recently has been in the *government employee unions*. Following legislative changes in the 1960's, which gave public employees broader rights to unionize, bargain and strike, government-employee unions grew rapidly; by 1985 about 90 percent of government employees were unionized and the three largest unions in Canada were government-employee unions.

Organization and structure

The basic units of labor union organization are the **locals**. In industrial unions, whose members usually work in industrial plants, each local typically covers a single plant. In craft unions, union members such as construction workers move frequently from job site to job site, so it is common for locals to cover a geographical area, within which the local represents all its members employed on various sites.

Each local is headed by an executive elected by the union members. The members of local executives often work in the plant and perform their union duties on a part-time basis. Locals perform various services for union members, of which two stand out. Local officials are always involved in *contract negotiations* when new contracts (known as "**collective agreements**" in industrial relations) are being negotiated on behalf of their members, and it is the responsibility of locals to *police the contract* to ensure that management does not violate it. In cases where it is alleged that management has violated the collective agreement (for instance, through improper disciplining of workers), the local will file a grievance against management. Should the union and the employer be unable to resolve the grievance between themselves, the matter must by law be settled by an arbitrator—a neutral third party.[3] This mechanism for enforcing collective agreements, and the locals' role in it, is essential to the protection of workers' interests through contracts between unions and employers.

The next level of union organization is the national or international unions, or *headquarters*, such as the Canadian Union of Public Employees and the United Steelworkers of America. If the union is based in Canada, it is called a **national union**, while unions with headquarters in the USA are known as **international unions**. Headed by an elected executive of full-time union officers, (inter)national unions often have a large staff, which provides a variety of services, including recruiting (organizing) new members, assisting in the contract negotiations of locals, administrating strike funds, publishing union newspapers, and lobbying the government on behalf of the union and its members. In many respects, (inter)national unions are the most influential bodies in the union movement. They have had an increasingly dominant role in the contract negotiations of their locals in recent years, as more and more complex bargaining issues have required more research and expertise than that possessed by local union officers.

---

[3] It is not legal to strike over an alleged violation of an existing collecting agreement in Canada. Strikes are only legal as the final step in disputes over the negotiation of the terms of *new* collective agreements, as we will see later.

Still at the national level in the labor movement, there is the *Canadian Labour Congress (CLC)*. The CLC is not a labor union, but rather a *federation* of unions, an umbrella organization to which national and international unions belong. In 1988, unions comprising 2.2 million members, or 58 percent of total Canadian union membership, were affiliated with the CLC. While the CLC appears at the top of the organizational structure of the labor movement shown in Figure 13-9, it is important to note that the CLC is *not* the key decision-maker in Canada's labor movement. The CLC is a loose federation of labor unions which act together through the CLC in pursuit of certain common objectives; however, these national and international unions determine their own independent policies in many areas, regardless of CLC policies. For this reason, the CLC is often compared to the United Nations, which has no real authority over its member nations, and can lead only through persuasion. The only real disciplinary power the CLC has over its affiliated unions is to expel them from the national federation; however, this is not a severe penalty for many unions. The Teamsters' union was unaffected by its expulsion from the CLC,[4] and the United Automobile Workers remained outside the CLC for several years, after withdrawing over policy differences. The main functions of the CLC are in the areas of research, political lobbying, and the settling of jurisdictional disputes in which different unions lay competing claims to the right to represent the same group of workers. While the CLC is by far the largest federation in the country, it is not the *only* one—there are four other federations, the largest of which are the *Canadian Federation of Labour (CFL)*, which consists of construction trade

FIGURE 13-9 *Main Elements of the Labor Movement in Canada*

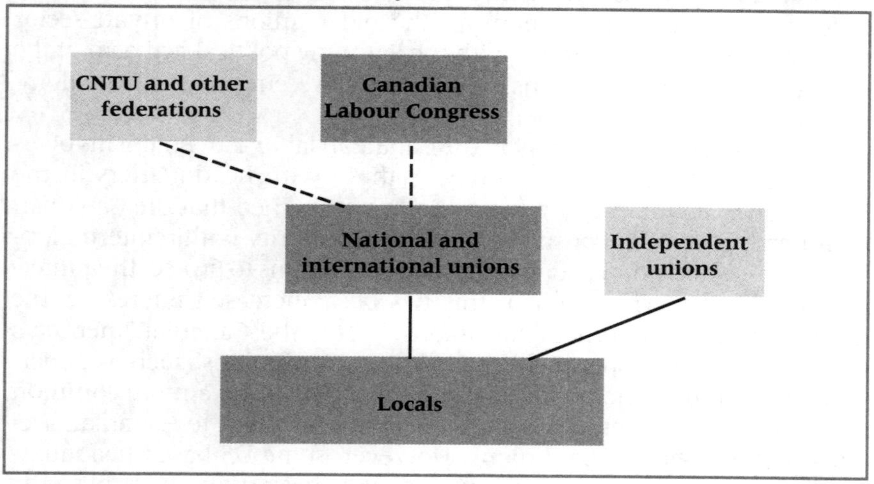

[4] Unions such as the Teamsters, which are not affiliated with any federation of unions, are called *independent unions*.

From 1978 to 1988, the percentage of Canadian union
members who belonged to unions with headquarters in the
USA declined from nearly 50 percent to 35 percent. This was
more the result of the growth of Canadian-based unions
(mainly of government employees) than of replacement of US
unions with Canadian ones.

unions representing 5.4 percent of the total Canadian union membership
in 1988, and the *Confederation of National Trade Unions (CNTU)*, which is
comprised of various unions in Quebec with 5.3 percent of 1988 total
union membership.

With 750 different unions organized into five different federations, the
labor movement is far from the united force that its name implies. Deep
philosophical differences have always existed between the craft unions
and industrial unions. While industrial unions, and particularly the government employee unions, believe that unions should be involved in
politics (supporting the New Democratic Party) and social issues (such
as minority rights, women's rights, combating poverty) the craft unions
take a narrower view of unionism, believing that unions should focus
almost exclusively on gaining economic benefits for their own members.
Earlier, we saw that these differences were overcome in the 1956 merger
of craft and industrial union organizations that formed the Canadian
Labour Congress. However, the long-standing differences opened up
again in 1982, when ten construction unions left the CLC over policy
differences. Furthermore, many of the older unions of private-sector
workers are not in agreement with the left-wing political activism of the
government-employee unions, which have in recent years come to dominate the CLC.

Another area of controversy in the Canadian labor movement involves
the so-called "international" unions—those with headquarters in the
USA. Some Canadian union members are concerned that the Canadian
membership—which constitutes a political minority within international unions—could not rely upon international unions to protect their interests in all cases. The result of this has been increased interest in the
Canadianization of international unions. While the Canadian members
have in some cases split into separate Canadian unions (such as paper-
workers, and most notably the autoworkers in 1984), a more common
development has been the granting of *greater autonomy* to Canadian sections by the international unions. However, some US-based headquarters, particularly in the building trades, have been quite resistant to the
trend toward Canadianization, to the point where consideration has been
given to the establishment of rival Canadian unions in these areas.

Some questions and answers

How do workers become unionized?

A basic principle of Canadian labor law is that workers should decide democratically whether to form or join a labor union. Their view can be expressed in various ways, including the signing of a union card and the payment of a small deposit; however, if there is doubt as to the view of the majority, a vote—known as a *certification vote*—will be conducted by the Labour Relations Board, which is a government agency that oversees labor relations. If the majority of workers vote in favor of being represented by a particular union in a certification vote, that union becomes "certified" as the exclusive representative of those employees, meaning that management must deal with the employees through the union. Conversely, if a group of workers no longer wishes to be represented by a particular union, they can vote to decertify it.

Should union membership and dues be compulsory?

The law provides for workers *as a group* to decide democratically whether or not they wish to join a labor union. However, once a union is established, a controversial question is whether or not *individual workers* should be forced to join the union or pay dues to it.

These matters are covered in a section of the collective agreement with the employer known as the **union security clause**, of which there are several very different types. At once extreme is the **open shop**, under which individual workers are completely free to *decide for themselves* whether or not to join the union and pay dues. While employers generally support the open shop on the grounds of freedom of choice, unions are strongly opposed to it. They point out that since the union is required by law to bargain for everyone in the plant, every worker should be required to support the union. Also, the open shop tends to weaken a union: the existence of "free riders" (workers who get the benefits of the union contract but pay no dues) divides the workers, and discourages others from continuing to support the union.

At the other extreme is the strongest form of union security clause—the **closed shop**, which exists in many craft unions, such as the building trades. In a closed shop, the collective agreement specifies that *only workers who are already union members can be hired;* as a result, the supply of labor available to such employers consists of union members only. This gives the union the opportunity to restrict the supply of labor by restricting entry into the union, and thus to force wages to high levels by virtually acting as a monopolist in the marketplace. It should be noted that such great power is possessed only by skilled trades unions, and that most unions are not in this position.

Between the extremes of the open shop and the closed shop lie the union shop and the Rand Formula. Under the **union shop**, the employer may hire anyone, but *new employees must join the union* after a specified time, usually at the end of their probationary period. The union shop places the union in a much stronger position than the open shop because it guarantees not only membership, but also dues revenue. Employers are generally opposed to the union shop on the grounds that forcing people to join any organization is a violation of their rights, and the union shop has encountered opposition from people who have religious, moral or political objections to joining labor unions.

Obviously, the issue of union security is a contentious one, involving the rights of individuals as well as the potential power of the union vis-à-vis the employer. On many occasions in first contract negotiations for newly formed locals, the insistence of management on the open shop and the insistence of the union on the union shop has led to long and bitter strikes. As a compromise between the two, the **Rand Formula** was developed in 1946. Under the Rand Formula, each worker may choose whether or not to actually join the union, but *all workers must pay dues*, through payroll deductions. Thus, although individuals who object to joining the union are not forced to do so, all must pay dues to the union in return for the economic benefits they derive from it. While the Rand Formula is not a perfect compromise, it is the most acceptable alternative to the other union security clauses. In some provinces the open shop is in effect illegal because the law specifies that workers represented by unions must at least pay dues, as per the Rand Formula.

How are collective agreements negotiated?

To most workers, the most important service provided by their union is the negotiation of their labor contract, or collective agreement. Collective bargaining—the process through which employers and unions negotiate a new collective agreement—usually begins a few months before the old contract expires. Both sides usually open bargaining with complete sets of demands, or proposals, which are quite unrealistic—they merely represent the opening positions of the parties. The process can best be likened to a poker game, as both sides bluff, conceal their true positions and try various tactics. Gradually, as the probability of a strike increases, to the discomfort of both sides, the union and management shed their bluffs and their positions become more reasonable and compatible. Many contract negotiations are settled at this stage. However, it is quite common for the parties to require third-party assistance before reaching an agreement.

This third-party assistance takes the form of **compulsory conciliation**, through which a government-appointed conciliator attempts to help the union and employer to reach a negotiated settlement. It is important to note that the conciliator has no authority to impose a settlement on the parties; rather, his or her role is to assist them to reach their own agreement. By law, employers and unions must go through compulsory conciliation before a work stoppage (strike by the union or lockout by the employer) can occur. Should conciliation prove unsuccessful, the law requires a further delay (a cooling-off period of two weeks, usually) before a strike or lockout can take place. Should the parties fail to reach a settlement under pressure of this strike deadline, a work stoppage will occur that will impose losses on both sides until an agreement is reached.

In recent years, somewhat less than half of contract negotiations have been settled before conciliation, about the same number through conciliation, and about ten percent of negotiations have ended in strikes or lockouts. At whatever stage a settlement is reached, however, a final requirement is that it be approved by the membership of the union, through a *ratification vote*.

Why permit strikes?

Many people see strikes as an archaic way of settling labor disputes through a form of "trial by combat," and feel that the government should not permit strikes (or lockouts).

However, it is important to appreciate that a basic premise of labor legislation is that industrial relations disputes are best worked out *by those directly involved*—the employer, through management, and the employees, through their union. As a result, the law does not provide for the imposition by government of a decision or a contract, but rather establishes a framework within which unions and employers are expected to negotiate their own solutions to their problems, even if that involves a work stoppage.[5]

The law also recognizes that work stoppages can be economically harmful to third parties and to the economy. That is why the compulsory conciliation system is used. However, should the conciliator fail, the law generally leaves the parties on their own to settle—or face the consequences of failing to do so, which may include a strike or lockout.

It is also important to recognize that the threat of a work stoppage plays a very important *positive role* in the collective bargaining process. Over 90 percent of all contract negotiations end in agreement without a work stoppage, mainly because both parties fear the consequences, should one occur. Thus, the right to strike/lock out (or, more precisely, the *threat* of a strike or lockout), serves the important purpose of forcing *both* the employer *and* the union to adopt more realistic negotiating positions, with the usual result being an agreement.

---

[5] We are discussing here bargaining situations in which the union has the right to strike. Other situations, involving mostly essential public services, will be considered later.

When are strikes not legal?

There are two basic types of disputes between employers and unions. The first type includes disputes over the negotiation of a new collective agreement, as described in the foregoing sections. In general, it is legal to resort to a strike or lockout in contract negotiations such as these, but there are two exceptions to this general rule: first, a strike or lockout is only legal after compulsory conciliation and a "cooling-off period," as required by law; and second, in the case of workers who provide essential public services, such as police and firefighters, work stoppages are usually forbidden by law.

There is, however, a second distinct type of labor dispute, in which strikes and lockouts are expressly forbidden by law. These are disputes not over the terms of a new contract that is being negotiated, but rather over *alleged violations of an existing contract*. For instance, suppose that management disciplines a worker in a way that he or she and the union consider to be a violation of the collective agreement. How should they pursue this matter?

The law does not allow strikes (or lockouts) over such disputes. Instead, the worker must file a **grievance** concerning the alleged violation of the contract, which will lead to a series of discussions between management and the union to resolve the matter. If these discussions fail, the dispute must by law be taken to **arbitration**, which is a court-like process in which a neutral third party (an *arbitrator*) hears the evidence of both sides and makes a binding decision in favor of one or the other.

In summary, there are two different types of labor disputes. Disputes over the negotiation of a contract are usually, in the final analysis, allowed to go to a work stoppage if necessary, or to a test of raw economic power. However, disputes over alleged violations of an existing collective agreement that the parties cannot resolve by themselves must be settled through the court-like process of arbitration, in which evidence, logic and argument are the key factors.

Aren't strikes costly?

Is it true that there are certain costs involved in strikes—the employer loses profits, the employees lose wages, and the society in general loses the output that could have been produced. However, the economic costs of strikes are greatly exaggerated by the general public. Often, both sides recover part of their losses after the strike, because of the backlog of orders. Also, the working time lost due to strikes is an extremely small fraction of total time worked in the economy: on average, about one-third of one percent of total time worked.[6] This is about the same amount

---

[6] During the second half of the 1980's, time lost due to industrial disputes was about half this level.

of working time that would be lost if all working Canadians were given one additional holiday per year. So, while industrial disputes do impose economic costs on society, it cannot be argued that strikes in general are ruining the nation's economy. This is not to deny that particular strikes involving important public services have severe effects, but these constitute a special case which we will consider shortly.

What would happen if strikes were banned?

While the time lost due to strikes is only a small proportion of time worked in the economy, Canada's strike record is nevertheless one of the worst of all industrial nations. This poor showing has led some people to advocate that governments should pass legislation banning strikes altogether.

As a practical matter, it is far from certain that a government *could* actually enforce a general ban on strikes in the face of determined resistance from hundreds of thousands of unionists. However, assuming that strikes were successfully outlawed, our present industrial relations system would cease to function—without the threat of a strike, there would be no pressure on either party to bargain seriously, so contract negotiations would drag on endlessly. As a result, contract disputes would have to be settled by some alterative method: either by allowing market forces to determine wages and salaries, or by having a third party impose a contract on the two sides. Since the first alternative amounts to *eliminating unions*, it cannot be considered a practical possibility. That leaves only the alternative of *arbitration* of contract disputes by a third party, such as a government agency or a private expert. Despite their strong differences over many matters, most unions and employers agree that they have strong reservations about allowing a third party—especially the government, but also a private expert—to decide their collective agreements for them. Both sides believe that these matters are too vital to be handed over to an outsider whose lack of familiarity with them could lead to a decision that was unfair or unworkable.

While our system of negotiations with the right to strike may be less than ideal, so are the alternatives to it—and, in general, both employers and unions prefer the present system to the alternatives.

How successful have unions been in raising wages?

Unions have had varying degrees of success in raising their members' wages. Much depends on the *economic limits* on wages, which are determined by the economic environment of the industry in which the union operates. In some industries strong competition makes profit margins so low that employers cannot grant large wage increases without impairing their *competitive position*, while in others, wage increases may be limited by the fact that higher labor costs may make it more economical for employers to introduce *labor-saving machinery*. In both cases, the upper limit on wages is the point at which the employees' jobs would be endangered by further wage increases.

Whether wages actually approach these upper limits, however, depends to a great extent on the *bargaining power of the union*—a strong, well-organized union is much more likely to succeed in pushing its members' wages closer to the economic limits than a weaker union. However, not even a strong union can increase wages much in a situation where the economic limits are tight, at least not without causing many union members to lose their jobs. In some industries, these economic limits are quite confining. For example, the clothing industry is besieged by domestic and foreign competition, with the result that the wage increases won by its unions have tended to be lower than average. On the other hand, in situations where competition is weaker, such as in some oligopolistic industries and government monopolies like the Post Office, larger wage increases are possible, if the union has the bargaining power to win them.

Generally, unusually high wages or wage increases are the result of a combination of powerful unions and economically strong employers who face relatively loose economic limits—situations where employers have the ability to pay high wages, and unions are strong enough to force the employers to do so. More specifically, high wages may originate in the *oligopoly power of employers*, who may decide to pay above-average wage increases in order to avoid strikes, then pass the cost increase along to the consumer in the form of higher prices. Many economists believe that it was through such a process that automobile workers achieved a wage and benefit package roughly 50 percent larger than the average industrial worker's by the early 1980's. Another factor that can increase the employer's ability to pay is *rising productivity*, or output per worker, usually due to technological progress and capital investment. This is another factor underlying the high wages of auto workers, although the petroleum industry provides an even better example. Finally, there are the high wages of the *closed shop* craft unions. While these have been described as the result of the restriction of the supply of labor by the unions, the other factor making such wages possible is the inelastic demand for many types of construction, which enables construction contractors to pass high wages on to the buyer.

In conclusion, the ability of unions to raise their members' wages varies greatly from industry to industry and occupation to occupation, with much depending on the elasticity of the demand for labor. Estimating the actual extent to which unions have increased their members' wages over the levels that would have prevailed without unions is a difficult matter, for the same reasons that estimating the effect of oligopolists' market power on prices in Chapter 12 was difficult. Statistical comparisons of the wages of unionized and non-unionized workers doing essentially same work are not always easy to find or make. Studies that have attempted such comparisons have found that the effect of unions on their members' wages varies greatly, from increases of as much as 50 percent for some skilled trades, to negligible gains for groups working in highly competitive industries or lacking in bargaining power. On average, such studies suggest that unions have probably increased their members' wages by something like 10 or 15 percent over the level that would have prevailed without unions. This effect is probably smaller than most people suppose it to be, because many people tend to overlook the economic limits on unions' bargaining and wage gains.

Doesn't Canada have a real labor problem due to strikes?

We have already said that, as a general matter, Canada's strike situation does not threaten to ruin the nation's economy—over 90 percent of contract negotiations are settled without a strike, and only about one-third of one percent of time worked is lost due to strikes.

On the other hand, the statistics indicate that there is some reason for concern. Generally, Canada has had the second-worst record of all industrialized nations for time lost due to strikes and lockouts. When considering Canada as a possible destination for investment, many foreign investors have expressed reservations about this country's industrial relations climate and the apparently high risk of strikes. While Figure 13-10 shows that the proportion of working time lost due to labor disputes declined in the 1980's, Canada's labor relations climate and record remained poor by international standards, and a matter of concern.

FIGURE 13-10 *Percentage of Working Time Lost Due to Work Stoppages*

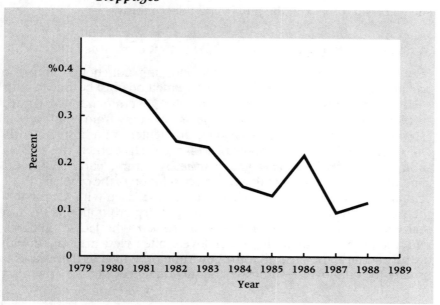

Canada's record in this respect [time lost due to work stoppages] has been among the worst in the industrialized world. Viewed from the perspective of direct production losses and revenue forgone, the amount of time lost due to work stoppages still represents a very small proportion of total working time. Indeed, the time lost due to industrial accidents and illness is more than double that due to industrial disputes. However, to the extent that work stoppages are an indication of the state of industrial relations, Canada's recent performance in this area compared with its main competitors is a matter of some concern.

> Hon. Michael Wilson, *A New Direction for Canada:
> An Agenda for Economic Renewal*
> (Ottawa, Department of Finance, 1984).

Simple statistics on percentage of working time lost due to labor disputes probably underestimate the impact of work stoppages on the Canadian public. This is because, compared to other countries, a higher proportion of Canada's work stoppages involve government employees and thus the *interruption of monopoly public services*. So, unlike private-sector work stoppages, the public has no alternative supplier. Work stoppages in public services such as postal service, education, public transit, garbage collection, airlines and health care, represent a particularly difficult and serious problem in Canadian industrial relations, because they have such a broad impact on the public and the economy.

What can be done about public service strikes?

As with labor disputes in the private sector, it is not enough simply to ban public service strikes; some alternative method must be used to settle such disputes promptly and fairly. Generally, governments have tended to follow the rule of *withdrawing the right to strike* only from employees in essential public services, such as police, firefighters, and hospital workers; unresolved contract disputes involving such workers are usually submitted to *compulsory binding arbitration* by a third party. While the general public tends to see this as a simply solution to the problem, those actually involved in the process are much less satisfied with it. Probably the major difficulty associated with compulsory arbitration is the fact that vital decisions must be made by an *outsider* who lacks familiarity with the problems. In addition, employees often view arbitration with distrust because they fear that the government, which in these cases is usually the employer, will possess undue influence over the arbitrator.

Whether or not this happens, another very real problem is the *long delays* in arbitration, with wage increases often held up for a year or more. Such delays happen partly because neither side (particularly the employer) feels any need to negotiate quickly in the absence of a strike threat, and because the arbitration process itself usually lasts several months. During such delays, it is not uncommon for the frustration of employees to result in illegal (wildcat) strikes.

LET'S PLAY ARBITRATOR

If you think compulsory arbitration of labor contract disputes is a simple matter, take the following opportunity to show how easy it really is.

A married couple whom you know only slightly is having severe marital problems and disputes, largely because their marriage is not living up to the expectations that each held for it. They agree that it would have been better if, before they were married, they had written up a marriage contract specifying the rights and responsibilities of each partner. However, given the present state of deterioration of their relationship, they are unable to agree on the terms of such a contract. They have asked you, as an impartial third party, to resolve the matter for them in the following way: you will listen to the views and arguments of each of the parties, their proposals for the terms to be included in the contract and the exact wording of each clause; then you will, on your own, *write for them a complete, detailed marriage contract* which will provide a workable basis for a renewed marriage.

Good luck!

Management is not always pleased with arbitration either, because it removes matters of great importance from management control. Major decisions are placed in the hands of an outsider whose decisions cannot be appealed, but which may impair management's ability to deliver the service for which the organization is responsible. Thus, arbitration is far from the ideal and simple solution to labor disputes that it may appear to be.

Some industrial relations experts believe that the severity of public service strikes in Canada is the result of an immature bargaining relationship, between newly formed unions anxious to prove their worth and insecure management fearful of the new unions. The same experts forecast that strikes will become less frequent as the relationship between the parties matures. Otherwise, it is likely that the right to strike will be withdrawn from some public service unions, and be replaced either by compulsory arbitration or by some formula for setting public employee wages that will be comparable to private-sector wages for similar jobs. Generally, Canadian policy has been to allow government employees considerably more freedom to unionize, bargain collectively and strike than is the case in most other nations. This policy has been controversial, and experts are divided on the question of whether it will prove to be sustainable in the future.

A perspective

The one generalization that can be made about labor unions is that all generalizations about labor unions are invalid. Some unions are very strong, others are very weak; some are autocratic, others are democratic; some are corrupt, others are very honest; some union-management relationships are characterized by virtual warfare, others by cooperation.

Public opinion certainly seems to overrate the power of unions. Union membership represents less than one-third of the labor force, and this proportion has not increased significantly in over a decade. The union movement is not a monolithic giant; indeed, unions spend considerable time fighting among themselves. Friends and foes of unions alike exaggerate the economic effects of unions—on the whole, they do not seem to have had the effects on wages that are often attributed to them; they are constrained by the economic limits of the industry in which they operate (which is not to deny that the limits are in some cases quite loose, and that the result in these cases has been fairly high wages). The economic damage done by strikes seems to be similarly exaggerated; the strike is in fact not used very often and is less costly economically than is generally supposed. It seems likely that the practices of some particularly powerful unions have given a bad public image to all labor unions, including the vast majority that are small and possess relatively little power.

The collective bargaining process, whereby the terms and conditions of employment of over five million Canadian workers are determined, is not fully satisfactory in several respects. It relies more on power than on rationality, and sometimes results in work stoppages that affect innocent third parties. Despite the effect that contract negotiations between large employers and unions have on the public, the public has no voice in these decisions—they are a matter of a private contract between unions and employers. Still, the alternatives to our industrial relations system, which involve either the elimination of unions or the replacement of collective bargaining by decisions of arbitrators, are not attractive either. Consequently, most Canadians seem to prefer their present industrial relations system, in spite of its flaws.

While most Canadians do not appear to want to change their industrial relations system radically, there is nonetheless considerable interest in improving its performance. This view was frequently expressed in submissions to the Royal Commission on the Economic Union and Development Prospects for Canada (the Macdonald Commission) which said in its 1985 report:

Some of the existing labour legislation, such as compulsory conciliation, may well be having its intended effect. Commissioners believe, however, that the scope for further legislative initiatives to reduce the incidence of collective bargaining disputes is probably very limited. Lower levels of collective bargaining disputes are more likely to result from increased co-operation, consultation and exchange of views and information between labour and management than for additional legislated restrictions on the use of the strike or lock-out.

The Commission went on to suggest various ways in which a more positive labor relations climate might be fostered, including a more open and communicative style of management, more consultation by management with workers prior to making decisions, and more "gain-sharing" arrangements whereby employees gain financially if their employer prospers, through profit-sharing, employee stock-ownership or plans which reward employees for increased efficiency. Such arrangements, which often work to the advantage of both employees and employers are relatively rare in Canada. However, the Commission cautioned against expecting rapid improvement in Canada's labor relations environment, largely because of the attitudes of both labor and management that have built up over the years.

DEFINITIONS OF NEW TERMS

Minimum Wage   A legal minimum wage set by law.

Collective Bargaining   The process through which employers and unions negotiate a new collective agreement.

Local   The basic unit of labor union organization.

Collective Agreement   A contract agreed upon by an employer and labor union, specifying the terms and conditions of employment of the employees for a specified period of time.

National Union   A labor union whose headquarters are in Canada.

International Union   A labor union whose headquarters are in the USA.

Union Security Clause   The clause of a collective agreement specifying whether or not the employees must pay union dues and/or join the union.

Open Shop   A union security clause under which employees may choose whether or not to join the union and pay dues.

Closed Shop   A union security clause under which the employer agrees to hire only workers who are members of the union.

Union Shop   A union security clause requiring that the new employees join the union and pay dues after their probationary period.

Rand Formula   A union security clause requiring that all employees pay union dues but leaving to each employee the decision whether or not to actually join the union.

Compulsory Conciliation   A procedure, required by law before a strike is legal, in which a government-appointed officer (conciliator) attempts to help a union and employer to reach an agreement on the terms of a new collective agreement.

Grievance   An alleged violation of a collective agreement by an employer.

Arbitration   The resolution of union-management disputes by the decision of a third party; required by law for grievances that the union and employer cannot resolve by themselves; used to settle disputes over the terms of new collective agreements in cases where strikes of essential employees are prohibited.

CHAPTER SUMMARY

1. In the non-union sector of the labor force, incomes are determined by supply and demand, which generates large differences in income between different occupations.

2. Minimum-wage legislation can increase the wages of low-income groups, but at the cost of fewer jobs for those groups.

3. For employees who are covered by labor union collective agreements, wages and conditions of employment are negotiated by unions and employers.

4. Except for workers in essential services who are not allowed to strike, it is the threat of a strike that provides an incentive for both

unions and employers to bargain seriously and to reach agreements on new collective agreements.

5. Overall, this system works reasonably well. Strikes are relatively infrequent, and the alternatives to this system (abolishing unions or arbitrating all disputes over the terms of new collective agreements) are not attractive.

6. Nonetheless, Canada has in recent years experienced considerable problems related to work stoppages in various public services. Work stoppages are legal in Canada for employees in many public services.

QUESTIONS

1. "Under no circumstances should a person be forced to join an organization, or contribute money to an organization, against his/her will." Do you agree or disagree? Why?

2. Is the Canadian Medical Association a union?

3. Could organization into a union raise the incomes of hairdressers by very much?

4. "From a publicity viewpoint, when a labor dispute ends in a work stoppage, the union is almost bound to look bad." Do you agree or disagree? Why?

5. What limits are there on the economic power of the closed-shop unions such as those in the printing and building trades?

6. To resolve labor disputes in essential public services, a procedure known as Final Offer Selection is occasionally used. Under this procedure, negotiations for a new collective agreement proceed as usual, but should the parties be unable to agree on a contract, each must make a *final offer* to the other at a final bargaining session. If no agreement is reached at that session, these final offers must be submitted, *unchanged*, to an arbitrator who must select as the terms of the collective agreement *that one* of the two offers deemed the more reasonable. How is this procedure supposed to work? What advantages and disadvantages does it have over conventional compulsory arbitration?

7. The text refers to the *attitudes* of labor and management as an obstacle to improving Canada's labor relations environment. What are some of these attitudes, and why have they developed?

8. "If employers had profit-sharing with their employees and employee stock ownership plans whereby employees could

become shareholders, there would no longer be any need for unions." Do you agree or disagree? Why?

9. In 1989, the federal government introduced proposals for changes to the Unemployment Insurance system. These proposals included increased spending on (re)training as well as new U.I. programs such as paternity leave. To pay for these changes, the government proposed tighter restrictions on U.I. payments to workers who quit their jobs voluntarily, which amounted to 10 percent of the approximately $10 billion in U.I. benefits paid out in 1988. Under the proposals, voluntary quitters would have to wait twice as long for their U.I. benefits, and their benefits would be reduced from 60 percent of insurable earnings to 50 percent. Explain why you agree or disagree with these proposals.

CHAPTER 14

The distribution of income and employment

In Chapter 13, we examined the operation of labor markets, both non-union and unionized, in Canada. In this chapter, we will consider two other important aspects of labor markets: the distribution of income between various groups, which is determined in these markets, and the trends in employment that have been occurring and are forecast to occur in labor markets.

Distribution of income

In Chapter 13, we saw how incomes are determined in labor markets, under conditions ranging from the free interplay of supply and demand to the craft unions and professional bodies that regulate entrance into some occupations. In determining the incomes of various individuals and groups, these labor markets also determine the division of the economic pie, or the *distribution of income* among various groups. Not surprisingly, as Figure 14-1 shows, there are wide differences in the incomes of various occupational groups. Some of these differences are the result of natural obstacles to entry to certain occupations, while others are partly due to artificial barriers erected by unions and professional bodies that restrict entrance, keeping the supply of people with particular skills low and their incomes high.

FIGURE 14-1 *Incomes by Occupation, 1987*

Occupation	Number	Average Income
Self-employed medical doctors and surgeons	36 790	$99 195
Self-employed dentists	8 700	82 717
Self-employed lawyers and notaries	21 930	76 331
Self-employed accountants	11 780	60 198
Self-employed engineers and architects	5 820	41 771
Other self-employed professionals	66 840	28 114
Investors	1 027 820	25 626
Employees	11 226 240	23 711
Fishermen	40 190	22 804
Self-employed salesmen	41 120	21 027
Property owners	134 570	20 972
Farmers	265 910	17 365
Business proprietors	566 640	15 541
Pensioners	1 800 140	13 445
Self-employed entertainers and artists	21 640	13 382
Unclassified	1 795 210	5 203
TOTAL	17 071 350	20 693
Business Proprietors		
Finance	1 810	$53 961
Real estate	2 810	33 992
Insurance agents	2 010	32 552
Wholesale trade	6 440	25 818
Forestry	8 940	20 955
Construction	89 790	18 767
Recreation services	7 730	17 137
Retail trade	137 850	15 320
Other businesses	7 830	15 299
Utilities	66 240	15 223
Business services	21 800	14 664
Manufacturing	16 050	14 515
Other services	197 370	13 095
TOTAL	566 640	15 541
Employees		
Teachers and professors	252 110	$38 290
Provincial crown corp.	152 580	35 715
Federal crown corp.	192 910	32 482
Federal government	307 590	31 497
Armed forces	83 590	30 911
Provincial governments	380 320	28 019
Municipal governments	645 620	26 791
Business enterprises	7 693 570	22 742
Institutions	982 610	22 438
Unclassified	535 350	14 145
TOTAL	11 226 240	23 711

SOURCE Revenue Canada, *Taxation Statistics,* 1989 ed. (p.79).
Reproduced by permission of the Minister of Supply and Services Canada.

On a broader scale, there is the question of the distribution of income among different *income groups*—what share of the economic pie goes to the lowest-income 20 percent of families, what share goes to the highest-income 20 percent and to the various groups in between? As Figure 14-2 shows, the distribution of income between various income groups has remained remarkably constant over the years, with roughly 40 percent of total family income going to the top 20 percent of families, 24 percent of income to the second-highest 20 percent, 18 percent to the middle 20 percent, and only 13 percent and 6 percent to the second-lowest and lowest 20 percent of families, respectively. These statistics show a degree of *inequality* in the distribution of income that is not only considerable, but also persistent. For over thirty years, the share of the economic pie going to the top fifth of Canadian families has been nearly seven times the share going to the bottom fifth.

FIGURE 14-2 *Distribution of Family Income in Canada*

	Percentage of total income received by each fifth							Maximum family income for each quintile, 1987
	1951	1961	1971	1973	1979	1983	1987	
Lowest-income fifth of families	6.1	6.6	5.6	6.1	6.1	6.2	6.5	$20 733
Second fifth	12.9	13.4	12.7	12.9	13.0	12.3	12.4	33 019
Third fifth	17.4	18.2	18.0	18.2	18.4	17.8	17.8	44 765
Fourth fifth	22.5	23.4	23.7	23.9	24.3	24.1	24.0	60 912
Highest-income fifth	41.1	38.4	40.0	38.9	38.3	39.5	39.4	—
All families	100.0	100.0	100.0	100.0	100.0	100.0	100.0	

SOURCE Statistics Canada, *Income Distributions by Size in Canada*.

Reproduced by permission of the Minister of Supply and Services Canada

Is the distribution of income reflected in Figure 14-1 and 14-2 *fair?* To some, higher incomes represent a *reward* for effort and education; they reflect those people's contribution to society, and provide *incentives* for Canadians to improve themselves and work harder. To others, these differences in income are much greater than can be explained by differing contributions, or by the need to provide incentives. These people view the income-distribution process as one in which relatively few Canadians possess the economic power to extract an *excessive share* of the economic pie from the system, leaving only the crumbs for the poor.

Which view is correct? How much of this inequality is necessary in order to provide incentives? Is this distribution of income fair or not? The economist can help to explain *why* such a distribution of income exists, but is of little help in making value judgments as to whether it is a *fair* or appropriate distribution of income.

Characteristics of various income groups

In the following sections, we will examine the characteristics of the highest-, middle-, and lowest-income groups in Canada. While the most recent study of these characteristics used 1981 incomes, it is unlikely that the characteristics noted have changed much since then.

The highest-income group

Figure 14-3 provides a profile of the highest-income group. As the statistics show, this group consists mainly of two-earner families with children, with wages and salaries their major source of income. The husband is mostly likely to be between 35 and 54, with at least some post-secondary education.

Figure 14-4 highlights the importance of second incomes and working wives in high-income households, 84 percent of which had two or more income-earners in 1981. In 1981, 60 percent of Canadian families had

FIGURE 14-3 *Profile of the Highest-Income Group*

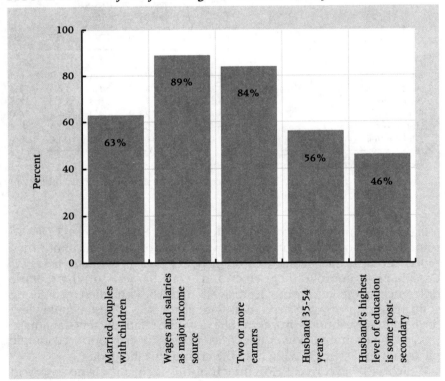

SOURCE Statistics Canada, *Charting Canadian Incomes, 1951-81* (1984).
Reproduced by permission of the Minister of Supply and Services Canada.

FIGURE 14-4 *Wives' Participation in the Labor Force and
Contribution to Family Income*

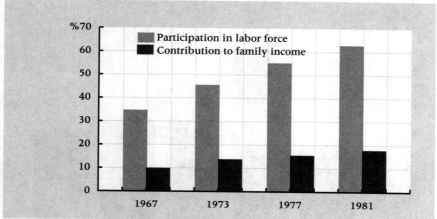

SOURCE Statistics Canada, *Charting Canadian Incomes, 1951-81* (1984).
Reproduced by permission of the Minister of Supply and Services Canada.

two or more incomes, almost twice the proportion in 1951. The participation of wives in the labor force and their contribution to family income
are shown in Figure 14-4.

The middle-income group

As Figure 14-5 shows, the middle-income group differs from the highest-
income group in its number of income-earners, age, and level of education. These families tend to be younger than the highest-income group,
suggesting that some of them may simply be at an earlier stage of their
careers, when their incomes are lower. However, two other aspects of
the middle-income group are also noteworthy. Fifty-three percent are
one-earner families (as compared to only 16 percent for the highest-
income group), and the education level of the husbands is considerably
lower than the highest-income group. The highest level of education for
half of the husbands in this group is some high school, while a similar
proportion of the highest-income group had at least some post-secondary
education.

The lowest-income group

As Figure 14-6 (on page 261) shows, the lowest-income group consists
mostly of individuals who are either young or elderly. Two-thirds of this
group are unattached individuals, and they are predominantly women,
either under 25 or over 65, with no earned income. Many members (56
percent) of the lowest-income group are women who are heads of fam-

FIGURE 14-5 *Profile of the Middle-Income Group*

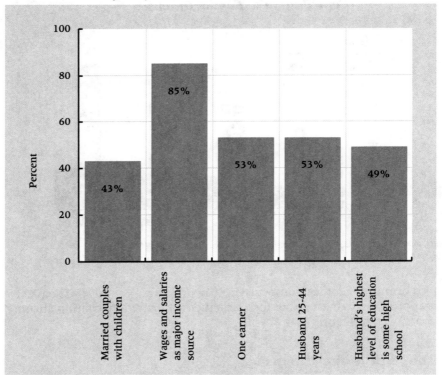

SOURCE Statistics Canada, *Charting Canadian Incomes, 1951-81* (1984).
Reproduced by permission of the Minister of Supply and Services Canada.

ilies. About a third of all low-income families are single-parent families, and married couples are likely to be past retirement age.

Almost half the lowest-income group has Grade 8 or less education, 63 percent are not in the labor force (that is, neither working nor seeking work), and for 57 percent their major source of income is social benefits.

The male-female pay gap and pay equity legislation

The income differentials that have attracted the most attention by far in recent years have been the pay differences between men and women. Most studies show that women earn between 62 and 67 percent of what men earn for full-time work, raising questions of sex discrimination in labor markets.

Some of this difference between the incomes of men and women can be explained by economic factors. Most studies estimate that if differences in hours worked are considered, the male-female wage gap shrinks by about two-fifths. Somewhat less than another one-fifth of the gap can

FIGURE 14-6 *Profile of the Lowest-Income Group*

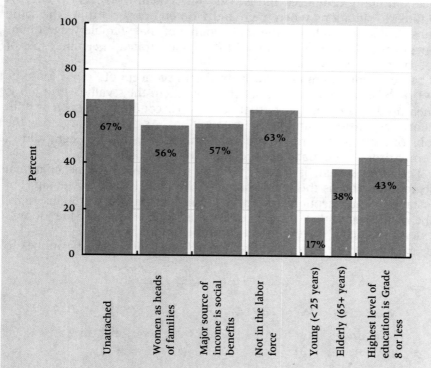

SOURCE Statistics Canada, *Charting Canadian Incomes, 1951-81* (1984).
Reproduced by permission of the Minister of Supply and Services Canada.

be attributed to "productivity" factors, such as training, education and experience.[1]

This leaves a male-female wage gap of about 10 to 15 percent that can best be explained by gender factors. First and foremost, there is what is called occupational segregation: 77 percent of female employees work in five occupational groups: clerical, service, sales, medicine/health and teaching. Since many of the jobs within these occupational groups are relatively low-paid, the average income of women tends to be below average.

Such male-female wage gaps raise important issues of government policy. The first step toward dealing with this matter was legislation ruling that people who do the same work must receive the same pay—

[1] For instance, the fact that some women interrupt their career for child-raising holds down their advancement and incomes, and the fact that the participation rate for women is much lower after age 55 depresses the average income of women due to the lower number of them working during these higher-income years.

"*equal pay for equal work*" legislation. Such legislation has existed for many years in many provinces and is widely accepted. However, its effect is limited to situations where men and women are performing the same jobs. It does not address the main source of male-female wage differences—the fact that women tend to be concentrated in certain types of jobs with below-average pay.

More recent and more controversial is the concept of "**equal pay for work of equal value.**" Under this approach, the "value" of a job is measured by a point system that takes into account factors such as skill, effort, responsibility and working conditions. As the box comparing the jobs of receptionist and warehouseman shows, such a system allows comparisons to be made between quite different jobs.

The point system is flexible enough to deal with the occupational segregation that is the main source of the male-female wage gap. For instance, if the receptionist were being paid less than the warehouseman, she would be entitled to an increase to his pay level because her job was assessed as being worth the same number of points as his.

"Equal pay for work of equal value" legislation already applies to

---

COMPARING TWO EMPLOYEES

How a Toronto auto company evaluated two jobs using a pay equity point system

Job	Receptionist	Warehouseman
Hourly wage	$8.01	$11.01
Education	106	80
Experience	79	86
Complexity	81	76
Supervision of others	0	0
Independence of action	55	55
Consequence of errors	46	51
Confidentiality	14	0
Contacts	48	33
Physical skill and effort	44	76
Working conditions	19	38
Total	492 points	495 points

Jobs rated within three points of one another are considered of equal value. The company would have five years to make adjustments to the receptionist's wage to match the warehouseman's wage.

SOURCE: Coopers & Lybrand Consulting Group, in the *Financial Post*, Aug. 21, 1989 (p.1)

government employees in several jurisdictions. However, the application of the same legislation to private employers is much more controversial, due to concerns regarding employers' ability to compete with others not subject to such requirements. As of 1990, only Ontario had extended "equal pay for work of equal value" legislation to private-sector employers. Under the Ontario law, governmental employers and private employers with more than ten employees must post detailed pay equity plans and, where raises are required, must spend a minimum of 1 percent of their payroll each year on pay equity until the discrepancies disappear.

Reactions to "equal pay for work of equal value" have been mixed. While there is wide agreement on the need to end discrimination, many employers have reservations about how. They point out that the *administration* of pay equity laws is not simple, that it involves complex systems for assessing jobs, the preparation of extensive pay equity plans, mechanisms for employee complaints regarding inequity to be investigated, government officials to enforce the law, and a hearings/tribunal system to make final decisions concerning complaints. These concerns are especially worrisome for smaller businesses, which lack sophisticated personnel departments and whose managers are often already overworked. The *costs* of pay equity are also a concern of small business and of businesses subject to strong foreign competition.

Economists tend to be particularly interested in the possible side-effects of pay equity laws on labor markets. As pay equity legislation increases the wages of females, will there be any negative effects upon employment of women? If there is a shortage of workers in one male job class, forcing employers to increase their wages in order to attract workers, will they be required to raise the wages of all female employees doing work of equal value, even though there is no shortage of such employees? And will employers seek to avoid or control such cost increases by employing fewer female employees?[2] There is considerable disagreement among economists as to whether this will become a problem. Some foresee negative effects upon job opportunities for women, while others believe that a combination of low unemployment and the spreading out of the increased costs over several years will cause the effect to be minimal. Certainly, many observers will be watching with interest the results of Ontario's law, which is the first to extend "equal pay for work of equal value" legislation to the private sector.

Poverty in Canada

Discussion of the distribution of income brings us to the question of poverty in Canada. It is difficult to define or measure poverty with any precision, because people's ideas of what constitutes poverty vary, as do living standards and living costs in different regions of the country, as

[2] The basic economic issue here is the same as that of price supports as discussed in Chapter 8: if the price (here, the wage rate) is increased, how will the demand for the product (here, female worker) be affected?

well as the circumstances of individual families that could be considered poor. As a result, some experts would call a particular family poor while others would not.

Aggregate distribution of income statistics such as those in Figure 14-2 are not very helpful in determining the extent of poverty. While they appear to show that, for instance, 20 percent of families lived in continuing poverty over the years shown, earning only 6 percent of all incomes, this is not so. The composition of this lowest group does ot remain constant, but rather shifts to some extent as time passes. For instance, this group in 1951 included students whose incomes were low because they only worked for part of the year, but who moved into the higher-income groups after graduation, whereas the bottom group in 1973 consisted partly of another generation of students temporarily in similar circumstances. Thus, the statistical fact that the bottom 20 percent of families consistently earn only 6 percent of income is not an accurate measure of either the extent or the persistence of poverty.

Poverty lines

To define and measure poverty, statisticians use **poverty lines** or income levels below which families or individuals are considered to be poor. The most widely-used poverty lines in Canada are the *low-income cut-offs* which Statistics Canada uses to produce data on the low-income group. These are based not on some absolute level of income, but rather on the expenditure patterns of the poor as compared to the average family. Specifically, if a family's expenditures on the essentials of life (food, shelter and clothing) are more than 20 percentage points above the average percent of income spent by families on these items, that family is considered to be poor.[3] Since Statistics Canada's 1978 Survey of Family Expenditure found that Canadian families on average spend 38.5 percent of their income on food, clothing and shelter, the low-income cut-offs were set at income levels where 58.5 percent or more of family income (20 percentage points above the average) go to the essentials of life.

There is no single poverty line for all of Canada, because what constitutes a poverty-level income depends on two other factors that affect living costs: *family size* and *place of residence*. Poverty lines are lower for smaller communities and rural areas, where living costs are generally lower. Figure 14-7 shows the *National Council of Welfare's* estimates of low-income lines for 1989; as can be seen from the table, these poverty lines vary widely, depending on family size and place of residence.

The other major set of poverty lines for Canada are those established

---

[3] Statistics Canada itself does not consider its low-income cut- offs to be poverty lines, but they are widely used by others as such.

| Family size | Population of area of residence | | | | |
	500 000 and over	100 000-499 999	30 000-99 999	Less than 30 000	Rural
1	$12 037	$11 432	$10 725	$ 9 915	$ 8 901
2	15 881	15 074	14 063	13 048	11 634
3	21 245	20 132	18 815	17 502	15 578
4	24 481	23 266	21 749	20 231	18 009
5	28 526	27 011	25 189	23 469	20 942
6	31 157	29 437	27 516	25 593	22 862
7 or more	34 294	32 473	30 349	28 223	25 189

¹These are technically known as the "low income cut-offs (1978) base." The "1978" refers to the Family Expenditure Survey data on which the cut-offs are based.

by the *Canadian Council on Social Development*. These are set for a family of three at one-half of average family income, and adjusted for varying family size by a point system. Unlike Statistics Canada's low-income cut-offs, the CCSD poverty lines do not vary with the size of the place of residence, because the Council does not agree that living costs vary significantly or systematically by community size. The CCSD poverty lines are mostly higher than Statistics Canada's low-income cut-offs. For 1989, the CCSD method of calculation resulted in poverty lines estimated at $11 800 for a single person, $19 667 for two, $23 600 for three, $27 533 for four, $31 467 for five and $35 400 for a family of six.

Who are the poor?

As Figure 14-8 shows, poverty is most common among certain groups, such as single-parent families (especially those headed by women), the old, the young and the poorly educated. A disproportionate number of the poor are women, especially elderly women living on their own and women heading single-parent families. Traditionally, the over-65 age group has had a high incidence of poverty, mainly due to the inadequacy of many pension plans. However, as pensions and government assistance to the elderly have improved, and many retirees have benefited from selling their homes at high prices, poverty has been becoming less of a "seniors' problem" and more of a "women's problem." In 1989, over 40 percent of unattached elderly women and nearly 57 percent of sole-support mothers had incomes below the poverty line.

FIGURE 14-8 *The Likelihood of Poverty in Canada, 1981*

Characteristics	Percentage of each category with incomes below the low-income cut off	
	Families (head)	Individuals
Age		
Less than 24	22.7	38.4
25 – 34	12.6	18.2
35 – 44	10.7	22.4
45 – 54	9.0	30.3
55 – 64	10.5	40.9
65 + (Male)	12.9	48.4
65 + (Female)	24.7	62.2
Education		
0 – 8 years	18.9	62.9
High school	11.6	33.3
Post-secondary, no diploma	8.4	34.2
Post-secondary, with diploma	7.0	22.8
University degree	4.7	17.3
Sex/Family Structure		
Children		
Married couple	8.3	—
Married couple, child	8.9	—
Married couple, children and/or relatives	8.0	—
Male single parent family	13.8	—
Female single parent family	42.8	—

SOURCE Canadian Council on Social Development, Task Force on the Definition and Measurement of Poverty in Canada, *Not Enough: The Meaning and Measurement of Poverty in Canada* (Ottawa: The Council, 1984).

Figure 14-9 points out other aspects of poverty, showing that it is by no means confined to the elderly and to single-parent families. In fact, the largest number of poor people live in families consisting of a couple with children. Many of the poor are the *working poor*, who struggle to get by on low wages and with little help from the social welfare system.

Many of the working poor live on incomes that are actually *lower* than they would receive if they were on welfare. Nonetheless, the social welfare system has provided little help for these people. People working for the minimum wage generally fall below the poverty line, but if the minimum wage were increased to above-poverty-line levels, job opportunities for the low-income group could be reduced.

Finally, as Figure 14-10 shows, poverty in Canada has a *regional* character, being most severe in the Atlantic provinces, where for years general economic conditions such as slow growth and high unemployment have generated considerable poverty. As industries such as coal mining, shipbuilding and shipping declined, the failure of other industries to expand

FIGURE 14-9   *Composition of Canada's Poor Population, 1982*

Family type	Percentage of all poor persons
Unattached individuals:	
Over 65	13.9
Under 65	20.1
Families:	
Couples, no children	10.9
Couples, with children	35.3
Single parent, male	3.5
Single parent, female	11.8
Other	4.5
TOTAL	100.0

SOURCE   Canada Employment and Immigration Commission analysis of data from the Survey of Consumer Finances, 1982 (unpublished).
Reproduced by permission of the Minister of Supply and Services Canada.

FIGURE 14-10   *Distribution of Families and Unattached Individuals by Income Groups and Regions, 1987*

Income	Canada	Atlantic provinces	Quebec	Ontario	Prairie provinces	British Columbia
(			Percent			)
Under $10 000	12.7	16.0	14.9	9.6	13.2	14.2
$10 000 – 14 999	10.0	11.4	10.4	8.9	10.7	10.8
$15 000 – 19 999	9.9	10.8	9.3	9.4	10.8	10.6
$20 000 – 29 999	16.8	18.5	18.1	15.0	16.9	17.6
$30 000 – 39 999	14.9	15.8	15.5	14.5	14.5	14.8
$40 000 and over	35.6	27.6	31.7	42.6	34.0	32.1
TOTAL	100.0	100.0	100.0	100.0	100.0	100.0
Average income	$35 965	$30 627	$33 409	$40 326	$34 524	$33 998

SOURCE   Statistics Canada, *Income Distributions by Size in Canada*, 1988.
Reproduced by permission of the Minister of Supply and Services Canada.

and replace them led to depressed economic conditions. Attempts by governments to foster, through subsidies, the growth of other industries such as electronics, steel and petroleum refining have generally been disappointments, proving too costly to the taxpayer to be sustained. The basic alternative to moving industry into these regions is for people to move out of them. While migration of workers from lower-income provinces to more prosperous regions to Canada has occurred on a significant scale, this has not been a simple or complete solution, either. Canada is a nation with at least five very distinct regions (the Atlantic provinces, Quebec, Ontario, the Prairies and British Columbia), and migration from region to region is not always easy. Besides the obvious problem of distances (which can be offset by the federal government's grants to assist migrating families), there are cultural obstacles to migration (many people in low-income regions are reluctant to migrate to more prosperous but unfamiliar areas) and language obstacles, which limit migration both into and out of Quebec. As a result, the problem of regional economic disparities has been a persistent one in Canada, and seems likely to remain so.

The extent of poverty

As Figure 14-11 shows, a significant number of Canadians live on low incomes. The extent of poverty declined considerably from 1961 to 1981, but began to increase again under the pressure of the severe recession of the early 1980's and the high unemployment that followed it. According to the National Anti-Poverty Organization (NAPO), the increase in family poverty in 1982 and 1983 wiped out the gains that had been registered in the previous six years. After 1983, however, improved economic conditions reduced the degree of poverty to lower levels.

FIGURE 14-11 *Percentage of Canadians with Low Income, 1961-87*

Year	Unattached individuals	Families	Persons
1961	49.2	27.9	N.A.*
1971	43.1	18.3	20.6
1981	37.8	12.0	14.7
1983	41.3	14.0	17.1
1985	36.8	13.3	16.0
1987	33.5	11.3	14.1

SOURCE For 1961–1981, F. Vaillancourt, "Income Distribution and Economic Security in Canada: An Overview," in *Income Distribution and Economic Security in Canada*, vol. 1, prepared for the Royal Commission on the Economic Union and Development Prospects for Canada (Toronto: University of Toronto Press, 1985), Table 12. Since 1981, Statistics Canada, *Income Distribution by Size in Canada*.

*N.A. = not available.
Reproduced by permission of the Minister of Supply and Services Canada.

By conservative estimate 3 535 000 Canadians—one in seven—lived on low incomes in 1987. The provincial poverty rate ranged widely from 10.3 percent in well-off Ontario to 20.8 percent in economically disadvantaged Newfoundland.

National Council of Welfare,
1989 Poverty Lines (April, 1989)

By international standards, the degree of inequality in Canada's distribution of income is neither unusually high nor unusually low. Compared to other industrialized countries, Canada ranks approximately midway in income inequality.

Nonetheless, poverty in Canada represents a persistent economic, social and political problem. On the positive side, *significant progress* has been made over the past quarter century in reducing the extent of poverty. There has been considerable disagreement as to the reasons for this trend, with some observers giving the credit to *government programs* to redistribute income (which will be examined in the next chapter) and others attributing it to the *rapid economic progress* of the era, in which most Canadians have shared to some degree.

THE SHIFTING DEFINITION OF POVERTY

Statistics Canada's low-income cut-offs increase as living standards rise: for instance, in 1961, Canadians were considered poor if they spent more than 70 percent of their income on essentials, whereas since 1978, Canadians who spend more than 58.5 percent of their income on essentials are considered poor. As a result, the definition of poverty is not constant, but rather changes over time. By the 1978 definition of poverty, 11.3 percent of Canadian families were poor in 1987, whereas by the 1961 definition, less than 8 percent of families were poor in that year.

There is an important relationship between poverty and the general condition of the economy. It is far easier to reduce poverty during periods of economic prosperity, not only because good economic conditions provide more opportunities for the poor, but also because prosperity makes higher-income groups less resistant to programs that redistribute income to lower-income groups. Much of the progress that has been achieved has occurred during periods of prosperity, when a rapidly increasing economic pie made it possible for *all* groups to gain economically. On the other hand, recessions such as that of 1982-83, have the opposite effect: not only are job opportunities for the poor reduced, but the incomes of the poor also tend to lag behind other groups, leaving the poor farther behind in an intensified struggle for a larger share of the static economic pie.

POVERTY: AN ILLUSTRATION

Takes, as an illustration, a single mother on welfare who supports one child aged two and lives in the largest city in her province. Her family's total income from provincial social assistance and refundable tax credits and federal family allowances and the child tax credit ranged from 59 percent to 84 percent of the poverty line in 1986, depending on her province of residence. If she lives in Toronto, her income in 1989 will be an estimated $12 311, which represents just 65 percent of the amount the Social Planning Council of Metropolitan Toronto considers necessary for her family to maintain "an adequate but modest" standard of living. The gap between her income and the Social Planning Council's basic income level is wide—over $6 500.

National Council of Welfare, *1989 Poverty lines*

Employment trends in Canada

As Figures 14-12 and 14-13 show, there have been major changes in the nature of work in Canada since the Second World War. Broadly speaking, the major trend has been a large increase in the proportion of Canadians producing *services*, and a corresponding decline in the proportion producing *goods*, as illustrated in Figure 14-12. Figure 14-13 breaks this trend down into its component parts: a dramatic decline not only in the proportion, but also the actual number, of Canadians employed in *agriculture*; a gradual but steady decline in the proportion of employment accounted for by the *manufacturing* sector; a slight increase in the proportion of employment provided by *trade, finance, insurance* and *real estate*; and a dramatic increase in employment in a variety of community, business and personal *service industries* and *public administration*, or the government sector. In the following sections, we will examine the causes and implications of these trends, both today and in the future.

FIGURE 14-12 *Shares of Total Employment of the Goods-Producing and Service-Producing Sectors, 1951-88*

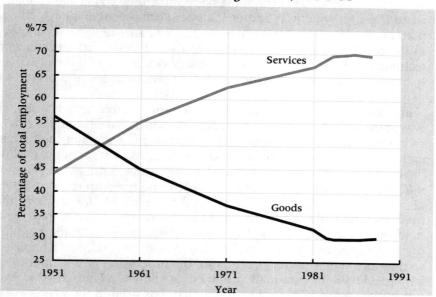

FIGURE 14-13 **The Changing Nature of Employment in Canada**

	Percent of labor force employed in each sector in:				
	1951	1961	1971	1981	1988
Agriculture	18.4	11.2	6.3	4.4	3.6
Non-agricultural primary industries	4.4	3.0	2.7	2.9	2.4
Manufacturing	26.5	24.0	21.8	19.3	17.2
Construction	6.8	6.2	6.0	5.9	5.9
Total goods-producing sector	56.1	44.5	36.9	32.5	30.2
Transportation, storage, communication and utilities	8.8	9.3	8.7	8.3	7.4
Trade	14.1	16.9	16.5	17.1	17.7
Finance, insurance, real estate	3.0	3.9	4.9	5.4	5.9
Community, business and personal services and public administration	18.0	25.3	33.0	36.7	39.8
Total service-producing sector	43.9	55.5	63.1	67.5	69.8
Total all industries	100.0	100.0	100.0	100.0	100.0

SOURCE Statistics Canada, *The Labour Force: Labour Force Annual Averages,* 1981–88.

Reproduced by permission of the Minister of Supply and Services Canada.

The demand side: Technological change . . .

Technological change is the most basic force underlying the changing nature of employment. While technology affects the production methods used in all industries, it has generally proven easier to apply technology to the production of *goods*, which lend themselves to mass-production techniques, than to the production of services, many of which (such as haircuts, medical services and education) require more of a person-to-person approach.

In Canada as in other nations, the first impact of technological change was in the *agricultural sector* of the economy, which is well-suited to extensive use of capital equipment. The result has been a major increase in agricultural productivity over this century, and a corresponding decline in the number of workers required in the agricultural sector. Viewed differently, technological change in agriculture freed up large numbers of workers from that sector, making them available for work in the manufacturing and service sectors of the economy. While employment (and output) increased rapidly in the *manufacturing sector* for a while, manufacturing is also quite well suited to mass-production technology, so that for the past thirty years or so, the proportion of the labor force employed there has gradually declined, as shown in Figure 14-13. As a result, the largest increase in employment has been in the *services sector*, whose share of total employment has increased greatly. During this century, then, the nature of work done by Canadians has undergone major changes: early in the century, most young people stayed and worked on the farm; later, many would go to work in manufacturing plants; now, most take jobs in offices or service industries.

Within the manufacturing sector, the nature of work is also changing. In the past, manufacturing operations have been characterized by large numbers of workers performing physical production work. Today, however, Northern Telecom, a large Canadian manufacturer of telephone systems, estimates that one-fifth of its workforce physically makes things. The rest are involved in planning, designing, programming, problem-solving and selling.

. . . And changes in consumer demand

Obviously, such significant growth in service-industry employment could not occur without major increases in the *demand for services*. By increasing output per worker (productivity), technological changes have *increased the standard of living* of Canadians. And, as people grew wealthier, they tended to spend an increasing proportion of their incomes on services such as restaurants, entertainment and travel. This growing demand for services provided employment in the service sector for many of those people no longer needed in the goods-producing sector. Since most service industries are labor-intensive, the rising demand for services generated a vast number of service-industry jobs, sufficient to allow the economy to absorb labor freed up from the agricultural and manufacturing sectors by technological change. And so, the shift of employment from the goods sector of the economy to the service sector was generally achieved quite smoothly, without undue increases in unemployment.

The shifts in employment that we have been describing have had other implications for Canadians. As technology progressed, jobs became more complex and sophisticated, causing an increase in *educational and training requirements*. Also, there was a large increase in the *number of women working*, as many women found jobs in the rapidly-expanding service industries and white-collar (office) sector.

Finally, these shifts in employment also had major effects upon the nature of Canada's union movement. In the mid-1960's, US-based unions had dominated the Canadian labor movement, representing 70 percent of union members. Most unions were based in the manufacturing and trades sectors. Over the next two decades, however, these sectors were severely undercut by technological change, and unions began to seek out other sectors in which to maintain their share of the labor force. In Canada, union growth was maintained to a significant extent by the formation of unions of government employees. These unions quickly replaced the US-based unions as the dominant voice within the Canadian labor movement and, coupled with the Canadianization of some American-based unions, reduced the US share of Canadian union membership to 35 percent.

However, with nearly 90 percent of government employees now covered by union contracts, the Canadian union movement must look elsewhere to sustain its growth. Specifically, unions must succeed in organizing the rapidly growing service and white-collar (office) sectors, which are not traditional areas of union strength and which are often quite resistant to unionization. In 1985, only 43 percent of white-collar employees were covered by union contracts, and an even smaller proportion were union members. Unions were anxious to increase their white-collar membership by organizing large employers such as the chartered banks.

The supply side: Working women

On the supply side of the labor market, there is no doubt that the most dramatic and important development in recent years has been the great increase in the number of *working women*. In 1950, the percentage of women of working age participating in the labor force—the *participation rate*—was 23.2 percent. By 1988, it was 57.4 percent.[4] Participation rates increased most rapidly for married women, who accounted for only one-eighth of the labor force in 1961, but over one-quarter in the 1980's. Overall, women comprised 44 percent of the labor force in 1988, compared to less than 22 percent in 1950.

> Perhaps the most important labor force development in this period (the 1970's) was the increase in the proportion of married women in the labor force.
>
> Industrial Relations Centre,
> Queen's University at Kingston
> *The Current Industrial Relations Scene in Canada*, 1980 (page 64).

These trends are reflected in Figure 14-14, which highlights the rising participation rate of women since the 1950's. As we saw earlier in this chapter, this was a key factor in the rise in family income over this period, with 84 percent of the highest-income families having more than one income by 1981.

Several reasons have been advanced for this remarkable growth of the female work force. Probably the most frequently mentioned factor is the *squeeze on family incomes*. After the mid-1970's, wages and salaries in general did not keep up with inflation, making it more important for families to have a second income. However, as Figure 14-14 shows, the increase in female participation rates was underway long before this became a factor. This suggests that other factors were also at work.

Another reason for the change is the *rising education levels and aspirations of women*. Many more women are completing high school and going on to college and university for higher education than in the past. And, as women's education levels have risen, so have their expectations concerning their jobs, incomes and careers. However, these factors only increase the numbers of women *wanting* to work. For this to be translated into more working women, there have to be more job opportunities for women.

These opportunities were provided by *the rapid growth of the service sector* of the economy, as described earlier in this chapter. Service-industry jobs are well suited to women for various reasons. Unlike many goods-industry jobs, they do not require physical strength so much as the ability to think and to deal with people. Also, many service industries, such as retail trade, provide part-time work, which appeals to women with

---

[4] Over the same period, the participation rate for males declined gradually, from 84 to 77 percent, largely as a result of a trend toward earlier retirement.

FIGURE 14-14 *Participation Rates of Men and Women, 1950-88*

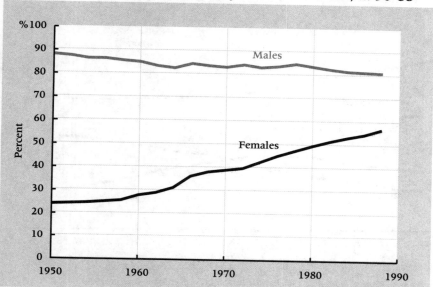

SOURCE   Statistics Canada, *The Labour Force* Reproduced by permission of the Minister of Supply and Services Canada

family responsibilities. The importance of the growth of the service sector to the increase in the number of working women can be measured by the fact that over 82 percent of Canada's female labor force works in the service sector of the economy.

An important difference between male and female labor force participation rates occurs after the age of 50. After age 50, female participation rates are considerably lower, as the figures for 1988 below show. Male participation rates also decline, but not nearly as rapidly.

Age Group	Males	Females
15 years and over	76.6%	57.4%
15-24 years	72.2	66.9
25-44 years	94.4	75.5
45-54 years	91.5	66.6
55-64 years	66.6	35.5
65 years and over	11.5	3.9
55 years and over	38.9	17.8

SOURCE: Statistics Canada, *Labour Force Annual Averages, 1981-88* (71-529), p.15

FIGURE 14-15 *Labor Force Composition by Demographic Groups 1966-88*

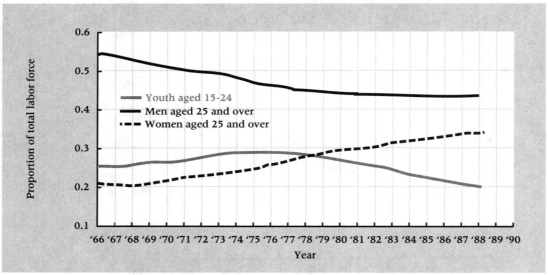

SOURCE Department of Finance, *Quarterly Economic Review,* Annual Reference Tables, June 1989.

Finally, many more women are self-supporting than in the past. It is estimated that six in ten women at some time in their life will be self-supporting. More women are opting for careers, and more marriages break down now than in the past.

Figure 14-15 shows the changes in the composition of the labor force from 1968-86. Due to the rising female participation rates already discussed, the proportion of women in the labor force rose steadily over this period. The 1970's saw a similarly rapid increase in the proportion of *young Canadians* (age 15-24) in the labor force, as the postwar "baby boom" came of working age. However, in the early 1980's, this surge of young entrants to the work force waned, while the proportion of women in the labor force continued to rise.

The question of unemployment

The entry into the labor market of large numbers of baby boomers and women also affected the level of unemployment in Canada. As Figure 14-16 shows, the unemployment rate—the percentage of the labor force unemployed—moved upward from 1965 until 1980, despite the fact that the number of jobs also grew quite rapidly during most of these years.

By the 1980's, most of the baby boomers had entered the labor force, but the "Great Recession" of the early 1980's and its aftermath of slow employment growth left unemployment high until the late 1980's. At the end of the decade, after several years of economic recovery from the

FIGURE 14-16 *Unemployment Rates, 1960-88*

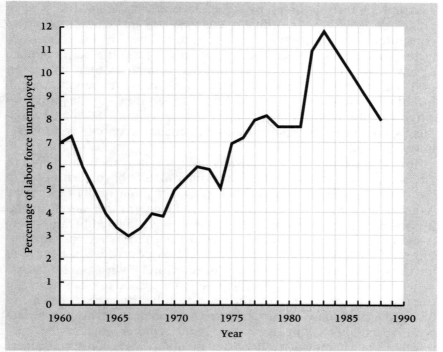

SOURCE Statistics Canada, *Historical Labour Force Statistics (71-201).*

recession, the unemployment rate was finally reduced to its lowest level since 1979. And, while most forecasts foresaw an economic slowdown and higher unemployment rates in the early 1990's, the general view was that unemployment rates would be relatively low for much of the 1990's, thanks to a combination of slow labor-force growth (due to the low birth rates of the 1970's) and modest economic growth.[5]

Will technological change cause unemployment?

When unemployment rises, fears are often raised that technological change is displacing people from jobs and condemning ever-higher numbers of people to unemployment. Such concerns have accompanied the introduction of various types of technology in the past, from farm machinery to industrial equipment to computers. During the recession

---

[5] "Reasonably low" refers to the Canada-wide average unemployment rate. Unfortunately, a "reasonably low" national average unemployment rate generally consists of a very low unemployment rate in central Canada and uncomfortably high rates in some regions, especially the Atlantic provinces.

of the early 1980's, the focus of concern was the expanded use of micro-electronics which was seen by some observers as a new kind of technological revolution. According to this view, the introduction of micro-computer technology was occurring more swiftly than previous technological changes that had transformed agriculture and manufacturing. It was feared that in the process, computerization would cut swiftly and heavily into the clerical, office, sales and service sectors, including small business, that had provided so much of the growth of employment in Canada over the past quarter century. Such a development would generate serious strains on Canada's economy and society, it was claimed.

However, economists are generally quite sceptical about such doomsday scenarios. They point out that similar alarms have been raised in the past when agricultural technology and manufacturing technology reduced labor requirements, but that no long-term increase in unemployment resulted.[6] In large part problems were averted because there is another, less-noticed aspect to technological change that tends to offset its negative effect on employment. As technology progresses, rising output per worker generates *higher living standards* and *higher disposable incomes*. When the increased income is spent, jobs are created in other sectors of the economy, most notably the service-industry sector, which has received a large share of rising consumer spending over the past quarter century. As labor-saving technology reduces the production costs and prices of some items (such as food and manufactured goods), consumers have more income available to spend on other items, such as services (entertainment, restaurants, etc.). This means that there are powerful *automatic job-creation forces* at work in the economy to offset the potentially destructive effects of technological change.

> From 1978 to 1988, the output of the manufacturing sector of the Canadian economy increased by about 30 percent. Over the same period, employment in manufacturing increased by only 7.6 percent. However, employment in the service sector of the economy grew by 30.3 percent over the same period.

The key to the level of unemployment is the general condition of the economy, as Figure 14-16 illustrates. When the economy is growing rapidly (as in 1961-66, 1972-74 and the period following the 1982-83 recession), the unemployment rate falls. On the other hand, when the

[6] It is generally accepted that changing technology generates *short-term* increases in unemployment, as labor must shift from industries and sectors where employment is declining to those where it is expanding. However, the disruption is regarded as mostly transitional in nature, rather than representing an addition to the long-term level of unemployment.

economy slides into a recession (such as 1958-61, 1970-71, 1975-78 and 1982-83), the unemployment rate rises. Technological change was occurring throughout the nearly 30 years covered by Figure 14-16, but the unemployment rate did not increase steadily; rather, it rose during recessions and fell when the economy grew more rapidly.

These overall economic conditions are determined by the level of *aggregate demand* for goods and services, or the amount of total spending in the economy by consumers, businesses, governments and foreign purchasers of exports. If aggregate demand is high, the economy will boom and unemployment will decline. If, on the other hand, aggregate demand is low, there will be a recession and unemployment will increase. If the general level of unemployment in the economy is considered to be too high, the government can boost aggregate demand—and thus employment—by increasing the volume of money in circulation (**monetary policy**) and increasing government spending and/or reducing taxes (**fiscal policy**). These policies must be used with some moderation, however, because if aggregate demand rises excessively, the result will be more severe inflation, as excess demand pulls up prices throughout the economy.

There is no significant evidence that the massive unemployment of the 1930s or of the present day resulted from technological change. Most of those examining both periods would agree that the sharp rise in unemployment resulted from the fact that total demand for goods and services in the economy fell considerably short of the economy's ability to produce them.

Royal Commission on the Economic Union and
Development Prospects for Canada
(Ottawa: Minister of Supply and Services, 1985)

Finally, any consideration of unemployment in a country with an economy as open to *foreign trade* as Canada's has to take into account the ability of the nation's industries to compete internationally. Many Canadian jobs depend upon the ability of Canadian businesses to export to foreign markets or compete with imports in Canadian markets. An ongoing concern about the Canadian economy is that the efficiency of Canadian producers in general (as measured by labor productivity, or output per worker per hour) has lagged behind their foreign competitors, undermining Canada's ability to compete internationally. Over this period, Canada's share of world trade has declined, with negative effects upon employment in Canada. Therefore, rather than posing a threat to employment, many economists believe that technological change and

---

LABOR FORCE FACTS FROM 1978 TO 1988:

- Approximately 2.3 million new jobs were created in Canada.
- Over 2 million of these new jobs were in the services sector.
- More than two-thirds of the new jobs (68 percent) went to women, as 1.6 million females entered the labor force (as compared to only 765 000 new male entrants).
- About 30 percent of the new jobs were part-time, bringing part-time jobs up to 15.4 percent of total jobs (as compared to 12.1 percent in 1978).

---

higher productivity are important for the protection and creation of Canadian jobs, because they improve Canadians' ability to compete internationally. In generally, economists are not nearly as concerned that technological change will cause unemployment as are the media and the general public.

Trends in the future

It is difficult to forecast future trends in labor markets, but a few broad developments seem likely. On the *supply side* of the labor market, one safe prediction is that *the labor force will mature*, as the postwar baby boom group ages and the 1970's ''baby bust'' group enters the labor force.[7] These trends reduced the proportion of the labor force in the 15-24 age group from its 1979 high of 27 percent to only 19 percent by 1989. As the 1990's progress, the average age of Canada's labor force will continue to rise.

It is also expected that the proportion of the labor force accounted for by *women* will increase. The increases in the participation rate for women shown in Figure 14-14 are expected to continue, although less rapidly, and the participation rate for men is expected to continue its gradual decline, mainly due to earlier retirements.

After the year 2010, the baby boomers will move into retirement age, and Canada will be faced with a new economic challenge: the ratio of retired people to working people will reach unprecedented highs. In the simplest economic terms, the wealth produced by a relatively small group of working Canadians will have to be shared with a relatively

---

[7] The low birth rates of much of the 1970's mean that there will be fewer young people entering the labor force for much of the 1990's.

large group of non-working (retired) Canadians. Unless changes are made, this could place a serious burden on working Canadians during this period. One such change that some observers are predicting is the extension of retirement age beyond the traditional age of 65. This would not only reduce the numbers of retired people to be supported, but also add to the numbers of Canadians working and thus contributing to their support. As lifespans increase, the concept of mandatory retirement at 65 is now being challenged, and pressures to at least provide people with the option of working beyond 65 seem likely to grow.

Forecasts on the *demand side* of the labor market are particularly difficult, because the demand for labor is affected by changes in both consumer demand and technology, both of which are notoriously difficult to predict. In general terms, even moderate economic growth with a moderately-rising overall demand for labor is likely to keep *unemployment rates low*, considering that the labor force is projected to grow slowly over much of the 1990's. In this environment, *shortages of particular skills* are quite likely, even during economic slowdowns. As the trends toward higher-technology production methods and more service-industry jobs continue, employers are likely to face increased difficulty recruiting the more skilled and educated work force that they will require (see Figure 14-17). This will place increased pressure on educational institutions to provide more and *better skills training*, perhaps in cooperation with employers. The failure to provide such training has been a long-standing weakness of Canadian industry and educational institutions, and will require attention in the economic environment of the future.

FIGURE 14-17 *Skill Requirements in the Canadian Economy*

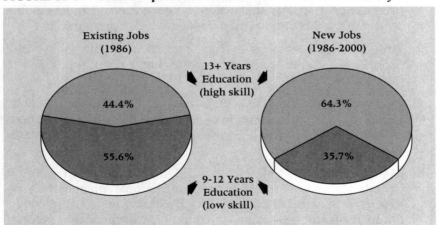

SOURCE Statistics Canada; Employment and Immigration Canada, Canadian Occupational Projection Systems (COPS), in *Adjusting to Win: Report of the Advisory Council on Adjustment, 1989 (p. 24).*

DEFINITIONS OF NEW TERMS

Equal Pay for Work of Equal Value   The concept that the value of *different* jobs may be measured against each other using a point system that incorporates a variety of criteria, including skill levels, effort, degree of responsibility and working conditions.

Poverty Lines   Income levels below which families or individuals are considered to be poor.

Monetary Policy   The control of aggregate demand by government through increasing the volume of money in circulation.

Fiscal Policy   The control of aggregate demand by government through increasing government spending and/or reducing taxes.

CHAPTER SUMMARY

1. There is considerable inequality in the distribution of income among various occupational groups in Canada, partly due to natural obstacles and partly due to artificial barriers to entry into various occupations.

2. There also exists a pay differential between men and women of about 10 to 15 percent that is attributed to gender factors. In particular, women tend to be concentrated in certain occupational groupings, in which many jobs have below-average incomes. To deal with this, "equal pay for work of equal value" legislation has been passed in several jurisdictions for government employees, but as of 1990, only Ontario had extended it to the private sector.

3. Poverty, which tends to be concentrated in certain groups and regions, is a significant economic, social and political problem in Canada.

4. Over the years, the extent of poverty in Canada has gradually decreased, with the exception of the early 1980's, when a serious economic recession and high unemployment temporarily reversed this trend.

5. Due to changes in technology and demand, the composition of Canada's labor force has changed greatly: employment in the services sector has increased rapidly and employment in the goods-producing sector (especially agriculture) has declined as a percentage of the labor force.

6. The increased participation of women in the job market has been the outstanding trend in the labor force since the early 1970's.

Working wives are now a key factor in the vast majority of Canada's highest-income families.

7. It is expected that Canada's labor force in the future will be comprised of an increasing proportion of women and older workers, as female participation rates continue to rise and the population ages.

8. While some Canadians are concerned that technological progress will generate high unemployment in the future, most economists are not so pessimistic.

QUESTIONS

1. "Only a totally fouled-up society would pay an uncouth lout of a hockey player ten times the salary of its Prime Minister or a doctor." Discuss this statement.

2. What are some of the obstacles to the recruitment of service- industry and white-collar workers by unions? What factors may assist unions in their attempts to organize these workers? Do you believe that unions will succeed or fail in these attempts?

3. Why has the labor force participation rate of women, especially married women, increased so greatly?

4. Suppose that, in order to allow a major Canadian industry to remain competitive with foreign producers, technological changes had to be made which would result in the layoff of thousands of employees. What could be done to minimize the problems associated with such a situation?

5. Critics of job evaluation systems such as those used to compare jobs for the purpose of "equal pay for work of equal value" argue that such systems merely replace incomes that are determined in the marketplace with incomes that are determined by someone's arbitrary assessment of how many points a job is "worth."

   Try your hand at job evaluation by comparing the jobs of *nurse* and *police constable*. Use the points assigned to the jobs of receptionist and warehouseman on page 262 as a guide in assigning points to the jobs of nurse and police constable. Have a friend make a similar assessment and compare your results.

CHAPTER 15

Government and the economy

As discussed in Chapter 3, the Canadian economy is basically "market" in nature, with most economic activity being carried out by private businesses in response to consumer demand. However, there is also a substantial amount of government involvement in the economy, and this government involvement has grown over the years.

The most commonly used measure of this growing role of government in the economy is the size of *total government spending* (by all three levels of government—federal, provincial and local) as a percentage of Gross Domestic Product (GDP). By this standard, as Figure 15-1 shows, the extent of government involvement in the economy has grown considerably since the 1950's.

Figure 15-2 breaks total government spending down into some of its major components, and shows the growth of government spending in each area from 1950 to 1983.[1]

As a *purchaser of goods and services*, the role of government has grown substantially. In 1950, government current spending on goods and services amounted to 13.4 percent of total current expenditures (of both households and governments); by 1983, this had doubled to about 27 percent. As a *redistributor of income*, the role of government has also increased considerably. In 1950, the proportion of total personal income that consisted of transfer payments was 7.1 percent;[2] by 1983 this had

---

[1] 1983 was the year in which most such measures of government spending relative to the size of the economy peaked. This was partly due to the recession of 1982-83, which sharply increased spending on Unemployment Insurance. Since 1983, as we will see, these measures of government spending have declined somewhat, as governments have tried to restrain their spending.

[2] Transfer payments are payments whereby governments redistribute income from some people to others, such as Welfare, Family Allowances and Unemployment Insurance.

FIGURE 15-1 *Total Government Expenditure as a Percentage of
GDP,*[1] *1950-88*

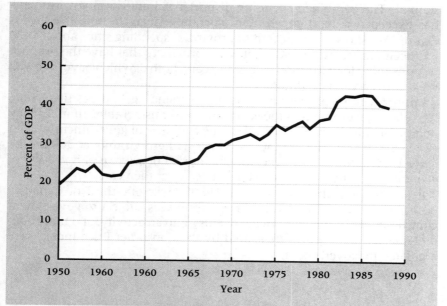

1 Gross Domestic Product (GDP) is an approximation of the total value of output
produced and incomes earned in the economy in any given year.

SOURCE Department of Finance, *Quarterly Economic Review.* June 1989.

FIGURE 15–2 *The Growth of Government Spending, 1950-83*

	1950	1983
Government current expenditure on goods and services as a percentage of total (household plus government) current expenditure on goods and services	13.4%	26.8%
Government transfer payments to persons as a percentage of total personal income	7.1	14.9
Government wages and salaries as a percentage of total wages and salaries	11.7	27.6

SOURCE Department of Finance, *Quarterly Economic Review*, June 1989.

reached 14.9 percent. Finally, the role of government as an *employer* has
expanded greatly as well. In 1950, government wages and salaries
amounted to only 11.7 percent of total wages and salaries in Canada,
while in 1983 they were well over twice that proportion at 27.6 percent.

While most discussions of government spending in Canada focus on *federal* spending, spending by *provincial* and *local* governments is also substantial. The combined spending of provincial and local governments has exceeded federal government spending since the mid-1960's. As Figure 15-3 shows, the growth of provincial spending since about 1970 has been particularly rapid, as it is the provinces that have the primary responsibility for education and health care, both of which have involved major increases in spending.

Impressive though they may be, these spending statistics understate the role of government in the economy by a considerable amount. They do not include the rapid increase in the activities of government-owned *Crown corporations,* the number of which had grown to over 300 by the early 1980's. Nor do they include the myriad of *government regulations* of economic activity that have been enacted over the years.

It is estimated that in the early 1980's over one-third of Canada's economic activity (as measured by output) was subject to government controls over production, pricing or entry into an activity, and that about one-quarter of the prices measured by the Consumer Price Index were regulated by government.

FIGURE 15-3 *Spending[1] by Federal, Provincial and Local Governments, 1950-88*

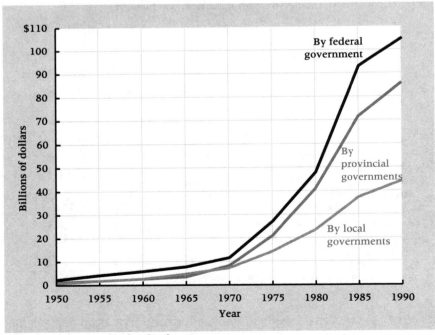

1 Net of transfers to other levels of government.
SOURCE Department of Finance, *Quarterly Economic Review,* June 1989

REGULATION

Canada, like other western industrialized nations, has become a regulated society. In the morning the clock radio awakens us with the sound of music subject to Canadian content regulations. The price, at the farm gate, of the eggs we eat for breakfast has been set by a government marketing board. We drive to work on tires that must meet federal minimum safety standards and in a car whose exhaust is subject to pollution emission regulations. At lunch, the restaurant in which we eat has been subject to the scrutiny of public health inspectors. The monthly rate for the telephone we use at the office is set by a federal or provincial regulatory agency. Shopping in the supermarket on the way home, we note the unpronounceable names of certain chemical preservatives that, by government regulation, are disclosed to us on a finely printed label. As we turn down the thermostat before retiring, we are confident that a government agency has protected our purse by setting the price we will be charged by the local monopoly supplier of natural gas. Putting on our sleepwear, we are secure in our knowledge that it is not impregnated with a hazardous substance. . . .
. . . If we live in certain cities, we approach our rest reassured that the smoke detector we were required to install will stand on guard throughout the night. In the words of Samuel Pepys, ''And so to bed.'' . . .

The Council defines regulation as the imposition of constraints, backed by government authority, that are intended to modify economic behaviour of individuals in the private sector significantly. Regulation is effected by government departments and by statutory regulatory agencies primarily through the use of statutes and subordinate legislation in the form of regulations. The scope of regulation in Canada is so great that it is difficult to think of an activity, good, or service that is not subject to government regulation, directly or indirectly. . . .

Economic Council of Canada, *Responsible Regulation;*
An Interim Report, November 1979

Thus, the role of government in the Canadian economy has expanded greatly over the past half-century. In this chapter, we will examine the reasons for this growth, the present extent of government's role, some concerns and criticisms, as well as possible future trends with respect to the role of government in the Canadian economy.

The growth of the welfare state

As we have seen, Canadian governments spend substantial amounts of money on social welfare, with most of it going to the three key areas of *income security* (such as Unemployment Insurance, Welfare and pensions), *health care* and *education*. Government spending on these programs has risen dramatically during the twentieth century. Why has this happened?

In the most basic sense, the rise of the welfare state was brought about by the transition from a rural, agrarian society of small communities to a modern, urban society with a large industrial work force. In the earlier society of small, closely-knit and stable communities, *traditional institutions* such as the family, the Church, the local community and private charity were able to take care of the social needs of those who required assistance. However, as Canada evolved into an *urban society* with a large, mobile work force comprised largely of industrial employees, the situation changed greatly. People and families were exposed to increased risks of loss of income due to unemployment (or layoff), illness, disability and old age. The traditional social institutions were less and less able to provide for Canadians' social needs, making it increasingly necessary for governments to extend assistance to those who needed it. The growth of the welfare state acquired considerable momentum from the *Great Depression* of the 1930's. The depression destroyed faith in the ''laissez-faire'' philosophy that the economy could be counted upon to automatically provide employment for all who wanted it, and made much more acceptable the idea that the government should intervene in the economy and provide assistance to the victims of economic dislocations and insecurity.

> Income security, health and education represent central supports of the welfare state.
>
> Royal Commission on the Economic Union and
> Development Prospects for Canada
> (Ottawa, Minister of Supply and Services, 1985).

Income security programs

In the decades that followed, Canada's welfare state expanded greatly. In the field of *income security programs*, Unemployment Insurance was introduced in 1942, Family Allowances in 1945, Old Age Security in 1952, various social assistance programs in the 1950's, the Canada and Quebec Pension Plans in 1965, the Canada Assistance Plan for social welfare and the Guaranteed Income Supplement in 1966, the Spouses' Allowance in 1975 and the Child Tax Credit in 1978. Also, in the 1970's, the Unemployment Insurance and Family Allowance programs were enriched significantly, and many programs were *indexed* so that transfer payments to beneficiaries would keep pace with increases in the Consumer Price Index. Figure 15-4 traces the growth of government spending on Canada's major income-security programs from 1956 to 1987.

FIGURE 15–4 *Expenditure on Major Income Security Programs, 1956-87*

Programs	1956	1960	1964	1968	($ millions) 1972	1976	1980	1984	1987
Federal									
OAS-GIS*	376	587	871	1 478	2 430	4 305	7 020	10 999	14 006
Unemployment Insurance	210	482	344	438	1 869	3 332	4 332	9 859	10 369
Family allowances	394	502	559	615	611	1 942	1 812	2 393	2 552
Canada Pension Plan	—	—	—	11	190	775	1 903	4 045	6 948
Provincial									
Social assistance direct relief	20	24	59	381	751	1 392	2 414	4 509	5 618
Old age and blind pensions	60	80	116	40	23	334	565	673	829
Mothers' and disabled allowances	37	73	93	69	41	64	116	254	295
Workers' Compensation	70	92	124	177	280	701	1 192	2 144	2 940
Quebec Pension Plan	—	—	—	4	58	261	664	1 554	2 326
Local									
Direct relief	24	57	80	131	244	270	394	726	957
TOTAL	1 191	1 897	2 246	3 344	6 497	13 376	20 412	37 156	46 840

SOURCE Statistics Canada, *National Income and Expenditure Accounts.*

*Old Age Security-Guaranteed Income Supplement.

Another important, although less visible, way in which governments support people's incomes is through *tax credits* in the income tax system. These tax credits reduce the income tax payable by Canadians in order to offset a variety of factors that adversely affect their living standards, from children and other dependents to sales taxes and property taxes. Some of these tax credits are structured so as to be of benefit only to lower-income individuals and families.

Health care

Health care represents the second key element of Canada's social welfare system. Following the introduction of hospital-insurance and medicare programs, government expenditures on health care grew very rapidly. From the mid-1950's to the mid-1980's, health expenditures rose from 5.7 to 8.4 percent of Gross Domestic Product, and the government's share of health expenditures increased from less than half to more than three-quarters of total costs. By the late 1980's the prospective costs of providing health care to an aging population had become a major concern of many provincial governments.

Education

Education—the third pillar of Canada's social welfare system—has also become a major expenditure of governments. While education costs as a percentage of GDP declined after the baby boomers had completed their education, the provision of an educational system suited to the demands of a modern society and economy such as Canada's remains a major expenditure item for governments.

Government in the Canadian economy as of the mid-1980's

By the mid-1980's, the role and cost of government in the Canadian economy had grown to a substantial size. Canada's welfare state, and especially its income-security system, consisted of the complex mix of federal, provincial and local programs shown in Figure 15-5. Some programs, such as Unemployment Insurance and the Canada Pension Plan, were *social insurance plans* to which Canadians made contributions or paid premiums. Others, such as welfare and family allowances, did not involve such contributions by those eligible for benefits; they were *direct government expenditures.* Still others, such as income-tax credits for dependents, sales taxes and property taxes, took the form of *tax expenditures,* or reductions in the taxes payable by beneficiaries. In 1984-85, the total cost of these progams was over $60 billion, or 13 percent of GDP.

In addition to these programs for individuals and families, governments provided many *services and subsidies to businesses.* The 1985 Nielsen Task Force on government program review found 218 federal and federal/provincial progams that provided services and subsidies to business at an annual cost of over $16 billion, and employed 68 000 people.

During the 1980's, the years of recession placed a heavy burden on many of these government programs, lifting government spending to unprecedented levels. By mid-decade, total spending by all levels of government in Canada amounted to nearly 47 percent of Gross Domestic Product.

Financing problems

The growth of these government expenditures placed serious financial strains on Canada's system of government, because of the way in which the powers to *spend* and *tax* were divided between the three levels of government: federal, provincial and local. Broadly speaking, the origin

FIGURE 15-5 *Estimates of Government Social Security Programs in Canada, 1984-85*

Target group	No. of persons (thousands)	Costs (billions)	
		Federal	Provincial
Poor			
Canada Assistance Plan	3 000	$ 4.1	$ 4.1
Provincial tax credits	107	—	1.6
Veterans' allowance	—	0.5	—
Social assistance to on-reserve Indians	—	0.2	—
Guaranteed Income Supplement & Spouses' Allowance	1 440	3.1	—
Child tax credit	5 000	1.1	—
Social housing	—	1.1	—
Total		10.1	5.7
Families			
Child care expense deduction	370	0.1	0.0
Family Allowance	370	2.4	—
Child tax exemption	6 600	0.9	0.5
Married & equivalent to married	3 230	1.4	0.6
Total		4.8	1.1
Employment Assistance			
Unemployment Insurance	3 200	11.6	—
Training allowance	64	0.1	0.1
Workers' Compensation	620	—	1.6
Employment expense deduction	—	0.8	0.4
Total		12.5	2.1
Elderly			
Canada/Quebec Pension Plan	2 330	4.4(CPP)	1.6
Old Age Security	2 700	8.3	—
Tax assistance (RRSP, RPP, C/QPP)	—	4.7	2.3
Age exemption	0	0.3	0.2
Pension deduction	903	0.1	—
Veterans' pensions	655	0.7	—
Total		18.5	4.1
Total Income Security		45.9	13.0
Grand Total		61.6	

Note: Calculations supplied by Ministry of State for Social Development, based on 1984-1985 estimates and Department of Finance figures.

SOURCE Royal Commission on the Economic Union and Development Prospects for Canada, 1985.
Reproduced by permission of the Minister of Supply and Services Canada.

of the problem lies in an interpretation of the *British North America Act* which gave to the federal government wide powers to *levy taxes,* while granting to the provincial governments the widest responsibilities for *spending money.* More specifically, the *federal government* possesses the largest single source of revenue—the *personal income tax*—while the *provincial governments* have heavy responsibilities for such major areas of spending as *education, health* and *welfare.* And, as spending in these areas rose rapidly after the mid-1960's, the responsibility (or power) to make major government spending decisions in Canada shifted increasingly toward the provincial governments and away from Ottawa. In 1950, federal government spending was roughly 10 percent greater than the combined spending of the provincial and municipal governments, but by 1980, the provincial and municipal governments were spending about 50 percent more than the federal government. As measured by government spending statistics, this made Canada's system of government one of the most *decentralized* in the world, with a high proportion of spending decisions at the provincial level.

Federal transfers to the provinces

As spending by provincial governments on health, welfare and education increased sharply after the mid-1960's, the provinces experienced problems financing these programs. By contrast, the federal government was well endowed with tax sources, especially the personal income tax. To deal with the provinces' problems, a considerable amount of tax revenue that was being raised by the federal government was *transferred to the provincial governments,* through various federal-provincial fiscal arrangements.

These federal funds were not, however, always handed over to the provinces unconditionally. The federal government has attempted to ensure that certain Canada-wide standards are maintained with respect to public services, and has done so by making federal transfers to the provinces conditional upon the provincial governments following certain *federal guidelines.* While the provinces tended to regard such federal standards as an improper federal intrusion into areas of provincial jurisdiction, they nonetheless often accepted the conditions in order to get the funding.

By the 1980's, these transfers of funds from the federal government to the provinces had grown very large, amounting to about 20 percent of total provincial government revenues, and 40–50 percent of the revenues of some provinces. In 1988, the federal government spent nearly $25 billion of its revenues, or nearly $1000 for every Canadian, on transfer payments to the provincial governments, mostly to help pay for health care, postsecondary education and welfare.

Reassessing the role of government

By the mid-1980's, total government spending (by all levels of government) was over $250 billion, or $10 000 for every Canadian man, woman and child. With its expenditures far larger than its tax revenues, the federal government was borrowing as much as $30 billion per year ($1200 for every Canadian) to pay its bills. Such heavy borrowing accumulated federal government debt in excess of $300 billion, on which the government was paying interest of over $30 billion per year by the late 1980's. As ever-rising interest payments on past borrowings forced the government into further borrowing (and higher interest payments in the future), concern over the sheer cost of government grew. In addition, there was concern that too much money was being wasted, because of inefficiency and ineffectiveness in government programs. In the rest of this chapter, we will consider some of the concerns and proposals for reform regarding:

(a) Canada's social welfare system, and

(b) the size and cost of government in general.

Concerns regarding the role of government

Part A: The social welfare system

As noted earlier, Canada has an extensive social welfare system, the centerpiece of which is a series of *income support programs* such as unemployment insurance, family allowances, the Canada Pension Plan, old age security, welfare, workers' compensation, mothers' allowances, disability allowances and so on. While the majority of Canadians support this social welfare/income security system, critics argue that it is *too complex*, that it is *inequitable*, that it has *undesirable side-effects*, or *disincentives*, and that it is *ineffective*. We will consider each of these in turn.

(i) The social welfare system is too complex and inefficient

It is generally agreed that Canada's social welfare system consists of too many programs with too many people administering them. As a result, it is often difficult for Canadians to discover what benefits they qualify for, and some programs overlap each other in costly duplication. In other cases, needy people are unable to get assistance because of gaps between the jurisdiction and responsibility of the various agencies. Each agency has its own administrative structure, or bureaucracy, which adds to the

> The welfare system in each province is governed by a complex and extensive set of rules. The complexity of the system makes it difficult to understand and be knowledgeable about eligibility or degree of entitlement.
>
> National Council of Welfare,
> *Welfare in Canada: The Tangled Safety Net* (1987)

cost of the welfare system, absorbing tax dollars intended for the assistance of needy Canadians. According to research done by the Fraser Institute, a conservative research think-tank in Vancouver, if transfer payments were given directly to the poor, rather than filtered through the welfare system, every Canadian household below the poverty line in 1984 could have been given an annual subsidy of more than $17 000.

(ii) The social welfare system is inequitable

One basic purpose of a social welfare system is to redistribute income from higher-income to lower-income groups. But under Canada's welfare system, many Canadians who need assistance fail to get it, while billions of dollars of benefits go to those who don't, strictly speaking, need them. This is the trade-off Canadians accept for the long-standing principle of **universality** under which some benefits, such as unemployment insurance, are available to all Canadians, regardless of their income. For example, in the mid-1980's, a larger proportion of UI benefits (20 percent, or about $2 billion per year) went to individuals whose family income was more than $40 000 per year than went to individuals below the poverty line. In addition, the social welfare system provided very little or no assistance to the ''working poor''—people who worked for wages so low that they would have been better off on welfare.

> ''I think that at the present time, if I could find a job, I would refuse it since I would only be about $10 ahead a month by working as compared to welfare. It is not very encouraging. After paying transportation, food, babysitting and the extras you need when working . . . I would come out about $10 ahead . . . So you stay where you are.''
>
> Welfare recipient quoted in National Council of Welfare,
> *Welfare in Canada: the Tangled Safety Net* (1987)

(iii) The social welfare system generates disincentives and side-effects

A major criticism of Canada's social welfare programs is that they often have a negative effect upon the *incentive to work.* While some members of the middle class believe that welfare recipients live so comfortably that they feel no need to work, this is not the case. As a general rule, welfare benefits are well below the poverty line, and most recipients would be better off with even a low-paying full-time job. Not many people would quit a full-time job to go on welfare.

Why, then, do people on welfare often not take jobs that are available, such as part-time work? The answer to this is that the welfare system itself often provides disincentives to work: *for every dollar a welfare recipient earns by working, his or her welfare benefits are reduced,* often by so much that there is little or no incentive to work.[3] It is not the intention of the welfare

---

THE MARGINAL TAX RATE

It is important to note that the *marginal* tax rate is different from the *average* tax rate, which is more commonly known simply as "the tax rate". For instance, in 1988, a person with a taxable income of $27 500 would pay an average tax rate of 26 percent, or about $7200 of income taxes. However, the tax story is quite different for any *increases in income* that this person might earn—the marginal tax rate on these for a person with a taxable income of $27 500 in Ontario* was about 39 percent. Consequently, if this person earned an additional $1000, the income tax payable on that extra $1000 would be $392.

As this example shows, the marginal tax rate is *considerably higher* than the average tax rate—usually about one and one-half times as high. Thus, the answer to the question, "What tax rate do you pay?" depends on wheather you are considering the tax payable on your total income (the average tax rate) or on any *increases* in your income (the marginal tax rate).

*Because provincial income tax rates vary, marginal tax rates are different in different provinces.

---

[3] Welfare agencies attempt to ease this disincentive effect by providing special assistance for work-related expenses. However, experts agree that this is far less desirable than letting clients keep most of the income they earn. Having to give up all or most of that income and then ask for special allowances for work-related expenses merely reinforces their dependency on welfare authorities and discourages them from working.

agencies to erode the incentive to work; their problem is that they only have so many dollars to distribute, so they tend to channel them to those people who need them the most—and people who are earning some money by working don't need as much welfare. However, this tends to have a negative effect upon the welfare recipient, who is in effect told, "If you earn some money, the system will take it away from you." Economists refer to this as paying a high **marginal tax rate**. Many recipients of social welfare gain so little by working that they in effect pay a marginal tax rate of from 80 to 100 percent. By contrast, even the highest-income earners pay a marginal tax rate of less than 50 percent on any extra income they earn.

In conclusion, it is high marginal tax rates that often lie at the root of the disincentives to work associated with welfare programs. To break out of this trap, a person usually has to find a reasonably steady full-time job, so as to move beyond the low income levels where such disincentives prevail. Unfortunately, it can be quite difficult for those at the margin of the labor force, such as the unskilled and the inexperienced, to find such jobs, so the *welfare cycle* tends to go on and on, from year to year and even from generation to generation.

THE MARGINAL TAX RATE AND THE ECONOMIC INCENTIVE TO WORK

The **marginal tax rate** is the percentage of any extra income that is earned which goes to taxes. Because it decides how much of any additional income a person gets to keep, the marginal tax rate is very important to the incentive to work; specifically, the higher the marginal tax rate, the lower the economic incentive to do additional work.

We will consider the marginal tax rates of two people. Joan, a teacher, is wondering whether to teach a night course. The course would pay $1000, but after taxes, Joan would receive only $600, because her marginal tax rate is 40 percent. Joan complains that there is little incentive for her to teach the night course because of these high taxes, which go to support "lazy welfare bums."

Sandy is on Welfare, receiving $600 per month. If she earns $100 per month working part-time, her Welfare will be reduced to $520 per month, leaving her $20 better off for having earned $100. In other words. Sandy's marginal tax rate is 80 percent. Sandy declines the job on the grounds that it's not worth the trouble. Is Sandy a "lazy welfare bum"?

Canada's social welfare programs are also criticized because they tend to *increase unemployment* amongst those who are looking for work. The *unemployment insurance* system has been criticized considerably on these grounds. UI benefits are relatively generous and are available for a year, which causes some recipients to be selective regarding the jobs they will accept, prolonging the duration of their unemployment. To the extent that UI provides the unemployed with the opportunity to take the time to seek out jobs that make the best use of their abilities rather than accept the first available job, UI helps the economy to make the most efficient use of its labor resources. On the other hand, to the extent that UI permits unemployed people not to seek work seriously until their UI benefits run out, UI generates a burden on the economy by creating a disincentive to work.

On reviewing the evidence compiled by a number of researchers, Commissioners have concluded that the unemployment insurance program:

- Contributes to an increase in the duration of unemployment
- Increases the volume of temporary lay-offs
- Reinforces the concentration of temporary and unstable jobs in high-unemployment and low-wage regions
- Provides too generous a subsidy to Canadians whose labour-force behavior is characterized by repeated unstable employment.

We are convinced, therefore, that Canada's UI program does not fully satisfy the objectives of facilitating adequate adjustment in the labour market and developing stable and productive jobs. Consequently, the UI system should be revised to make it more efficient in the coming years.

Royal Commission on the Economic Union and Development Prospects for Canada
(Ottawa, Minister of Supply and Services,1985).

Because UI benefits are more attractive in regions with high unemployment, such as the Atlantic provinces, the UI system also tends to slow down the migration of labor from these regions to other regions with more job opportunities. According to one major study, the changes in the UI system in the early 1970's reduced out-migration from the Atlantic provinces by about 8000 per year. To the extent that UI reduces the migration of unemployed people to regions where job opportunities exist, it increases unemployment.

UI is criticized for slowing labor-force adjustments and contributing to unemployment in another way. Many of the unemployed lack skills, and need retraining if they are to become employed again. However, UI has traditionally focused on income support and provided neither incentives nor resources for retraining.

Minimum wage laws have also been criticized as contributing to unemployment. As noted in Chapter 13, if the minimum wage is too high, it can reduce employment opportunities for some low-wage workers. The irony of this situation, of course, is that while minimum wage laws benefit low-income Canadians, if they are too high they can also harm the very people they are intended to help.

Another side-effect of minimum-wage laws appears to be that they reduce the opportunity for young people to benefit from *training programs*. The report of the Macdonald Royal Commission on the Economic Union and Development Prospects for Canada (1985) stated that

> Raising minimum wages also affects the training opportunities available in the labour market. This effect is particularly important for younger workers whose training and labour-market experience is limited. The expense of providing on-the-job training is often covered by the payment of low wages to employees undergoing a training period: in effect, the training is partly financed by the trainee. Higher wages and higher productivity come into play in the post-training period. High minimum wages tend to discourage such financing methods and, with them, on-the-job training and subsequent wage increases. European countries such as Germany, Austria and Switzerland rely much more on apprenticeship programs than does Canada, for smoothing the transition from school to work. Apprentices' wages are typically quite low compared to those of trained workers: in Germany, for

---

Increases in minimum wages will benefit some low-wage earners: those whose employment opportunities are not reduced. Others, however, will suffer from the reduced employment opportunities. The ones who suffer may well be those with the least skills and the fewest opportunities.

On the basis of these studies, it is estimated that a 10-percent increase in the minimum wage, relative to the average wage, will raise the unemployment rate by 0.2 to 0.5 percentage points.

Royal Commision on the Economic Union and
Development Prospects for Canada
(Ottawa, Minister of Supply and Services, 1985)

example, the average wage for first-year apprentices is about one-fifth the economy's average industrial wage. However, youth minimum wages in most Canadian jurisdictions are equal to a substantially higher proportion of average industrial wages. Several analysts have suggested that this factor accounts for much of the apparently-low incidence of apprenticeship programs and other on-the-job training in Canada.

(iv) The social welfare system is ineffective

Despite expenditures of billions of dollars and a tripling of real per-person welfare expenditures in recent years, the distribution of income remains almost unchanged. Many Canadians still live in poverty, with the poorest fifth of Canadian families and individuals continuing to receive about 4 percent of all income—about the same share as thirty years ago.

One reason for this problem is that the *overall effect* of government expenditure and taxation programs has not been to redistribute income from higher-income Canadians to lower-income earners as much as is generally thought. In considering the effect of government on the distribution of income, most Canadians tend to focus on the welfare system, which transfers income to the poor, and on the progressive income tax, which takes a higher percentage of high incomes than of lower ones. They conclude that government programs generate a substantial redistribution of income from higher-income earners to lower-income ones.

The overall effect of government on the distribution of income in Canada is, however, much more subtle and complex than a simple discussion of income taxes and welfare suggests. While the personal income tax is **progressive,** in that it takes a higher percentage from the rich than from the poor, it is in fact one of the few taxes that has this effect. Many other taxes are **regressive**—they take a greater percentage from low incomes than from higher ones. For instance, an increase in *sales taxes* would have a greater impact on the poor (in percentage terms) than on the rich, and *property taxes* are often regressive. Even a tax that apparently has no effect on the poor may turn out, upon examination, to have quite an unexpected impact. For instance, a large increase in *corporate profits taxes* might look like a progressive tax, because it taxes corporations and their wealthy shareholders. However, if it leads to higher prices for the corporations' products, its effect could well be as regressive as a sales tax. Mainly as a result of the large number of regressive taxes in Canada, the *overall* tax system—when *all* taxes are considered—is not nearly as progressive as most people suppose it to be. In fact, studies in the past have found the tax system to be quite regressive for very low-income groups.

However, the effect of government on the distribution of income is not confined to *taxation*. We must also consider *government expenditures*

Eva owns a house; Ray lives in an apartment. Ray qualifies for a property tax credit (refund), while Eve does not. Is this fair?

Eva earns $30 000 per year and lives in a house on which she pays property taxes of $1200 per year .

Ray earns $15 000 per year and lives in an apartment for which he pays rent of $350 per month, or $4200 per year. Of this, approximately 20%, or $840, goes to property taxes paid by the landlord.

Eva's property taxes amount to 4.0% ($1200 ÷ $30 000) of her income.

Ray's property taxes amount to 5.6% ($840 ÷ $15 000) of his income.

Thus, even though Ray does not own a house, he pays a higher percentage of his income to property taxes than Eva does, which entitles him to a property tax credit. The objective of these tax credits is to relieve the burden of regressive property taxes on lower-income Canadians.

on lower-income groups, such as unemployment insurance and welfare, as well as subsidies for the poor such as low-rent housing provided by governments. Studies indicate that when all these things are taken into account the overall effect of government programs is *only mildly and gradually progressive*. The perception of many people that they are being taxed to death in order to pay for the luxurious idleness of others is not supported by economic studies.

Part B: The cost of government

These concerns about the social welfare system were only part of a larger concern regarding the cost of government in general. After the mid-1970's, government spending increased much faster than tax revenues. By the mid-1980's, governments in Canada were spending more than $30 billion more per year than they were taking in through tax revenues, and huge *government budget deficits* had accumulated, as shown in Figure 15-6.[4]

[4] While Figure 15-6 shows large budget deficits for the federal government only, it must be remembered that much *provincial government* spending is financed by transfer payments from the federal government. Therefore, the problem of budget deficits is really one of *all* levels of government, not just the federal government as Figure 15-6 seems to suggest.

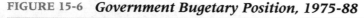

FIGURE 15-6 *Government Bugetary Position, 1975-88*

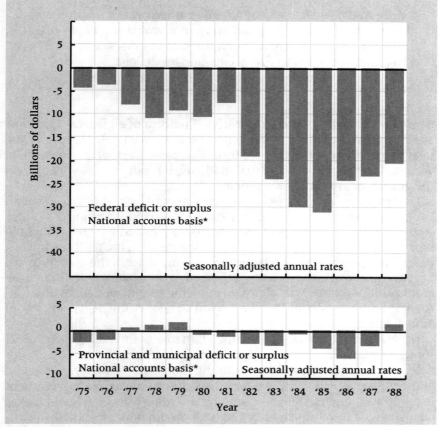

*Excludes the Canada and Quebec Pension Plans
SOURCE Toronto Dominion Bank, *Canada's Business Climate*

To finance such budget deficits, the federal government had to *borrow vast amounts of money*, mostly by *selling bonds*. By borrowing in this way, the government was able for some time to continue spending far in excess of its tax revenues.

However, by the mid-1980's, another problem had arisen—the government had borrowed so heavily to finance its past spending that its debt[5] had grown to such massive levels (over $300 billion) that interest had become a major expenditure. In 1988, *interest payments on the federal*

[5] "Debt" refers to the National Debt, or the total of government debt owed as a result of past borrowing. The budget deficit is the *annual addition* to the National Debt as a result of government borrowing to cover spending in excess of tax revenues. For instance, if the National Debt were $200 billion and the government's budget deficit for this year were $30 billion (spending of $90 billion; tax revenues of $60 billion), the National Debt would rise to $230 billion.

By the mid-1980's, the federal government was spending about $1400 more per Canadian than it was receiving in taxes, and borrowing (mostly through the sale of bonds) over $30 billion per year to finance its budget deficits.

government's debt accounted for nearly 25 percent of all federal spending, as compared to less than 12 percent in 1968. Viewed differently, in 1988, nearly one-third of all taxes paid by Canadians to the federal government went not to provide services to Canadians, but rather to pay interest on the government's $330 billion debt.

This situation raised serious concerns about the cost of government. Unless something were done, a vicious circle could develop, in which soaring interest payments on past borrowing forced the government to borrow even more, forcing future interest costs even higher. With interest payments absorbing such a large and growing share of the government's tax revenues, the government was forced to *cut spending* on existing programs and/or *increase taxes*. Only by reducing its budget deficits and borrowing requirements in this way could the government regain control of its finances.

These financial realities forced upon Canadians and their governments some very basic questions about the desirable, appropriate and affordable size and role of government in the Canadian economy. Reduction of the budget deficit became a basic objective of the federal government in the 1980's, forcing difficult decisions regarding priorities. Should taxes be increased? If so, which ones and who should pay? Or should government spending be reduced? And if so, which programs should be cut and who should bear the burden? In the final section of this chapter, we will consider what government has been doing, and may do in the future, to answer these questions.

Debt-service (interest) costs as a percentage of government expenditures are higher in Canada than in any major industrial country. The reality of compound interest rates is forcing the government to consider program cuts and tax increases to bring the deficit under control.

Policy Review and Outlook, 1985: A Time for Decisions
(C.D. Howe Institute, 1985).

In each of the past ten years the expenditures of the federal government have exceeded its tax revenues. These continuing deficits have led to an enormous growth in the burden of debt and the (interest) costs of servicing that debt. Moreover, unless we begin now to put our fiscal house in order, the burden of debt will continue to mount rapidly in the future. We are on a very dangerous treadmill.

Hon. Michael Wilson, Minister of Finance, *Economic and Fiscal Statement*, Nov. 8, 1984, in the House of Commons

Directions for reform

As the 1990's approached, several directions for reform of the role of government in the economy seemed to be taking shape. Some of the major directions for such reform, which are related to each other in several ways, are outlined in the following sections.

Social welfare reform

The main directions for reform of the social welfare system are towards the *"targeting" of social welfare expenditures* toward those who need assistance and the *increasing of incentives* for recipients of social welfare to work.

As noted earlier, some social welfare assistance is available to all Canadians, regardless of their income. In the future, government programs are likely to try to target social welfare expenditures toward those who *most* need assistance while reducing the benefits paid to higher-income Canadians. One way in which it is likely to be done is through the provision of additional tax credits, which will make income-tax reductions or refunds available to lower-income Canadians. In addition, benefits such as family allowances may no longer be paid to higher-income families, or may be taxed back from them at high tax rates. More effective social welfare spending is considered to be one key to reducing the government's budget deficit, since social welfare expenditures are such a large part of government spending.

Another direction for social welfare reform is the increasing of incentives to work. For unemployment insurance, the most commonly suggested reforms involve tightening up the UI system by raising eligibility requirements and reducing benefits and benefit periods, so as to encourage (some would say force) UI recipients to seek work more quickly and more earnestly. Others would tie UI assistance (or the level of assistance) to recipients' participation in retraining programs, so as to increase their employability.

The reforms usually recommended for welfare involve some relaxation, rather than a tightening, of the system, so as to give welfare recipients an incentive to work by not reducing their welfare benefits by too much if they take a job.

THE GUARANTEED MINIMUM INCOME

The **Guaranteed Minimum Income** represents a particularly imaginative approach to social welfare reform. While specific proposals vary, they all tend to have the following characteristics:

(a) The government would pay everyone whose income was below a certain level sufficient benefits to bring them up at least to a guaranteed minimum income level. These benefits would be paid instead of, rather than in addition to, existing welfare benefits, and would be intended to ensure that no one's income was insufficient to provide for basic needs, however defined.

(b) The higher a person's earned income from work rose, the lower his or her benefits under the GMI would be. People with incomes above a certain level would receive no payments from the government; they would pay taxes instead. Thus, Guaranteed Minimum Income would mean, not that everyone receives subsidies from the government, but that *no one's income falls below a certain level.*

(c) The reduction of the GMI benefits, as earned income from work increased, would be structured so as to preserve the *incentive to work.* Specifically, for each dollar earned income rose, the GMI benefits would be reduced by significantly less than one dollar. By so doing, the system would allow the GMI recipient to keep a significant proportion of any earned income, thereby providing an economic incentive to work. This plan to maintain work incentives is the key aspect of the proposed welfare reforms commonly known as the Guaranteed Minimum Income.

A Guaranteed Minimum Income plan could probably be administered through the personal income tax system: people whose incomes were above a certain level would pay taxes, as at present, while those below a certain level would receive benefits, which are sometimes called *negative taxes.* For this reason, the Guaranteed Minimum Income is also known as the *Negative Income Tax.*

While the very term, Guaranteed Minimum Income, encounters resistance among many people who feel that such ideas are fanciful and could not be afforded in reality, supporters of the GMI argue that the opposite is true. According to them, Canada already has a guaranteed minimum income which puts a floor under people's incomes. We call it Welfare and we are not very pleased with it. Its coverage is uneven, it consists of many poorly coordinated agencies that are inefficient and costly to operate, and it imposes disincentives to work upon those who receive it.

This emphasis on incentives to work represents a departure from the traditional approach, which aimed to *redistribute income* from higher income-earners to the poor. According to some economists, while the distribution of income has not changed significantly over the past few decades (despite all attempts made by government programs and taxation policies), the living standards of all Canadians, including the poor, have risen, due to economic growth. Consequently, many economists

Suppose that the government decided to impose a tax rate of 80 percent on any income over $70 000 per year, in order to raise tax revenues to provide increased benefits for the poor.

In 1986 (the most recent year for which statistics were available at the time of writing), only 290 040 Canadians reported earnings of over $70 000. The total of their income over and above $70 000 was about $16 billion, which was taxed at a rate of about 50 percent. An increase in the tax rate to 80 percent would have produced additional tax revenues of about $4.8 billion (30 percent of $16 billion). While this may sound like a lot, the benefits to the poor of even so severe a tax increase would have been disappointingly small: about $23 per week, spread evenly among the nearly 4 million Canadians living below the poverty line. A practical limitation is therefore imposed upon redistribution of income by the fact that, while the rich have high incomes that make them attractive targets for heavy taxation to benefit the poor, there are simply not enough of the rich to provide significant benefits without risking serious effects on people's incentives to work.

have become sceptical concerning the value of large-scale attempts at income redistribution, and believe instead that the best way to benefit the poor is through a growing economy in which everyone's real income is rising.

Reduction of the federal budget deficit

As noted, the federal government's budget deficit had grown so large by 1984 that deficit reduction had become a top priority. The new government did not introduce any dramatic spending cuts or tax increases in order to reduce the deficit. Rather, it introduced a considerable number of relatively small expenditure reductions and tax increases that were intended to reduce the deficit over a period of years.

The government was assisted in this effort by the years of economic recovery during the second half of the 1980's. As economic growth brought production, employment and sales up, the government's revenues from personal income taxes, profits taxes and sales taxes rose. And, as better economic conditions reduced unemployment, government expenditures on transfer payments such as unemployment insurance were held down. From fiscal year 1983-84 to 1987-88, government spending on UI benefits declined from 2.4 percent of Gross Domestic Product to 1.9 percent, as the number of unemployed Canadians fell from 1.434 million to 1.031 million.

The overall results of these policy changes and improved economic conditions are shown in Figure 15-7. Over the period from 1984 to 1988,

FIGURE 15-7 *Major Components of the Federal Government Budget, 1984 and 1988*

	1984 Billions of $	1984 % of GDP	1988 Billions of $	1988 % of GDP
Goods and services (excluding national defence)	$13.1	2.9%	$15.0	2.5%
National defence	8.0	1.8	10.5	1.7
Transfers to persons	29.7	6.7	36.1	6.0
Interest	20.9	4.7	31.9	5.3
Transfers to other levels of government	19.9	4.5	24.7	4.1
Total federal government spending	$106.5	24.0%	$130.6	21.7%
Total federal revenues	$76.5	17.2%	$110.1	18.3%
Federal budget deficit	$30.0	6.8%	$20.5	3.4%

SOURCE Department of Finance, *Quarterly Economic Review*, June 1989.

the federal budget deficit declined from $30 billion to about $20 billion. Spending restraint showed in the reduction of federal government spending as a percentage of GDP from 24 percent in 1984 to 21.7 percent in 1988. All major areas of federal spending (with the exception of interest on the government's debt) declined as a percentage of GDP. On the revenue side, federal revenues increased from 17.2 percent of GDP to 18.3 percent. The overall result of these changes was a reduction in the federal budget deficit from 6.8 to 3.4 percent of GDP over this five-year period.

On the other hand, the situation as of 1988 was still not regarded as satisfactory. After five years of good economic conditions and attempts at deficit reduction, the federal deficit was still over $20 billion in 1988. Furthermore, the deficit remained this large under good economic conditions, with low unemployment. (It is considered appropriate for the government to have a balanced budget under such good economic conditions, and to have budget deficits during recessions, when unemployment is high.) According to some projections, this $20 billion budget deficit could readily swell to as large as $40 billion if the economy were to slump into a recession and unemployment rose again, as it did in the early 1980's. Such budget deficits would create major financing problems for the federal government, which would have to borrow $40 billion per year. Total personal saving by Canadians in 1988 was only $36 billion, and that was invested in many ways besides buying federal government bonds. Thus, a $40 billion federal budget deficit could not be financed by borrowing within Canada, and would require heavy borrowing from foreign lenders.

While there was widespread agreement that the federal budget deficit should be reduced further, the task of deficit reduction was not an easy one. As Figure 15-7 shows, spending restraint in other areas was largely offset by *increases in interest payments*, as the government's debt rose each

ASSET SALES TO REDUCE GOVERNMENT DEBT?

During the 1980's the federal government "privatized" several Crown corporations, including Air Canada, by selling them to private interests. According to some observers, one motive for these sales was to raise funds to reduce the federal government's debt—and with it the interest payments that were becoming such a problem for the federal budget. In such a case, the federal government would be not unlike a household or a business that was selling assets to reduce an excessively burdensome debt.

year due to its annual budget deficits. From 1984 to 1988, a period of federal spending restraint, the federal government's interest payments increased by $11 billion, and rose from 4.7 to 5.3 percent of GDP. Interest payments had become a large and growing component of federal spending that would prove difficult to control unless federal deficits and borrowing were reduced.

To reduce the deficit by a meaningful amount would require significant reductions in government spending and/or increases in taxes.[6]

On the *expenditure side* of the federal budget, deficit reduction faced serious obstacles. As Figure 15-8 shows, nearly 80 percent of all federal expenditures excluding interest payments consisted of transfer payments. The vast majority of these went to persons (mainly in the form of *pensions* and *unemployment insurance*) and to provincial governments, to finance provincial spending on *health care, postsecondary education* and *welfare*.[7]

Any significant reduction in federal spending would involve reductions in transfer payments, which was a very sensitive matter politically. Tentative attempts by the government to reduce spending on UI and pensions met with fierce political resistance. Cutting transfers to the provinces was not much easier, as this would reduce provincial budgets for health care, education and welfare, provoking opposition from all of the provincial governments as well as those provinces directly affected. Thus, attempts to reduce the federal government's budget deficits through expenditure reductions would encounter strong political resistance.

1989.

FIGURE 15-8 *Federal Government Expenditures, 1988*

	Billions of dollars	% of total
Goods and services (excluding national defence)	$15.0	11.5%
National defence	10.5	8.0
Transfer payments to persons	38.5	29.5
Transfers to other levels of government	24.7	18.9
Interest on the public debt	31.9	24.4
Subsidies	6.1	4.7
Capital assistance	1.7	1.3
Gross capital formation	2.2	1.7
	$130.6	100.0

SOURCE Department of Finance, *Quarterly Economic Review*, June 1989.

[6] To completely eliminate the deficit in 1988 would have required government spending cuts and/or tax increases of $800 for every Canadian man, woman and child, or nearly $2500 per family.

[7] A third type of transfer payment was *federal subsidies to business*. These, however, amounted to only about one-eighth of transfers to persons and provincial governments. Also, over the 1984-88 period, subsidies had been reduced from $10.8 billion (2.4 percent of GDP) to $7.8 billion (1.3 percent of GDP).

On the *revenue side* of the federal budget, obstacles to further deficit reduction through tax increases were growing. Since 1984, the government had introduced a number of tax increases, culminating in its 1989 budget, in which tax increases outweighed spending cutbacks by a ratio of about three to one. Later in 1989, the federal government proposed a national sales tax (the Goods and Services Tax, or GST) to replace the existing federal tax on manufactured goods. Despite the government's description of the GST as not increasing tax revenues on balance, public opposition to the new tax became so strong that it was described as a "tax revolt."

In conclusion, the federal government entered the 1990's with a very heavy public debt and budget deficits of about $20-22 billion adding to that debt each year. However, attempts to reduce those deficits, either through spending cuts or tax increases, faced strong political opposition from Canadians.

Tax reform

Broadly speaking, governments can raise tax revenues by taxing *incomes* (of persons and of businesses), by taxing *consumption spending* (through sales taxes) and by taxing *assets* (through taxes such as property taxes).

Each of these types of tax is subject to its own economic and political difficulties. If personal income tax rates become too high, they can impare incentives to work, save and invest, and damage the performance of the economy. Similarly, excessively high tax rates on business profits can reduce the incentive to invest and expand, and even drive businesses to other countries.

Sales taxes, on the other hand, are particularly burdensome for low-income people, who must pay the same amount of tax on the items they buy as high-income people. Sales taxes are regressive taxes—they take a higher percentage of the incomes of the poor than of the rich.

Property taxes have various flaws. They apply only to a narrow base (those who have chosen to invest in taxable assets, such as real estate), they discriminate against those who invest in those assets, and they are regressive.

Concerns regarding Canada's tax system

The personal income tax

As government spending grew rapidly in Canada, so did taxation. To an increasing extent, governments came to rely upon the personal income tax as a source of tax revenue.

As governments' reliance on the personal income tax grew, the personal income tax rates paid by Canadians increased. Of particular interest to economists is the *marginal tax rate*, since this affects the incentive to work, save and invest. In 1950, a typical Canadian wage-earner paid a marginal tax rate of 22 percent on any overtime worked or bonuses earned; by the 1980's this had risen to more than 33 percent, and many were paying 40 to 45 percent.[8] Such high marginal tax rates generated not only complaints, but also real concerns that taxes were undermining incentives. While the government was eager to raise additional tax revenue to reduce its budget deficits, further increases in personal income taxes did not seem to be the way to go, for both economic and political reasons.

> In 1950, the personal income tax provided about one-quarter of all federal government revenues. By the 1980's, over half of the federal government's revenues came from the personal income tax.

Consumption taxes (sales taxes)

The other major source of tax revenue for governments is taxes on consumer spending, or sales taxes. While most provincial governments levy a retail sales tax, the federal government has not had such a tax in the past. Instead, the major **consumption tax** levied by the federal government has been the *Federal Sales Tax* (FST), which applied to about one-third of all goods manufactured in Canada, at a tax rate of 13.5 percent. In 1988-89 the FST yielded about $17 billion in revenue for the federal government, or nearly 20 percent of its tax revenues. Relatively few Canadians were aware of its existence, as it was added into the price of products at *wholesale*, and was therefore *not visible* at the retail level, as provincial retail sales taxes are.

By the late 1980's, there was general agreement that the FST was an inappropriate and economically damaging tax, since it applied a high tax rate to a narrow range of manufactured goods only. About one-third of FST revenues came from four products: alcohol, tobacco, gasoline and automobiles. While these products were taxed heavily, two-thirds of manufactured goods and all services escaped the FST altogether, making it a *discriminatory tax*.

More serious was the fact that the FST damaged the ability of Canadian producers to *compete internationally* in a world economy that was becoming increasingly competitive. Because the FST was added at the wholesale level, it increased the prices of Canadian exports subject to the FST,

---

[8] Tax rates are for Ontario; these vary from province to province due to variations in provincial tax rates.

making them less attractive in export markets. In addition, it taxed imports more lightly than Canadian-made goods, and hurt the ability of Canadian-made goods to compete *within* Canada. By the late 1980's the FST was the only tax in the industrialized world that *favored imports over domestically-produced goods.*

In other countries, governments facing similar economic and financial problems to Canada's had moved away from income-tax increases and toward broad-based consumption taxes (often known as "Value-Added Taxes") as a major source of government revenue. By 1989, 19 of the 24 most highly industrialized countries in the world had implemented such sales tax systems.

Tax reform in Canada

In the mid-1980's, the federal government began a series of tax reforms, to be completed by the early 1990's. In broad terms, the reforms consisted of three major aspects:

(a) the reduction of marginal tax rates on personal incomes,

(b) increased tax credits for lower-income earners, and

(c) the introduction of a broadly-based federal consumption tax (the Goods and Services Tax, or GST).

(a) Reduction of marginal tax rates on personal incomes

The reductions in marginal tax rates were especially pronounced for high income earners, as the top marginal tax rate went from a peak of 63 percent in the early 1980's to 44 percent (excluding surtaxes) in 1988. For average income earners, the marginal tax rate declined from about 33 percent to about 26 percent (Ontario tax rates).

The objective of these reductions in marginal tax rates was to *improve incentives* for Canadians to earn additional income by working, saving and investing. This was considered to be important in view of the need to improve Canada's competitiveness in the increasingly competitive world economy.

(b) Increased tax credits for lower income earners

During the 1980's a number of tax credits were added to the income-tax system that benefited Canadians with low incomes. Some of these, such as sales and property tax credits, were introduced in order to offset the effect of regressive taxes such as property and sales taxes on low-income people. In addition, a number of tax deductions were converted to tax credits, which were of more benefit to lower-income taxpayers.[9] The objective of the changeover to tax credits was to *reduce the tax burden on low-income Canadians.*

In addition, a major new tax credit providing $2.4 billion per year to lower-income families was to be introduced as part of the proposed Goods and Services Tax.

(c) Tax on consumption (the Goods and Services Tax)

The third—and most controversial—aspect of tax reform was the proposed introduction of a new, broadly-based tax on consumer spending, known as the Goods and Services Tax, or GST. The stated objective of the GST was to replace the Federal Sales Tax on manufactured goods with a consumption (sales) tax on a wider range of goods and services. The government hoped the GST would raise sufficient revenues to offset the personal income-tax rate reductions, the introduction of tax credits for lower-income taxpayers, and the elimination of the FST.

The operation of a GST is illustrated in the simplified example shown in Figure 15-9. When a forest products company sells $100 of wood to a furniture manufacturer, it must pay a GST of $7 (7 percent) to the government. When the furniture manufacturer sells the furniture it has made from the wood to a retailer for $400, the manufacturer must pay $28 GST (7 percent) to the government. However, the manufacturer can deduct from this $28 the $7 tax it had paid on the wood it bought from the forest products company. Therefore, the manufacturer pays a net GST of $21.[10] When the retailer sells the furniture to the consumer, a similar process occurs. The retailer must pay a GST of $42 (7 percent of the $600 selling price), but can deduct the $28 that was included in the price it paid the manufacturer. As a result, the retailer pays a net GST of

[9] Consider, for example, a taxpayer with a spouse who is not working and two young children. In 1987, this taxpayer would have claimed $9040 in tax deductions, meaning that tax would not have to be paid on that $9040. How much tax these deductions would save the taxpayer would depend on the taxpayer's income. If his/her taxable income was $64 000, the saving would be the $4610 that would have been payable on that $9040 by someone with such a high income. However, for someone with a low taxable income, the tax saving would be much less, because they would have paid a much lower tax rate. And for very low-income people with no taxable income, the deductions would be worthless, as there would be no taxable income to deduct them from.

In 1988, all Canadians with a non-working spouse and two young children claimed tax credits of $2002. Since these tax credits were deducted from their tax *payable, each* of them saved $2002, regardless of their income. Canadians with no taxable income and no tax payable could claim income-tax *refunds* of $2002 as a result of these credits.

[10] In effect, the manufacturer only pays GST of 7 percent on the value it has added to the wood ($300) in transforming it from a $100 piece of wood into a $400 piece of furniture. That is why taxes of the GST type are referred to as "value-added" taxes.

FIGURE 15-9 *The Operation of the Goods and Services Tax*

Seller	Buyer	Item	Price	Tax	Refund	Net Tax
Forest products company	Furniture manufacturer	Wood	$100	$7	$0	$7
Furniture manufacturer	Retailer	Furniture	$400	$28	$7	$21
Retailer	Consumer	Furniture	$600	$42	$28	$14

$14. When the furniture reaches the consumer, the GST has added a total of $42, or 7 percent of its price, to the selling price.

The GST is different from a retail sales tax in an important way: businesses do not pay 7 percent GST on all of their sales. They pay this amount *less* the GST they paid on their inputs. (For instance, the manufacturer in Figure 15-9 with sales of $400 pays a GST of $21—$28 on its furniture sales less the $7 GST it paid on the wood used to make the furniture.) While such a system of taxes paid and refunded at each stage of the production process makes the GST more complicated to administer than a simple retail sales tax with no refunds, it also has an important advantage. Under the GST, *producers do not pay GST on the inputs they buy*, so it does not add to their production costs and force price increases that make it more difficult for them to compete with foreign producers.[11] In effect, the deductions would help Canadian producers to *compete internationally*, by ensuring that the GST on inputs would not be added to the price of Canadian exports. Also, the GST would not favor imports over Canadian-made goods, as the FST has done.

Since sales taxes are regressive taxes, the government also proposed a new *GST tax credit* for lower-income Canadians, to offset the effect of the GST upon them. Under this plan, lower-income families would receive GST rebates, which would be mailed to them every three months, in advance of actually paying the GST. When the tax credit was taken into account, the government projected that families with an annual income under $30 000 would be better off under the new tax system than under the previous one, since the burden of the GST would fall upon those with incomes over $30 000 per year.

[11] For instance, in Figure 15-9, if the manufacturer sells the furniture to a foreign dealer, the price need include only $28 of GST. Under a simple 7 percent tax without the refund, the price would have to include $35 of GST—the $28 payable by the manufacturer on its sale *plus* the $7 included in the price of the wood.

Tax reform in review

The overall strategy of tax reform was to shift some of the tax burden from the personal income tax to consumption taxes (the GST). It was hoped that a broadly-based consumption tax such as the GST would be able to raise the tax revenues necessary to reduce the government's massive budget deficits without imparing economic incentives to work, save and invest, as increases in personal income tax rates would. Because the GST was regressive, a system of tax credits was introduced to ease its effects on lower-income Canadians. The tax-reform strategy could therefore be summarized as follows.

(a) personal income-tax rate reductions to *improve incentives*,

(b) consumption tax increases to *raise tax revenue*, and

(c) tax credits to *provide relief* from the higher consumption taxes for those with lower incomes.

However, at the beginning of the new decade, the future of the GST was uncertain. Surveys indicated that nearly 80 percent of Canadians were opposed to the new tax, which was seen as yet another tax increase following several years of tax increases to reduce the federal budget deficit. Adding to the public's hostility was the perception (again, as indicated by public-opinion surveys) that about 38 percent of the taxes they paid were spent wastefully by governments, anyway. Finally, there was a suspicion among many Canadians that, once the GST was introduced, it would be gradually increased again and again, providing governments with a virtually endless source of tax revenue for them to spend (wastefully). As a result, while a 7 percent GST was planned for January 1, 1991, the future of the tax remained uncertain.

Government spending in perspective

Generally, Canadians have welcomed the expansion of their nation's social welfare system and the benefits it has brought them in terms of income security, and services such as health care and education. However, since the mid-1970's, Canadians have been receiving substantially more benefits from their social welfare programs than they have been paying for in taxes, and the federal government has been borrowing very heavily. As a result, the size of government debt and annual interest payments has become a serious problem, especially for the federal government.

Underlying the debate over government benefits and services is the basic economic reality of scarcity, as discussed in Chapter 2. Since society's economic inputs are limited, the more resources such as labor and capital that are used by the government sector of the economy, the less are available for private consumption and investment. In short, the opportunity cost of improved health care services might be that Canadians make do with less beer and pizza.

As of the start of the 1990's, Canadians were still trying to decide the level of government spending (and taxation) that they wanted for their society. Maintaining the current level of government benefits and services would mean higher taxes for the majority of Canadians. If, instead, they were unwilling to pay more taxes, they would have to accept a reduction in the level of government benefits and services available to them. The choice was not an easy one.

DEFINITIONS OF NEW TERMS

Universality   The principle that some social programs should be available to all Canadians, regardless of their income.

Marginal Tax Rate   The percentage of any additional income that is earned that goes to taxes.

Progressive Tax   A tax that takes a higher percentage of high incomes than of low incomes.

Regressive Tax   A tax that takes a higher percentage of low incomes than of high incomes.

Consumption Tax   A tax based on the amount of personal income that is spent on consumer goods and services.

Guaranteed Minimum Income   A proposed welfare system intended to support incomes at a minimum level while providing incentives to work.

CHAPTER SUMMARY

1. The role of government in Canada's mixed economy has grown greatly over the past half-century, with government spending rising to nearly 47 percent of GDP by the mid-1980's. Governments are major purchasers of goods and services and employers as well as providers of services to the public. In addition, governments redistribute income from higher-income to lower-income Canadians, and regulate business and economic activity in a wide variety of ways.

2. The three main aspects of Canada's social welfare system are income security programs, health care and education.

3. By the mid-1980's, Canada's social welfare system was under considerable criticism for its complexity and inefficiency, its inequity,

its ineffectiveness and the distincentives and side-effects that it generated.

4. Also by the mid-1980's, the cost of government had become a major concern, as the federal government had very large budget deficits.

5. Likely directions for social welfare reform include better targetting of social welfare expenditures toward those who need assistance, and the increasing of work incentives for recipients of social welfare.

6. After 1984, the federal government introduced a series of tax reforms that included reductions in marginal tax rates on personal income, increased tax credits for lower-income Canadians and the introduction of a new, broadly-based federal consumption tax (the Goods and Services Tax, or GST).

7. In the 1990's Canadians are likely to continue to face difficult choices as to whether to pay higher taxes or accept cutbacks in government programs and services.

QUESTIONS

1. What have been the most recent trends concerning
   (a) government spending as a percentage of GDP, and
   (b) the size of the federal budget deficit?

   What are the reasons for these trends?

2. What changes, if any, have been made in federal-provincial cost-sharing arrangements regarding health, postsecondary education and welfare?

3. In the USA, taxpayers can deduct from their taxable income the interest that they pay on mortgage payments. Who would benefit economically from such a plan? Who would be hurt economically? Would this plan have any economic side-effects?

4. Would import duties (tariffs) on imported goods be a regressive or progressive tax?

5. If faced with the need to reduce the federal budget deficit through either spending cuts or tax increases, which would you choose? Which types of spending would you cut, and/or which types of taxes would you increase?

6. An interesting educational reform that has been suggested is that, rather than have students assigned to a particular school in their district, each student be given a voucher for the value of a year's

education. They would then be free to spend this voucher by enrolling at the school of their choice, with the school receiving the funds associated with the voucher.

How would such an approach be intended to improve the operation of the school system?

Do you believe this approach would be effective in improving the school system? Why or why not?

7. One idea to prevent the accumulation of outdated government programs is *sunset legislation*. Under such legislation, government programs would automatically be terminated at the end of a given number of years of operation, *unless* they were specifically renewed by the government.

   Do you believe such legislation would be a good idea for Canada? Why or why not?

8. In the eighteenth century, Scottish historian Alexander Tytler made the following observation, based on his study of democracy in ancient Greece:

   > A democracy cannot exist as a permanent form of government. It can only exist until a majority of voters discover that they can vote themselves largesse out of the public treasury. From that moment on, the majority always votes for the candidate who promises them the most benefits . . . with the result that democracy always collapses over a loose fiscal policy.

   Does Tytler's observation bear any relevance to Canada's democracy in the last quarter of the twentieth century?

9. The Goods and Services Tax was scheduled to be introduced in January 1991. Was the GST introduced on schedule and in the form outlined in the text? If not, what changes were made, and why?

10. In 1989, as a deficit-cutting measure, the federal government introduced the "clawback." Under the "clawback," family allowance benefits and old age security pensions would be "taxed back" from recipients with net incomes above roughly $50 000 per year. Taxpayers with net incomes above about $55 000 per year would pay back through taxes all of their family allowance benefits, and pensioners with incomes above about $76 000 per year would pay back all of their old age security pensions.

    The National Council of Welfare opposed the clawback on several grounds, one of which was that it ended the principle of universality. It recommended that, instead of taking back social welfare benefits from higher-income Canadians, the government should increase income taxes on higher-income Canadians, by raising the maximum marginal tax rate from 45 to 50 percent.

If both measures reduced the deficit by the same amount, would you prefer to use the clawback method or to raise the top marginal tax rate to 50 percent? Why?

11. To reduce the federal government's large budget deficits without major cuts in expenditures would require large increases in the taxes paid by Canadians. List the economic and political advantages and disadvantages of increasing each of the following taxes:
   (a) personal income taxes
   (b) corporate income taxes
   (c) gasoline taxes
   (d) consumption taxes (such as the GST)
   If taxes had to be increased, which of the above would you choose, and why?

CHAPTER 16

The politics of economics

As Chapter 15 suggests, the fields of economics and politics are closely intertwined. Because they affect people in so many important ways, economic issues often become major political issues, and there are sharply divided views regarding the appropriate role of government in the economy. Often, profoundly different philosophies concerning economic and social matters and values emerge from such disagreements. This chapter provides a rudimentary guide to these different philosophies, which are usually described as *right-wing* (or simply right), and *left-wing* (or left), and how they apply to economic issues.

The right-wing view

The right-wing view is characterized by a strong belief in *free enterprise*, the *market system* and *individual responsibility* for one's own economic fate or fortune. Right-wingers tend to believe that, generally, the best solution to economic problems lies in the operation of free markets. Through these markets, they see society's prosperity enhanced by free enterprise, competition and the profit motive. In their view, *consumer sovereignty* directs businesses to produce what consumers want, the *profit motive* induces private producers to operate as efficiently as possible, and *competition* ensures that the consumer is well-served regarding price, quality and service.

The value system of right-wingers emphasizes factors such as *incentives*, *efficiency* and the *creation of wealth*. They view free enterprise and private ownership of business as the most effective way of achieving this, largely through the profit motive. Right-wingers are less concerned about how

319

equally the benefits of prosperity are divided—their individualistic philosophy tends to make them believe that one is responsible for one's own share of the economic pie, and that people generally get what they earn in the marketplace. To them, personal responsibility is an important aspect of the incentive system associated with the marketplace.

In summary, right-wingers are believers in individualism, economic freedom, the marketplace and private enterprise. They believe that through the incentives for efficiency provided by these values, a society can best achieve the creation of wealth and economic prosperity.

The left-wing view

While left-wingers also value economic prosperity as an objective, they do not agree that the right-wing approach is the best way to achieve it. In particular, left-wingers *lack faith in free markets* as a means of achieving prosperity. They believe that in a free market the economically powerful can and do take advantage of the economically weak—that big business can exploit consumers and employers can exploit workers, so that the *distribution of income* in a free market will inevitably be unfair.

Another aspect of free markets that disturbs left-wingers is the *insecurity* that accompanies the marketplace—the exposure of people to the risk of layoff due to factors such as recession and competition. Again, left-wingers point out, the victims of layoffs are usually the economically weak—those with limited experience and skills. Thus, they argue, the free-market system is so biased in favor of the powerful and wealthy that it cannot provide an equitable share of its wealth for the large numbers of people who lack the economic power to wrest it from the marketplace. The rich and powerful devour most of the economic pie, leaving the crumbs for the weak.

To remedy these weaknesses of the market system, left-wingers advocate an *active role for government* in the economy. In particular, they favor government policies that redistribute income from the rich to the poor, and laws that regulate and restrict the behavior of the economically powerful. Such a role for government, they believe, will improve the overall prosperity of society, by ensuring a fairer distribution of economic welfare.

To summarize, the value system of left-wingers stresses the collective (as opposed to individualistic) aspects of society, and so emphasizes *fairness, security* and *an equitable distribution of income*. If it can be said of right-wingers that they focus on incentives for the creation of wealth and more or less take the distribution of wealth for granted, it could also be said of left-wingers that they stress a fair distribution of wealth, and tend to take the continuing creation of wealth for granted. Because they see the free market as a threat to their objectives of security and fairness, left-wingers advocate a more collective approach to economic questions, with the government actively working to overcome the free market's tendency to inequality.

THE EXTREMES

There are varying degrees of both right-wing and left-wing philosophies. In the extreme the right-wing view would leave almost all economic activity to the free market, in which economic decisions would be made almost entirely by individual consumers and businesses. The role of government would be restricted to providing physical security (through the army and police) and a court system for the enforcement of contracts. There would be no government programs to redistribute income or provide economic security, as these would interfere with incentives. Those who wanted to help the needy could do so voluntarily, through private charity, but no one would be forced to do so through taxes.

In the opposite extreme, the left-wing approach would replace private enterprise with government ownership of business. Through democratic socialism, elected governments would engage in thorough economic planning, which would decide (or strongly influence) the key economic decisions regarding what to produce, the production methods to be used and the distribution of the economic pie. The distribution of income would be much more equal, or possibly even completely equal. In effect, economic decisions would be made collectively, through the government, rather than by individuals in the marketplace.

Right versus left on various issues

In this section, we will consider the left and right views on a variety of economic policy issues.

Business enterprise

Right-wingers believe in *private ownership* of business, with competition and the profit motive as vital incentives for the productive efficiency that generates prosperity. They agree that *monopolies* are undesirable, but argue that, in a free market, monopolies do not tend to last for long, because monopoly profits will attract competition from other businesses or new products. Most long-lasting monopolies, they argue, are government-owned (or regulated) enterprises, which the government itself protects against competition by law. Right-wingers are generally opposed to government ownership of business enterprises, which they criticize as inefficient because of the absence of competition and the profit motive.

Left-wingers tend to question the social value of private ownership of business and the profit motive. In private enterprise, they see incentives leading not so much toward efficiency and service to the consumer as toward abuse of businesses' market power and exploitation of both consumers and employees. In the view of left-wingers, private business is a basic source of the problem of the inequitable distribution of income. As a result, they believe that there should be *considerable government regulation* of business activities as well as considerable *taxation of business profits* in order to redistribute income in favor of the poor. Some left-wingers would place government regulations (such as price controls) on larger businesses, or take over ownership of them (nationalization). Generally, though, left-wingers are considerably more sympathetic toward *small businesses*, which are usually subject to such strong competition that they lack the market power that concerns left-wingers.

Profits

Right-wingers regard profits in the most positive terms: as an *incentive for efficiency*, as a *reward* for good management and as a *major source of funds* for capital investment, which provides employment and productivity gains. In short, right-wingers view profits as a key to economic prosperity for society as a whole, and oppose heavy taxation of profits as damaging to prosperity.

Left-wingers tend to view profits (at least above a certain level) as evidence of market power which has been used to *exploit consumers and employees*. To left-wingers, profits are a prime cause of the *inequitable distribution of income* that concerns them, because the money that profits take from consumers and employees goes to the wealthy shareholders of businesses. As a result, left-wingers would favor relatively heavy taxation of profits as part of a policy of income redistribution.

Investment income

To right-wingers, investment income (interest, dividends and capital gains) provides an incentive to people to save and invest their capital in business enterprises which provide employment and prosperity. They regard such income as *well-deserved*, not only because of the risks undertaken by the investors (especially shareholders), but also because of the contribution their capital makes to the *general economic prosperity* of society. Left-wingers generally regard investment income, or the return on capital, as *less socially productive than wages*, or the return on labor. Also, because investment income goes to higher-income people who have money to invest, left-wingers tend to see investment income as adding to the problem of an inequitable distribution of income.

The distribution of income

Right-wingers accept inequalities in the distribution of income quite readily. They regard high incomes as a way of encouraging people to become educated or trained, and to work, save and invest. To right-wingers, higher incomes are *earned* by those who receive them, and reflect their contribution to society, as measured by the marketplace—that is, by the willingness of others to pay them for their services. Right-wingers are generally *not very sympathetic to the poor*, believing that they should do more to help themselves.

> "Capitalism is the unequal sharing of plenty; socialism is the equal sharing of misery."

Left-wingers view the income-distribution process and its results quite differently. They see the issue mainly in terms of *market power*—the ability of some groups and individuals to extract from society, through the marketplace, an excessively large share of the pie, leaving only a small share for the less powerful. To left-wingers, incomes do not measure people's contribution to society so much as their *ability to take from society*, through their bargaining power in the marketplace. As a result, left-wingers generally regard the poor as the *victims* of an economic system which allows some people to take advantage of others.

> "Rugged individualism makes ragged individuals."

Social welfare

Right-wingers tend to see social welfare and income-redistribution programs in terms of their effect upon *incentives*. They are concerned that excessive redistribution of income will have negative effects upon the incentives of all concerned, by taxing the rich too heavily and encouraging the poor to rely on welfare rather than help themselves. Right-wingers are sceptical regarding the propriety and the value of government programs to redistribute income.

By contrast, left-wingers see redistribution of income as *one of the most essential functions of government*. Because the marketplace results in an unjust division of the pie, they believe it is the responsibility of government to promote *social justice* by redistributing income from the rich to the poor, through both taxation and transfer payments.

GIVE ME THAT OLD-FASHIONED RIGHT-WINGISM!

The following is an excerpt from a famous speech by an American preacher named Conwell in the 1880's. The speech was given six thousand times and earned a total of $8,000,000. Its popularity derived from the fact that it reflected attitudes that were widely held at the time.

> To secure wealth is an honourable ambition and is one test of a person's usefulness to others. I say get rich, get rich . . . Ninety-eight out of a hundred of the rich men of America are honest. That is why they are rich. I won't give in but what I sympathize with the poor, but the number of poor who are to be sympathized with is very small. To sympathize with a man whom God has punished for his sins, thus to help him when God would still continue a just punishment, is to go wrong, no doubt about it.

Labor unions

Right-wingers generally view labor unions with great mistrust. To them, unions tend to *reduce productive efficiency and prosperity* in various ways: by interfering with management's right to make decisions, by opposing efforts to increase labor productivity (because unions are wary of threats to workers' job security) and by reducing the amount of business profits available for capital investment in improved facilities and equipment. Right-wingers are also quite disturbed by *Canada's bad strike record* and its possible effect upon the willingness of business (both Canadian and foreign) to invest and create jobs in Canada. On the issue of public-service strikes, such as postal strikes, right-wingers can become quite agitated; many would remove the right to strike from all government employees.

Left-wingers are generally sympathetic to unions, which they see as organizations of workers trying to *protect* themselves against *exploitation by employers* who enjoy more market power than individual employees. One value which unionists and left-wingers share strongly is *economic security*—the desire to be secure against the marketplace or arbitrary decisions of management. Left-wingers mostly support the right of government employees to strike, but will usually draw the line when the broader public interest is endangered. Similarly, some left-wingers are not very supportive of unionized groups, such as doctors, which have acquired sufficient market power that they are no longer underdogs.

The role of government in the economy

Not surprisingly, right-wingers believe in a *smaller role* for government in the economy. They believe in the market system as the best way to handle most economic decisions, and are sceptical about the value of government intervention in the economy. They regard "big government" as the main threat to economic prosperity because it *pre-empts economic resources* (through taxation and borrowing) that would be better used for private consumption and especially private investment. Also, they believe that government *damages incentives to work, save and invest* through its tax and welfare policies and through over-regulation of the business sector. Generally, right-wingers see less government (taxation, spending, borrowing and regulation) as a key to solving many economic problems.

Left-wingers have exactly the opposite view. Because they are not confident that free markets promote general prosperity, they believe in a *large and activist role* for government in the economy. In particular, left-wingers favor government policies *to protect workers and consumers* against business, and to *redistribute income*. Unless government actively plays these roles, they believe, the economically powerful will increasingly enrich themselves at the expense of the less powerful.

Politics

The views of left-wingers and right-wingers regarding politics are interesting, because each seems to think (or at least fear) that the other is in control of the political process. Right-wingers express with dismay the view that democratically-elected governments tend toward left-wing policies, because there are more lower-income voters than higher-income ones. As a result, right-wingers fear a continual growth of government and policies to redistribute income and regulate business (socialism), with very damaging effects on the economy in the long run.

Left-wingers are often equally cynical about politics, but for a different reason. They tend to see big business and the wealthy and powerful as exercising undue influence on governments and their policies. The result, according to left-wingers, is that government policies (especially tax exemptions and deductions) tend to favor big business and the rich, and government programs on balance do far less for the poor than they could or should.

The need for balance

Most people intuitively feel that the most effective approach to economic issues generally lies in a reasonable balance, or blend, of the left and right approaches, rather than an extreme of either one. Indeed, both extremes hold real dangers.

A society that went too far toward the right-wing approach, or *laissez-faire*, would place nearly total reliance upon free markets to make its economic decisions and resolve its economic problems. In such circumstances, some powerful private-interest groups (both businesses and labor unions) would be free to use their market power to enrich themselves at the expense of others. There would be no protection for groups that lacked the economic clout to take care of themselves, such as consumers, or unskilled non-union workers, nor would there be social welfare programs for those who lacked an income due to unemployment, accident, illness, disability or old age. The result would be a very *unequal distribution of income*; the rich might tend to stay rich over generations, inheriting both wealth and access to educational and career opportunities, while the poor would have difficulty getting out of the poverty trap, having no access to either money or education. In the extreme, the poorer classes could even strike back at the establishment, causing *social instability* such as has characterized some South American countries.

Another possible problem could be *economic instability*. With income so heavily concentrated in the hands of the wealthy few, the economy would lack the consumer-spending support of a broadly-based middle-income class such as exists today, and would therefore be *more vulnerable to economic downturns*, or recessions. Without social welfare programs, economic insecurity would be a much greater problem—even a disaster—for many people.

Probably the left's favorite horror story about such matters is the United States' economy before and during the Great Depression of the 1930's. During the 1920's, passive governments watched benignly as the top 5 percent of income-earners received 33 percent of total personal income, and a largely unregulated business and financial sector erected very unstable financial structures that contributed to the collapse of the stock market after late 1929. Once the Depression had started, even with the unemployment rate in the 20-percent range, the government took years to come to grips with the problem and attempt to alleviate it. The American economy of that era graphically demonstrated the major flaws of the laissez-faire approach: extreme wealth for a few, but poverty and insecurity for many, together with general economic instability.

On the other hand, societies that go too far toward the left approach tend to wind up with problems which, through different, are no less severe. Socialist governments can become so big, so costly and so interventionist in the economy that they *erode incentives to work, save and invest*. Very high taxes on business and higher-income individuals can have this effect, as can excessive government regulation of business. Excessive government borrowing (or even, in extreme cases, printing) of money to finance its heavy expenditures tends to generate high interest rates (and possibly inflation), which depresses capital investment spending and slows economic growth. As incentives and capital investment are undermined, productivity and living standards stagnate. The government's preoccupation with redistribution of wealth and income can thus interfere with the creation of wealth, to the disadvantage of society generally.

Right-wingers enjoy discussing their own favorite horror story, that of Great Britain after the Second World War. In Britain, left-wing governments built a massive welfare state centered on income redistribution and free government services to the public. However, the financing of all this extensive government spending required such heavy taxation of business and higher-income earners that incentives were seriously affected. Business investment languished, productivity performance was weak, British producers lost competitive ground to imports and unemployment rose as a result. Capital—both business and personal—was taken from the country by investors seeking better returns elsewhere, and Britain lost many of its younger, more aggressive and able people to nations that offered greater opportunities. Many observers believe that Britains's leftist economic policies were primarily responsible for the nation's economic decline in the postwar period.

Trends

The foregoing reinforces the argument made earlier that the most effective approach to economic policymaking should involve a judicious blend of the left and right approaches. However, it is much harder to reach agreement on what the most appropriate blend actually is, and whether getting to it requires moving toward the left or toward the right.

Certainly, the long-term trend has been toward the left, as the growth of the welfare state outlined in Chapter 15 shows. This trend gained momentum after the Great Depression of the 1930's highlighted the flaws of the market system, and was especially pronounced in Canada from the mid-1960's to the mid-1970's, when government spending and the role of government in general grew very rapidly. Similar trends occurred in most other industrialized countries, at different paces and with different timing.

By the late 1970's, however, changes were beginning to occur. As the performance of most industrialized economies stagnated, disillusionment with big government and the welfare state began to grow. These ideals did not seem to have achieved the great economic promises that had been held out for them—inflation was severe, unemployment high and productivity and living standards had practically stopped rising. Rightly or wrongly, increasing numbers of people came to blame the size and the policies of government for many of these problems, and the pendulum began to swing back toward the right. In Britain and the United States, new governments placed renewed emphasis on the "old virtues" of incentives, work, investment and productivity. Attempts were made to rein in the growth of government and to ease the regulatory and tax burden on business, in order to promote capital investment. By the mid-1980's, Canada had joined in this trend, as the new federal government attempted to get its budget deficit under control while improving incentives, especially for private-business investment, which was hailed as the engine of growth and provider of jobs for Canadians. In the view of many observers, the time was appropriate both economically and politically for such a shift in emphasis, especially since Canada faced the need to compete in international trade with nations whose policies were shifting in that direction.

So, driven in part by the financial problems presented by its budget deficits and in part by a desire to improve the performance of its economy, Canada shifted the orientation of its policies, reversing the long-term trend toward more government spending and regulation. As befits a nation known for its moderation, this change was neither sudden nor dramatic. Nonetheless it was regarded as significant that, in seeking the optimum blend of the left and right approaches, Canada was moving somewhat back toward the right.

CHAPTER SUMMARY

1. Right-wingers believe that economic prosperity is best promoted by free markets, with minimal government interference. This view emphasizes private enterprise, incentives, efficiency and the creation of wealth.

2. Left-wingers emphasize the importance of economic security and a fair distribution of income. They believe that to provide real prosperity and equality, the government must actively intervene in the economy, particularly in order to redistribute income from higher-income earners to lower-income ones.

3. Theory and evidence both suggest that neither the left nor the right approach in itself will ensure good economic performance. Rather, some blend of the two, intended to retain the advantages of the free market while rectifying its disadvantages, seems to be the most effective approach.

4. The long-term trend has been toward the left, but since the late 1970's, there has been a shift in policy back toward the right in the United States, Great Britain and, more recently, in Canada.

QUESTIONS

1. How would a strong right-winger and a strong left-winger feel about:

(a) a surtax on investment income (interest, dividends and capital gains) in order to finance subsidized daycare centers for the poor

(b) a tightening of the unemployment insurance program, including more restrictive eligibility rules and a general reduction of benefits

(c) tax reductions on corporate profits

(d) the bail-out by government of a near-bankrupt corporation that employs many people in the Atlantic provinces

(e) the removal of rent controls

(f) deterrent fees for medicare (that is, the charging of a small fee for each visit to the doctor)

(g) increased government subsidies for passenger rail service

(h) the replacement of the progressive income tax with a flat tax of 20 percent of all income earned by everyone, regardless of income

(i) the removal of the postal workers' right to strike

(j) the sale of Crown corporations to private buyers

(k) an increase in tuition fees for postsecondary education.

2. As they grow older, do most people become more left-wing or more right-wing? Why?

CHAPTER 17

The economics and politics of oil

To a great extent, modern industrialized societies rely upon oil to provide the energy requirements not only of their industry, but also their consumers. Yet few industrialized nations produce sufficient oil to meet their own requirements; most are dependent on imports from other nations.

Energy in general is not a major concern for Canada, which is more fortunate than other industrialized nations in being richly endowed with natural gas, coal, hydroelectricity and uranium. The one area of concern to Canada is oil, which provided just under one-third of the nation's energy requirements in the 1980's. While Canada has been fortunate in the past in being able to provide much (about three-quarters) of its own oil requirements at quite low costs, the nation's oil reserves were projected to be seriously depleted by the late 1990's.

Because Canada is not only a large *consumer* of oil, but also a large *producer* of oil, developments in the remainder of this century with respect

> . . . Canada has the highest per capita total energy consumption of any Western industrialized country—double that of Germany and almost three times that of Japan.
>
> C.D. Howe Research Institute,
> Policy Review and Outlook,
> *Investing in Our Own Future*, 1980 (page 39).

to world oil markets and the oil industry are of special importance to Canadians. Oil prices and supply in the future will have a major impact upon Canada's economic growth, industrial structure, the international value of the Canadian dollar and ultimately the prosperity of all Canadians.

Background: Canada's oil situation

Canadian oil sources

Since the 1950's the **conventional** oil reserves of Alberta have provided an accessible and low-cost source of about three-quarters of the oil consumed by Canadians. However, it is expected that these conventional oil reserves will be largely depleted by the late 1990's.

There are several possible alternative oil sources in Canada. The best-known, due to their vast size, are the *Athabasca Tar Sands* of northern Alberta. The Tar Sands are believed to contain between 200 and 300 billion barrels of recoverable oil—300 to 400 years' oil supply for Canadians at the rates of use prevalent in the 1980's. The problem with the Tar Sands is *production costs*, because the oil is difficult and costly to extract and process. When world oil prices reached very high levels in the late 1970's and early 1980's, it became economical to produce oil from the Tar Sands, but when oil prices declined, development was postponed. By the late 1980's, only a small proportion of Canada's total oil requirements was being produced by Tar Sands oil plants.

There are several other potentially major sources of oil in Canada, including heavy oil deposits in *Saskatchewan*, *Arctic* oil deposits and *East Coast* offshore deposits. Some production of heavy oil is already taking place, and the potential production from one East Coast offshore well—Hibernia—has been estimated at 200 000 barrels per day.

All of these projects, including the Tar Sands plants, have two characteristics: first, they involve *high costs*, so that the oil from them will not be cheap, and second, these projects are so *large in scale* and so complex that they take many years to plan and complete.

THE TAR SANDS IN PERSPECTIVE

It is believed that the Tar Sands contain approximately fifteen times as much oil as has *ever* been discovered in Western Canada, and four times as much as is likely to be discovered in the Arctic and off the East Coast.

The legal framework

Legally, natural resources such as oil are owned by the provinces in which they are situated.[1] The *provincial governments* (mainly Alberta) derive tax revenues from **royalties** charged on the oil extracted from their lands. But while the provinces *own* the oil, they do not under the law possess the power to *price* it as they wish. The *federal government* has considerable powers over interprovincial and international trade, including strong powers over the *pricing* of oil.

In the past, the federal government has used these powers to negotiate the price of crude oil with the oil-producing provinces. However, in the event of a disagreement, the federal government possesses—and has used—the legal authority to *impose* a price decision upon the producing provinces. As we will see, the conflicts between the provinces' rights over the ownership of oil and the federal government's rights over the pricing of oil have led to considerable tension between the federal government and the producing provinces, particularly Alberta.

Supply and distribution

Unlike most industrialized countries, Canada supplies most of its own oil. During the 1980's, roughly three-quarters of Canada's oil requirements were produced within Canada, mostly from Alberta's conventional oil reserves.

Figure 17-1 shows Canada's oil supply situation under the National Oil Policy established in 1961. Most Alberta oil was to be used in Ontario, the Prairies and the Western provinces, with a major pipeline bringing Alberta crude oil to refineries in Sarnia, Ontario. The remainder of Alberta's oil production would be exported to the USA. Quebec and the Mari-

> The federal government's authority over oil prices derives basically from its regulatory authority over trade and commerce in section 91.2 of the British North America Act. Also, the Petroleum Administration Act, passed in 1975 and amended in 1980, authorizes the federal government to fix domestic oil and gas prices if the federal government and the producing provinces fail to reach a negotiated agreement.

[1] Oil located outside provincial boundaries, such as in the Arctic or the offshore waters, falls under federal government ownership. These areas are known as the "Canada Lands" (see Figure 17-3).

FIGURE 17-1 *Canada's Oil Supply Situation Under the National Oil Policy, 1961*

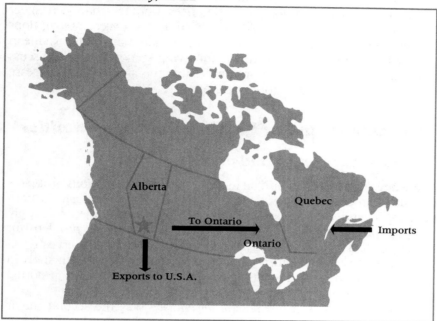

times would be supplied through imports of oil, mainly from Venezuela and Saudi Arabia.

Until 1973, imported oil was cheaper than Alberta oil. As a result, the National Oil Policy assisted, or subsidized, the development of Alberta's oil industry, by guaranteeing it the Canadian market west of Quebec. However, this situation was not to last long: by late 1973, it became apparent that Alberta's reserves of conventional oil were being depleted unexpectedly rapidly. Experts predicted that annual oil production would decline more or less steadily, forcing Canada to rely increasingly on imported oil. And, to make matters worse, imported oil was no longer cheap; in fact, it had become far more expensive than Canadian oil, due to the new economic power of the OPEC nations.

OPEC

The Organization of Petroleum Exporting Countries (**OPEC**) is a cartel of nations, mostly Arab states, which produce and export oil.[2] For many years, the multinational oil companies had succeeded in buying oil from the Arab states at low prices because the Arabs were not united and

---

[2] A cartel is an oligopoly whose members have entered into a formal agreement to suspend competition among themselves.

could be played off against each other. However, in late 1973 the OPEC producers succeeded in presenting a united front on prices, the result being a dramatic quadrupling of world prices, from less than $3 (US) per barrel to nearly $12 per barrel. At the same time, there were interruptions of international oil supplies and shortages of oil in many nations, due in part to the Arab-Israeli War. In the following section, we will discuss both the problems and the opportunities that this sudden large increase in world oil prices created for Canada.

The early seventies: Problems and opportunities

(a) Problems: Supply and prices

These developments in world oil markets created some serious problems for Canadian policy-makers. One concern was *security of supply*: Eastern Canada depended on imported oil, which had been subject to supply interruptions. Over the longer term, this was not just a problem for Eastern Canada, however, because the conventional oil reserves upon which the rest of the country depended were expected to run short in about 13 years, possibly increasing the nation's dependence on imported oil.

The sharp increase in *the price of imported oil* was the second major concern, as it would hit Eastern Canada oil consumers particularly hard. Whether to allow *the price of Alberta's oil* to rise to world (OPEC) levels was another question. If Canadian crude oil prices rose to world levels, they would provide strong incentives for exploration and development which could expand Canada's limited and depleting oil reserves. On the other hand, such a price increase would transfer vast amounts of money from consumers (mostly in Ontario) to the Alberta government (through royalties) and the multinational oil companies.

(b) Opportunities: Who should get the benefits?

A more positive way of looking at the oil situation was that Canada (Alberta) possessed in its established, low-cost conventional oil reserves a major economic resource that had just increased dramatically in value. This sharp increase in the value of Canada's oil would generate vast amounts of what economists call **economic rent**—an excess of income over and above production costs plus a reasonable profit.[3] A major question facing Canadians in the 1970's was "who will get the economic benefits of rapidly rising oil values?" Broadly speaking, there were four possible recipients of these benefits: consumers, the provincial govern-

---

[3] Economic rent is often referred to as *windfall profits* in the media.

ments involved in oil production, the federal government and the oil industry.

The *provincial governments* of the oil-producing provinces claimed that much of the economic benefits should go to them (and their people) as legal owners of the oil. The *oil industry* argued that it should receive a substantial share of rising oil revenues, as these would provide it with the funds needed for oil exploration and development that could make Canada self-sufficient for many years. The federal government argued for a more equal distribution of the benefits across Canada. If the price of Alberta's oil were held down, *Canadian oil consumers* would receive much of the benefit of Canada's low-cost oil. Or if the *federal government* took much of the economic rent from rising oil prices through higher federal taxes on oil, these funds could be used for the benefit of all Canadians. Clearly, the question of who should receive the benefits of Canada's low-cost oil was to be a controversial issue.

The government's cheap-oil policy

The federal government decided to hold the price of Alberta oil down, through *price controls* which kept Canadian oil prices far below world prices. The security of supply issue was addressed by *extending the Western oil pipeline* to Montreal, reducing the need for imported oil. To make more Alberta oil available to Montreal refineries, *exports* to the United States were to be *phased out* over a ten-year period. Finally, a *federal tax* was placed on oil exports to the USA to bring their price up to the world price, and the revenues from this tax were used to subsidize the cost of imported oil. This move kept the price of crude oil across Canada down to the same level as the price of Alberta oil. Overall, the policy was popular but controversial. It spread the economic rent quite evenly across the country, distributing most of the economic benefits of Canada's low-cost oil reserves to *Canadian consumers*, who enjoyed prices much lower than in other countries.

However, it was also politically divisive. *Western Canadians* found the policy *discriminatory*, as they were forced to sell their valuable and depleting oil resources to Eastern Canadians at prices far below the world price, which they regarded as its real value. They felt that simply because a majority of voters lived in the East, the federal government was forcing them to subsidize Eastern consumers.

From the viewpoint of security of supply and the goal of oil self-sufficiency, the policy had serious flaws. Its low prices actually *encouraged consumption* of this depleting resource, as Canadians moved much more slowly than other nations toward energy conservation in the 1970's. Furthermore, the low controlled price of Canadian oil *discouraged exploration and development* in Canada, as oil companies found Canadian projects less attractive.

An overview

The government's oil policy had three basic objectives:

(a) low oil prices,
(b) increased government oil-tax revenues, and
(c) security of supply.

Ultimately, the government's oil policy failed because these objectives were themselves in conflict with each other. In particular, the objective of security of supply conflicted with the objectives of low prices and high tax revenues. For Canada to develop its alternative, higher-cost oil sources, higher prices would be needed. However, if government policy held prices down while taxing oil considerably, the industry would have insufficient funds and incentives to develop the alternative oil sources necessary for self-sufficiency.

The only way to resolve the conflicts between these policy goals would be to increase the price of oil sufficiently to provide the industry with the necessary funds to develop Canada's oil resources while giving governments the tax revenues they wanted. The question was not whether Canadian oil prices would rise, but when and how rapidly.

1974-79: A period of relative stability

Following its major price increases of 1973-74, OPEC encountered difficulties in maintaining its prices. While the cartel members had agreed on prices in 1973-74, they had never reached an agreement on *production quotas* for each to follow. Consequently, when the demand for oil grew more slowly after 1974 in response to higher prices and slower economic growth, OPEC failed to adjust the oil supply accordingly, and the period from 1974 through 1978 was characterized by oil surpluses on world markets and slowly rising prices, as Figure 17-2 shows. In fact, the price of OPEC oil failed to keep up with inflation during this period—in other words, the *real price* of OPEC's oil actually *fell*.

OPEC's difficulties from 1974 to 1978 led many observers to believe that OPEC had lost its power over oil prices. It was pointed out that higher prices had reduced the demand for oil and, more important, stimulated much greater oil exploration efforts, which would increase the supply of oil and undermine the cartel's monopoly. Furthermore, the OPEC nations were not united among themselves: while those with relatively low oil reserves wanted higher prices for the limited quantities of oil they possessed, those with large reserves (such as Saudi Arabia) were concerned that excessive price increases would speed the development of alternative sources, threatening their markets in the future. These nations, particularly Saudi Arabia, held oil-price increases down by threatening to use their large reserves to undercut the more militant members of the cartel.

FIGURE 17-2 *World Oil Prices, 1972-80*

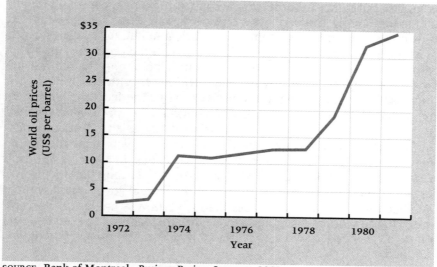

SOURCE Bank of Montreal, *Business Review,* January, 1981

In Canada, the federal government allowed the price of Canadian oil to increase gradually, from just over half the world price in 1974 to over three-quarters by 1978. This approach represented an apparently workable compromise between the interests of consumers, oil-producing provinces and the oil industry, as oil prices gradually rose toward the levels needed to provide long-term security of supply.

The 1979-80 OPEC price increases

The period of stagnant OPEC prices ended dramatically in 1979-80, as oil prices soared from about $13 (US) to $32 per barrel, as shown in Figure 17-2. This was partly the result of OPEC's efforts to reduce oil production in order to regain control over prices, and partly the result of supply interruptions, due to political instability in Iran and the Iran-Iraq War. When OPEC indicated its intention to exercise greater control over supply and prices in the future, oil markets seemed poised for a prolonged period of substantial and regular price increases.

In Canada, the OPEC price increases left the government-controlled price of Canadian crude oil at only 45 percent of the world price in 1980. To keep imported oil as cheap as Canadian oil, the federal government had to spend over $20 to subsidize the price of every barrel of imported oil. The cost of oil subsidies surpassed $3 billion per year, adding to the federal government's already-high budget deficits. The situation became unsustainable, with the federal government in effect borrowing billions of dollars of Canadians' savings (more than the oil industry was spending on exploration and development) *not* to invest in projects to increase oil supplies, but rather to subsidize the consumption of a scarce and rapidly depleting energy resource. The cheap-oil policy had led to a massive misuse of the nation's economic resources, and had to be reconsidered.

Major policy decisions had to be faced, with the problems and issues similar to those confronted in 1974. Both Alberta and the oil industry wanted a rapid move toward the *world price*, with the bulk of the increased revenues going to themselves, while the federal government remained in favor of *relatively low prices* and *higher federal oil-tax revenues*, which it saw as more widely beneficial to all Canadians. A new element in the picture was the large *federal budget deficit*, which made the federal government anxious to acquire new tax revenues. In 1980, Alberta and Ottawa sought to negotiate a new agreement regarding the pricing and taxation of energy resources. However, the federal government wanted a larger share of energy revenues than Alberta was prepared to accept, and Alberta wanted faster and larger price increases on its conventional oil reserves than Ottawa was prepared to allow, and no agreement was reached.

The National Energy Program (NEP)

Following its failure to reach agreement with the producing provinces, the federal government enacted its National Energy Program (NEP) in the fall of 1980. The NEP increased the federal government's control of the oil sector considerably, in various ways. While little of the NEP remains today, it is worth examining its main provisions and the problems it encountered.

(a) Federal control of the price of Canadian oil and natural gas

Prices were to remain under federal control and rise slowly toward a maximum of 75 percent of the world price.

(b) Increase in the federal share of oil revenues

Through a host of new and complex *taxes* on both producers and consumers of oil and gas, the federal government intended to increase its share of oil and gas revenues from 10 percent to 24 percent.

(c) Security of supply

The NEP sought to move toward oil self-sufficiency by both reductions in the demand for oil and by increases in supply. To reduce the demand for oil, the NEP offered incentives for *oil conservation* and for consumers to substitute natural gas for oil in home heating.

The federal government also increased its control of *oil exploration and development*. Prior to the NEP, companies decided where to explore for oil and deducted the costs of exploration. Under the NEP, this tax incentive system was replaced by a system of *federal grants*, under which the federal government would only pay grants to companies that explored areas *designated by the government*. These federal grants directed exploration toward the *Canada Lands* (see Figure 17-3), which were comprised of frontier and offshore areas that fell under federal (as opposed to provincial) government jurisdiction. Through these grants, the federal government hoped to promote the discovery of an "elephant find" of oil that would be *outside of provincial jurisdiction* (and taxation) and that would provide oil self-sufficiency for the future.

In addition, the NEP allowed a special higher price for Tar Sands oil, so as to provide incentives for production in that area.

FIGURE 17-3 *The Canada Lands*

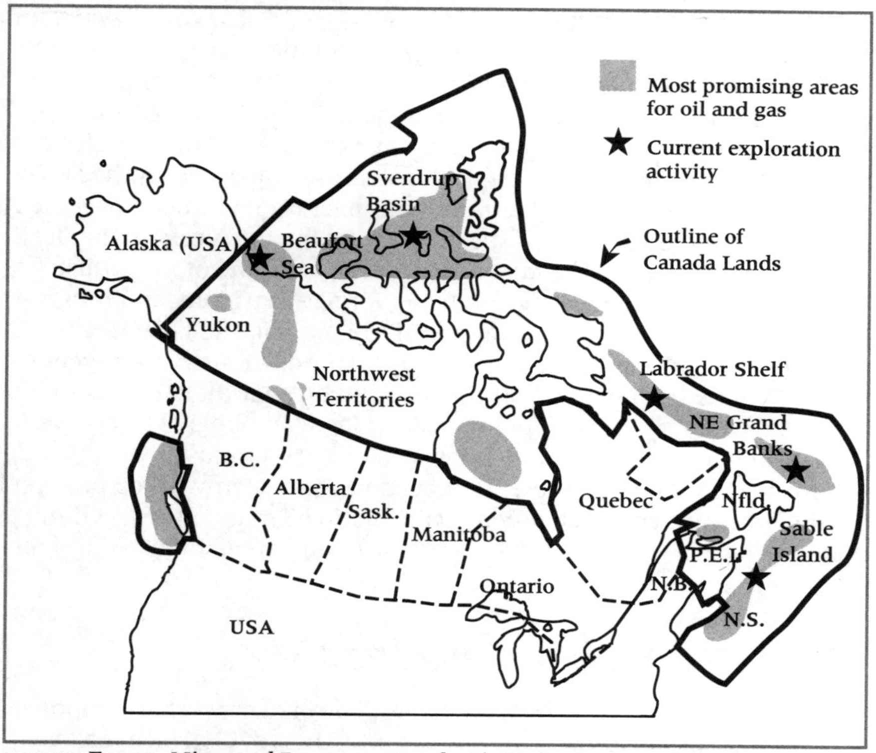

SOURCE Energy, Mines and Resources Canada, *The National Energy Program 1980*,
Ottawa, 1980
Reproduced by permission of the Minister of supply and Services Canada

(d) Canadianization of the oil industry

The NEP also sought to increase the degree of Canadian ownership and control of the oil and gas industry, from about 25 percent in 1980 to 50 percent by 1990. First, the federal exploration and development grants referred to earlier were structured so as to *favor Canadian firms* and promote their growth. Second, *Petro-Can*, the federally-owned Crown corporation, was to take over some foreign oil companies, with the funds for the take-overs to be provided by a special tax on consumers.

Modification of the NEP

The oil industry objected strenuously to virtually all aspects of the NEP. It was argued that the combination of low prices, heavier taxation and increased regulation would discourage investment in Canada's oil sector, especially by foreign firms. In turn, this lack of investment would make it impossible for Canada to reach its goal of self-sufficiency by 1990, and would expose the country to international price and supply disruptions. Alberta complained strongly that the NEP's pricing, taxation and grant/incentive system all discriminated against Alberta.

In September 1981, Alberta and Ottawa signed a *five-year agreement* on significant modifications to the NEP. Most notably, the agreement provided for *much more rapid price increases* toward the "cap" of 75 percent of the world price than the NEP had planned. Tar Sands oil and new oil (discovered after 1981) would receive the world price. These (projected) large price increases made possible the second main aspect of the agreement: *major tax revenues* for Alberta and the federal government, projected at over $60 and $50 billion respectively over the five years of the deal. Further adjustments to the tax regime addressed some of the industry's concerns, and the stage seemed to be set for new harmony and progress in the oil and gas sector. It is important to note that the federal-Alberta agreement, which gave Alberta, Ottawa and the oil industry the revenues they all wanted, was based on the assumption that the world price of oil would continue to rise rapidly, making large amounts of funds available to both levels of government as well as the oil industry.

However, by the time these modifications had been worked out, yet another unexpected development in the world oil market was beginning that would cause further problems for the Canadian oil industry and for policy-makers.

World oil-price cuts in the 1980's

By the early 1980's, OPEC was losing its control over world oil supplies and prices. The huge oil-price increases of the 1970's had weakened OPEC's power from both the demand side and the supply side of the world oil market. On the *demand* side, world demand for oil declined by 11 percent from 1979 to 1985,, largely due to oil-conservation measures in response to higher prices. On the *supply side* of the world oil market, the high prices had attracted a number of new producers, including the United Kingdom, Mexico and Norway. As a result, non-OPEC, non-communist oil production, which had increased by 20 percent from 1973 to 1979, grew by another 27 percent from 1979 to 1985. With supply rising and demand falling, OPEC faced a growing problem of oil *surpluses* on world markets, and world oil prices slipped from a peak of about $34 US per barrel to less than $28 by mid-1985.

In Canada, the decline in world oil prices caused uncertainty and concern in the oil industry, which had undertaken exploration and development projects with relatively high costs, while prices were still held by federal controls to a maximum of 75 percent of the world price.

Strains on the NEP

Declining world oil prices also played havoc with Canadian oil policy. The NEP (and the 1981 Ottawa-Alberta agreement that modified it) had been built almost entirely upon the assumption that world oil prices would increase rapidly, reaching $70 US per barrel by 1990. In effect, the governments involved had assumed away the policy conflict between low prices, high tax revenues and security of supply by assuming that prices would be so high that there would be ample money for both governments and the oil industry.

The assumption of high and rising oil prices proved woefully incorrect. As oil prices fell in the 1980's, the NEP began to unravel. Most notably, the *security of oil supply* aspects of the NEP looked increasingly unworkable. Under a combination of declining prices, heavy taxation and rising interest rates, and with investor confidence undermined by the NEP's extensive regulatory measures, the industry cut back on its exploration and development efforts. The oil-price decline was especially serious for high-cost projects such as the Tar Sands. In 1982, two Tar Sands megaprojects were cancelled after being caught in a squeeze between oil prices that were lower and interest rates that were higher than had been expected. Furthermore, the federal government's grant system for oil exploration was a disappointment. Despite putting billions of dollars into frontier exploration (paying up to 90 percent of companies' exploration costs), the grant system had failed to come up with the ''elephant find'' that had been hoped for as the source of oil self-sufficiency for the 1990's.

Oil-industry representatives argued that the entire thrust of the NEP was wrong. According to the industry, the way to move toward self-sufficiency was for the government to reduce its involvement in their industry and let private producers and market forces operate. Specifically, the industry wanted an end to government control of oil prices, less government regulation of the oil industry and better tax incentives (rather than grants).

The end of the NEP

In 1985, the new federal government made major changes to Canada's energy policy that seemed to respond to most of the oil industry's concerns. On June 1, 1985, the federal government deregulated Canadian oil prices, allowing the price to rise from its controlled level of $21.70 US to the world price at that time of $26 to $27 US. The federal exploration grants were to be dropped, and replaced with tax-based incentives for exploration and development that would leave more decision-making to private companies.

> We're satisfied that our total regime is one of the most attractive in the world. [New York investment dealers] Salomon Brothers have said we are more attractive than the US, the UK and Norway.
>
> Energy Minister Pat Carney, 1985

With oil-price controls lifted and the NEP gone, oil-industry representatives expressed confidence that Canada was poised for major exploration and development activity, with economic benefits not only for the oil-producing provinces, but also for Eastern Canada, whose industry supplies much of the materials and equipment (especially vehicles) for the oil industry.

TIME WORKED BY AN AVERAGE WORKER TO EARN AN AMOUNT SUFFICIENT TO PURCHASE A LITRE OF GASOLINE*

1961—2.7 minutes
1979—1.7 minutes
1984—2.6 minutes
1989—2.3 minutes

*Based on the average hourly wage for a manufacturing worker and gasoline prices at the pump for each year in Toronto.

The 1986 price collapse

By early 1986, however, oil-price deregulation looked like a mixed blessing at best for the industry. World oil prices plunged from about $28 US per barrel a year before to below $15 US per barrel in 1986, carrying the

> Each $1 per barrel change in the price of crude oil translates into six-tenths of a cent per litre at the gas pump.

price of Canadian oil with them. As a result, in August 1986, Gulf Canada was forced to stop its drilling in the Beaufort Sea.

Underlying this trend was a major development within OPEC. As world oil prices slumped in the 1980's, OPEC had attempted to support prices by reducing its own output, to offset production increases by non-OPEC nations. As a result, OPEC's share of the world non-socialist oil market had fallen from nearly 60 percent in 1979 to less than 38 percent in 1985, and OPEC's production had declined from 31 million barrels per day to 14 million per day over the same period. This shrinking market share had serious financial implications for the OPEC nations, whose oil revenues fell by more than half, from $287 billion US in 1980 to $132 billion US in 1985.

The key player in the OPEC oligopoly was *Saudi Arabia*, the largest OPEC oil producer. In the early 1980's, Saudi Arabia acted as a *swing producer*, reducing its output as necessary in order to keep total OPEC production from becoming so large as to cause a price collapse. As a result, the main burden of oil oversupply had fallen on the Saudis. Due to the growth of non-OPEC production and the unwillingness of some OPEC nations to obey OPEC's production quotas, Saudi Arabia's production had fallen from a peak of 9.9 million barrels per day in 1980 to a low of 2.2 million barrels per day in mid-1985.

Having suffered a massive decline in its oil revenues, Saudi Arabia changed its strategy dramatically. Starting in early 1986, it increased its output sharply, to the 5-7 million-barrels-per-day range. This created a *glut of oil* on world markets, precipitating a price collapse, as shown in Figure 17-4.

OPEC's lower prices did bring the cartel a larger share of world oil production and sales, but at a tremendous cost to OPEC's oil revenues, which fell by almost half. Following the 1986 price collapse, OPEC attempted to stabilize the market by establishing a new ''reference price'' and production quotas for its members. This attempt was not particularly successful. For instance, in 1989, OPEC nations were producing about

FIGURE 17-4 *World Oil Prices, 1972-89*

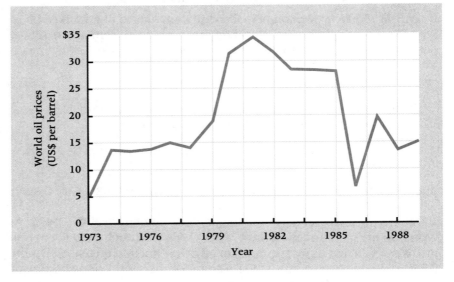

21 million barrels of oil per day, which was well above the cartel's total quotas of 18.5 million barrels per day. The biggest over-producers were *Kuwait* and the *United Arab Emirates*, both of which felt they had been assigned unfairly low production quotas. As a result, prices were generally below OPEC's "reference price" of $18 US per barrel.

Many energy economists considered OPEC's 1989 target price of $18 US per barrel to be too high to allow OPEC to sell its target (quota)

INTERNATIONAL DOWNSTREAM INTEGRATION

By 1988, some OPEC nations were revising their strategy so as to adapt to lower crude oil prices. By buying oil refineries and gasoline stations in the industrialized countries (what the industry calls "international downstream integration"), they planned to protect themselves against low or falling oil prices.

When crude oil prices fall, producers such as the OPEC nations lose money. However, oil refiners and distributors tend to have higher profits, because of the lower cost to them of crude oil. By investing in such operations, these OPEC nations hoped to be able to cushion the effect upon themselves of lower world oil prices.

production of 18.5 million barrels per day. They pointed out that at that price too many non-OPEC oil sources and non-oil energy projects were economical to make it a sustainable price. Many economists believed that, in these circumstances, the "equilibrium" price (in the sense of a sustainable price) was probably about $15 US per barrel.

The basic economic reality that emerges from these numbers is that OPEC had lost control of world oil prices. By the mid- to late-1980's, OPEC producers were not only badly disunited, but also controlled too small a proportion of the world oil market (a 40 percent market share as compared to 60 percent in the 1970's) to be able to determine world oil prices. In fact, as of late 1988, the real price of oil (that is, adjusted for inflation) was actually *lower* than it had been *before OPEC's first major price increase of 1973*.

The outlook for the future

Many economists believed that OPEC's problems after 1986 would prove to be temporary. They pointed out that low oil prices were encouraging rising consumption, while depressing both oil exploration and development and the development of alternative (non-oil) energy sources. For instance, US producers need about $18–20 per barrel in order to make US oil production economical on a significant scale. Non-conventional Canadian oil sources are vast, but are so costly that a price of $25-30 US is required to make them economical. Therefore, if OPEC's pricing and production strategies kept the world price of oil below $18 US per barrel, a combination of rising consumption and depressed production in the industrialized countries would make us *increasingly dependent upon OPEC oil* in the future.

And that dependence is expected to grow. A 1987 US report forecast that the USA would become dependent upon imports for over half of its oil needs during the 1990's. Projections for Canada were similar: as Alberta's reserves of conventional oil run out, Canada's dependence on

In these circumstances, a logical policy for both the USA and Canada would be to impose heavy taxes on oil consumption. Such taxes would encourage oil conservation by raising oil prices, as well as raise large amounts of tax revenues that could be used to reduce the massive budget deficits of the US and Canadian governments. However, Canadians and Americans are so fond of cheap energy that such taxes were considered politically unacceptable.

imports is expected to reach 600 000 to 700 000 barrels per day, or two-fifths of Canadian oil consumption. Thus, while the return of low oil prices was pleasant, it was contributing to a growing North American dependence on OPEC, and vulnerability to another major OPEC price increase.[4]

Despite its problems in the 1980's, OPEC still possesses about three-quarters of the world's oil reserves, putting it in a position to again become the dominant player in world oil markets before the end of the twentieth century. In addition to its vast reserves of oil, OPEC has tremendous production-cost advantages over other producers. While many major non-OPEC oil sources have production costs of $12 US per barrel or higher, Saudi Arabia can produce oil for 50 cents per barrel. Such large reserves of oil and such low production costs could allow OPEC to wait out the period of oil surpluses and low prices. After several years of low oil prices that encourage rising consumption while depressing oil exploration and development, the industrialized nations could again become vulnerable to OPEC's market power before the end of the century. Unfortunately, this scenario leaves Canada's oil industry, which has vast reserves but high production costs, with an uncertain future.

The Economic Council of Canada has recently assessed the costs of recovering oil from various non-conventional sources. The Council's study suggests that regardless of the method used to increase Canadian oil production, projects will have to be virtually free of taxes if they are to succeed. Economic rents cannot be extracted if there are none to be had. Yet even projects that yield no economic rents can be of immense benefit to the economy if, while yielding a reasonable return to the operators, they provide employment and produce oil that is competitive with world prices, thus reducing our reliance on imports.

Royal Commission of the Economic Union
and Development Prospects for Canada
(Ottawa, Minister of Supply and Services, 1985).

[4] In 1973, when the USA proved very vulnerable to the first OPEC price increases, the USA imported only 35 percent of its oil. At the time of the second major OPEC price increase in 1979, the USA imported 46 percent of its oil.

DEFINITIONS OF NEW TERMS

Conventional Oil   Oil from older, established wells as opposed to Tar Sands oil and heavy oil, which require considerably more processing.

Oil Royalties   Taxes levied on oil production by provincial governments, as owners of the oil.

OPEC   Organization of Petroleum Exporting Countries; established to control the supply and price of oil in world trade.

Economic Rent   An excess of income over and above production costs plus a reasonable profit; in the case of oil, the result of rapidly rising oil prices.

CHAPTER SUMMARY

1. While Canada is richly endowed with energy resources, oil is an important exception, as reserves of low-cost conventional oil are limited.

2. Legally, oil and natural gas are owned by the provinces within which they are located; however, the federal government has the power to control their prices.

3. In 1973-74 and 1979-80, OPEC increased world oil prices dramatically, thus increasing the cost of oil imported into Canada.

4. Despite this, the federal government held Canadian oil prices far below world levels through a combination of controls on the price of Canadian oil and subsidies on imported oil.

5. By 1980, rapid increases in the world price of oil made federal subsidization of imported oil extremely costly, and Canada's cheap-oil policy unsustainable.

6. Canada has domestic sources, such as the Tar Sands, which could replace imports; however, the price of oil from these sources would have to be high due to its high production costs.

7. Government oil policy has had three broad objectives: security of oil supply, high tax revenues for both provincial and federal governments, and low oil prices. Unfortunately, the third objective conflicts with the other two.

8. In 1980, the federal government introduced the National Energy Program, which undertook to continue to hold Canadian oil prices

well below world prices while significantly increasing the federal government's share of oil and gas revenues at the expense of the industry and the producing provinces. The NEP also undertook to increase Canadian ownership of the oil and gas industry and to shift exploration toward the frontier areas, or Canada Lands. A major aspect of the NEP's plan to achieve security of oil supply was a planned reduction in Canadian oil consumption.

9. In September 1981, the federal and Alberta governments reached agreement on substantially higher energy prices under the NEP, with higher tax revenues for both governments.

10. However, the NEP and the 1981 Alberta-federal agreement were based on assumptions of rapidly-increasing world oil prices. When oil prices fell, the results were disappointing, both in terms of oil exploration and development and in terms of tax revenues for the governments.

11. In 1985, the federal government ended the NEP, deregulating Canadian oil prices and making the tax incentive system more conducive to exploration and development.

12. However, in 1986, world oil prices fell sharply as oil surpluses developed due to falling consumption and rising production. The resultant lower price of oil threatened to make important Canadian oil sources uneconomical due to their high production costs.

13. As the lower oil prices increased consumption while depressing exploration and development, it was forecast that the industrialized world would grow increasingly dependent upon imported oil, and vulnerable to another OPEC price increase later in the 1990's.

QUESTIONS

1. Is the present world price of oil higher or lower than the $18 US per barrel considered necessary to make many North American oil projects economical?

2. Would the current financial condition of Canada's oil industry best be described as prosperous or troubled? What are the reasons for this?

3. Some Canadians want the federal government to make oil self-sufficiency a top priority of the federal government. Under this proposal, the federal government would ensure that development of the Tar Sands went forward, with sufficient production to elim-

inate Canada's dependence on imported oil. Assess the economic advantages and disadvantages of such a proposal.

4. "Another sharp increase in OPEC's price would represent more of an opportunity for Canada than a burden." Explain the reasoning behind this statement.

5. What would be the effect upon the international value of the Canadian dollar if
   (a) Canada's conventional oil reserves were to run down unexpectedly rapidly, forcing Canada to import large volumes of oil;
   (b) the Tar Sands and other oil projects were to go ahead rapidly, financed by substantial foreign investment?

The economics and politics of oil

CHAPTER 18

Environmental economics

During the second half of the 1980's, the environment became a major public issue in Canada. The seriousness and the scale of environmental problems—acid rain, global warming and the depletion of the ozone layer—made earlier concerns over air and water pollution seem minor by comparison. According to some projections, the environmental side-effects of our economic growth and prosperity were well on the way to threatening our very existence. By the early 1990's, environmental concerns were becoming a major political issue in Canada and other countries.

Environmental concerns are not a new phenomenon. During the late 1960's and early 1970's, concerns over air and water pollution led to the first legislation governing automobile emissions and air pollution. From the mid-1970's to the mid-1980's, however, environmental issues took second place to "bread and butter" economic issues such as unusually severe inflation and unemployment. During the second half of the 1980's, a combination of better economic times and serious environmental problems brought these issues back to the forefront.

Rather than focusing on the *causes* of these problems, and setting realistic *objectives* and effective *strategies* for reaching them, public discussion of environmental issues too often focuses on *fixing blame*, usually on someone else. Often, the problem is simply blamed on "industry," with the implication that if "industry" (someone else) were more responsible, there would be no environmental problems.

A more productive approach is to *analyze the reasons* for these problems. By doing so, we can not only gain a better understanding of them, but also formulate government policies that are most likely to be effective in dealing with them.

Economic analysis of this sort shows that environmental problems are much more than the result of industrialists' negligence. Environmental problems are deeply rooted in the very nature of our society and our economy, in at least two fundamental ways. The first of these is our *desire for material benefits*. To a significant extent, pollution is a by-product of the high levels of production and consumption that we have come to enjoy. For instance, the largest single source of air pollution in North America is automobiles. The second reality is that there are strong *economic incentives to pollute* the environment. Whether you are a corporation dumping waste into the water and air, or a driver disconnecting the emission controls on your car to save on gas, it is to your economic advantage, in the short run, to pollute the environment.

The economic incentive to pollute

As noted in Chapter 3, in a market system the profit motive provides important economic incentives for producers to produce what consumers want and to produce it as efficiently as possible. These incentives help greatly to increase the economic prosperity of consumers.

However, the profit motive also generates other incentives that are socially undesirable. One of these is for producers to join together in price-fixing agreements, as discussed in Chapters 10 and 12. Another problem is that there is an economic incentive to pollute the environment.[1]

In discussing this problem, economists distinguish between two types of costs incurred in the production of a product:

(a) private (internal) costs, and

(b) social (external) costs.

Private costs are ordinary production costs such as labor and materials. These costs are paid by producers, and ultimately included in the price paid by the consumer. Because these costs are contained within the production/consumption system, they are called "internal costs."

Social costs are the costs to the environment, and thus to society at large, of actions such as the dumping of industrial wastes into the air and water. These costs may or may not be measurable in dollar terms, but they are real and often high. Because they are not paid for by the

---

[1] This does not mean that pollution is only a problem in market economies that have profit incentives. Command economies such as the Soviet Union have generated serious pollution problems, too. The origin of the problem seems to be that the society fails to invest in pollution control because it values industrial output more than a clean environment. In this sense, the basic problem is similar in both systems.

business and not included in the price of the product paid by the consumer, but rather are passed on to the environment and to society at large, they are called "external costs."

The economic incentive is for producers to *minimize* their internal costs by being as efficient as possible. However, this also encourages them to *maximize* their external costs by dumping as much of their waste as possible into the environment rather than paying to prevent or clean up the resultant pollution. It is important to note that such behavior is economically beneficial (in the short run) not only to the *producer* (who gets higher profits), but also the the *consumer* (who gets the product at a lower price). However, the result can be serious effects upon the environment.

"We have met the enemy and he is us."

Externalities

When the production or the consumption of a product inflicts incidental costs such as pollution on others, and these costs are not paid by those who inflict them, economists say that an **"externality"** exists. This is also known as a "spillover effect," because the effects of the actions of some people spill over onto others. Pollution is among the most serious of these effects.[2] In our pursuit of material prosperity, we—including

You need to buy a great deal of paper and are on a limited budget. You can buy this paper from the Purewater Paper Company, which has invested heavily in pollution-control equipment, and charges $10 per kilogram for its paper, $3 of which covers the cost of the company's pollution control program. Alternatively, you can buy the same paper for $7 from Consolidated Killfish Inc., which is famous for having annihilated virtually all life in the rivers below its Northern Ontario pulp mills.

Which company's paper do you buy?

---

[2] External effects can involve benefits as well as costs. For instance, if someone thinks of an idea that improves auto safety, many people may benefit from it without paying that person for thinking of it.

GOVERNMENT VERSUS THE ENVIRONMENT

In addition to the marketplace's incentives to pollute the environment, governments have at times provided incentives of their own.

Despite the known serious environmental effects of burning fossil fuels, governments have chosen to subsidize oil and gas developments (and thus encourage their consumption) rather than to tax and discourage the use of these fuels.

Governments have also chosen to subsidize the use of agricultural fertilizers and pesticides that pollute the environment.

And, by underpricing trees (through low "stumpage fees" charged to forestry companies for cutting timber) governments have encouraged a disastrously neglectful forestry industry that strips forests without adequate provisions for replacement.

Why do you think governments have ignored the environment in these cases?

both producers and consumers—are choosing to avoid paying some important costs of our prosperity, and to pass these on instead to our environment, with potentially devastating results.

As a result, we cannot rely upon the marketplace to solve this problem; government action will be required.

The cost of a cleaner environment

Another fundamental reality of environmental economics is that pollution is mostly the by-product of the production and consumption of goods that most people value highly. You may be upset about the quality of air in your community, but are you willing to reduce your driving by one-third and do without some electrical appliances in order to reduce air pollution from cars and electrical generating plants? Alternatively, would you be willing to pay significantly more for these and other consumer products in order to pay for the costs of making the producers' plants and the products themselves less damaging to the environment?

Many people have been reluctant both to accept these realities and to pay the cost, preferring instead to view the situation with alarm while blaming others. Such attitudes could explain the reluctance of politicians to mount an effective attack on environmental problems. If government leaders believe that voters really prefer more consumer goods to paying for a cleaner environment, their efforts will tend to consist of strong words but weak action.

At the most basic economic level, a cleaner environment is like any other good, or economic benefit: we can have more of it if we are prepared to sacrifice other things. As we saw in Chapter 2, the fact that society has limited economic resources means that using more of these to produce one thing necessarily means having less available to produce other things. For instance, if we choose to devote more of our economic resources, such as capital and labor, to producing pollution control equipment and thus a cleaner environment, we will have less of other products, or a lower material standard of living.[3] This is a trade-off, like other economic choices, that we somehow have to make. So far, we have for the most part opted for more consumer goods and tolerated the resultant dirtier environment.

The trade-off between consumer goods and a cleaner environment can be shown with a production-possibilities curve of the sort discussed in Chapter 2 and illustrated in Figure 18-1. We could choose point A, at which we would have the maximum possible amount of consumer goods but devote no resources to pollution control and therefore have

FIGURE 18-1   *Trade-Offs Between Consumer-Goods Production and the Environment*

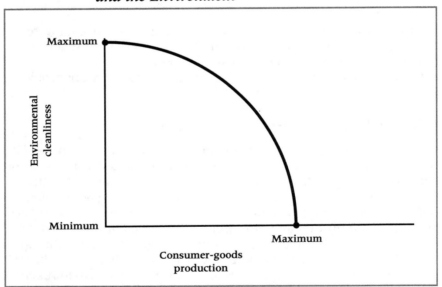

[3] This trade-off between a cleaner environment and fewer consumer goods is the way the economist sees the issue. The *consumer* sees it as having to forego consumption of, or pay *higher prices* for, certain products. The result is the same: a trade-off in which the outcome is a cleaner environment and lower production of other products. The money that the consumer must pay for emission controls on his/her automobile cannot be spent on other consumer goods.

ACID RAIN: THE COSTS AND THE BENEFITS

According to Environment Canada, the damage inflicted by acid rain on Canada's natural resources amounted to about $1 billion per year in the late 1980's. More than 300 000 lakes were considered vulnerable to acid rain, about 150 000 were being damaged, and more than 14 000 were described as having "acidified." The main source of acid rain is emissions of sulphur dioxide into the air from coal-fired power generating stations and nonferrous ore smelters.

In 1980, sulphur dioxide emissions from Canadian sources amounted to 4.5 million metric tons. By the late 1980's, under a program established by the federal government and the governments of the seven provinces east of Saskatchewan, emissions were down 38 percent to a level of 2.8 million metric tons per year. By 1994, the governments planned to reduce total Canadian emissions to 2.3 million tons, or about half the 1980 level.

To reduce emissions to this level will cost Canadians about $500 million annually, or about $20 per Canadian per year. In the USA, which accounts for approximately half of the acid rain falling in Canada, emission-control programs are estimated to be costing Americans about $12-18 each.

the dirtiest possible environment—perhaps one in which we would have to wear gas masks to work. At the other extreme, we could choose point B, at which we would have the cleanest possible environment, with highly restricted consumer-goods production, due to extremely strict environmental controls.

Points A and B represent the two extremes of environmental decision-making. In reality, it would be reasonable to expect a choice between A and B that represents an acceptable balance between our material wants and the quality of our environment.

Diminishing returns and the environment

As with other economic benefits, the cleaning of the environment is subject to the Law of Diminishing Returns described in Chapter 11. That is, it may prove quite easy to reduce the level of pollution by, say, 20 percent, through relatively simple and inexpensive measures. However, to achieve a further 20 percent reduction of pollution may well involve higher costs, while reductions beyond this are likely to prove even more costly. To approach the objective of very low levels of pollution could

> The main source of economic expansion, employment
> growth, and improvement in the quality of life is investment.
> . . . Although Canadians direct a high proportion of their
> private and business income into savings, Canada has
> traditionally needed to supplement its domestic savings with
> foreign borrowings in order to achieve rates of investment
> consistent with the desired growth of the economy and
> employment.
>
> Economic Council of Canada
> *Fourteenth Annual Review,* 1977 (page 45).

prove so costly that it might well be considered not worth doing.[4]

This reality makes it all the more important that we have reasonable
estimates of the costs of pollution and of the costs of pollution-control
measures, so that we can make rational decisions concerning pollution
control.

Environmental decision-making and cost-benefit analysis

Economists cannot tell society *which one* of the various possible combinations of environmental cleanliness and consumption is best, or
whether we should improve our environment by *x* percent at the cost
of a *y* percent reduction in the volume of our consumption. These are
decisions for the people of society to make, mainly through their
governments.

However, economic analysis can assist in the decision-making process
by providing estimates of the *costs* and *benefits* of any given level of pollution; that is, who loses due to the pollution, and how much, and who
gains economically due to the pollution, and how much?

For instance, suppose a pulp and paper company is polluting a river.
Those who benefit from this situation would include the company itself,
its shareholders and employees. Less obvious beneficiaries would
include consumers of paper, who get cheaper paper, and the local community, which benefits from the employment created by the paper mill,
the taxes paid by the mill, and the spending of money by mill employees.
Some of the social costs of the pollution could be estimated, such as
damage to commercial fishing and tourism, water purification costs and
health costs. Other costs, such as damage to wildlife and the quality of

---

[4] The exception to this generalization is where the particular pollutant is so dangerous
that complete (or near-complete) eradication of it is worth even very high costs.

the environment, would be more difficult to determine. However, it would be possible to at least make estimates of the costs and benefits of the situation as it is now, and the benefits and costs of reducing the volume of pollution.

Such estimates can help in making decisions concerning matters such as:

(a) *the objective of the pollution-control program*:
    Is the target to be total elimination of the pollution, or would that prove too costly? What would be the cost of reducing the pollution by 90 percent? 80 percent? 70 percent? Having estimates of the costs and benefits of these decisions can be quite helpful in setting targets for pollution-control programs.

(b) *how to attack the problem*:
    As we will see shortly, there are a variety of possible approaches to protecting the environment. An understanding of who benefits and who loses from the situation can help in deciding the most effective approach.

(c) *who should pay the costs of attacking the problem*:
    Depending on the costs and benefits involved, it may be appropriate for the cost to be paid by the producer and/or the consumer and/or the government. Economic analysis can help to determine who should pay these costs.

The current environmental situation

In the past, society has generally been prepared to accept the trade-off of additional pollution in exchange for economic growth and higher living standards. The environment *seemed* capable of handling most industrial by-products—those that were not recycled by natural processes seemed to be spread sufficiently thinly so as not to constitute a serious concern. During this era, the prevailing attitude was summed up in the phrase "the solution to pollution is dilution."

By the late 1960's, however, growing problems of air and water pollution made it clear that dilution was *not* the solution. A wave of public concern led to legislation providing some protection for the environment; however, this movement lost momentum in the second half of the 1970's and the first half of the 1980's, when public concern over severe inflation and high unemployment pushed economic concerns ahead of the environment.

After the mid-1980's, however, environmental concerns again came to the fore. Not only was the *volume* of waste larger than ever, but also much of it was *more toxic* than before, and included a variety of new chemicals. Most seriously, however, environmental concerns moved to a *global scale*. Problems such as *acid rain*, *the greenhouse effect* and *the depletion of the ozone layer* threatened worldwide disaster.

While many economic problems are best solved by the marketplace, environmental pollution is not one of these. As noted earlier, there are economic incentives for both producers and consumers to pollute the environment. As a result, environmental problems call for *action by governments*, not only on a national level but also internationally.

What can governments do?

We have seen that the basic reason for pollution is that there is an incentive for producers and consumers to pass on the external costs of their activities to the environment and to society at large. From the economic viewpoint, then, the objective of anti-pollution policy should be to *internalize* the external costs of pollution, so that polluters are forced to pay all of the costs arising from their activities. Three ways of doing this, which are described in the following sections, are *direct regulation*, *fines and taxes*, and *legal liability*. In addition to these, we will consider the possibility that in some cases the government should pay for, or *subsidize*, pollution control.

(a) Direct regulation

By far the most common form of government anti-pollution action is the imposition of direct controls. Under this approach, the polluter is required by law, or by a government agency empowered by law to set pollution standards, to reduce the pollution to a certain level. The emission controls set by governments for automobiles are probably the best-known form of direct pollution control.

While controls have the appearance of simplicity ("pollution is bad, so make it illegal"), in practice they encounter certain problems. Foremost among these is the setting of the limit, or standard, for the pollution. From the environmental viewpoint, it would seem desirable to set a standard of zero pollution, or ban pollution outright. However, as we have seen, it would prove extremely costly (and in some cases technically impossible) to achieve zero pollution. As a result, outright bans are used only for substances that have such extremely severe environmental effects that they must be banned at virtually any cost. Generally, direct controls allow some pollution, but specify the acceptable limits. Setting such standards is a difficult and controversial matter, especially when the environmental costs and the costs of pollution control are not completely known. Almost always, polluters complain that the costs of meeting the standards are excessive and will result in lost jobs, while environmentalists find the standards too lax and complain that they will allow serious pollution to continue.

Once the standards have been set, there remains the problem of enforcing them. Enforcement of complex regulations requires considerable

THE ENVIRONMENT INDUSTRY

While many people see industry and the environment as being in direct conflict with each other, the fact is that Canada is developing a significant "environment industry". By the late 1980's, there were about 3500 environmental equipment and service firms operating across Canada, employing about 110 000 people and generating sales of about $7 billion annually. Furthermore, the environmental sector was regarded as a growth industry, with projected growth rates of 20–40 percent per year. Nonetheless, compared to European nations, Canada's environment industry has been described by knowledgeable observers as "less developed."

A TAX ON CARBON

During the 1970's, when oil prices increased sharply, there was a major reduction in the amount of energy used per dollar of output produced. This experience indicates that making energy more expensive does cause people to use it more economically. Therefore, an effective way to reduce the air pollution caused by the burning of fossil fuels such as gasoline would be to charge higher taxes on those fuels, so as to raise their prices and reduce consumption of them.

In 1986, when oil and energy prices fell sharply, there was a great opportunity for the governments of both Canada and the United States to take major steps toward dealing with both environmental problems and their budget deficits. As oil prices fell, governments could have increased taxes on oil and gasoline. This would not only have reduced consumption of these fuels and the associated pollution, but also would have generated massive tax revenues to reduce governmental budget deficits.

Instead, governments in both countries chose not to increase these taxes. Oil and gasoline prices fell, consumption of oil and gasoline increased, the environment deteriorated and the budget deficits continued.

But voters were pleased.

resources, and environmentalists argue (often with justification) that governments tend to pass environmental legislation but fail to provide the resources to enforce it effectively.

Finally, the penalties for violating environmental protection laws must be sufficiently high to discourage polluters. Often, both the risk of prosecution for violating pollution control legislation and the fines levied on violators are so low that polluters are actually encouraged to violate the law, and pay the fines if caught.

Notwithstanding these difficulties, direct controls are the most commonly used form of pollution control. When properly set and enforced, direct controls do force polluters to pay the costs of pollution prevention or cleanup. By forcing producers—and consumers of the products, if their prices rise—to pay these costs, direct controls have the effect of internalizing the previously external costs that had been passed on to the environment and society at large.

(b) Taxes on pollution

Another approach to pollution control is to levy a tax on polluters (a "pollution tax") equal to the external costs caused by their pollution. Such a tax would force polluters to pay the full external costs of their activities. More importantly, it would provide an incentive for polluters to invest in pollution-control equipment. For instance, suppose that a firm is paying pollution taxes of $150 000 per year. If by investing $1 million in pollution-control equipment it can cut its pollution so as to pay no pollution tax, it would save itself $150 000 per year—a rate of return of 15 percent (after tax) on the investment of $1 million. Such a rate of return would warrant investing the $1 million in pollution-control equipment.

While attractive in theory, this approach also has certain disadvantages. In many cases, it may be difficult if not impossible to measure the external costs imposed by a polluter, making it very difficult to establish the amount of pollution tax to be paid. In addition, the pollution-control authorities would have to monitor each polluter's performance so as to levy the appropriate taxes. Finally, there are political obstacles to this approach. While economists see pollution taxes as an incentive to invest in pollution-control equipment, the public tends to see them as a "licence to pollute" that wealthy firms will cheerfully pay while continuing to destroy the environment. As a result of these problems, governments have seldom employed this approach, and have relied mostly on direct controls.

(c) Lawsuits for damages

Another way to force polluters to pay for the external or social costs of their activities is to allow the victims of their pollution to sue them for damages. If damages could be proven and the amount established, such lawsuits—whether by groups of citizens, other businesses or governments—could provide a strong incentive for polluters to invest in pollution-control equipment.[5] While this approach is seen as a useful part of anti-pollution policy, the complexities, cost and time involved in using the court system have tended to restrict it to a relatively minor role.

(d) Subsidies

A frequently-expressed concern of business is that if Canada forces them to invest in costly pollution-control equipment, they will be placed at a competitive disadvantage vis-à-vis foreign competitors who are not subject to such requirements. In the extreme, these costs might become so high that Canadian producers are unable to compete and must close. A variation of this argument is that corporations—both Canadian and foreign—will tend to establish new plants outside of Canada, where pollution controls are less strict and costly. This argument can be quite telling, because it places protection of the environment in direct conflict with another very high policy priority—employment. Such concerns are particularly relevant in communities that rely on one or a few industries for employment, such as pulp and paper towns.

> If you want this town to grow, it's got to stink.
>
> Mayor of a Northern Ontario town,
> in the 1970's

If pollution control regulations would really seriously impair a firm's competitive position, government policymakers are faced with a difficult choice between allowing the firm to continue to pollute at an unacceptable rate and imposing regulations that might cost the firm's employees their jobs. In either case, an undesirable social effect will result. In such circumstances, it may be justifiable for society at large, through the government, to use public funds to *subsidize* the cost of pollution-control equipment, so as to permit the firm to reduce its pollution without causing severe economic hardship.

Energy and the greenhouse effect

Our lifestyle is tied to high energy consumption. We use energy to transport ourselves, to heat us in winter and cool us in summer, to fuel our industrial activity and to operate the myriad of electrical appliances that

---

[5] It is helpful if the law allows "class action" lawsuits, in which large numbers of private citizens can pool their resources and sue as a group.

RECYCLING: THE MARKET AT WORK

Another environmental concern is the exhaustion of certain types of non-renewable natural resources, such as minerals. Some futurists have painted economically disastrous scenarious in which the world runs out of many such resources.

However, market forces appear to be dealing, at least in part, with this concern. As the most attractive low-cost sources of some minerals have run down, their prices have risen. These rising prices have provided incentives for both consumers and producers of these minerals to do some useful things. Faced with higher prices, users of these minerals have found ways to economize on their use and/or find substitutes. Meanwhile, rising prices have not only encouraged the development of new sources of such materials, but also have made it more economical to *recycle* them. In effect, higher metal prices can change scrap metal into an economically valuable alternative to mining.

In such circumstances, the market provides the necessary economic incentives for recycling, as recycled metals become cheaper than newly mined minerals. By the mid-1980's, the western world was obtaining 48 percent of its lead, 38 percent of its copper, 25 percent of its aluminum, 24 percent of its zinc and 21 percent of its tin from recycling.

we use daily. Even much of our leisure time is spent consuming energy through travel, the use of recreational vehicles and so on.

The simple fact is that there is no known large-scale source of energy that does not generate significant amounts of pollution. The main problem is the burning of fossil fuels, mainly gasoline. The automobile is the largest single source of air pollution, followed by the coal and oil burned to generate much of the electricity that our lifestyle requires.

Some of the pollutants from the burning of fossil fuels can be controlled, but not all. The most intractable pollutant is *carbon dioxide*, which, unlike other pollutants from automobiles, cannot be controlled with pollution control equipment. The resultant ongoing large-scale emission of carbon dioxide into the air has contributed greatly to the *"greenhouse effect"*—the global warming trend that environmentalists fear will cause disastrous climatic changes around the world, including the raising of ocean levels and widespread flooding of coastal areas.

Unless technology can solve the carbon dioxide problem, the fundamental conflict will remain between our high-energy-consumption life-

RECYCLING: THE GOVERNMENT AT WORK

Another area in which recycling can be helpful is with respect to household garbage. The recycling of some types of garbage, including paper, tin cans and bottles, not only provides reusable materials, but also reduces the volume of garbage and the strain on disposal facilities.

A major obstacle to recycling household garbage is sorting it into different categories, such as paper, glass, cans and other materials. This task is most easily and economically done at the household level, but there is no direct economic incentive to do so. In fact, such sorting involves a cost to householders: the time spent and the containers used to sort the garbage.

Some municipalities have dealt with this problem by providing households with free containers to put recyclable garbage into (a form of government subsidy) and by providing considerable publicity stressing the advantages to their community of using these containers. Thus, by spending a relatively small amount of public money, governments have been able to promote environmentally beneficial recycling.

style and the environment in which we live. At present, the only way to control carbon dioxide emissions is through conservation: that is, by controlling and reducing our energy consumption. We would have to switch from a value system based on economic growth and rising living standards to one that embraced conservation and quality of life, and accepted limits on our lifestyles and energy consumption. This is understood by all involved at the scientific and government level, but it would mean such a drastic change in established attitudes and practices that leaders are very reluctant to confront the problem.

As a result, this fundamental problem has gone virtually unaddressed, and seems likely to remain so until such time as a deterioration of the situation forces a more drastic reassessment of society's basic values and attitudes.

A tax of $.12 per litre on gasoline would not only discourage excessive consumption of gasoline and the associated pollution, but also raise about $3.6 billion per year in tax revenues.

The outlook for the environment

What is the outlook for improving our environment? Certainly, the rising public concern of the late 1980's makes it more likely that governments will take some action to curb pollution and protect the environment. However, there was a similar wave of concern in the late 1960's and early 1970's, and while that did lead to some environmental legislation, it did not solve the basic problems. A major criticism of much of the legislation passed at that time was that while it appeared impressive, it was not very effective. Many observers believe that governments wanted to respond to the public's concerns, but did not really believe that the public was willing to pay the economic cost of effective pollution control.

The key to an effective attack on pollution is not whether the public is *concerned* about the environment, but whether the public is *willing to pay* to protect and improve the environment. Will people accept a lower material standard of living as a necessary trade-off for a cleaner environment? As the 1990's began, it was still not clear whether Canadians had weighed the costs and the benefits of pollution control and come down on the side of the environment.

> Reversing the deterioration of the environment on a global basis is the most important challenge facing Canadians and citizens of the world.
>
> Thomas d'Aquino, President, Business Council on National Issues, May, 1989

DEFINITIONS OF NEW TERMS

Private (Internal) Costs   Production costs such as labor and materials, that are paid by producers and ultimately included in the price paid by the consumer.

Social (External) Costs   Costs to society at large and the environment of dumping wastes into the environment.

Externality   An incidental cost, or side effect, inflicted on others by the production or consumption of a product. Also known as a spillover effect.

CHAPTER SUMMARY

1. There are economic incentives for both producers and consumers to pollute, by passing the external costs of their production or consumption on to the environment.

2. There is an economic trade-off in which society can have a cleaner environment if it is willing to accept a lower level of production and consumption of goods and services.

3. As with other economic benefits, the cleanup of the environment is subject to the Law of Diminishing Returns: as the level of pollution is lowered, it becomes increasingly costly to reduce it further.

4. Economic analysis of the costs and benefits of pollution control can help in making decisions concerning the objectives of a pollution-control program, how to attack the problem and who should pay the costs of the program.

5. By the late 1980's, problems such as acid rain, depletion of the ozone layer and the greenhouse effect had raised public concerns about the environment.

6. Four types of action that can be taken to protect the environment are direct regulation, taxes on pollution, lawsuits for damages due to pollution and government subsidies to help pay the cost of pollution controls.

7. The key to whether the public concern over the environment in the early 1990's will be translated into effective action is whether Canadians will be prepared to pay the costs of environmental protection.

QUESTIONS

1. One source of pollution is throwaway drink containers.
   (a) Identify some of the costs and the benefits of using such containers.
   (b) Identify the advantages and disadvantages of each of the following approaches to the problem of throwaway drink containers:
      (i) prohibition of throwaway containers
      (ii) taxes on throwaway containers

2. "Setting pollution-control standards is simple—the standards should require that pollution be reduced to the maximum extent possible using modern technology."

Do you agree or not? If not, how should pollution-control standards be determined?

3. "The real problem with pollution is that people do not understand the side-effects of their actions. What is needed to combat pollution, therefore, is a comprehensive educational program pointing out how pollution is caused and the dangers of it."
   Do you agree or disagree? Why?

4. Do you believe that the values of your generation concerning the environment and material goods and services are different from those of your parents' generation?
   Would you be prepared to reduce your living standard by 10 percent in order to create a much cleaner environment?

5. If a gasoline tax of $.12 per litre would discourage excessive gasoline consumption while raising nearly $4 billion per year in tax revenues for a government with massive budget deficits, why has such a tax not been enacted ?

CHAPTER 19

The agricultural sector

While much of the Canadian economy is dominated by large corporations, in the agricultural sector the family farm is the most common form of enterprise, and competition among large numbers of relatively small producers is so intense that it has threatened the long-term stability of the industry. And if public debate over government policy has often stressed the market power of big business and the need for government to *restrict* its power, the problems of Canada's agricultural sector make it the best example of the opposite situation: one in which governments have felt compelled to *support* producers. To understand the nature of Canadian agricultural problems, we must first consider the nature of the industry, as well as the changes that have swept through it over the past few decades.

Profile of agriculture

Agriculture is an extremely varied sector of the Canadian economy. Canadian farms range from highly mechanized Prairie wheat farms of over 1000 hectares to small vegetable farms of less than 40 hectares. The

> Agriculture accounts for about 10 percent of Canada's total economic activity, including the food processing, wholesale and retail sectors.

one feature which seems to hold true of Canadian agriculture is that the vast majority of operations are family farms. According to the 1986 census, over 99 percent of Canada's 293 089 farms were controlled by families, the vast majority being sole proprietorships. Almost 95 percent of total gross farm sales in 1986 were generated by family-controlled farms. Figure 19-1 provides a brief statistical profile of Canadian agriculture.

While the agricultural sector's production amounts to less than 4 percent of the total output of the Canadian economy and employment in primary agriculture is less than 5 percent of total employment in Canada, the performance of the agricultural sector is of great importance to Canadians. Agricultural exports such as wheat make an important contribution to Canadians' prosperity, and the typical Canadian family spends a considerable proportion of its income (although a lower proportion than in most countries) on food, which represents about 20 percent of the Consumer Price Index.

Canada is a leading force in the world agricultural marketplace. Agriculture is a pillar of the economy in the west, and the mainstay of many communities in the east. The sector has demonstrated its resilience in responding to change to an extent probably unmatched by other industries.

Canadian farmers must compete, in most products, with foreign suppliers on both domestic and export markets. This competition has contributed to the development of a sector that is efficient by world standards, as witnessed by a continuously improving trade performance in the face of an increasingly adverse international market environment.

Hon. Michael Wilson, Minister of Finance
A New Direction for Canada: An Agenda for Economic Renewal
Ottawa, November 1984.

The agricultural revolution

Figure 19-2 summarizes the tremendous changes in the agricultural sector that have come to be called the *agricultural revolution*. The driving force behind the agricultural revolution has been *technological change*, which has greatly increased farm productivity through the use of more and improved equipment and fertilizers, improved strains of crops, and better farming techniques. The result, as Figure 19-2 shows, has been a long-

FIGURE 19-1 *Structure of Agriculture by Province, 1984*

Province	Number of farms	Average farm size (hectares)	Farm cash receipts 1984 (millions)	Top three commodities by value of farm cash receipts		
Newfoundland	679	49	$40.9	Poultry and eggs	Dairy	Hogs
Prince Edward Island	3 154	90	186.7	Fruit and vegetables	Dairy	Cattle
Nova Scotia	5 045	92	261.2	Dairy	Poultry and eggs	Fruit and vegetables
New Brunswick	4 063	108	229.4	Fruit and vegetables	Dairy	Poultry and eggs
Quebec	48 144	79	3 073.2	Dairy	Hogs	Cattle
Ontario	82 448	73	5 284.3	Cattle	Dairy	Small grains (excluding wheat)
Manitoba	29 442	263	1 926.4	Wheat	Cattle	Small grains
Saskatchewan	67 318	394	4 221.2	Wheat	Cattle	Small grains
Alberta	58 056	348	3 863.8	Cattle	Wheat	Small grains
British Columbia	20 016	123	964.5	Dairy	Fruit and vegetables	Poultry and eggs
Canada	318 365	214	20 051.6	Wheat	Cattle	Dairy

SOURCE Canada, Agriculture Canada, *Handbook of Selected Agricultural Statistics 1984*; and Statistics Canada, *Farm Cash Receipts*; December 1984.

term trend toward fewer but larger and more mechanized farms, operating much more efficiently as they produce more output with fewer farm workers.

The agricultural revolution has provided the economic basis for our high standard of living, because it has freed up a tremendous number of workers from employment in agriculture and thus made them available for employment in the manufacturing and service sectors of the economy, where they can produce the goods and services that make our present lifestyle possible. Without these improvements in agricultural efficiency, a high proportion of Canada's labor force would still be tied up in the agricultural sector, the nation's economic progress would have been much slower and its standard of living much lower.

In 1900, 45 percent of Canada's labor force was employed in the agricultural sector. By 1989, this proportion was just over 3 percent.

Moreover, the workers freed up from the agricultural sector have generally been absorbed by the expanding manufacturing and service sectors of the economy,[1] largely because aggregate demand for goods and services has been sufficiently high to keep output and employment in the economy rising. But while these changes did not create an unemployment problem, they *were* related to other problems that the agricultural sector experienced.

FIGURE 19-2 *The Changing Face of Canadian Agriculture*

	1941	1951	1961	1971	1981	1986
Number of farms	732 858	623 091	480 903	366 128	318 361	293 089
Number of people on farms	3 152 400	2 912 000	2 128 400	1 489 600	—	—
Percentage of population on farms	27.4	20.8	11.7	6.9	—	—
Percentage of labor force employed in agriculture	—	—	—	5.9	4.1	3.7
Average size of farm (hectares)	96	113	145	187	214	231
Number of tractors	159 752	399 686	549 789	596 698	657 700	728 024
Number of combines	19 013	90 500	155 611	162 751	161 110	157 934

SOURCE Canada Year Book; Statistics Canada, *Historical Labour Force Statistics* (71-201).

[1] The transition from the farm to other types of employment has been made easier by the fact that it has generally been the *children* of farmers, rather than farmers themselves, who have made this transition.

The farm problem

Low farm incomes

The statistics in Figure 19-2 do not seem to portray an industry in economic difficulty; if anything, such rapidly rising output per person would seem to reflect a prosperous sector of the economy. However, while farmers did everything producers are supposed to do—invest in capital equipment, improve productivity, and not band together to fix prices—the result was not prosperity for farmers. In fact, farmers have not only had *low incomes* compared to other Canadians, they have also had *unstable incomes;* that is, their incomes have fluctuated greatly from year to year. We will consider each of these problems in turn.

The great productivity improvements in agriculture have made possible large *increases in the supply* of agricultural products; however, this has not benefited farmers because the *demand for food is inelastic*. The farmers' problem is illustrated in Figure 19-3. Suppose that S and D represent the original supply and demand curves, with an equilibrium price of $10 and sales of 100 units for a total revenue (farm income) of $1000. If technological improvements increase the supply to S_1, the price will fall to $7, and total revenue will fall to $840 ($7 × 120). Clearly, the problem is that the demand for food is inelastic: *people do not buy much more food simply because its price is lower.* As a result, it takes a big price cut to sell the increased supply—such a big price cut that farmers' incomes actually fall. If the demand were elastic, as shown by demand curve D_1, only a small price cut (to $9) would be needed to sell the increased supply, and the farmers' total revenues would rise. Unfortunately for farmers, however, the demand for food generally is inelastic, so that the farmers' efforts to increase productivity are self-defeating, as the increased supply drives farm prices and incomes down.

FIGURE 19-3 ***With an Inelastic Demand Rising Supply Means Lower Farm Incomes***

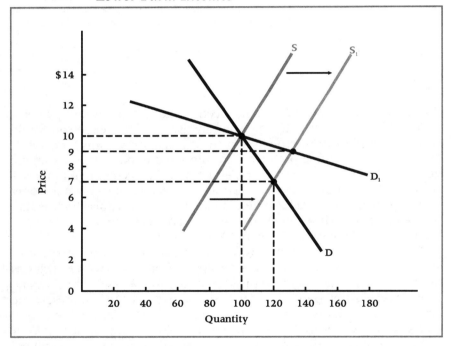

An additional problem facing agriculture is that the *income elasticity of demand* for farm products is quite low. This means that, as consumers' incomes have risen, the amount of food they buy has not increased as rapidly. As a result, farmers have not benefited as much as other industries from the growing prosperity of Canadians. This slow growth of demand has combined with rising supply to generate surpluses, low prices and low farm incomes.

Unstable farm incomes

It is a well-known fact that variations in the weather cause fluctuations in crop sizes (the supply of food) and farm incomes. However, varying weather conditions are only part of the problem, the other part being the *inelasticity* of *both* the *supply of* and the *demand for* food, as Figure 19-4 illustrates. Once a crop is harvested, the supply cannot readily be increased or reduced; and, as we have seen, the demand for the product is not likely to change much in response to price reductions. In graph (a), which portrays the market for an agricultural product, both the demand and the supply are inelastic—the supply curve (S) is in fact perfectly inelastic, meaning that 70 000 units have been harvested, and must be sold. Regardless of how high (or how low) the price goes, 70 000 units will be sold; with the demand curve D the result will be a price of $6. However, if good weather conditions result in a big crop next

FIGURE 19-4 *Supply Fluctuations Affect Prices Much More When
Supply and Demand are Inelastic*

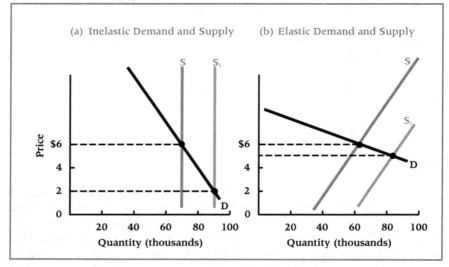

(a) Inelastic Demand and Supply   (b) Elastic Demand and Supply

FIGURE 19-5   *Farm Income, 1972-87*

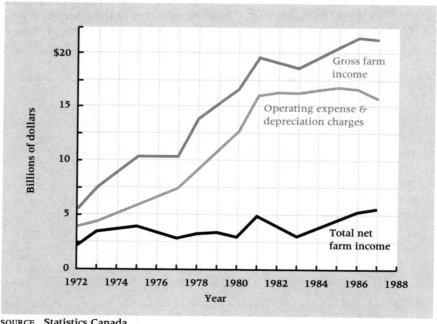

SOURCE Statistics Canada

year, as shown by S_1, the price of this product will *plunge* to $2. The reason for this large price decline is not simply the increase in supply— an equally important factor is the *inelasticity* of both supply and demand. This can be seen clearly from graph (b), in which the same increase in supply (20 000 units) occurs but the supply and demand curves are both quite elastic. The result, as graph (b) shows, is a very moderate price decline of less than $1.

The results of this combination of fluctuating supply and inelastic supply and demand are shown in Figure 19-5, which shows Canadian farm incomes from 1972 to 1987. Note that Figure 19-5 shows *total* farm income; for *individual* crops, the fluctuations have been much greater.

What to do about the farm problem?

Since the inelastic demand for food is beyond the control of farmers, the key to supporting and stabilizing farm prices lies in *controlling the supply* of farm products. In other words, farmers would benefit from an oligop- olistic price-and-supply agreement among themselves. The major obsta- cle to this, of course, has been the very nature of farming (and, some would say, farmers)—an excellent illustration of a highly competitive industry consisting of many small, independent producers selling sub- stantially similar products. Under these conditions, it has proven very difficult to achieve any coordinated action on the part of farmers, even when it would be in their best interests to do so.

> • From 1977 to 1988, Canadian farm debt more than doubled, from $10.3 billion to $22 billion.
>
> • From 1979 to 1988, 3681 farmers went bankrupt in Canada—more than one per day.

Farm cooperatives (co-ops) are one means by which farm prices could be supported and stabilized. Organized by farmers themselves, cooperatives could be the means by which farmers agree to restrict the production of various crops. However, co-ops have not generally proven very success- ful in these efforts, mainly because such agreements are voluntary, and too many farmers tended to ignore or break them. As a result, co-ops have tended to be of more benefit to farmers in areas such as research, advertising and securing volume discounts on purchases of supplies and equipment, rather than in restriction of the supply of farm produce.

When efforts at self-help proved largely unsuccessful, farmers turned to *government assistance* of various sorts. The Canadian Wheat Board (CWB) was established to stabilize the prices of wheat and feed grains. In the

Even 'world's best potatoes' have their cyclical problems

*By Barbara MacAndrew
For The Financial Post*

BANGOR, P.E.I.—Henry Compton was one of a family of 11 children raised on the family farm. It was a typical Prince Edward Island farm of the time: a few dairy cows, a few hogs, a few potatoes in the fields.

Compton, 54, and two brothers today work 1,400 acres dedicated entirely to potatoes. In one generation, the Comptons have expanded the original acreage five fold and invested more than $3 million in their operation.

In the past five years, they have marketed one million 10-pound bags of potatoes—90% for the fresh market, the rest as feed. Henry and brothers John, 42, accounting/sales manager, and Ralph, 49, mechanical manager, will gross about $1 million in a good year.

Not all years are good, though. The Comptons are totally dependent on the vagaries of not only nature, but the prices Ontario and Quebec consumers are willing to pay.

Henry Compton accepts the market ups and downs as part of the business, just as natural in their own way as the effects of the weather. "I'm a free-enterpriser," he says, "The boom-and-bust cycle has always existed. Our markets are based on supply and demand."

During the [1982-87] period, it cost the Comptons $4.31 to grow and market a hundredweight of potatoes, leaving an average profit of 24¢ per hundredweight.

The Comptons, as grower/dealers, have invested in warehousing and packaging equipment that allows them to wait for an improvement in market conditions before they ship their "Island Tradition" family brand to central Canada by truck.

They estimate their total production cost at about $1,200 per acre. That includes a payroll of 15 local people, employed from harvest in September through the winter, when two tractor-trailer rigs a day pull away from the Compton warehouses.

This summer, Henry Compton is watching a bumper crop mature in his fields and listening to talk that drought in Ontario and potato-producing areas of the U.S. will drive prices up. This could be a good year for the Comptons.

Total acreage

Henry and his brothers bought up land in the 1960s as other farmers went out of business. At the time, there were almost 6,000 potato farmers in P.E.I. There are 678 registered potato growers today, but the total acreage in potatoes has increased by 16% since 1978.

For Henry Compton, former chairman of the P.E.I. Potato Marketing Board, a director of Potatoes Canada and recent appointee to the Federal Stabilization Board, the idea of supply-management in potatoes is alien to his free-enterprise philosophy.

Just because about 72% of Canadian potato farmers voted recently for some form of supply-management system does not necessarily mean they want it, he argues. "They do want to look at improvements in marketing, for wider markets, quality control, organized production and distribution."

Compton has concerns about the future of the family farm. "Where does farming go from here? It's the only life I ever want, but most of our children don't want to farm."

(Nor does brother Ralph, who comments quietly: "I would like to do something else now with my life.")

SOURCE *The Financial Post*, August 22, 1988 (p. 13).

Prairie provinces, the CWB buys almost all of the crop entering commercial channels, providing minimum prices guaranteed by the federal government, and handles all exports. During periods when excess supply threatens to depress prices, the CWB also attempts to regulate the production of grains so as to support prices.

The other major government agency providing farm price stabilization in Canada is the Agricultural Stabilization Board (ASB), established in 1958. The ASB is required to support the prices of nine commodities—cattle, hogs, sheep, butter, cheese, eggs, wheat, oats and barley (the latter three outside the Prairie provinces only)—at not less than 90 percent of the previous five-year average price. The intention of the ASB is obviously not to stabilize farm prices and incomes against *any* market fluctuations, but rather to prevent farmers from suffering *extreme* hardship when prices are particularly depressed by market conditions.

In the following sections, we will consider various means by which governments attempt to support and stabilize farm prices and incomes.

Offers to purchase

Under the offer-to-purchase method, the government establishes the price of the farm produce and undertakes to purchase any unsold produce at that price. As we saw in Chapter 8, and as Figure 19-6 shows, the result of farm price supports will be *surpluses* of farm produce. At the supported price of $2 per bushel, farmers will produce 65 million bushels but only 45 million will be sold, the result being a surplus of 20 million bushels that the government will have to buy and store. Unless market conditions turn favorable, the government will likely accumulate embarrassingly large *crop surpluses* that are costly to store and for which there is no ready use. Possibly for these reasons, the offer-to-purchase approach is not widely used, being restricted to a few products such as butter, cheddar cheese and skim milk powder, of which the Canadian Dairy Commission has accumulated massive surpluses in the past.

Acreage restriction

To avoid the problem of crop surpluses, governments have sometimes used acreage restrictions. Under such a program, farmers are either *required* to reduce their acreage under cultivation or are given *financial incentives* to do so. The result, as shown in Figure 19-7 is that the supply curve shifts to the left (to S_1) and the price is increased (from $1.25 to $2.00). Acreage restrictions have not always proven a reliable method of restricting supply, however, because farmers sometimes take their least productive land out of cultivation and cultivate the remainder more intensively.

FIGURE 19-6 *The Effects of Farm Price Supports*

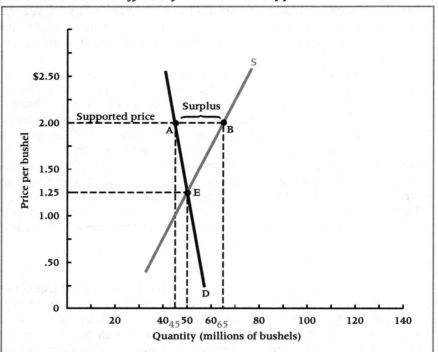

FIGURE 19-7 *The Effect of Acreage Restrictions*

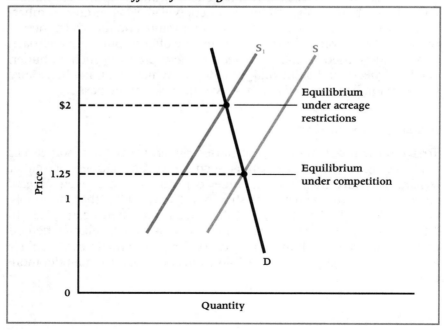

Deficiency payments

Under the previous two programs we have examined, crop prices are increased by *reducing the amount of produce available to consumers*—either by the government buying surplus produce and holding it off the market, or by allowing less produce to be grown. A completely different approach, which does *not* reduce the amount of produce available to consumers, is known as **deficiency payments**. Under this approach, the government does not attempt to reduce the supply of produce on the market; instead, it sets a *target price* for the produce and undertakes to pay farmers the difference between this target price and the actual market price. Figure 19-8 shows how the program works: in a free market, the price would be $3; however, the government establishes a target price of $5, which is considered to provide a fairer return to producers. Knowing that they are guaranteed a price of $5, farmers undertake to produce 50 million units, as shown by point A on the graph. To sell this output of 50 million units, point B on the graph shows that the price must be $2. Thus, the government must pay each farmer a deficiency payment (or subsidy) of $3 for each unit sold at $2, to bring the farmers' return up to $5 per unit.

The deficiency-payments approach eliminates the problems of surplus disposal and is the best from the consumer's point of view, because it does not restrict supply and results in lower prices. On the other hand,

FIGURE 19-8 **The Effects of Deficiency Payments**

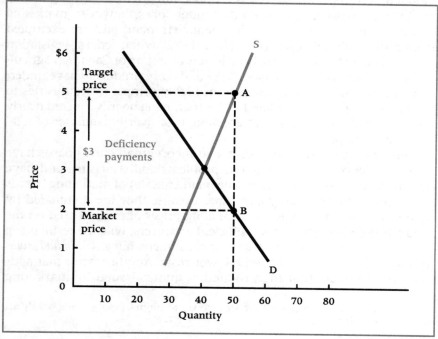

it can require considerable direct payments from the government to farmers and therefore tends to be more costly to the government (or taxpayer).

The Agricultural Stabilization Act is a form of deficiency payments program. By paying farmers the amount necessary to keep prices at 90 percent of the average of the previous five years, it achieves two objectives. First, it protects farmers against *short-term price declines*. Second, in the event of a *long-term price decline*, it delays and cushions the effects of the depressed market on farmers, giving them more time to adjust.

Marketing boards: From competition to monopoly

A more recent development in Canadian agricultural policy has been the concept of *supply management* through marketing boards. **Marketing boards** are government-sponsored organizations of farmers that are intended to regulate the production and price of various types of farm produce.[2] In theory, the marketing board establishes the size of the market for a particular product, then assigns *production quotas* to individual farmers so as to restrict the amount they can legally produce and prevent overproduction. Individual farmers then sell their produce to the marketing board, which acts as a monopoly sales agent on their behalf, selling the produce to processors and distributors at a price that is set by the marketing board to give the average producer a fair profit.

Because they have the legal power to set production quotas for individual producers, and thus control supply and prices, marketing boards are in effect *monopolies*. Unlike other monopolies, however, marketing boards have been encouraged by the government, and are exempted from anti-combines legislation. Since 1972, when federal legislation paved the way for marketing boards, many sectors of Canadian agriculture (including eggs, chickens, turkeys and dairy products), have undergone a dramatic transformation from highly-competitive industries to virtual monopolies. By the late 1980's, marketing boards covered nearly 80 000 Canadian farmers, and accounted for over one-quarter of total farm cash receipts.

While they seem relatively simple in theory, marketing boards have in practice encountered numerous problems and criticisms, and have become a center of controversy. The main criticism of marketing boards is that they cause *excessively high prices*, because they are dominated by producers. Their formulas for calculating prices often are based on the production costs of smaller, less efficient producers, with the result being not only unnecessarily high prices for consumers, but also *windfall profits* for more efficient producers with lower costs. Another factor that adds to costs is the fact that the production quotas issued by marketing

[2] Not all marketing boards possess the legal power to control supply; some simply act as a sales agent for farmers.

boards—which are in effect a piece of a monopoly—acquire a market value. Producers who are starting or expanding operations are *forced to buy production quotas* from other producers; for instance, the quotas for a 25 000-hen egg operation in Ontario in 1981 cost about $450 000. The costs of these quotas add to the cost, and, ultimately, to the price, of farm produce.

Related to the question of costs and prices is the complaint that marketing boards *foster inefficiency* in agriculture. Because of the high prices

In sum, by restricting foreign and domestic supply, supply-management marketing boards raise the prices of agricultural commodities and thus augment farm incomes. They appear to accomplish this, however, at a significant efficiency cost to the Canadian economy as a whole. Nor do they benefit all producers equally. They bring very little benefit to new farmers, who must buy their quota. Indeed, it may be that few of the beneficiaries of marketing boards are still on the land; many have sold their quota and retired. Again, Commissioners would repeat that these criticisms are levelled at national supply-management marketing boards controlling the supply of agricultural products such as eggs, chickens, turkeys, tobacco and milk; we are not criticizing those marketing boards which do not restrict supply, many of which operate at the provincial level.

Commissioners assume that in general, Canadians support the goal of augmenting and stabilizing farm incomes. Nevertheless, national supply-management marketing boards represent an expensive way to meet a perfectly acceptable social goal. One alternative would be a scheme that reduced the extent of income fluctuations experienced by the producers, instead of supporting their level of income, as such marketing boards do. Unlike the boards' methods, an income-stabilization scheme would smooth out market risks without generating efficiency losses. This Commission recommends that the federal government, the provinces, farm groups and consumer associations commit themselves to the task of designing and implementing other possibilities such as an income stabilization scheme. We further recommend that Canada move gradually to phase out supply-management marketing boards.

Report of the Royal Commission on the Economic
Union and Development Prospects for Canada, 1985
Reproduced by permission of the Minister of Supply and Services Canada.

established by marketing boards, small, inefficient producers are kept in business. Furthermore, there is little incentive for producers to consolidate into larger, more efficient units because *growth is discouraged by quotas*. Not only does the cost of buying quotas discourage growth, as we have seen, but also the quotas themselves can prevent growth to efficient sizes: while production costs per dozen eggs decrease substantially for operations with 50 000 or more hens, only Alberta and Manitoba allowed flock sizes in excess of 50 000 hens in 1980. Finally, by forcing producers to operate below their capacity levels, marketing boards reduce efficiency and add to costs and prices.

In addition, marketing boards have experienced *administrative problems* that have led to considerable criticism. In particular, boards have sometimes found it easier to control the price of produce than the supply of it. There are problems in administering quotas that apply to thousands of scattered producers (and don't apply to producers below a certain size), especially when the high prices caused by marketing boards provide an incentive to increase production and sell it directly to processors, distributors and even consumers, rather than to the marketing board. As a result, despite their quota systems, marketing boards have experienced some embarrassingly large *surpluses*. To reduce its problem of surplus production, the Canadian Egg Marketing Agency in the spring of 1981 paid farmers a $2 200 000 subsidy to slaughter 1 500 000 laying hens—a decision that prompted considerable public criticism.

In summary, marketing boards represent the most recent government approach to supporting and stabilizing farm prices and incomes. While they have been generally quite effective in improving the economic position of farmers, they are quite controversial, mainly because they grant to farmers an unusual amount of legally sanctioned monopoly power, and many observers are concerned about the negative effects of this monopoly power on agricultural prices and efficiency.

Free trade and marketing boards

Another problem facing marketing boards is the trend toward freer international trade. Marketing boards limit production of farm products in order to raise prices. Such control of supplies requires restrictions on imports, which runs counter to the trend toward freer trade.

Under the **General Agreement on Tariffs and Trade (GATT)**,[3] countries may limit imports if they also limit their own production. This provision is intended to prevent countries from dumping surplus products into the world market. Through the *Import Control List*, (ICL) Canada protects its supply management system by limiting imports of various agricultural products.

---

[3] **GATT** is an international agreement governing global trade and tariff reductions. Its aim is to promote freer trade among nations.

While the Import Control List protects farmers, it creates problems for many Canadian *food processors*, who must buy their food inputs at high Canadian prices. Under free trade, these processors may face competition from American food processors who pay much less for food inputs. The key to this issue is whether GATT's article 11—which permits countries to limit imports of supply-managed products—also applies to packaged goods made with those supply-managed products. For instance, Canadian marketing boards limit the production of chickens and mozzarella cheese, and imports of these are also limited under the ICL. However, it is not clear whether Canada can limit imports of packaged goods such as TV chicken dinners and pizza that are made from these supply-managed products.

WHY CANADIAN FARMERS AND FOOD PROCESSORS WORRY

According to Agriculture Canada, in 1988 prices in Canada (after adjustments for the exchange rate) were higher than in the USA by:

- 94 percent for eggs
- 27 percent for broiler chickens
- 54 percent for turkey hens
- 49 percent for industrial milk

If the GATT disallows Canada's limits on such imports, increased imports of low-priced packaged food products could create serious problems for Canada's food processors (and as many as 150 000 of their employees) and the marketing boards and farmers that supply them. This would generate strong pressure on Canada to alter its agricultural supply-management practices.

Canadian farmers themselves were not united on the matter of free(r) trade. While marketing boards and supply management were supported by farmers in eastern Canada who wanted protection against US imports, western Canadian farmers favored free(r) trade because they wanted access to the US market for their exports of grain, oilseeds and beef.

The international subsidy war

During the 1980's, there was a large-scale effort by a number of major food-importing countries to increase their agricultural output and become more self-sufficient. The main policy approach used by these countries was heavy government **subsidies** to farmers, through price supports and/or direct payments to farmers. The result was *major increases in farm output* and inventories of farm products in many nations. For instance, during this period, Europe went from being a net importer of cereal grains to the third-largest wheat exporter in the world.

> Canada is among the top seven food-exporting nations in the world. In 1985, 51 percent of all Canadian agricultural production was exported (wheat accounted for half of these exports). Agricultural and food exports accounted for 10 percent of Canada's total exports.

Faced with a problem of growing domestic food surpluses, some governments *subsidized the export prices* of agricultural products in an attempt to unload their surpluses onto world markets. Other food-surplus nations retaliated with subsidized exports of their own, creating a "subsidy war."

In some markets, such as the wheat market, the effects were very disruptive for Canada, which exports three-quarters of its production. During the first half of the 1980's, world stockpiles of wheat grew by two-thirds, and wheat prices fell by almost 50 percent. After the 1986-87 record world grain crop of 1.7 billion metric tonnes, there was a surplus of nearly half a billion metric tonnes in storage.

> When adjusted for inflation (i.e., expressed in "real" terms), the average price of wheat of $3 per bushel in 1987 was *lower* than the average price in the 1930's.

As world food prices fell, government subsidies to farmers escalated dramatically. Figure 19-9 shows the growth of government subsidies to farmers over this period.

As the international subsidy war intensified, the cost to the governments involved soared. By the late 1980's, the total cost of Canadian

FIGURE 19-9 *Growth of Farm Subsidies, 1979-86*

	Percent of total farm income that comes from government	
	1979	1986
United States	15%	35%
Canada	24	46
European Economic Community	44	49
Japan	64	75

farm subsidies was estimated at nearly $9 billion per year, including about $2 billion from consumers, through higher prices.

As governments not only subsidized exports, but also placed restrictions on imports in order to keep domestic farm prices up, the matter became the subject of a major trade dispute in GATT negotiations. Until this issue is resolved, it will continue to create major problems for farmers and governments in major food-exporting nations such as Canada.

Agricultural policy in perspective

As we have seen, Canada has a variety of programs to support and stabilize farm prices and incomes, including price supports, acreage restriction, deficiency payments and marketing boards. As with all government policies, there are *benefits* and *costs* associated with agricultural policy.

Ultimately, of course, the cost of agricultural programs falls upon the public, through *higher food prices* and *taxes* to finance subsidies to farmers. There are various estimates of the total cost of Canada's farm support programs, ranging as high as $9 billion per year in the late 1980's, or about $350 per Canadian.

There are various economic and social benefits associated with agricultural policy. Support of farmers ensures a *more healthy agricultural sector*, not only today, but well into the future, because producers are protected against severe price fluctuations, low incomes and bankruptcies, and there are sufficient economic incentives to attract young, capable people into farming. Another argument on behalf of programs to support farm incomes is that they *help to preserve farmland*. By making farming a more economically attractive use of land, they reduce the incentive for farmers to sell their land for industrial or residential use, and help to preserve the amount of good agricultural land available to Canadians in the future. In these ways, agricultural policy represents a trade-off, in which consumers are asked to pay higher food prices today in exchange for a more stable and healthy agricultural sector tomorrow.

Finally, assistance to farmers can be defended on the grounds of *equity*, or fairness. Because farming tends to be one of the most competitive sectors of the economy, farm incomes have tended to be significantly lower than the incomes of other Canadians, many of whom belong to labor unions or professional associations, or work for large corporations or governments that have the means to pay higher incomes. Consequently, it can be argued that it is only fair that farmers have some protection against the harshness of a marketplace that is not only extremely competitive, but also quite unstable.

While support of farmers is generally accepted as a policy objective, there has been criticism of some of the support methods used in Canada. In particular, there are concerns about supply management and the operation of marketing boards, which tend to hold down output, foster inefficiency and boost production costs and prices. With the trend toward freer international trade generating stronger international competition, there has been increased interest in developing agricultural policies that promote efficiency rather than inefficiency.

The most likely policy approach to achieve increased efficiency and output while still protecting farmers against periodic price and income declines would be *deficiency payments*, as described earlier. While this approach guarantees the farmers a price for their produce, subsidized by the government if necessary, it does not reduce production or discourage the development of improved efficiency, as marketing boards do. Deficiency payments are not a completely simple approach to agricultural policy: the problem of setting an appropriate target price that is neither too high nor too low is a difficult one. However, even if the target price is higher than necessary, limits can be placed on payments to individual farmers. This would reduce the incentive to produce excessive quantities of output and direct relatively more assistance to smaller farmers, preventing larger farmers from reaping windfall profits as often occurs under marketing boards. Agricultural policy in the USA has shifted toward deficiency payments, and unless the criticism of the performance of Canada's marketing boards subsides, pressure will increase for Canadian policy to follow.

While you may think that there is all kinds of land available for agriculture in a country the size of Canada, this is not the case. Eighty-nine percent of Canada's land is not suitable for agriculture of any kind, and less than 0.5 percent is rate as class one—suitable for all types of crops. Furthermore, not all suitable land is being used for agriculture: 37 percent of all class one land can be seen from the top of Toronto's CN tower, and is within commuting distance of Canada's largest and fastest growing city.

DEFINITIONS OF NEW TERMS

Offer-to-Purchase   A farm-income support program under which the government establishes the price of the farm produce and undertakes to purchase any unsold produce at that price.

Acreage Restriction   A crop supply management program that either forces farmers to reduce their acreage under cultivation, or gives them financial incentives to do so.

Deficiency Payments   A program for supporting farm incomes under which the government guarantees farmers a target price for a crop by subsidizing all sales of that crop which fall short of the target price.

Marketing Boards   Government-sponsored organizations of farmers that support farm incomes by restricting the supply of produce, usually through a system of quotas on individual farmers.

General Agreement on Tariffs and Trade (GATT)   An international agreement under which many nations have, since 1947, negotiated reductions in tariffs in order to promote freer international trade.

Subsidy   Government financial assistance to an industry, through measures such as grants, loans or special tax treatment.

CHAPTER SUMMARY

1. During the twentieth century, technological progress has greatly increased agricultural productivity, making farms larger, more mechanized and more efficient, and freeing up labor from the agricultural sector, allowing the manufacturing and service sectors to expand more rapidly.

2. Farmers, however, have tended to have incomes that were low and unstable. Low incomes have been the result of increasing supply interacting with an inelastic demand, while unstable incomes have been caused by an inelastic and fluctuating supply interacting with an inelastic demand.

3. When farmers proved unable to organize themselves adequately through voluntary organizations such as co-ops in order to restrict supply and support and stabilize their incomes, governments undertook to help them.

4. One type of government program is offers to purchase, under which the government establishes the price of the farm produce and purchases any unsold produce at that price; however, this program tends to result in crop surpluses.

5. Under acreage restrictions, the government either requires or pays

farmers to reduce the amount of land under cultivation, so as to reduce the supply of produce and increase its price.

6. With a system of deficiency payments, supply is not restricted; rather, the price of the produce is directly subsidized by the government up to the target price level.

7. Marketing boards are government-sponsored monopolistic organizations of farmers that increase farm incomes by restricting the supply of produce, usually through production quotas for individual farmers.

8. Since their inception in 1972, there has been considerable criticism of marketing boards, focusing mainly on the high prices they cause, the deterrents they create to improving efficiency, and various administrative problems related to difficulties in actually controlling supply.

9. During the 1980's, growing subsidization of farming by many nations led to worldwide food surpluses and low prices. This caused problems for both farmers and governments in Canada, which is a major agricultural exporter.

10. While Canada's various farm price and income support programs are quite costly to consumers and taxpayers, they can be defended on the grounds that they help to support farm incomes at more equitable levels, and that they help to preserve a healthy agricultural sector for the future.

11. Nonetheless, there remains considerable dissatisfaction with the operation of marketing boards. It is possible that, under the pressure of freer international trade, agricultural policy may shift in the direction of providing incentives for improved efficiency.

QUESTIONS

1. For decades, the agricultural revolution has made large amounts of labor available for increasing output in the manufacturing and service sectors of the economy. Now, however, with less than 4 percent of Canadians on the farm, there is little scope for continuing this process. In the future, what are possible or likely sources of increased output in the manufacturing or service sectors?

2. From the viewpoint of low-income families, which would be the more desirable approach to stabilizing and supporting farm incomes: marketing boards or deficiency payments?

3. As noted in this chapter, the production quotas assigned by marketing boards have acquired market values, so that new or expanding producers must buy them. What would determine the price of such quotas?

4. When some marketing boards inadvertently accumulate surpluses of produce, they place a special levy, or charge, on the farmers to finance the purchase, storage and disposal of the surplus. As a result, they argue, the problem of the cost of surpluses is really the farmers', not the consumers' or the taxpayers'. Is this argument totally correct?

5. Has criticism of marketing boards continued or subsided recently? Are any changes in agricultural policy considered likely?

6. Most industrialized nations tend to experience agricultural surpluses like Canada's. Why don't they simply give their surplus food to underdeveloped nations as part of their foreign aid programs?

7. The text notes that imports of low-priced packaged food products from the USA, where food costs are lower, could cause serious problems for both Canadian food processors and the farmers who supply them.

In 1989, the Advisory Council on Adjustment (to the Canada- US Free Trade Agreement) proposed a two-price system for poultry and dairy farmers. Under this plan, farmers would sell the small proportion of their produce that goes to processors at the same low prices that prevail in the USA, enabling Canadian food processors to compete with American imports. In return, the farmers' marketing boards could charge slightly higher prices for the vast majority of their output that goes directly to Canadian consumers. What problems might such a two-price system create for farmers?

CHAPTER 20

The Soviet economy

After nineteen chapters, many of which have dealt with the problems associated with a market type of economic system, one is entitled to wonder whether there isn't a better way of organizing an economy. The major alternative to the market system is the *command system*, the best-known example of which is the Soviet Union. In this chapter, we will examine how the Soviet economy is organized and how well it performs, so as to be able to compare it to our own system.

Structure and organization

The two most fundamental differences between a command economy and the market system are that in a command economy, there is *state ownership* of production facilities rather than private ownership, and that most economic decisions are made by *central economic planners* rather than through markets. It is the government planning agency (in the USSR, "Gosplan") that makes the decisions regarding the three basic economic questions of what to produce, how to produce it and for whom to produce it (or how to divide up the economic pie). Furthermore, the central economic planners make the crucial decisions regarding the division of the economy's output between consumption (that is, consumer goods for present enjoyment) and investment (in capital goods to increase future output).

Under the central economic plan, each individual enterprise is given a set of targets by the central economic planners. The most important of these are its *production quotas*, which specify how much of each type of product the enterprise is to produce. In addition to the production quotas,

> The Soviet economy is governed by an overall state plan—this is possible because the means of production are socially owned. The result is that production can be organized in the most effective way, society is free of the ruinous consequences of anarchy in production, from economic crises and recessions, and the working people no longer have to fear unemployment. The economy can develop without hindrance.
>
> Nikolai Rogovsky,
> *Work and Employment in the USSR*
> (Novosti Press Agency Publishing House,
> Moscow, 1975).

the plan for the enterprise will include labor and material allotments provided the enterprise and a variety of financial targets for wages, costs and other variables.

It is the task of the planners to coordinate the plans of many thousands of individual enterprises into a master plan for the entire economy, so as to ensure that there are no shortages or surpluses of industrial commodities. To do this, planners prepare a set of preliminary production figures

> A modern highly developed economy was created in the USSR within an extremely short time. It took the Soviet people less than four decades to transform pre-revolutionary Russia, which in 1917 was 50-100 years behind developed countries in the West economically and technically, into a powerful industrial state. About half this period, moreover, was taken up by repelling invaders and rehabilitating the war-ravaged economy.
>
> The fact that public ownership of the means of production has been established, an end put to the exploitation of labor, the soil for economic crises removed, unemployment ended and planned economic management introduced has given socialism decisive advantages over capitalism in the sphere of production.
>
> Nikolai Rogovsky,
> *Work and Employment in the USSR*
> (Novosti Press Agency Publishing House,
> Moscow, 1975).

for commodities, based on projected production data. These are broken down into proposed production quotas for regions and then for individual enterprises, which are asked to suggest adjustments to the plan based on their ability or inability to meet the proposed quotas. The planners then prepare the final plan, which is supposed to reflect a realistic plan for achieving the state's economic goals. Because this planning process is so complex and time consuming, it must apply to considerable periods of time—hence the famous Soviet *Five-Year Plans*.

The Russians have claimed that their centrally planned economic system is superior to the market system in every important way: that it has no recessions, no unemployment, no inflation and no serious economic inequality, and that it can achieve economic growth so rapid that Soviet living standards will ultimately surpass even those enjoyed by North Americans. However, as we will see (and as Russian economists now acknowledge), the situation is considerably more complicated—and less favorable—than that. In fact, Soviet economic problems became so severe in the 1980's that a major overhaul of their economic system has been undertaken.

Capital investment and growth

At the time of the Communist takeover of Russia in 1917, the country was quite underdeveloped economically, far behind the industrialized nations of the West. The most remarkable economic achievement of the Soviet Union has been its transformation in less than half a century into a major industrial nation.

This rapid economic growth and industrial development was achieved mainly through a *great emphasis on capital investment*, as the central economic planners allocated economic resources toward the production of capital goods rather than consumer goods. Capital investment on such a vast scale required low levels of consumer-goods production over a period of many years. Because relatively few consumer goods were available, there was *forced saving* (doing without consumption) by the public, who were given no choice in the matter. Through this mechanism, the Soviet planners were able to achieve the high levels of capital investment essential for their ambitious growth objectives.

Another important source of the USSR's rapid economic growth has been its *rapidly increasing labor force*, and particularly the number of *women* in the labor force. According to Soviet statistics, in 1974 women accounted for 49 percent of those working in Soviet industry, 85 percent of health-service workers, 72 percent of the staff of educational establishments and 45 percent farm workers. Thus, while the USSR's population was only 17 percent larger than the USA's, its labor force was 45 percent larger, in large part due to the greater participation of women.

Soviet economic problems

While the Soviet Union's central planning system has achieved remarkable economic growth, it has also encountered many serious problems.

Consumer goods and services

The most glaring weakness of the Soviet economy is in the area of consumer goods and services. Since the establishment of central economic planning after the 1917 Bolshevik Revolution, the production of consumer goods and services has been a relatively low priority of Soviet planners, ranking well behind military and capital goods. As a result, the typical Soviet citizen's volume of consumption is less than half that of a typical North American, or roughly equivalent to North American living standards around 1940 (see Figure 20-1). In addition to *low volume* per person, Soviet consumer goods are characterized by *low quality*, *little variety* and *limited availability*—that is, there are long waiting lists for many

FIGURE 20-1 *Consumption Levels, USSR vs USA, 1986*

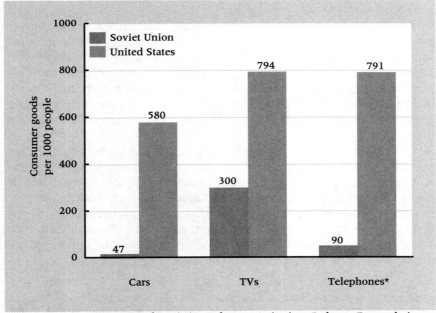

SOURCE Aganbegyan, National Statistics: Telecommunications Industry Research, in *The Economist*, April 9, 1988.
*1985 figures.

items, especially major ones such as apartments, appliances and automobiles.

To keep the level of consumer spending as low as the volume of consumer-goods produced, three basic approaches are used. First, the central economic planners *keep wages and salaries low*—since the state is the only employer, this is quite a simple approach. Second, *the prices of many consumer goods are made high* by the application of a sales tax (called the turnover tax), so as to restrict the demand for them. Finally, by requiring cash for virtually all purchases, and by paying interest on bank deposits, Soviet authorities *encourage saving*. Through these measures, the planners can avoid massive pent-up excess demand for the limited volume of consumer goods.

> As of the late 1980's, Soviet apartment rents had not increased since 1928. The most recent increase in the price of bread had been in 1954. It cost the state about $8 to produce a kilogram of average meat, but to keep its price at the 1962 level of $4, the government had to spend $4 on subsidies.

The prices of consumer goods bear little relationship to the costs of producing them. Essentials are generally low-priced, because they are subsidized by the government. For example, housing is so heavily subsidized that a typical worker may pay only 3 to 5 percent of monthly income for rent, as compared to 25 to 30 percent in Canada. (On the other hand, for this, a family of four gets about 40 square metres, reflecting the relatively low priority of housing construction with the Soviet planners.)

While essentials are low-priced, consumer items beyond essentials are scarce, heavily taxed and expensive. For example, an average Soviet car would cost the typical worker about four years' pay, as compared to about six months' pay in Canada,[1] and many major consumer goods are in such short supply that one of the most valued contacts in the Soviet Union is a store employee or manager who can provide information concerning the arrival of shipments of such goods, which often sell out very quickly.

---

[1] The scarcity of products such as cars makes such high taxes and prices necessary. If cars were low-priced and scarce, there could develop a black market in which those who had acquired cars could sell them at high prices, with the huge profits going to the black marketeers rather than to the state. Thus, even though the USSR does not use a market system, market considerations such as supply and demand do enter into pricing and taxation decisions.

Shortages of automobile parts are particularly frustrating for Russian citizens. Inability to obtain spare parts often forces cars to be off the road for months or even years. To protect against theft, many Soviet drivers keep their windshield wipers in the trunks of their cars, stopping to attach them when it starts to rain.

With consumer goods in such short supply, and so highly priced, it is inevitable that there would be a very active *black market* in the Soviet Union. Most Westerners have heard of the Soviet black-market prices on Western goods such as a Sony Walkman (US$620), blue jeans (150 roubles, or three weeks' pay and Japanese VCR's (6000 roubles, or two years' pay). However, much more than Western goods is available on the black markets. The Soviet economic journal *Eco* estimates that 84 percent of the Soviet population gets consumer goods through the black market. Most of these goods are believed to be produced in hundreds of underground factories across the USSR, through which perhaps as many as 20 million people earn their living. According to the Soviet newspaper *Literaturnaya Gazeta,* ''The black market passes through everyone.''

The low priority attached to consumer-goods production has been an increasing source of tension in the Soviet Union. With low morale a serious problem among the Soviet work force and general population, some Soviet leaders have come to the conclusion that it is time to shift their economic priorities somewhat, so as to increase the emphasis on consumer goods. However, these attempts have been resisted strongly by the old, established proponents of heavy industry (which has traditionally received very high priority), who have considerable influence within the Communist Party. As a result, progress in increasing the emphasis on the consumer-goods sector continues to be very slow.

Inefficiency

Probably the most basic problem facing the Soviet economy is *inefficiency.* Output per worker in the USSR has recently been estimated at only slightly more than one-half US levels. Worse yet, Soviet productivity performance appears to have actually deteriorated recently, leaving the Soviet Union even farther behind Western nations.

The most fundamental source of Soviet productivity problems has been the *lack of incentives,* for both employees and enterprises.

Many Soviet *workers* find that their pay is unrelated to the quantity or quality of work that they perform. Perhaps worse is the fact that even if they do earn additional income through extra effort, there is not much

> We've got the perfect economy. We pretend to work and they pretend to pay us.
>
> Popular Soviet joke.

for them to spend it on—all that it will buy them is a spot on the waiting list for whatever they want. Under these circumstances, many employees put in as little effort on the job as possible.

For Soviet *enterprises*, the problem is even more severe. Without the profit motive, there is no incentive to produce what buyers want and to produce it efficiently. If a plant produces exceptionally efficiently and earns profits, it does not get to keep them and reinvest them so as to improve its efficiency or its product. Instead, it will probably find its quotas increased for next year, perhaps to unreasonable levels. Under such a system, the incentive is to conceal from the planners the plant's potential output, so as to convince them to give the plant low quotas that are readily achieved.

In addition to these problems of incentives, Soviet industry is burdened with *inadequate capital equipment*. More than one-half of Soviet industrial plants and equipment date back to Stalin's industrialization drive of the 1930's. Most are badly outdated, and very few are automated. Of special concern is the computers field: experts believe that in 1985 the USSR had only about 30 000 mainframes and minicomputers, compared to about 620 000 in the USA, and that more than half of the Soviets' mainframes were copies of discontinued IBM models. By the late 1980's, experts estimated that the Soviet Union was 7-12 years behind the USA in advanced computer-related technologies.

It is important to understand the seriousness of this basic problem of inefficiency. Unless the USSR can achieve higher productivity, it will face a particularly difficult manifestation of the classic economic problem of *scarcity*—increasingly strong competition for a stagnant economic pie between the industrial, military and consumer-goods sectors. During the 1980's, the arms race between the USA and the USSR was particularly

> [An arms race such as Star Wars] will certainly make us reconsider our plans for economic development. You are richer; it is a heavier burden for us.
>
> Sergei M. Plekhanov,
Institute of the USA and Canada, Moscow

burdensome for the Soviet Union. Because the US economy was so much more productive than the USSR's, the Soviets found themselves diverting 15 percent of their economy's total output into military uses, as compared to only 7 percent for the USA.

Unless the USSR succeeds in increasing its efficiency and thus its potential output, it will be forced to continue to badly neglect its people's need for consumer goods in order to meet its objectives in the higher priority sectors such as capital investment and the military. The "Catch-22" in this situation is that higher consumer-goods production is needed to provide the Soviet people with the incentives that could help to generate increased productivity.

In the late 1980's, the Soviet Union initiated a number of disarmament proposals. This caused many economists to speculate that this might be part of an economic strategy in which economic resources would be shifted *from* military uses *to* the consumer-goods sector of the Soviet economy, so as to bolster the morale of and incentives for Soviet workers.

Agriculture

The agricultural sector has been and continues to be a major problem area in the Soviet economy, due to its *inefficiency* and *low productivity*. For a variety of reasons, the typical Soviet farm worker produces only one-fifth as much as a European farmer and one-tenth as much as an American farmer.

The consequences of low agricultural productivity are important for the entire Soviet economy. Improvements in agricultural productivity are vital to a society's economic progress because they free up large numbers of workers from agriculture for employment in the manufacturing and service sectors. Because Soviet agricultural productivity has

Collective farmers and state farm workers! Increase the efficiency of production! Make better use of land, machinery and fertilizers! Maximum care and attention to the future harvests!

Soviet Communist Party exhortation
urging increased agricultural
productivity, 1980.

lagged badly, a high proportion of the USSR's labor force continues to be tied up on the farm, and unavailable for employment in other sectors of the economy, particularly the consumer goods sector (see Figure 20-2). Also, when poor agricultural performance results in shortages of food, the Soviet Union has to use its scarce foreign currencies (particularly US dollars) to purchase food rather than the capital goods and technology which would spur economic growth. As a result, low and slowly rising agricultural productivity represents a drag on overall Soviet economic progress.

FIGURE 20-2 *Employment by Sector, USSR and USA, 1985*

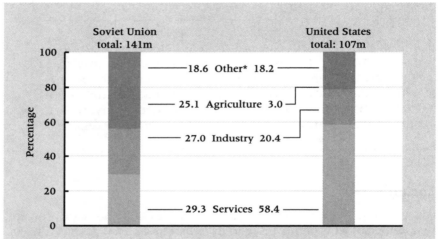

SOURCE Gorbachev's Economic Plans (study papers submitted to US Congress);
US Bureau of Labor Statistics
* Includes construction, transport, communications and others

The causes of the Soviet agricultural sector's low productivity are numerous and complex. In part, it is due to Russia's harsh climate and short growing season, which limit crop yields and increase the risk of crop failures. However, much of the problem is the result of decisions made by the Soviets themselves. Following the Bolshevik Revolution in 1917, the Communists abolished privately owned farms and reorganized the agricultural sector into large, government-operated farms known as *state farms* and *collective farms*. These enterprises are so vast as to be *unmanageable*, with Russia's 18 000 state farms averaging 40 000 acres and the 29 000 collective farms averaging 13 000 acres each. By contrast, Canadian farms, whose labor productivity is more than five times as large, have an average size of about 500 acres.

While such large farms would seem to call for extensive use of capital equipment, Soviet agriculture is in fact *undercapitalized*—a reflection of the low priority that the central planners have placed on agriculture over the years. In fact, the Soviet agricultural sector is estimated to have less than half the trucks and tractors used on US farms. However, the Soviet farm problem goes well beyond inadequate capital investment—it also includes a significant human element. While North American farmers are mainly self-employed entrepreneurs, Soviet farm workers are in effect state employees, and, as such, *lack incentives* to be efficient. While the Communist Party exhorts farm workers to work harder and improve productivity, the workers know that they themselves will not benefit from doing so, and respond accordingly.

Planning problems

On the surface, a centrally planned economy would seem likely to be able to operate smoothly, achieving through planning a high degree of coordination and avoiding many of the problems experienced by unplanned (market) economies. However, the Soviet Union's centrally planned system has in face experienced many serious problems that have arisen from the planning process itself—some from the imperfections of the planning system, and some from its basic nature. These problems have proved increasingly troublesome and frustrating for the Soviet authorities responsible for managing the economy.

Central economic planning is an enormously complex task, owing to the *vast numbers of inputs and outputs* that have to be coordinated in intricate ways. In the early years of Soviet planning, this task was relatively simple, since the planners were dealing with a comparatively underdeveloped and simple economy, the major requirements of which (military equipment and capital investment in basic industries) were clear cut and by their nature lent themselves to a planning approach. However, as the Soviet Union has grown and developed into a vast industrial economy, the task of economic planning has become much more difficult. The sheer numbers of inputs and outputs that need to be coordinated, and the relationships between them, make the planning process overwhelmingly complex and vulnerable to errors.

Also, the *increasing volume of consumer goods*, which by their nature are not as well-suited to central planning, has led to problems as the planning system has persisted in producing consumer goods that consumers do not want. The following sections examine these problems further.

> The latest index of products has twenty million articles. The plan can't detail that amount.
>
> Official of Gosplan, the Soviet State Planning Committee.

Quotas and incentives

As we have seen, Soviet plant managers often receive production quotas from the central planners, usually expressed in physical terms, such as 15 tons of chairs, 12 tons of chandeliers, 510 thousand pairs of shoes or 420 thousand suits. Faced with limited resources (labor and/or materials, depending on the situation) and great pressure to fulfill their quotas, plant managers would often *distort production* in order to meet their quotas. The major victim of this situation tends to be quality, as plants rush production, paying little attention to the final product. However, the quota system has also led to more bizarre distortions of production. Plants with adequate materials but too little labor to meet their production targets may solve their problem by producing unusually large products, such as overstuffed armchairs and very heavy chandeliers. By doing so, plant managers meet their production quotas (15 *tons* of chairs, 12 *tons* of chandeliers), even though the products are not very useful. In a similar way, other plants faced with materials shortages and quotas expressed in numbers of units may produce small items, so as to make enough units of output to meet their quotas; as a result, Russian consumers have tended to be plagued with small suits and too many shoes of smaller sizes, as well as overstuffed armchairs and overweight chandeliers.

The underlying cause of problems such as these is the Soviet planning and quota system itself. While each of the examples above represents an ineffective use of economic resources, the plant managers *did* meet their quotas: by official measures, they were successful. In view of the overall scarcity of consumer goods in the Soviet Union, this tendency of the planning system to produce inappropriate items represents a serious and wasteful use of economic resources.

Errors in planning

As noted earlier, the task of the central economic planners is to coordinate the plans for all enterprises, inputs and outputs in the economy so as to achieve efficient use of all economic resources. However, faced with the need to plan an ever-increasing number of goods, many of which are interrelated and many of which are consumer goods, the Soviet planning system has shown a tendency to make errors.

Failure to produce goods that serve consumers' needs is one such error: the Soviet system has persistently tended to produce too much of some goods, too few of others and many that consumers will not buy. *Failure to match the production of complementary goods* has resulted in many errors, such as two-year delays in the start-up of major hydroelectrical facilities due to the omission of a few key parts. Similarly, the system has produced large numbers of televisions sets that could not be sold due to the lack of one key component, many eyeglass lenses but not enough frames, cameras but no films, tape recorders but no tape and a wide range of small appliances but not the batteries needed to operate them.

Lack of feedback from consumers is one basic source of such errors. Since plants take their orders from the central planners rather than from retailers (and thus, indirectly, consumers), the system has a tendency to persistently turn out goods that consumers find inappropriate. Another source of errors has been *unrealistic production quotas*. Knowing that plant managers tend to understate their productive capacity in order to get easy quotas, the central planners often will increase quotas to tighten up the plan. Under these circumstances, however, there is a risk that unrealistically high quotas may be set for some plants, so that shortages of their products could result. Such breakdowns of the plan tend to cascade through the planning system, causing problems in other plants and products. This problem develops because of the complex interrelationships between various products, which can create a *chain-reaction effect* of errors. For instance, the failure of a plant to meet its quota for a particular chemical could lead to shortages of materials made with that chemical, which could cause below-quota production of all products made from that material, some of which may be parts for other products, and so on. Furthermore, the inflexibility of the plans can make it *difficult to correct errors promptly*. Economic plans are so complex that it is not feasible to revise them frequently in order to correct flaws and errors.

Finally, it is important to note that the problems described in this section are not the result of *imperfections* in the central economic planning system that could be corrected. Rather, these problems are an intrinsic part of central economic planning; that is, they are part of its essential nature.

Summary

In conclusion, central economic planning is not the effective, efficient process for organizing the use of a society's economic resources that it would appear to be in theory. Where it has been successful is in focussing economic resources on particular objectives considered important by the state, without regard for the cost. Examples of such selective development would include capital investment for industrialization and economic power, military and space equipment for security, and athletics and culture and the arts for public relations purposes. While the Soviet planning system has made notable achievements in all of these areas, it has done so at the expense of other sectors of the economy, such as consumer goods and agriculture.

Furthermore, experience with the command system shows it to suffer from serious intrinsic flaws. The most basic of these is that it tends to result in inefficient and wasteful use of economic resources. This happens not only because of the lack of incentives in the system and the errors to which the system is prone, but also because the quota system itself causes plants to produce low-quality and unwanted products in order to meet their quotas. In addition, because of the rigidities of the planning process, the command system is very slow to correct its own errors and problems.

Directions for reform

Most economists (including those in the Soviet Union) agree that certain basic reforms are required if the performance of the Soviet economy is to improve. Virtually all proposals for improving Soviet economic performance include a combination of *improved technology, stronger incentives* for employees and managers and changes in the very structure of the economy to provide a more *market-oriented environment* for Soviet enterprises.

(a) Technology

Modernization of Soviet industry and agriculture is a basic prerequisite for improving efficiency. In most cases, the readiest source of production technology (especially for consumer goods) and management expertise is Western nations. To acquire such technology from Western corporations the Soviet Union must either purchase it or enter into joint ventures with Western firms.

(b) Incentives

The second key to improving efficiency is to create strong incentives for both employees and managers. This requires that their work performance be measured, and that adjustments be made to their pay based on these measurements.

(c) Structural reform

The third and most fundamental—*and* most controversial—key to improving Soviet economic performance is to change the environment in which Soviet enterprises operate. The essence of these proposals is to replace central economic planning with a more market system approach in which enterprises produce in response to consumer demand, rather than according to quotas set by the planners.

Economic reforms prior to perestroika

In 1985, the Soviet Union undertook its famous program of **perestroika**, a wide-ranging series of economic reforms that, if completed, would reshape the very structure of the Soviet economy. Following this section, we will examine some of the details of perestroika. First, however, we will consider some of the measures taken to improve the performance of the Soviet economy prior to perestroika.

(a) Economic incentives for workers and managers

The use of economic incentives for both workers and managers is not a new idea to Soviet authorities. For many years, production workers have been paid largely on a piece-rate basis, and office workers and managers have been on a salary-plus-bonus system, in order to provide incentives for improved performance. The income figures in Figure 20-3 reflect these incentives: for instance, a skilled worker could earn as little as 100 roubles or as much as 250 roubles per month, with much of the difference attributable to his or her skills and/or output.

While these figures are from the early 1960's, they do reveal some interesting aspects of the Soviet system. On the one hand these differences in incomes exaggerate the differences in living standards associated with lower and higher incomes, since essentials are subsidized and cheap, and non-essentials are often expensive. On the other hand, these figures

FIGURE 20-3 *Soviet Incomes*

	Monthly earnings in roubles
Leading scientist	800–1500
Senior government official	700
Professor (science or medicine)	400–1000
Plant manager	300–1000
Engineer	100–300
Worker (skilled)	100–250
Physician	85–180
High school teacher	85–100
Worker (semi-skilled)	60–90
Worker (unskilled)	27–50

SOURCE George Leland Bach, *Economics: An Introduction to Analysis and Policy, 6th Ed.* (Prentice-Hall, Englewood Cliffs, N.J.), p. 566. Reprinted by permission of Prentice-Hall, Inc., Englewood Cliffs, N.J.

Lenin wrote of the need to build socialism 'not directly relying on enthusiasm, but aided by the enthusiasm . . . personal incentive and business principles.'

Nikolai Rogovsky,
Work and Employment in the USSR
(Novosti Press Agency Publishing House, Moscow, 1975).

exclude the special perquisites such as free housing, cars, vacations and so on that are enjoyed by the Soviet elite.

Figure 20-3 also illustrates another way in which Soviet planners have used incomes as incentives: *higher incomes* were paid to those occupations deemed important, in order to attract talented people to them. For instance, the Soviet system of incomes placed more emphasis on attracting people into engineering and the sciences, and into occupations such as plant management and skilled trades, than on occupations such as medicine or teaching, which contribute less directly to the state's objective of industrial growth. In a similar way, higher incomes were used to attract workers into industries that have high priority, or into remote regions, such as the far North.

All in all, the Soviet authorities have used an approach remarkably like a market system to allocate labor in their economy, using income differentials to attract workers into certain occupations, industries and regions and to motivate them to perform better. This runs counter to the widely held impression that workers were forced into certain jobs by the planning authorities: in fact, the only compulsory element in the allocation of labor in the Soviet Union was the planned allocation of graduates of full-time educational institutions to jobs for a period of two years following graduation.

> Work that differs in quantity and quality must be rewarded differently. This is what ensures that there is a material incentive for the worker to increase the quantity and raise the quality of his labor.
>
> Nikolai Rogovsky,
> *Work and Employment in the USSR*,
> (Novosti Press Agency Publishing House, Moscow, 1975).

Attempts have also been made to improve productivity by strengthening *financial incentives* in various ways. As already noted, many plant managers not only received personal bonuses, but also could reinvest some of their profits into their plant. Managers could dole out merit raises of up to 30 percent, and some workers earned bonuses of up to 50 percent of their pay. In 1986, half the nation's factories paid salaries to *brigades*, which are teams of a dozen or more workers who sign a contract to perform certain tasks. Upon completion of their plan, the factory would pay the brigade, and the leaders of the brigade would divide the money among the brigade's members on the basis of their contribution to the group's production.

(b) Acquisition of western technology

For many years, the Soviet Union has made efforts to acquire Western nations' technology and managerial expertise. Since the purchasing of these requires foreign currencies (especially US dollars), the USSR has had to increase its efforts to earn these, through exports to the West of products such as tractors, vodka and even automobiles. In addition, the USSR has attempted to attract investment by foreign corporations—for instance, the Vaz automobile plant was built by Fiat. While the volume of such transactions has not been large, they are indicative of the value placed by Soviet economic authorities upon Western industrial technology.

(c) The Kosygin reforms

After the Soviet economy stagnated in the early 1960's, Prime Minister Alexei Kosygin introduced a series of reforms intended to improve economic performance.

There were various aspects to Kosygin's reforms, including "recentralization" of the planning system (which had been decentralized in the 1950's into various regions), and price reform (prices were still to be set by the planners rather than by market forces, but according to more sophisticated rules).

However, the most radical aspect of the Kosygin period involved experiments with *structural reform* of some industries. The basic element of these experiments was to reduce the central planners' control of these industries through production quotas, and to give more decision-making power to consumers (regarding what to produce) and to plant managers (regarding how to produce it).

The most fundamental reform involved having plants take orders not from the central planners but rather from retailers (and thus, indirectly, from consumers). The introduction of this element of consumer sovereignty was intended to reduce the production of unwanted goods that were being produced to satisfy the central planners rather than consumers. As such, these experiments represented a challenge to the central planning system itself.

However, the experiments went well beyond the simple introduction of an element of consumer sovereignty. Without productions quotas to meet, plant managers had to be evaluated on a different basis. One criterion that was used was a target for *total sales volume*—presumably, the more effectively a plant used its resources to produce products that satisfied consumers, the higher its sales volume would be.

However, sales volume measures only the amount sold; it does not measure how efficient a plant is at producing its output. In economic terms, the real task of plants is to achieve a combination of *high sales* and *high efficiency*—that is, to produce as much saleable output as possible, as efficiently as possible, or at the lowest possible cost per unit. Plants that are more successful at this task will have higher sales income, lower production costs, and thus, *higher profits*.

Figure 20-4 provides an illustration of this concept. While plant A has a profit of 20 million roubles, plant B has a loss of 10 million roubles. Plant B's loss could be the result of two factors. First, its sales income is lower than plant A's by 10 million roubles. Second, to generate this lower volume of sales, plant B had 20 million roubles more of production costs than plant A. In short, plant B is failing to use its resources as effectively (in the sense of producing what consumers want) and as efficiently (in the sense of production costs per unit) as plant A is.

FIGURE 20-4 *Profit as a Measure of a Plant Manager's Performance*

	Plant Manager A	Plant Manager B
	(millions of roubles)	
Value of output sold (total sales revenue)	100	90
Value of inputs used (total production costs)	80	100
Difference = Profit	+20	−10

If plant managers' bonuses are based on their profits, there is a real incentive for the manager of plant B to improve profits. This could be done by a combination of *increasing sales* (perhaps by improving its products) and by *reducing production costs* (perhaps through better incentives for workers, or better technology). Thus, there is an incentive for plant managers to produce products that consumers will buy, and to produce them at the lowest possible cost—that is, to use economic resources effectively and efficiently to satisfy consumers' wants.

It is important to note the fundamental role of profits in these experiments. Profit is much more than a financial concept measuring a volume of money. It is also an economic concept—a measure of how effectively and efficiently economic resources have been used by an enterprise. Plant A used 80 million roubles of economic resources to produce saleable output of 100 million roubles—on balance, a contribution of 20 million roubles to society's economic welfare. The firm's profit of 20 million roubles is a measure of this contribution. Finally, profit is a key incentive prodding enterprises and their managers (whose bonuses depend on profits) to use their economic resources more effectively and efficiently.

An interesting side effect of the increased use of profit as a measure of managers' success was that managers sometimes found that it payed them to *advertise*, in order to increase their sales. Soviet advertising was still in a rudimentary stage, as the following advertisements suggest:

"The bread store offers an assortment of bread."

"You won't be making a mistake if you buy a Chaika TV set."

Nonetheless, Soviet authorities accepted advertising in principle, stating, "We must define the role and possibilities of advertising as a 'motive force of production'," and, "A properly designed and well-organized advertisement will quickly pay for itself many times over." Consumers were considerably less enthusiastic, even suspicious—it was widely believed that in a society in which consumer goods were in short supply, only over-produced junk needed to be advertised.

These pre-perestroika economic experiments should be viewed in perspective. First, the central planners did not relinquish their control of the overall direction of the economy. They still decided the share of the economy's resources that would be devoted to the capital-goods, military and consumer-goods sectors of the economy. However, while the planners still decided the *total volume* of consumer-goods output, the reforms attempted to give consumers more say in the *composition* of that output—that is, whether plants would produce radios or televisions, and so on.

Second, these experiments met with strong opposition within the Communist Party and the bureaucracy. The introduction of market-oriented reforms was viewed as a serious deviation from Communist principles by conservative and ideologically-conscious groups within the Party. On a more practical level, the central planning bureaucracy was opposed to any reforms that would reduce its power. In the conflict between the factories' supposedly greater independence and the authority of the central planners (ministries) to establish plans, the bureaucrats succeeded in sabotaging the Kosygin reforms, and the authority of the ministries was reasserted. After 1970, the Soviet economy drifted backwards into more tightly controlled central planning, with all of its problems.

(d) Private plots in agriculture

Probably the boldest and most successful Soviet economic reform has been the introduction of *private plots* in the agricultural sector. Soviet farm workers are allowed (in fact, encouraged) to work small plots of up to half an acre of land, the produce from which they are free to sell *in free markets at market prices*, rather than at prices dictated by the state. There are 8000 such farmers' markets in the Soviet Union, 30 in Moscow alone, where farmers bring the produce from their private plots that they farm part-time, to be sold for the best price they can get. While prices are higher in these private markets than in state stores, the quality and selection are better, and the *kolkhoz markets* (markets in which collective farm workers sell their produce) are popular with shoppers.

While Soviet authorities originally tolerated these private plots and the kolkhoz markets, they have recently begun to encourage them. This official encouragement of private enterprise stems from the fact that the private plots are *astonishingly productive*. While the private plots amount to between one and three percent of all agricultural land, they produced in the mid-1970's roughly 27 percent of the total value of Soviet farm output (official figures). The difference between the high efficiency of these plots and the low efficiency of the state farms and collective farms is obviously the result of the economic incentives associated with the private plots and the kolkhoz markets, as farm workers farm their private plots much more intensively.

More recently, the *brigade system* used in some parts of Soviet industry was introduced into agriculture, giving groups of farmers the opportunity to profit if they increase output: for farmers, this represented a radical departure from the past practice of low and equal pay for all. In some parts of the country, the brigade system amounted to the reintroduction of *family farming*, which had been ruthlessly stamped out over half a century earlier by the Communists as being unduly capitalistic.

Extensive vs intensive growth

The exceptionally rapid growth of the Soviet economy from 1917 into the 1960's was what economists call **extensive growth**. That is, it was achieved mainly by the use of ever-increasing *quantities* of capital and labor rather than by improving the *quality* and the *efficiency* of Soviet capital equipment and labor. As a result, even after a half-century of rapid industrialization, Soviet productivity (output per worker) was still far behind that of Western Europe and North America.

This low productivity has been of growing concern to Soviet planners in recent years. As the growth of the Soviet population and labor force slowed, it was no longer possible to achieve the extensive growth of the past. Rather, it became necessary to strive for **intensive growth**, or *efficiency*, which is achieved through improvements in the *quality* of labor and capital and the efficiency with which they are used.

However, in the period following the termination of the Kosygin reforms around 1970, the Soviet economy stalled again. There was no growth of output during the first half of the 1980's, and probably no growth or very little growth over the 1970-85 period. With Soviet population increasing at about one percent per year, such stagnant output meant a declining standard of living for the people.

The Gorbachev period

These severe economic problems generated renewed pressures for reform of the Soviet economy. When Mikhail Gorbachev assumed power in the mid-1980's, the time was ripe for change. Gorbachev seemed to be in a uniquely advantageous position to implement reform. At 54, he was much younger than previous Soviet leaders, and he could look forward to as much as twenty years of power, making the prospects better than ever for significant and lasting reform.

Under Gorbachev, ambitious goals were set for the Soviet economy. *National income* and *industrial production* were to double by the end of the century, which would require an ambitious average annual growth rate of 4.7 percent. However, there remained considerable uncertainty regarding the strategy that would be used to pursue these goals, as there were two quite different options facing the Soviet leadership.

One option was basic reform along more *market* lines. Such an approach is used in various Communist countries, including Hungary, where there is less centralized planning and more private enterprise, including the profit motive and emphasis on "encouraging the creative powers of the citizens by increasing individual responsibility and decision making in industry." China has also introduced market-oriented reforms, including experiments with agricultural markets, private farming, profit-making joint ventures between Chinese and foreign companies, and the possibility of individual workers owning shares in their factories. Officially, the Soviet Union under Gorbachev was not planning to move in the direction of such basic reform. According to government sources, the Gorbachev goals would be achieved "without any shift toward the market economy or private enterprise."

Instead, *reform of the existing planning system* was emphasized by the new Soviet leadership. The first step was to *impose discipline* on Russian workers and managers in an attempt to force higher productivity by curbing the slackness and alcoholism that have plagued the Soviet economy. Such measures had been undertaken in the past, with only short-term results.

A more basic strategy was implicit in the state's plan itself. Real (personal) incomes were planned to increase by only 13-15 percent from 1985 to 1990, but by 60-80 percent by 2000. In other words, the plan was to *hold down consumption* for a few years in order to make possible the capital investment needed to improve productivity and living standards in the last decade of the century. This, too, has been a basic Soviet strategy for most of the century; however, it risked failing to provide the consumer goods necessary to boost incentives for a work force which was growing impatient waiting for long-promised rewards.

Perestroika

In fact, the Gorbachev reforms went far beyond imposing discipline and holding down consumption in order to strengthen capital investment. Under the reform program known as *"perestroika"* (which translates as "restructuring"), much more fundamental changes were implemented.

The basic thrust of perestroika's restructuring was similar to that of the 1965 Kosygin reforms, in that it aimed in the direction of *decentralization of economic decision-making*. The power of the central economic planners to direct the economy was to be reduced, and more decision-making power was to be passed to consumers and plant managers, along "market" lines. Gosplan, the state planning agency, was to become more of an economic think-tank and individual ministries were to focus more on long-term planning, leaving detailed operational decisions more to individual factories and farms.

> The market is an indispensable means of gearing production to fast-changing demand, and a major instrument of public control over quality and cost.
>
> *The Kremlin's new chief ideologist, Yadim Medvedev.*

Some of the key aspects of perestroika involved:

- a reduction in the decision-making power of the ministries and central planners,
- increased decision-making by plant managers, with factories to become self-financing,
- development of widespread small private enterprises ("cooperatives"),
- a "technical reconstruction" of the Soviet economy, through the introduction of new technology, and
- increased decision-making by farmers, who were once again to become "masters of the land."

Perestroika was to be implemented in three stages, as shown in Figure 20-5. Some details of its implementation are outlined in the following sections.

> We will have to carry out profound transformations in the economy and in the entire system of social relations.
>
> Mikhail Gorbachev to Party workers, December, 1984.

FIGURE 20-5 *The Three Stages of Perestroika*

Stage 1 Preparation 1985–87	Stage 2 Transition 1988–90	Stage 3 Take-off 1991–?
Discipline, anti-alcohol campaign	Enterprises start to get more independence	Whole economy on new system
Replace incompetent and corrupt officials	Move to "self-financing" and wholesale trade	Still learning and adjusting
Tighten quality control	Bring research closer to production	Growth accelerates as motivation improves and investments come on stream
Merge some ministries, widen foreign-trade rights	Trim bureaucracy	
More legal scope for small private enterprise	Start price reforms	
Start investing heavily in modern machinery	Learning about new system	

SOURCE *The Economist.*

(a) Reform of the planning system

By the mid-1980's, the Soviet Union had accumulated a massive central economic planning bureaucracy employing 18 million officials. Under perestroika, the power of this bureaucracy to direct industrial production in detail was to be drastically reduced. About half of the 60 industrial ministries were to be scrapped, and about half the staff in the Moscow ministries and the Communist Party's economic planning bureaucracy were to be removed by 1990. About 600 000 bureaucrats were to be transferred from government ministries in Moscow to factories.

This was all part of one of the keystones of perestroika: the *decentralization of economic decision-making,* with a much smaller role for the central planners and a larger role for plant managers and consumers.

The remaining planners were to concentrate on grand economic strategy, not attempt as in the past to determine and control from Moscow every detail of Soviet industrial and agricultural production.

(b) Industrial reforms

With the reduction in the role of the central economic planners would come *increased decision-making power* for plant managers. Under the 1987 Law on the State Enterprise, factories were to draw up their own plans rather than receive plans from Moscow. Part of their production would still be obligatory "state orders"; that is, production determined by the ministries and the central planners. Eventually, however, up to 70 percent of their output would be produced according to orders from customers, along market system lines.

With these new freedoms came new responsibilities. Factories were expected to be *self-financing* rather than dependent upon government subsidies as in the past. To achieve self-financing, plants would have to make two fundamental changes: they would have to produce what customers would buy, and they would have to produce it efficiently. The objective of these reforms was to make Soviet industry *more responsive to consumer demand*, and *more efficient*.

In pursuit of these objectives, a variety of new practices were introduced. *Financial incentives* were strengthened, with managers able to dole out merit raises of up to 30 percent, and some workers earning bonuses of up to 50 percent of their pay. By 1986, it was reported that half the nation's factories were utilizing *brigades* similar to those introduced under Kosygin.

> Mikhail Gorbachev has repeatedly attacked the "levelling mentality," by which he means paying people more or less the same, regardless of their work. Gorbachev says that this "has a destructive impact not only on the economy but also on people's morality and their entire way of thinking and acting."

Some factories began experiments with *leasing*, under which groups of workers would lease all or part of a plant from the state. The workers would make fixed lease payments to the state for the period of the lease (usually around seven years), operate the plant and distribute whatever profits were earned as they saw fit. Some were sub-leasing operations to brigades, as described earlier. By 1989, over 500 enterprises in the Moscow area, ranging from small cafes to factories and employing some 100 000 people, were on such a lease system. In some cases, the results were impressive, with productivity improvements of 25 percent reported.

The requirement that their plants become self-financing pushed some plant managers to improve efficiency. Without government subsidies, inefficient plants would be forced to lay off workers in order to cut costs.

CANADA AND THE SOVIET UNION

Because Canada and the Soviet Union are similarly rich in oil, natural gas, forests, metals and minerals, there is little trade between the two countries. In 1988, Canada exported only $1.1 billion to the USSR, and imported only $156 million of Soviet goods. However, the similarities between the two countries makes them quite compatible for many joint ventures. In particular, the Soviet Union can use the technology developed by Canadian firms in the natural resources sector of the economy.

As an added incentive for plant managers to improve efficiency, plants were to be allowed to keep some of their profits in order to invest in improved technology.

Soviet enterprises also sought improved productivity performance in *joint ventures* with foreign firms. With the abolition of the Ministry of Foreign Trade, Soviet enterprises became free to deal directly with foreign exporters and investors. The Soviet government has been promoting these joint ventures, through which Soviet enterprises can not only gain access to western technology and management skills, but also obtain a yardstick by which to measure the performance of Soviet enterprises.

By the 1990, some 365 joint venture agreements had been signed between Soviet and western firms. However, only 50 of these were actually running, the most notable being McDonald's Moscow outlet, the largest in the world. Many western firms have been cautious about Soviet joint ventures because of problems repatriating profits (the rouble is not convertible into foreign currencies). In an attempt to make their joint ventures more attractive, the Soviet Union has begun to allow some forms of foreign ownership.

(c) Private enterprise in the USSR

Under perestroika, it became legal for Soviet citizens to operate small private businesses (known officially as *"cooperatives"*). This was done partly to bring into the open Soviet black-market operations. Another objective, however, was to stimulate both production and efficiency in the consumer goods and services sector, which has been a notorious weakness of the Soviet economy.

Within two years, there were more than 100 000 such private enterprises operating in the USSR in various fields such as restaurants, repair shops, bakeries and retail outlets. These enterprises employed perhaps 2.7 million people, or about two percent of the Soviet labor force. Generally, these cooperatives provide higher-quality goods and services than state-owned enterprises, at considerably higher prices. The chronic shortages and low quality of many consumer goods and services in the USSR provide considerable opportunity for private enterprise, and some cooperative operators have earned considerable amounts of money.

(d) Technology

Another key to improved productivity performance is improved technology. One basic aspect of perestroika's economic strategy was to hold down consumer-goods production (again) over the 1985-90 period, so that emphasis could be placed upon capital-goods production. The objective of this program was described as a "technical reconstruction" of the Soviet economy, stressing the introduction of computers into industry in a major effort to improve productivity.

Emphasis was to be placed on modernizing existing factories rather than building expensive new ones. Consequently, the heaviest spending was to be on machines and computers in an attempt to achieve a massive refitting of Soviet industry. Incentives were developed for plants to modernize both their products and their production methods. For instance, some plants are allowed to increase prices by up to 30 percent for modernized products, and can keep some of their profits for reinvestment in improved technology and production methods. More generally, the requirement that enterprises be "self-financing" has given plant managers considerably more incentive and freedom to seek productivity-increasing technology, not only in the USSR but also through joint ventures with foreign firms.

Obstacles to perestroika

The objectives and strategies of perestroika are economically logical, and if successfully implemented, would lead to a dramatic transformation of the Soviet economy. However, such a major overhaul of an economy as large and complex as the USSR's is a massive task. Over the first few years of perestroika, a number of problem areas and obstacles became apparent.

The bureaucracy

The first such obstacle was *the central planning system* itself, which had aborted the Kosygin reforms of 1965-70 by reasserting the ministries' central control of the economy. If perestroika succeeded, the size and power of the central ministries would be greatly reduced. The conflict began on January 1, 1988, when Gorbachev transferred important decision-making powers from the central planners to the factory managers. The planners responded by placing *special state orders* with factories, through which the central planners dictated up to 100 percent of their production, effectively reasserting their total control over Soviet industry. Gorbachev's response was to reduce the ministries' staff and instruct them to limit their orders to factories. However, as of 1989, most Soviet industrial output was still being produced according to central plans in terms of tonnes and numbers of pieces, and the prices of 95 percent of the products of Soviet industry were still centrally controlled. The ministries' attempts to maintain central control of Soviet industry were supported by old-line Communist Party members, who were suspicious of the market system and free enterprise nature of the perestroika reforms.

Workers' attitudes

Perestroika also encountered some resistance from Soviet workers. According to some experts, Communism, at the most fundamental level, involves a "silent deal" between the Communist Party and the citizens, in which the citizens receive economic security and government subsidies in exchange for their acceptance of rule by the Party. Put differently, in exchange for accepting totalitarian rule, the people are *relieved of responsibility* for their own economic welfare.

After three generations of such a relationship with their government, many Russians were reluctant to accept the responsibilities—and risks—that perestroika offered. For instance, by 1989, the opportunity for workers to lease and operate factories had been taken up in only 600 plants. Similar attitudes were an obstacle to perestroika in the agricultural sector, where many farmers were reluctant to take the risk of leasing land and equipment and operating in a more open market.

Shortages

Another problem was that perestroika was being introduced at a time when *shortages* were growing particularly severe, and was manifesting itself as a problem to which Soviet citizens were unaccustomed—*inflation*.

As we have seen, Soviet state industrial enterprises are very inefficient. To keep these plants solvent, and to keep the prices of their products from rising to levels that would cause unrest among the citizenry, the Soviet government spent billions of roubles to *subsidize* both state enterprises and the prices of their products, so as to keep prices artificially low. For example, in 1989 an average kilogram of meat sold in state stores for about $4—the same price as in 1962. However, it cost state enterprises about $8 to produce it, meaning that the government had to spend $4 to subsidize every kilogram of meat sold across the USSR. Similar heavy subsidies were required to keep down the prices of many consumer goods, including bread (which had not increased in price since 1954) and rents (which were frozen at 1928 levels).

To maintain this illusion of low prices, the government was by the late 1980's spending 60 billion roubles per year on food subsidies alone.

Government spending far outran tax revenues, leaving the Soviet government with *massive budget deficits* in the range of 100 billion roubles per year, mostly due to consumer subsidies. To finance its budget deficits, the Soviet government resorted to *printing money*. The newly printed roubles kept the government's finances afloat, but when the money found its way into circulation, it caused consumer demand to outrun the economy's limited production of consumer goods by an even greater margin. This excess demand forced consumer prices upwards, especially in the black markets and the unregulated markets in which operators of cooperatives and private plots sold their output. The result was inflation—a phenomenon that was both new and unsettling to Russians. By the late 1980's, the rate of inflation was placed at 5-7 percent per year by official Soviet sources, and estimated to be 10 percent in reality. In addition, as consumer demand outran supply, shortages grew more severe and waiting lists for many goods grew longer.

Thus, the average Soviet citizen came to see perestroika not in terms of needed economic reforms that would increase prosperity, but rather in terms of *more severe shortages, rising prices* and *declining living standards*. This posed a serious threat to perestroika, since it undermined the public understanding and support that would be needed for success.

> The most pressing problem is the gap between purchasing capacity and the supply of goods. Out of 200 groups of products today, 90 percent of them are in short supply. Now there is no incentive to earn a lot of money, because it is very difficult to spend it in a legal way.
>
> Soviet economist Abel Aganbegyan

The shortages also forced the Soviet government to postpone its plans for ending government control of prices, which was a key element in perestroika's shift toward freer markets. Given the huge "overhang" of unspent roubles (estimated to be as high as 300 billion, or 80 percent of total retail sales in 1987—a massive amount[2]), the government feared that decontrolling prices and ending food subsidies could lead to the doubling of the prices of meat, dairy products and bread, causing riots in the streets. As a result, in 1989 the government postponed its planned

[2] The huge "rouble overhang" was ironically in large part related to the government's anti-alcohol campaign. Liquor sales, which in 1984 had accounted for 16 percent of retail sales, had been cut in half by 1988. Without an increase in the availability of other consumer goods to absorb the purchasing power that could no longer be spent on liquor, there was a massive backup of unspent roubles.

price reform for two or three years, further delaying the progress of perestroika toward a more market-oriented economy.

Shortages and inflation also dampened the Soviet government's attempts to encourage private enterprise and entrepreneurship through cooperatives. While some of the USSR's new entrepreneurs earned considerable incomes through their enterprises, the incentive provided by these opportunities was reduced significantly by the fact that there were few consumer goods and services available for them to buy with their new-found wealth. For instance, consumers faced a one-year wait for a washing machine and a wait of up to ten years for a car.

A more serious threat to the development of private enterprise lay in the public's value system and attitudes. In an economy of shortages, operators of private enterprises were able to charge high prices and earn high incomes selling consumer goods and services. Many Soviet citizens became resentful of these private operators. They saw them not as more efficient producers who contributed to society's prosperity, but rather as profiteers, who exploited consumers. Partly in response to such public hostility, the Soviet government placed new controls on cooperatives. In December 1988, cooperatives were banned from many fields, including book publishing and medical services, new controls were established on their prices, and taxes were raised from a maximum of 5 percent of cooperatives' revenues to an obligatory 35 percent.

Perestroika in perspective

By 1990, partly due to resistance from various quarters, perestroika represented at best a halfway reform of the Soviet economy. As such, it involved conflicting elements of traditional central planning and newly-introduced market approaches. For instance, under perestroika, much of Soviet industry was expected to produce in response to consumer demand; but in reality plants still produced mostly according to quotas set by the central planners, and had to draw up annual plans, get these approved by the planners, and stick to them even if conditions (such as consumer demand) changed. In addition, the prices of the vast majority of the products produced by the plants continued to be determined by the central planners, again without regard for consumer demand. Meanwhile, after actively encouraging private enterprise, the government

> Mr. Gorbachev hopes to create a system that combines central control with local initiative. "Impossible," say the critics. "Imperative," says Mr. Gorbachev.
>
> *The Economist*, April 9, 1988.

placed new controls and higher taxes on these enterprises when they proved unduly successful. In short, perestroika had disrupted the established central planning system, but had not yet replaced it with a market system, leaving the Soviet Union with an awkward combination of two very different economic systems.

Finally, it should be stressed that, in certain ways, perestroika was in fundamental conflict with established Soviet economic and political practices. Under Communism, all political power and economic decision-making had for decades been *centralized* under the rule of the Party. This system was firmly entrenched, in that it involved the "silent deal" described earlier, in which the citizens receive security and subsidies in exchange for their acceptance of Party rule.

However, by the 1980's, Soviet economic performance had deteriorated badly. As a result, the "silent deal" was beginning to break down, and the system was increasingly failing to provide its citizens with the economic benefits needed to maintain their acceptance of the status quo.

In an attempt to improve Soviet economic performance, perestroika was moving—quite rapidly—toward a very different type of economic system, in which economic decision-making would be much more *decentralized*. Such basic changes in the economic system could not be achieved without breaking the control of the Communist Party on economic planning and the economy. In a real sense, then, perestroika represented a move toward altering the fundamental nature of Soviet society, not only economically, but also politically.[3] As such, it was bound to encounter strong resistance from established and conservative elements within the Party and society. Because of this, even perestroika's staunchest supporters acknowledged that the implementation of so ambitious a reform program could take 20 years.

> We've had two decades of inertia, and it's going to take time to get the country moving again.
>
> Alexandr Bovin, *Izvestia*

On the other hand, several Communist nations, including Hungary, Czechoslovakia, Yugoslavia, Poland and China have implemented major programs of economic reform along the lines of freer markets and private enterprise. In most cases, these reforms have been quite successful. While

[3] The political changes took various forms. One was a purge of old-line conservatives within the Central Committee of the Communist Party. Another was a move, in the late 1980's, toward freer elections, in which the election of reformers pushed back the interference of the Party in the day-to-day management of Soviet industry.

the USSR—the most conservative of the Communist nations—has moved slowly toward economic reform, the increasingly poor performance of its economy has put great pressure on Soviet leaders to take similar steps.

Seeking a happy medium

The problems of the Soviet economy that we have considered show that a centrally planned command system has certain *basic inherent flaws*, particularly with respect to *incentives* and the operation of the *planning system itself*, which often fails to meet its objectives. Attempts to remedy these flaws have led the Soviet Union and other Communist countries to implement reforms that contain strong elements of the market system, such as economic incentives to allocate and motivate labor, a degree of consumer sovereignty, the use of profits to evaluate the performance of plant managers, and a degree of private enterprise, such as private plots in agriculture. In response to their own shortcomings, the command systems of the Communist nations have shown a tendency to move more in the direction of a market system in dealing with economic problems.

On the other hand, the experience of the market economies has indicated that a totally free-enterprise market system (called "cowboy capitalism" by some) is far from perfect. As we saw in Chapter 15, market economies tend to develop their own types of problems, which require a degree of government planning and control. As a result, the tendency in the western market economies has been toward an increasing degree of command in the form of government planning, regulation and control.

As the command economies introduce elements of the market, and the market economies move toward a greater degree of command, some observers have expressed the opinion that the two systems are converging, or becoming alike. This is a debatable point, since there remain *fundamental differences* between the command and market systems. However, there is general agreement that neither system is *the* answer to the basic economic problems that face all societies. The most effective type of economic system must contain substantial elements of both the market and command systems, and the challenge is to find the optimum balance.

DEFINITIONS OF NEW TERMS

Perestroika A radical reform program that aims to restructure the Soviet economy by decentralizing economic decision-making.

Extensive Growth Economic growth achieved through increased volumes of inputs such as capital and labor.

Intensive Growth Economic growth achieved through improvements in the quality of capital and labor and the efficiency with which they are used, the result being increased productivity.

CHAPTER SUMMARY

1. The two main features of the Soviet command economy are state ownership of production facilities and the making of most economic decisions by central planners.

2. Capital investment is a high priority of the central planners; through a combination of high investment and rapid increases in the labor force, the Soviet economy has achieved rapid growth of an "extensive" nature.

3. The consumer-goods sector is a low priority of Soviet planners; as a result, consumer goods are generally limited in volume, availability and variety, and of low quality.

4. Inefficiency is a basic problem of the Soviet economy, largely due to the lack of incentives in a command system.

5. The Soviet agricultural sector suffers from very low productivity, which causes it to be a drag on Soviet economic progress.

6. The Soviet planning system has often failed to achieve its objectives, partly due to errors in the planning process, but also due to lack of feedback from consumers and the use of physical production quotas, which induce plant managers to reduce quality and distort production in order to meet their quotas.

7. When their economic growth slowed after the early 1960's, the Soviets experimented with a number of economic reforms. These included stronger financial incentives for workers and managers, improvement of production technology, decentralization of economic decision-making authority from the central planners to plant managers, and the introduction of private plots and free markets in agriculture.

8. In 1985, the Soviet Union introduced a major reform program known as perestroika (restructuring). Some of the key aspects of perestroika were:

   • a reduction in the decision-making power of the ministries and central planners,

   • increased decision-making by plant managers, with

   • the development of widespread small private enterprise "cooperatives"

   • a "technical reconstruction" of the Soviet economy, stressing the introduction of computerized production technology

   • increased decision-making by farmers, and the introduction of a system of long-term leases.

9. There were several obstacles to perestroika, including the central planning bureaucracy, the attitudes of Soviet workers and farmers, and growing problems of shortages and inflation that undermined public support for perestroika. Nonetheless, the Soviet economy's continuing poor performance, together with the success of economic reforms in other Communist countries, kept the pressure on Soviet authorities to implement reforms.

10. Neither the market nor the command system is ideal; as each system evolves and seeks better performance, it has tended to adopt some of the features of the other.

QUESTIONS

1. The text refers to "fundamental differences" that remain between the Soviet economic system and market systems such as North America's. What are some of these differences? Are they likely to be eliminated or to remain?

2. Soviet economic strategy for most of the twentieth century has required the holding down of consumption in order to stress capital investment. How have Soviet authorities secured acceptance by the public of such a low material standard of living for such a long period of time?

3. Are the perestroika reforms proceeding more or less as planned? In particular, have prices been freed from the control of the central economic planners?

4. According to available reports, has the performance of the Soviet economy improved in recent years or not?

CHAPTER 21

The outlook for capitalism

Where does capitalism go from here? What changes will occur in the economic system in the future, and how will they affect us? Such futuristic and speculative questions do not lend themselves to the kind of systematic analysis with which many economists are most comfortable; however, they are questions that many people find fascinating. Certainly, such questions leave room for a wide range of opinions. In considering what the future may bring, we will first consider three popular but simplistic projections: first, that future prosperity is virtually assured; second, that disaster is inevitable; and third, that capitalism will eventually be replaced by socialism. We will then consider Canada's situation in the past and present, and possible directions for the future.

The optimistic view

During the 1960's and early 1970's, the rapid growth of output, productivity and living standards led futurists to assume that continuing technological progress would assure society of ever-increasing economic prosperity. In such a framework, the main concern of government was considered to be the *distribution of the benefits* of this prosperity. As a result, there was much discussion of how government policies could ensure a more equitable distribution of income in a society of affluence.

Futurists foresaw the time, before the end of the twentieth century, when technological progress would increase productivity to such high levels that only a small proportion of the population would be needed for work. In such a society, the *"what* to produce" and *"how* to produce it"* questions would fade into insignificance, leaving the *"for whom"*

422

question, or the distribution of the economic pie among the population, as the only major economic problem. Since so few people would be working, this question could not be left to the marketplace, in which relative incomes had traditionally determined the division of the economic pie. Rather, it was foreseen, the government would have to determine how society's affluence would be distributed among its population. It would be a society of unprecedented high living standards, in which people would be freed from the necessity to work and able to pursue higher goals, such as the arts, recreation and leisure.

A minority disagreed with this view, which they regarded as blandly optimistic. They believed that the consequences of advancing technology would not be affluence and leisure for all, but rather unemployment for those displaced from jobs by technology. In their view, unemployment would reach crisis proportions as many people failed to even qualify for the highly-trained jobs of the new high-technology society—a dilemma unflatteringly called the "stupidity problem" by some.

Others were less than sure about the supposed benefits of increased leisure, and the higher quality of life that would supposedly result from it. Questions were raised about the ability of a society conditioned to work to adapt to increased leisure in a positive way, with philosophical debates ensuing as to whether vastly expanded leisure would be a blessing or a curse. It was sardonically pointed out that, when a group of electricians moved below the magic 30-hour week, a study of their behavior showed that the main uses of their increased leisure time were watching television and drinking beer.

Such predictions seem unlikely to be realized now, at least during the twentieth century. Affluence on such a scale would require very high productivity, whereas in recent years the growth of real output per worker has slowed substantially. Most economists now regard these forecasts of undreamt-of prosperity as *simplistic projections* of trends from a past period of exceptional economic progress, when a combination of cheap food and energy, rapid technological progress and rapidly-rising productivity generated unprecedented gains in material prosperity. These gains were artificially inflated by society's refusal to pay the external costs of its prosperity, which were passed on in the form of an increasingly severe environmental problem that would have to be addressed (that is, paid for) in the future. With few of these factors likely to be as favorable in the future, the optimistic predictions are now generally seen as unrealistic. They were simplistic projections of past trends that could not reasonably be expected to continue indefinitely, and that focused on what was technically feasible rather than economically attainable.

The pessimistic view: The modern Malthusians

At the opposite extreme of the optimistic view is the opinion that not only is continued economic growth impossible, but also that it will inevitably lead to disaster. The most famous expression of this view is the Club of Rome's *The Limits to Growth*, published in 1972. Using sophisticated computer models, it was projected that a continuation of current trends regarding population, industrial output and pollution would result in a catastrophe before the year 2100 and probably much earlier than that. The reasoning underlying this view was remarkably like that of Thomas Malthus (1766-1834) who, as we saw in Chapter 1, believed that continuing pressure of population on the world's food supply would keep humanity in a constant state of deprivation. According to the Club of Rome's projections, the causes of these catastrophes would be a combination of pollution, resource depletion and food shortages, as relentless industrial growth would finally exert too much pressure on the finite resources of "spaceship earth." Even the most optimistic assumptions that were fed into the computer model only delayed the collapse of the system, which occurred before the year 2100 in any case. The pessimists therefore concluded that economic growth is inherently self-defeating, and we are doomed to a catastrophe.

> And always remember,
> the longer you live
> the sooner you're going to die.
>
> Anon.

Despite their computerized sophistication, the pessimists' predictions were not necessarily accurate, either. The *doomsday models*, like all forecasts, are based on certain assumptions, and are only as good as those assumptions. For instance, population and industrial production were assumed to increase continuously at exponential rates, while resources and technology were assumed to have certain fixed limits. However, these assumptions were not necessarily accurate; in fact, they were proved inaccurate. Population growth in the industrialized societies has tended to slow down, with birthrates in North America now at or even slightly below zero-population-growth levels. Also, technological progress can increase the efficiency with which resources are utilized, so as to make available resources go further. More importantly, technology can make valuable resources out of previously valueless substances, such as the Athabasca Tar Sands or waste materials that can now be recycled. Hydroculture, in which vegetables are now grown without soil, is another example of how technology is capable of overcoming resource scarcity.

Furthermore, the price system has built-in economic incentives to promote such technological changes. As a particular resource becomes more scarce, its price rises, providing stronger incentives to use less of it, find more of it, develop substitutes for it or recycle it. In large part, it was OPEC's price increases that made new oil fields an economical source of oil, and the rising prices of materials that have made recycling economical. Thus, critics of the doomsday models say, the computer models only tell us *what would happen if present trends were to continue unchanged* for many years. In doing so, their predictions of catastrophe ignore the facts that not only are changes in these trends possible, but also that the economic system contains mechanisms that create incentives for such changes. Like the extremely optimistic view, the doomsday forecasts are in effect simplistic projections of past trends that ignore important realities.

Socialism will replace capitalism

According to this view, capitalism and the market system cannot survive alongside democracy. In response to continual political pressures, it is believed that government intervention in the marketplace will eventually grow to the point where socialism replaces the market system. There are always political pressures to intervene in the economy in a variety of ways—to provide economic security, to redistribute income, to provide subsidized or free services to the public, to regulate business practices, to control inflation, to reduce unemployment, to control rents, to assist farmers, to protect Canadian companies and jobs against imports, to protect the environment, to bail out bankrupt corporations, to protect consumers, to protect workers, and so on. Clearly, it is argued, democracies have a built-in tendency towards socialism, whether their governments believe in it philosophically or not. The process occurs gradually, as governments respond to political pressures to do something about specific economic problems, until, in the long-run, the totality of these actions amounts to such tight regulation of economic activity that socialism prevails. As evidence to support their predictions, advocates of this view point to the great growth of the role of government in the economy over the past half-century or so, as outlined in Chapter 15.

However, as with the other two scenarios for the future, the situation is not as clear as it may seem. Since the late 1970's, most industrialized countries have experienced disappointing economic performances, including a troublesome slowdown in productivity growth. This failure to meet their economic expectations has led governments to *reassess their economic policies*, and place increased emphasis on *productivity growth* as an objective. This emphasis in turn has led to renewed appreciation of factors that enhance productivity, such as incentives, investment, competition and the market system generally. To promote better productivity performance, some governments shifted their policy emphasis back toward the market approach, reducing the extent of government regulation and promoting competition and incentives for both work and business investment. In the United Kingdom, the United States and, more recently, Canada, government policy has tended to place increased emphasis on the private sector and the marketplace as the most effective route to economic recovery.

It is also interesting to note that this phenomenon is not confined to the capitalist economies. As we saw in Chapter 20, several Communist nations, including the Soviet Union, have also been moving in the same general direction, in response to similar concerns regarding productivity performance.

All of these experiences serve to highlight the fundamental value of certain basic elements of the market system, or capitalism; in particular, the effectiveness of markets in organizing and allocating economic resources to serve the wants and needs of consumers, the importance of economic incentives to increase efficiency, and the role of profits as an incentive to use resources well by producing what people want efficiently. If, as many predict, the future does bring slower growth of productivity and living standards, society will be more concerned than in the past with the effective and efficient use of economic resources. In these circumstances, the basic advantages of the market system should not be forgotten by anyone concerned with the performance of the economy. As a result, it is probably more reasonable to expect countries to seek an effective balance between the marketplace and government planning as the best route to better economic performance, rather than to simply project that the market system will inevitably be replaced by socialism.

Recent Canadian experience

Canadian experience in recent years supports the view that there is no inevitable and irreversible trend toward socialism. As we saw in Chapter 15, the role of government in the Canadian economy grew rapidly in the 1960's and 1970's, causing some observers to conclude that Canada was moving inexorably toward a socialist economy. However, by the mid-1980's, the direction of government policy had changed, with increased emphasis being placed on private enterprise, entrepreneurship and incentives for work, investment and the creation of wealth. This

represented a significant departure from past policy, which had emphasized programs aimed at the redistribution of wealth rather than its
creation. In the following sections, we will consider some of the reasons
for this reorientation of government policy.

In the past, Canada relied considerably upon exports of natural
resources and resource products as a basic source of economic prosperity.
These exports, together with substantial inflows of foreign (mainly US)
business capital investment, provided Canadians with the foreign currency with which they purchased the large amounts of imported goods
and services that supported their high living standards.

With economic wealth so readily provided by resource exports and
foreign investment, government policy tended to focus on promoting a
fair distribution of wealth by providing assistance to individuals, businesses and regions that needed it. Over the years, governments established a wide variety of social welfare programs for individuals and
families, an extensive support system for weaker and less efficient producers (including tariff protection for manufacturers, subsidies for farmers and bail-outs of various sorts for many corporations in difficulty) and
various forms of assistance to economically weaker regions (including
equalization payments, regional development grants and subsidies to
people and businesses in those regions). According to some critical
observers, Canada developed a **resource wealth mentality**—the view
that wealth is not something that you *create* so much as something that
happens to you through the sale of resources, and the main role of government is to ensure that the nation's wealth is distributed fairly. Government policy tended to be more concerned with the *distribution* of
economic welfare than with incentives for the *creation* of wealth.

Recent trends

By the 1980's, however, the situation was changing in fundamentally
important ways. The world market for natural resources—Canada's traditional strength—was weakening. This was partly due to sluggish

> In 1966, we could get away with running a closely protected
> domestic market for manufacturers, and still export our
> resources. We don't have as good a market for resources
> anymore, and even with protection, the developing world is
> starting to take our market away. If we want to maintain our
> standard of living, we're going to need a more competitive
> stance in manufacturing and services.
>
> Donald Macdonald
> *Financial Post*, Sept. 14, 1985.

demand, as the growth of demand in the high-income countries of the world was shifting away from industrialized products that were major consumers of natural resources, and more toward services, and the products of high-tech and information industries. Competition in natural-resource markets intensified as well, as less developed nations entered the marketplace. The new markets for services and sophisticated manufactured goods offered great opportunities, but they were not markets in which Canadian firms (with some notable exceptions) had been particularly competitive. To succeed, Canadians would have to develop new skills, new approaches and new government policies.

> We must address the fact that natural resources will be less valuable in a low-inflation, knowledge-oriented world than they were during the inflationary 1970's. We will have to reduce costs and apply state-of-the-art technology throughout the economy. The outstanding question at the beginning of 1985 is whether Canada will ride the wave of change or be swamped by it.
>
> Edward A. Carmichael, *Policy Review and Outlook, 1985: A Time for Decisions* (Toronto: C.D. Howe Institute, 1985)

In particular, it was recognized that Canada would have to *improve its efficiency and productivity performance* in order to be able to compete successfully in the highly competitive world markets for goods and services. Over the previous two decades, Canada's productivity had lagged behind that of its major competitors, and Canada's share of world trade had slipped from fourth to eighth place. As markets "globalized" (that is, became more international and less national in character) and became more competitive, Canada was slipping even farther behind.

The future

Due to these changes, Canadian economic policy seems likely to place much more emphasis on *productivity* (creation of wealth) than in the past. As a means of achieving improved productivity performance, government policy will probably also rely more on market forces than in the past.

To this end, the federal government placed renewed emphasis on the *private sector* of the economy as the key to economic recovery and growth, employment and prosperity. Federal policies were shifted to provide greater encouragement for enterprise, entrepreneurship and business investment.

> For the first 100 years after Confederation, Canada lived off its
> resources. For the past 16 years, we have lived off our credit.
> Now we must live off our skills, our wits, our energy and our
> initiative.
>
> Hon. Michael Wilson, unattributed quotation in a speech delivered to the
> Centre on Foreign Policy and Federalism, 1984.

This trend was given reinforcement by the Report of the Royal Commission on the Economic Union and Development Prospects for Canada (the Macdonald Commission) in 1985, which stated that:

> Commissioners believe that, in some important areas, we Canadians must significantly increase our reliance on market forces. Our proposals to increase our openness to the international economy and, specifically, to enter into a free-trade arrangement with the United States reflect our general preference for market forces over state intervention as the appropriate means through which to generate incentives in the economy, from which growth will follow.

The 1989 Free Trade Agreement with the United States represented a landmark decision for Canada. It signalled Canada's intention to participate more fully in the increasingly globalized markets of the world. As such, it also meant a basic shift in Canadian policy, toward an emphasis on productivity and competitiveness rather than on sheltering Canadian industries and workers from world market realities.

Canadians want a great deal from their economic system. They want prosperity for themselves (high levels of private personal consumption), high levels of government services, including a strong social welfare system, health care and education, economic security and protection of the environment. To provide all these, the Canadian economy must be prosperous and productive. Only by becoming more efficient will Canadians find it possible to achieve all their economic and social goals. The challenge for government in this situation is to find an effective balance between the market and planning approaches that will retain and strengthen the advantages of the market system (especially its *incentives*) while maintaining the key elements of Canada's social welfare system (such as health care, education, security and fairness).

Many observers believe, therefore, there should be closer cooperation between business and government. In the past, the relationship between government and business has too often been adversarial rather than cooperative. Without consultation with the business sector, government policies have been introduced that have had negative economic side-effects that could have been avoided. With the government's new emphasis on improving Canada's economic performance, closer consultation and cooperation between government and business seems likely.

For a trading nation such as Canada, whose producers must be able to meet foreign competition, such an approach should prove beneficial to all concerned.

> Promoting growth in the private sector is a fundamental requirement if we are to secure our objective of sustained growth and productive jobs.
>
> Government has become too big. It intrudes too much into the marketplace and inhibits or distorts the entrepreneurial process. Some industries are over-regulated. Others are over-protected, not just from imports but also from domestic competition.
>
> First, government policies and programs must be changed to ensure that Canada's private sector can become the driving force of economic renewal in an increasingly competitive world marketplace. To foster growth in the private sector, Canadians must begin a process of change towards a new environment that encourages entrepreneurship and facilitates adaptation to new market realities.
>
> Michael H. Wilson, *A New Direction for Canada: An Agenda for Economic Renewal* (Ottawa, Department of Finance, 1984)

DEFINITIONS OF NEW TERMS

Resource Wealth Mentality   The view that society's economic wealth is derived mainly from the sale of natural resources, as opposed to efficiency in the production of goods and services.

CHAPTER SUMMARY

1. According to the optimistic view, technological progress will bring unprecedented economic prosperity to society, freeing people from the need to work and making possible a lifestyle of culture and leisure.

2. According to the pessimistic view (or "doomsday forecasts"), continued economic growth will lead to a catastrophe due to pollution, resource depletion and food shortages.

3. Another view is that the market system economies will inevitably become socialistic, as political pressures force continual expansion of the role of government in the economy.

4. None of these predictions seem likely to prove correct, as they are all essentially simplistic projections of past trends that ignore important realities.

5. With its traditional economic base of resource exports weaker than in the past, Canada faces the need to become more productive and competitive in other areas.

6. To this end, government policy in the mid-1980's shifted toward the encouragement of private enterprise, entrepreneurship, business investment, productivity and international competitiveness.

QUESTIONS

1. Do trends over the past five years indicate that any of the three scenarios for the future discussed in this chapter (the optimistic, the pessimistic and the socialistic) seem to be developing in reality?

2. Is the Canadian government's policy emphasizing private enterprise, entrepreneurship and incentives as described in the text regarded as successful in terms of improved performance of the Canadian economy?

3. Have Canadian businesses been able to improve their productivity and international competitiveness in recent years? Which Canadian industries and companies are succeeding in international competition, and why? Which are having difficulty, and why?

4. Generally, how does Canada's economic performance over the past five years compare to that of other industrialized countries? What reasons are given for this trend?

5. If the Canadian government had $5 billion per year of unexpected tax revenues to spend, do you believe that the public would favor using the money to increase unemployment insurance and welfare benefits or to provide incentives and assistance for industry to improve productivity?

Index